THE LIVERPOOL ENGLISH DICTIONARY

The Liverpool
English Dictionary

A Record of the Language of Liverpool 1850–2015 on Historical Principles

TONY CROWLEY

First published 2017 by
Liverpool University Press
4 Cambridge Street
Liverpool
L69 7ZU

British Library Cataloguing-in-Publication data
A British Library CIP record is available

ISBN 978-1-78694-061-2

Typeset by Carnegie Book Production, Lancaster
Printed and bound in Poland by BooksFactory.co.uk

Contents

For Teddy and Anne Crowley

and

in memoriam

Marie Midghall

Acknowledgements

Given the nature of this work, and the time it has taken to complete it, there are thousands of people who I should thank. Unfortunately, given that many of them are strangers or just casual acquaintances, I will need to express my gratitude generally to everyone I've bothered in the past with questions about Liverpool English; my thanks to them all. There are other people who can and should be named, since I am indebted to them both for help with this project and in other ways. They are: John Belchem, Tom Belger, Bridget Bennett, Phil Boland, Nigel Boyle, Deborah Cameron, Frank Cottrell-Boyce, the Crowleys – Nicky, Colette, Terry, Jacky (together with all my nephews and nieces), David Crystal, Michael and Geneviève Cuming, Fiona Douglas, Paul Farley, Anne and Bob Fyldes, Christiana Gregoriou, Emma Harding, Gail Hershatter, Patrick Honeybone, Hao Huang, Graham Huggan, Arthur Hughes, Alison Johnson, John Kerrigan, Grace Laurencin, Andrew Lees, Seán and Séimí Mac Aindreasa, Ann McKee, Peter McKee, Jen McCarthy, Andrew McNeillie, the Midghalls one and all – Marion, Yvonne, Shirley, Mark, Paula and Gary, Deborah Mulhearn, Rachel Mulhearn, Tom and Susan Mulhearn, Janet Muller, Bernard and Heather O'Donoghue, Francis O'Gorman, Michael O'Neill, Billy Ord, Mark Ord, Tom Paulin, Mally Pennell, Angela Poingdestre, Peter Robinson, Ray Ryan, Dion Scott-Kakures, Stephen Sheedy, Paddy Shennan, Julia Snell, Jane Taylor, Peter Trudgill, Sheila Walker, Mící Walsh, Bernard and Mary Weston, John Whale. I am also grateful to the staff at Liverpool University Press (thank God for university presses), particularly Anthony Cond, and my editor, Jenny Howard, and to my colleagues in the School of English at the University of Leeds.

The work is dedicated to Teddy and Anne Crowley (Uncle Ted and Aunty Anne) – mainstays both. And to Marie Midghall (née Crowley); like her brother Con, she is, I know, remembered and missed every day. Finally, I owe my deepest debt and therefore most heartfelt thanks, to Emily and our children Joseph and Louise – for their inspiration, their laughter, and their love.

The language of Liverpool

'The most deeply known human community is language itself', Raymond Williams, *The Country and the City*, 1973: 245.

'The city spoke in tongues and when it didn't speak it shouted', Linda Grant, *Still Here*, 2002: 1.

Introduction

In August 1950, a Liverpool schoolteacher, John Farrell, published two long feature articles in the *Liverpool Daily Post*: 'About that Liverpool accent (or dialect)' and 'This half-secret tongue of Liverpool' (Farrell 1950a; 1950b). There had been interest in the language of Liverpool before that date, as evinced by a number of letters and brief articles in the local newspapers in the 1930s and 40s. But Farrell's essays are landmarks that signal the first attempt to address the distinctive nature of Liverpool speech (his first essay begins with a complaint about the tendency of 'B.B.C. producers and others to represent the local speech-form as "Lancashire"' Farrell 1950a: 4). Farrell considered vocabulary, grammar and pronunciation in his relatively well-informed writing, and launched a staunch defence of Liverpool English. Noting that 'there are lots of intelligent people who look on any speaker of dialect as ill-bred and uneducated', Farrell's response was salutary: 'they should have more sense' (Farrell 1950a: 4).

Important as Farrell's work was in its own right, it is probably most significant in that it appeared to stimulate the interest of Frank Shaw, a Customs official on Liverpool docks, who called the first meeting of 'The Liverpool Dialect Society' in November 1950. The LDS flopped, but this didn't prevent Shaw from going on to become the founder of what he himself called 'the Scouse industry' (Shaw was the first person recorded as using the term 'Scouse' to refer to the language of Liverpool in '"Scouse Lingo" – How it all began' Shaw 1950b: 4). Shaw, a Tralee-born Irishman who moved to Liverpool in his twenties, claimed that his interest in the local form of speech began when he was trying to write short stories using Liverpool characters and places: 'I realised that there was so much to learn about Liverpool that I decided to compile a glossary' (Shaw 1950a: 5). The publication of a lexicon is always an important step in the institutional recognition of any form of language, and Shaw used the Liverpool Festival in 1951 (part of the Festival of Britain) to issue an appeal for the publication of an official glossary of Scouse. It failed, as did his second call in 1962 in response to the possibility of Britain entering the European Common Market. The glossary was

1

finally published in 1966 to exploit the fact that a number of matches in the World Cup were to be played in Liverpool, since this would bring tourists to the city who might need guidance when interacting with the locals. Entitled *Lern Yerself Scouse. How to Talk Proper in Liverpool*, the text was a collaborative effort between Shaw, Fritz Spiegl (founder of The Scouse Press) and Stan Kelly (a local folk-singer); it was the first published work that took the language of Liverpool seriously enough to record a selection of its vocabulary and idioms.

Lern Yerself Scouse led to a series of publications that were remarkably successful and ran to five volumes: *Lern Yerself Scouse. How to Talk Proper in Liverpool* (1966); *Lern Yerself Scouse. The ABZ of Scouse* (1966); *Lern Yerself Scouse. Wersia Sensa Yuma* (1972); *Scally Scouse. The Language of Law and Disorder* (1989); *Scouse International. The Liverpool Dialect in Five Languages* (2000). Taken together these works have dominated the popular understanding of language in Liverpool (their influence is clear, for example, in the numerous brief texts on Liverpool English, designed for the burgeoning local tourist market, that have appeared over the past decade or so). Due credit then has to be given to Shaw, Spiegl and the other pioneers of research into the language and indeed culture of Liverpool. And yet, that said, it is important to make clear that the *Lern Yerself Scouse* series, and its spin-offs, are folk-linguistic at best, and marked by a deep ambivalence towards Liverpool speech at worst. In addition to which, as will be shown below, the version of the history of language in Liverpool that they popularised is simply mistaken. The folk-linguistic nature of the work is understandable; none of the authors of these texts was a trained linguist, and Spiegl himself retrospectively described the *Lern Yerself* series as 'lighthearted – and unscientific – volumes of regional curiosities' (Spiegl 2000a: n.p.). But the negativity towards the Liverpool vernacular is deeply problematic and it can be found from the very beginning of Shaw's work in the 1950s. It is encapsulated in Spiegl's introduction to *The ABZ of Scouse* (volume 2): 'it is from the uneducated and in some respects uneducable stratum of Merseyside life that Scouse has arisen and developed. To a great extent it is the language of the ignorant' (Lane 1966: n.p.).

While acknowledging the important contribution of Shaw, Spiegl et al., therefore, the present text aims to adopt a scholarly approach to the language of Liverpool, and to avoid the ambivalent snobbery that characterised the *Lern Yerself* books. It also intends to evade the notion that Liverpool vernacular is 'always good for a laugh' (Lane 1966: n.p.), by heeding Farrell's advice that 'the tendency to regard dialect as a free source of laughter is to be deplored' (Farrell 1950a: 4). Instead, this glossary will treat the vocabulary of Liverpool as a topic of historical interest that can be considered using both traditional and contemporary methods. As will be discussed in more detail in the final section of this introduction, it will analyse the Liverpool lexicon as it has developed from the mid-nineteenth century to the present. It will do so according to the 'historical principle' enshrined in the *Oxford English Dictionary*, and it will be based on respect not just for the words themselves, but also for the people who use them. It will not be a 'scientific account', since lexicography is an art, but it will attempt to be as objective and accurate as possible in terms of definitions, the 'origins' and history of words and an account of their use in attested sources. But before turning to that task, I will outline briefly how the research that lies behind this work began.

A personal interest

I was born and bred(ucated) in Liverpool and I've spent a fair bit of time over the years quizzing Liverpudlians about language: 'have you heard this word?', 'what do you think it means?', 'do you use it?', 'where do you think it comes from?' and so on. One common response to these questions was 'why do you want to know?' (they were Liverpudlians after all). When I replied that I was writing a historical glossary of Liverpool English, I was often asked how long I'd been doing that. The answer is about thirty-five years, on and off. In fact, way back in 1981 I used examples with which I was familiar – 'bizzies', 'gansey', 'sag' and 'woolly back' – to write about word-invention and the historical study of meaning in the compulsory History of the Language paper in the Oxford University English degree. I was informed later, by one of the examiners, that I'd received great credit for discussing such words, despite the fact that he'd never come across them and had no idea what they meant (a comment that revealed a lot about both the generosity of some of my tutors, and their cultural provenance). In any case, one way and another, it has been a long-term project.

Differences in the use of language matter in that, for better or worse, they play a role in the construction of forms of social identity. In particular, as Raymond Williams once noted, 'the importance of speech as an indicator of social class is not likely to be underestimated by anyone who has lived in England' (Williams 1965: 237). Williams was surely right in this observation; certainly, as one of the few working-class students at Oxford in the early 1980s, the links between language and identity were all too obvious. In my case, my general experience at university provoked an interest in the language into which I had been socialised as a child. That provocation took many forms, ranging from relatively benign if ignorant encouragement, to explicit, antagonistic, cultural exclusion and social hostility. And it led me to consider and reflect upon the differences between the working-class Liverpudlian speech and cultural codes (including vocabulary, sounds and forms of social behaviour) with which I was familiar, and the varying sign-systems that I ran up against in Oxford. The differences were striking and significant and I thought about them a lot (there is, after all, always more to language than we already know). But what particularly engaged my curiosity (and, later, my professional interest), was the way in which such differences were evaluated. To be more precise, what I became concerned with was the social judgements that were made of forms of speech in Britain.

This wasn't just a personal concern, because it is an important social fact. To put it plainly, linguistic prejudice, still a socially acceptable form of prejudice, is an established norm in this society. And Liverpudlians, for the last four decades at least, have been on the receiving end of it. This was not, however, always the case. In an interview in the *Liverpool Echo* in 1959, the important Liverpool Welsh playwright Alun Owen reported familiar attitudes, claiming that he had 'fought for two years now to get plays performed in the Liverpool accent':

> I've had a battle to get a love scene played in the dialect. I was told the accent was ridiculous, comical, absurd and very ugly. But I believe it is a very lovely accent. People get married, live and die using the Liverpool accent, so I see no reason why they should not make love in the Liverpool accent. (Coles 1993: 203)

But such was Liverpool's central role in the emergence of British popular culture (including, but not just, The Beatles), that only a few years later Liverpool speech was being hailed as a prestige form. In 1966, for example, another report in the *Liverpool Echo* – 'That Scouser Accent … It's AN ASSET Now' – noted that 'in certain fields a Liverpool accent could be a positive help, implying a toughness and determination to get on with the job' (Frank 1966: 8). And yet, as the major historian of Liverpool, John Belchem, has observed, in more recent times the reception of Liverpool speech has been rather different: 'Scousers articulate a constant stream of prosodic patterns and segmental features which distinguish them unmistakably as Liverpudlians. Their identity is constructed, indeed it is immediately established, by how they speak rather than by what they say' (Belchem 2000: 33). Though Belchem has this the wrong way around (it is Liverpudlians whose identity is constructed as Scousers through speech), the point is well made: 'being from' Liverpool is a matter of language more than anything else. Yet if this were all there were to it, then it might not matter much. The significant issue, however, is the way in which this specific linkage of language and identity is evaluated socially. Because it is a simple historical fact that since the 1970s Liverpool speech forms, more particularly, Liverpool accents, have been heavily stigmatised. This has been established both in serious academic work (Giles and Powesland 1975; Coupland and Bishop 2007) and in the perennial surveys produced in the popular media. In 2013, for example, the *Daily Mail* gleefully reported an ITV survey finding that 'Scousers' have 'the least intelligent, least friendly and least trustworthy accent'. Of course, one response to this sort of thing is to dismiss it as petty nonsense; after all, it is surely silly to construct such a complex cultural phenomenon as an identity on the basis of how people speak rather than what they say. And it is a matter of idiocy to think that an *accent* can be evaluated in terms of intelligence, friendliness and trustworthiness (people are intelligent, friendly and trustworthy – accents aren't). Nevertheless, nonsensical though it is, linguistic prejudice is alive and flourishing in Britain, not least in relation to forms of class speech identified with cities such as Liverpool. The real question, therefore, is not whether such evaluations make sense (they don't), but what social work they perform, or, in other words, what social function linguistic prejudice has. In case there is any doubt about it, the role of linguistic prejudice, like other forms of prejudice, is to foster social division, antagonism and exclusion as a way of justifying and perpetuating inequality.

Needless to say, I didn't share many of the evaluations of speech that I heard vaunted frequently at Oxford, either from other students but also from people who really ought to have known better. On one occasion, for example, I sat in a seminar room listening to an educational theorist talking about verbal deprivation, inarticulacy, and the lack of confidence that went with it. And I realised with some surprise that he was citing 'working-class Scousers' as the exemplification of these social deficiencies. I'm afraid that I thought of the linguistic performance of many of the undergraduate students that I was teaching at the time (some of whom had attended major public schools), and I shook my head wryly at the rudeness and ignorance that was being flaunted as scholarship. The reality is that, historically, working-class Liverpudlians have been culturally dispossessed in all sorts of important ways. And, given that the effects of the dominant form of linguistic prejudice are hard to escape, they often evaluate their own forms of speech negatively as 'common'. But, linguistically deprived, inarticulate and unconfident? I don't think so. Quite the opposite in fact. Being good at narrating stories, telling jokes, making puns, linguistic inventiveness and playfulness; judging tone, using and responding to irony and sarcasm, being linguistically persuasive ... these were all highly valued social practices in the world I grew up in.

My belief that the language of Liverpudlians has been characterised inaccurately, and therefore treated unfairly, underpins this glossary. And, as noted above, the project started a long time ago and it has taken a fair while to complete. It began as a matter of personal interest and for a considerable period it amounted to nothing more than thinking about and looking up words that I used (or that I used in particular ways). Or recording (on index cards – that's how long ago it began) examples of vocabulary that I heard in the speech of relatives, friends and strangers, in Liverpool. Or just jotting down instances of the representation of Liverpool speech in popular culture, the media and general literary reading. But then, in the early 2000s, as I began work on *Scouse: A Social and Cultural History* (2012), I started to work as systematically as I could through all of the sources I could lay my hands on, including digital corpora, historical dictionaries (from Harman's *Caveat for Common Cursetors* 1567 to the online *OED*), local newspapers, history texts, sociological studies, the extensive literature of Liverpool (much of which is little known) and a considerable number of memoirs and autobiographies published by Liverpudlians (many of whom were working class). The result is not a defensive or nostalgic look back at the language of yesteryear, but an extended study which is the first to apply the methodology forged by the lexicographers of the *New* (later *Oxford*) *English Dictionary* to a local form of language. By doing so it presents a positive account of a linguistic vernacular which is tied to a particular place and which is part of a complex, stratified, multifaceted and changing culture, or way of life, that is embodied in the practice of its speakers. Indeed, the words recorded in this text are evidence of the tenacity of 'language as living form', to use Isobel Armstrong's memorable phrase (adapted from William Blake) (Armstrong 1982: title). This is not to suggest that language is organic, with a life of its own, still less that it is an abstract system (the model favoured by modern linguistics). But it is to claim that the language of Liverpool – like any other form – is constituted by history and *therefore* replete with openness, novelty and possibility, and yet subject to the real pressures that our social life exerts upon it. The marks of the dominant social order are all too present in the vocabulary documented in this work (and it is crucial that they are recorded). There are more than enough offensive examples of racist ('blammo', 'half-caste'), sexist ('charva', 'scrubber') and homophobic ('ship's Mary', 'turd burglar') terms. But there is also evidence of creativity ('marmalise'), innovation ('antwacky') and, most importantly, laughter and humour ('Ham and Egg Parade', 'Queen Anne front and Mary Ann back'). Carnivalesque at times in its irreverence towards authority ('bizzies', rozzers', 'scuffers'), funny about the body and its functions ('clean the pan'), sex ('Father Christmas') and religion ('dicky docker'), sardonic ('shit creek') and self-referential ('scouseology'), mocking ('bum-droops'), insulting ('sconehead') and absurd ('act soft and I'll buy you a coalyard'), this is a set of words that fits with the history that produced it. It is a lexicon of both common values and a keen sense of individuality, scored through with the recurrent themes of labour ('three on the hook and three on the book'), leisure ('jars out') and love ('cop off'). It can articulate sadness ('chocker') and joy ('made up'), tragedy ('churchyard luck') and comedy ('laughing bags'). And it reflects and refracts the city's role as an economic and cultural gateway that has opened out to the world, but also served to bring the world in to this particular place. It is no surprise then, given Liverpool's history over the past three centuries, including its central role in the development of the British Empire and the Slave Trade, that its language contains words lifted from around the globe. Described by Lees as 'resonating with the world's great ports' (Lees 2013: 134), Liverpool English includes items adapted from Afrikaans ('scoff'); American English ('ace'); Arabic ('akkers'); Australian English ('not much cop'); Cant ('kecks'); Chinese ('char'); Cornish ('scadge'); Danish ('kip'); Dutch ('mopus'); Fijian pidgin ('bullamacow'); Forces' usage ('doolally'); French ('barley'); Gaelic ('kaylied'); Guyanese Creole ('tonka'); Hindi ('dekko'); Irish English ('left-footer'); Italian ('carzy'); Lancashire dialect ('cob'); Latin ('cental'); Manx ('tanroagan'); Nautical usage ('hard lines'); Old English ('aleira'); Persian ('bukshee'); Polari ('tusheroon'); Portuguese ('bacalhoa'); Romani ('dixie'); Scots ('ming'); Spanish ('alicant'); Turkish ('burgoo'); Urdu ('cushy'); Welsh ('bad breath'); Yiddish ('nosh'). Little wonder then that the nineteenth-century writer Thomas De Quincey described Liverpool as a 'many-languaged town' (De Quincey 2000 [1821]: 2.228).

The history of language in Liverpool

The received version of the history of language in Liverpool is that 'Scouse' was created when the Lancashire dialect spoken in the town was mixed with the Irish English of Famine emigrants, together with a few other influences. There is something to this story, first articulated and popularised by Frank Shaw in the 1950s, but, in general and indeed specific terms, it is misleading and reductive. Ironically, given that it excludes so much of the multicultural history of Liverpool, Shaw's emphasis on the impact of Irish English on Liverpool speech was an attempt to insert an element of diversity in the city's story of its past during a period of everyday sectarianism. But laudable as the intention may have been, this populist version of history was inaccurate in a number of ways.

I have detailed the flaws in Shaw's account in detail in *Scouse: A Cultural History* and there is no need to repeat the critique here. A more accurate narrative of the history of language in Liverpool has to begin with demography. In the early eighteenth century Liverpool was little more than a small trading port of some 5,000 people. At the time, apart from its historical role as an embarkation point for troops engaged in the colonisation of Ireland, and as a contested town in the English Revolution, Liverpool was a relatively unremarkable place. By 1801, however, the population had grown by 1,400 per cent to some 77,000 and the town had become a crucial node in the global slave trade (between 1750 and abolition in 1807, two of every three slaves were transported by Liverpool-registered master-mariners). As the port continued to grow in the nineteenth century, the population increased correspondingly and reached 376,000 in 1851 (immediately following the post-Famine influx) and 685,000 in 1901. Clearly such growth could not have been internally generated and depended on large-scale immigration. Part of that great demographic flow came from relatively local areas since Liverpool, like most urban centres in Britain under early industrial capitalism, pulled in many people from its rural hinterland. But as it developed as a global port, the town brought in people from further afield in Britain – from Wales, Ireland, Scotland and other parts of England. And it drew in large numbers of sailors (usually temporary residents but culturally influential), on the basis of established connections with the Baltic and the newly formed trade links with China, Africa and the New World. In addition, once the town had become the most important port of emigration, it attracted significant numbers of refugees, from Ireland, of course, but also various parts of north and east Europe in particular; most left in short order, but many remained. And, finally, in the twentieth century, Liverpool's role as an important military port during the First and Second World Wars brought large numbers of personnel to the town and surrounding areas, again mostly on a temporary basis (though their presence was once more culturally significant).

There is little doubt that the Irish were an important element in this cultural mix. In fact, there was a long-established pattern of Irish emigration to Liverpool. In 1841, for example, before the inflow of Famine victims, there were some 50,000 Irish people in the town (approximately 17 per cent of the total). By 1861, the number had more than doubled to around 113,000, in a population of 462,000 (*c.*24.5 per cent). Evidently, the figures point to a significant presence, but it is necessary to put these numbers in context. Because in 1841, 45 per cent of Liverpool's population were immigrants, which means that 28 per cent of the total were immigrant but not Irish (or, to put it differently, 62 per cent of the immigrant population was not Irish). Even in 1861, when the number of Irish settlers was probably at its highest, 49 per cent of the total population was immigrant (a staggeringly high proportion). But of that number, 50 per cent were Irish and 50 per cent non-Irish. In other words, the Irish were evidently an important factor in the cosmopolitan construction of Liverpool, but there were many other components too. This is pertinent to the history of language in the town, since although there has been a lasting Irish cultural impact on Liverpool, the linguistic legacy is less clear. For example, the lexical evidence indicates that the influence of Irish English on Liverpool English since the mid-nineteenth century has been limited, particularly when compared with American English. And in terms of speech sounds, given the complex demographic picture, and the 'many-languaged' nature of the place, Shaw's claim that Irish pronunciations were simply adopted into Liverpool speech is implausible (not least because the Irish were one of the most stigmatised immigrant groups).

To return to the question then: what is the story of language in Liverpool? The answer has to be couched in general terms, but, in short, what happened to language in Liverpool is what happens in any location that has enormous population growth which is mostly constituted by immigrants. Which is that a new dialect is produced over generations by the contact between large numbers of people speaking different forms of the same language, and different languages, with their own respective vocabularies, idioms, grammars and modes of pronunciation. In the case of Liverpool, a physical and cultural borderland and a crucial site of 'languaging' (speaking between languages Mignolo 2012: 226), this new form – Liverpool English – was forged from the bitter, impoverished and often conflictual reality that lay beneath the town's gilded surface. The details of the process by which this new form emerged are hardly known. But it is clear that the circumstances in which this new dialect was created were highly complex and included, just to cite some of the more salient factors: multilingualism; difference in native language use between generations; highly variable levels of education and literacy (particularly before the introduction of compulsory schooling); the socio-spatial stratification of Liverpool and localism within the city; the nature, regularity and location of work and its status; the influence of trade languages; the distinctiveness of gender-related experience and the cultural formations that went with it; marriage patterns; confessional identity and sectarianism; the influence of prestige forms of language (whether national or local). To be clear: the exact inter-relation of these factors is unknown and perhaps, given the limited evidence available to us, now unknowable. But one thing is clear, Liverpool English cannot have been a hybrid of Irish English and Lancashire dialect. In fact, it is a wonderful mongrel form, forged within very narrow geographical limits and produced by, and often against, the best and worst aspects of modernity.

So what can be said in specific terms about the Liverpool vernacular? As noted earlier, hard historical evidence is difficult to find for a number of reasons. For example, there was no attempt to record the emergent language of Liverpool in the eighteenth and nineteenth centuries (even though there were various efforts to study the rudiments of Lancashire dialect in the same period). In addition, given that sound recording is a relatively recent development, and hardly available before the early twentieth century, there are few audio records of the sounds of Liverpool speech before the mid- to late 1950s. What is more, when dialectologists did begin to record and analyse regional speech forms in the mid-twentieth century, they ignored the cities (including Liverpool) and focused instead on the search for the sounds of rural (real, Old) England. And finally, even that other source for our knowledge of the language of the past – literature – is restricted, since the literature of Liverpool only began to appear from the mid-nineteenth century (hence the starting date of this glossary). In addition, although writing is by necessity one of our main sources of vocabulary (and it is treated as such in this work), the representation of speech in literary works is often highly stylised and conventional and needs to be treated with care.

The evidence about the specifics of language in Liverpool then is sparse and difficult to establish. But, as evinced in the following glossary, we do know that a distinctive vocabulary was forged in Liverpool from the many influences that constituted the cultural mix that developed in the town from the mid-eighteenth century. Many of the words in that lexicon are unique to the vernacular language of Liverpool, and these are indicated in the glossary. But precisely because words are great travellers and have little respect for borders, and because they cannot be owned exclusively, many more are shared either with surrounding areas (principally Lancashire and Northern dialects more generally) or with places linked historically to the town (Ireland and Scotland, Dublin and Glasgow, in particular). Many others were imported through language contact (from American English, Australian and New Zealand English and Forces' usage) or lifted from languages ranging from Arabic to Romani (as indicated earlier). In addition, with regard to pronunciation, we know that there are singular patterns used in forms of Liverpool speech, and that this is long-established (there is specific evidence for this claim in Farrell's work in 1950 mentioned earlier). Amongst others, these sound patterns include features such as TH-stopping (the use of 't' or 'd' in words such as 'thin' [tɪn] or 'then' [dɛn]); the lack of contrast in the pronunciation of 'SQUARE' and 'NURSE' ('square' [skwɛː] and [nɛːs] nurse, 'fare' [fɛː] and 'fur' [fɛː]); the lenition of plosives (/p, t , k , b , d , g /), leading to pronunciations such as 'lad' [lað], 'back' [bax], 'expect' [ɛxspɛxt], and 'time' [tsaɪm]; and, finally, a feature that distinguishes Liverpool English from contiguous dialects, 'happY tensing', or the tense 'ee' rather than lax 'i' at the end of words such as 'happy' ([api:] rather than [apɪ]).

Given this combination of a distinctive vocabulary, a small number of grammatical features ('youse' as plural *and* singular 'you', irregular past tenses), and an 'exceedingly rare' accent, Liverpool English fulfils the traditional definition of a 'dialect'. But 'dialect' is an increasingly problematic concept in the study of language, and I prefer to describe Liverpool English as a city vernacular. Whatever term is used to describe the form, however, one of its most striking features is that it is an anomaly in the 'English dialect continuum' (the phrase used to describe the way neighbouring dialects differ from each other and yet overlap), because it differs sharply from surrounding forms.

Even today, although Liverpool English has spread to surrounding areas (which is remarkable in and of itself given the stigma attached to it nationally), anyone travelling south-east from the centre of the city for some eight miles to Widnes, or fourteen miles east to St Helens, will find that the language deviates markedly from Liverpool English. This is a notable feature, though the historical evidence suggests that the spatial boundedness of this form is not a new phenomenon. Thus, in *Scouse,* I argued that there is textual evidence in an obscure play, *The Sailor's Farewell; Or, The Guinea Outfit* (1768), that appears to suggest that there was already a sense of a distinct form of Liverpool city speech (as opposed to the surrounding Lancashire vernacular), by the mid- to late eighteenth century. And certainly, by the end of the nineteenth century, there appears to be a clear sense that the vernacular language of Liverpool is singular. Sometimes the evidence is simply indicative. M. E. Francis's *Maime O' The Corner* (1898), for example, is set in 'Thornleigh', a village near 'Great Upton' (in reality Great Crosby, which lies less than eight miles from Liverpool city centre). Yet the representation of the dialect in the text is wholly Lancastrian: 'Yo'see, I think it's nobbut reet to larn her' (Francis 1898: 4). By contrast, Silas Hocking's *Her Benny* (1879), set for the most part in the Liverpool docklands, represents Liverpool speech in a distinctive manner: 'Be jabbers, it's a thripny ... Oh Glory! ... if it ain't haaf a bob ... If he'd a-catched me, I'd got a walloping' (Hocking 1966 [1879]: 1.14). As noted earlier, such representations of speech have to be weighed carefully as evidence, but more conclusively, perhaps, William Tirebuck's *Dorrie* (1891), again set in the inner-city, refers to 'Liverpudlian English' (Tirebuck 1891: 290). This is the first attested use of this phrase and it signifies a level of linguistic self-reflexivity. But the text is also interesting in its presentation of what may be the earliest recorded example of the sorry tradition of stigmatising Liverpool speech. This occurs when an impresario interviews Dorrie, the novel's eponymous heroine, for a stage role, before dismissing her because 'he didn't like the common Liverpool twang about her pronunciation' (Tirebuck 1891: 189). Further evidence, which asserts a clear awareness of a distinct vernacular form, and a pejorative attitude towards it, is presented in Dixon Scott's *Liverpool* (1907), in which he refers to the two main slum areas of the city as 'two dirty smears, one on either side of the clean-swept central spaces'. 'Here alone in Liverpool', he notes, 'do you get a specific dialect': 'a bastard brogue: a shambling degenerate speech of slip-shod vowels and muddied consonants' (Scott 1907: 144).

As noted earlier, from a historical perspective, this attitude to Liverpool English has been the norm, apart from one brief interlude. But given such sentiments, what is perhaps most remarkable about Liverpool dialect is the fact that it has persisted and developed. After all, it is reasonable to ask why such a consistently stigmatised form has not simply died away. The explanation, as sociolinguistic research attests, is the central role that language plays in identity-formation. For if language was simply a means of conveying linguistic meaning, then variation would in and of itself be nothing more than an unhelpful aberration. But language is a much more complex phenomenon than such a model might suggest since it is also the medium by which social meanings (including identity) are transmitted, and this is the reason that the vernacular language of Liverpool continues so distinctively to flourish. Alun Owen's observation is telling in this regard: 'the problem of Identity, which is to me one of the greatest the twentieth century has produced, is exaggerated in Liverpool, and the exaggeration makes it dramatic' (Owen 1961: n.p.). In short, Liverpool English is the most important means by which Liverpudlians reproduce themselves, and are recognised by others, as Liverpudlians; it is the key to their identity.

In summary, then, it is fair to say that we know a little of the history of language of Liverpool, but that a great deal of research remains to be undertaken. There has been some good work in the study of the contemporary sounds of Scouse, but even that work, when it moves to historical speculation, tends still to be tied to the old account. In truth, the field remains open and many of its central questions are still unanswered. But it is hoped that the lexical focus of this work will counter the tendency to reduce Scouse to a much-mimicked accent (an effect of its use in popular culture to 'index' Liverpool), by acting as a spur to further research. This might allow us to discover more about a form of language that is usually instantly recognised when spoken, yet whose history is much misunderstood.

Understanding and using this glossary

This glossary was compiled according to the 'historical principle' in language study, which is the method that underpins all modern historical dictionaries, most notably the *Oxford English Dictionary*. This approach regards any form of language as a product of history which is therefore best understood as a phenomenon that changes and develops over time. With regard to the language of Liverpool, the starting point is taken as 1850, although this is somewhat arbitrary and reflects the availability of linguistic material for analysis rather than a definite date at which this vernacular first form appeared. In fact, as already indicated, what little evidence there is suggests that there may have been a distinctive speech-form in Liverpool from the mid- to late eighteenth century, but, precisely because it was a spoken form, its precise nature is as yet unknown in any detail. This text began then, as noted earlier, with the compilation, over a considerable number of years, of a list of words and phrases that struck me intuitively, as a speaker of the form, as 'Liverpool words'. I then attempted to follow these words up using the traditional painstaking method of reading sources (literature, local newspapers, works of history, sociological studies) from the mid-nineteenth century to the present. In this reading, as is the nature of the enterprise, words led to other words, which led to other words … until I began to establish a set of words that are distinctive to Liverpool in specific ways. Now, given the unbounded mobility of language, it is important to make clear that this is not to assert that such words are only used in Liverpool (though there are many examples that are), but, rather, that they belong to Liverpool English, taken as a variable vernacular form whose boundaries are open rather than determinate. Nor is it to claim that all Liverpudlians will know all or even most of the terms included in this work, since, like any linguistic form, access to Liverpool English has been, and is, stratified by class, gender, ethnicity and age, to mention only some of the variables. But, those general caveats apart, once I had identified a base set, which took many years, it was then possible to use digital technology in the form of historical corpora and online sources, to check the findings, find earlier or later examples, ascertain meanings, and so on. In truth, the utility of the digital corpora was relatively limited, and certainly much better for more contemporary research. Hence the vast preponderance of this work derives from the most traditional mode of lexicography: the reading, annotating and analysis of written texts.

Once the words had been selected, although this is of its nature an unending (not to say interminable) process, they then had to be presented in a form that was accessible to readers and yet accurate and scholarly. For each word then the format is as follows. The word (or headword) is classified in terms of its function as a part of speech (adj. – adjective; adv. – adverb; int. – interjection; n. – noun; v. – verb; phr. – phrase; pron. – pronoun). If there are several clearly distinct meanings for the word, it is signalled by a separate entry with superscript numeral (for example *knock off¹ (v.) knock off² (v.) knock off³ (v.)*). Following the headword, a concise definition is give, with the aim of encapsulating the meaning of the term in as brief a form as possible. After the definition, the entry provides illustrative quotations taken from the various sources on which the glossary is based. These examples give a sense of how the word is used in context, but also when the word has been used and how it has developed through time. With the entries for *scouse*, for example, the quotations illustrate both the different senses of the term (*scouse¹* stew, *scouse²* person from Liverpool, *scouse³* Liverpool English) and the earliest recorded uses of the term (*scouse¹* from the late eighteenth century, *scouse²* from the early to mid-twentieth century, *scouse³* from around 1950). There are two points to note with regard to quotations, one significant and one technical. The first is that the earliest recorded use of a term does not necessarily indicate when it was coined, either in Liverpool English or English more generally, since dates are indicative rather than absolute (this is simply a fact about working with the linguistic past). Second, more technically, on occasion a text may have been most easily accessible in reprint form – for example, Silas Hocking's *Her Benny*. In such cases the reference will be given as (Hocking 1966 [1879]: page ref), where the figure in square brackets shows the original date of publication, and this will determine the place in the list of quotations (so Hocking 1966 [1879] would precede Tirebuck 1891). By contrast, however, given the fact that some autobiographies are consciously set in a particular period (for example, Jack Maddox's *In the Shelter of Each Other: Growing up in Liverpool in the 1930s and 40s*, published in 2008), two dates are given: date of publication and the period of historical reference – hence (Maddox 2008 [1930s–40s]: page ref.). In these examples, the date of publication determines the place in the list of quotations (so Maddox 2008 [1930s–40s] would come after Sampson 1998).

The final element in each entry is composed of two parts. First, an indication is given as to whether the term has previously been recorded in any dictionary

– from Thomas Harman's first work of English lexicography in 1567 through to the *OED* online, including dictionaries of cant, slang, dialect, varieties of English and etymology. When terms have not previously been treated in a dictionary, the entry is marked *NR (Not Recorded). The last part of each entry attempts to give the etymology or derivation of the term, but this is a complex matter and needs clarification. Etymology is not a science and the origins of many terms are unclear. Wherever possible, a precise derivation is given – for example, *ackers* 'money', from Arabic 'akka', 'Egyptian piastre' (a small coin). But in a case like this, the 'route' (rather than the 'root') of the word is significant, since *ackers* was imported into Liverpool English through First World War Forces' usage, rather than directly from Arabic, and this is made clear in the entry. In other cases, however, although a word may have appeared in English at a particular point, what is most interesting is again not its 'root', but the fact that it has been retained in Liverpool English. *Shift*, for example, is recorded in late sixteenth-century English as 'changing lodgings', and it has been kept in this specific sense in Liverpool usage rather than the now more common phrase 'move house'. And *parapet*, 'pavement' (an extension of sixteenth-century 'military defence'), was used in Liverpool till the late twentieth century. Other words, however, are obscure in and of themselves: the commonplace Liverpool term *ollies*, 'marbles', is unrecorded in any dictionary, though it is probably a variant of early eighteenth-century 'alley', 'marble', possibly an abbreviation of 'alabaster'. Other terms that are completely opaque include: *noak*, 'to keep watch', *Ardy Alligan*, 'old-timer'; *Basil*, 'fat man, policeman'; *ching*, 'five pounds'; *eenog*, 'back alley'; *fallies*, 'bananas'; *meff*, 'general insult' … and there are many more. Given the difficulty of establishing the derivation of terms, a conservative, non-speculative approach has been adopted: only when good evidence is available is an 'origin' indicated, or an influence noted, or the date of entry of a term into English more generally given. This is not quite as much fun as the speculative mode; *scuffer*, 'policeman', is claimed in one source to derive from the fact that after the Napoleonic Wars redundant soldiers who had served in France joined local constabularies and adopted the name 'escoffier' – 'someone able and ready to 'cook your goose' – from Auguste Escoffier, the famous French chef and restaurateur. But while the speculative mode is entertaining, it is also less reliable and therefore features only sparingly in this work.

Finally, it is worth specifying the limitation and purpose of this glossary. Like any study of a particular vocabulary, this work cannot pretend to be exhaustive, nor can it claim not to have included contentious items (for example, words that others may claim are not Liverpool English at all). No dictionary contains all the words of the language it covers and, as stipulated earlier, Liverpool English, like any other form of language, has porous boundaries. Is it possible that I have left words out that should have been included? Of course. Indeed, the traditional historical approach adopted in this text (specifically the focus on written sources – this is not a survey of contemporary usage) makes this inevitable. There are, for example, a number of words for which I could not produce evidence and which are therefore excluded ('mogger', a word recalled from my childhood, meaning 'a ride on the handlebars of a bike'). Are the definitions of the meaning of words always correct? Of course not. Meaning is a variable and contextual process – something created by users of a language as they interact with each other. All that a dictionary can do is to capture, in a relatively abstract way, the general sense of a term as evinced in the examples used to illustrate it. Are there words included in this text that others would regard as 'slang', and therefore not part of a local linguistic form ('dialect' to use the traditional term)? This is an important and contentious point and it is necessary to be very clear about it. I have never read or heard an account of slang that made sense, other than as a pejorative way of referring to the language of a specific group of people (the *OED* definitions of 'slang' are 'vocabulary used by any set of persons of a low or disreputable character; language of a low and vulgar type'; and 'language of a highly colloquial type, considered as below the level of standard educated speech'). And I asserted earlier that this work is predicated on a rejection of such prescriptivism. My account of Liverpool English is based on it forming part of a historical and cultural way of life, and stigmatising forms of language on the grounds of prejudicial and socially reactionary notions, or mystifying concepts (what *is* 'standard educated speech'?), is tantamount to rejecting that way of life. In my opinion, neither I, nor anyone else, is in a position to do that.

My aim is simple: to augment the history of Liverpool English by presenting an account of its lexicon. In doing so, I have found myself reflecting on Shaw's comment that 'one cannot be a narrator and a philologist too' (Shaw 1959a: 40) and my conclusion is that the exact opposite is true. A philologist – an old-fashioned term for a student of language and literature – cannot be anything but a narrator since words carry stories, and social histories, with them. This is as true of Liverpool English as it is of any other form of language. There is nothing more intimate to a city than its language, and the words of Liverpool reflect and refract the complex, multifaceted, bitter and glorious, comic and tragic, history of the place. My own journey with and through these words has been fascinating and enjoyable; I hope that will also be true for the readers of this work.

Note on the treatment
of offensive terms

As noted above, Liverpool English, like all other forms of English, contains words which are offensive or derogatory in various ways. It is crucial to record such terms for historical purposes, but it is also important to signal their abusiveness, and in doing so I have followed the method adopted in the *Oxford English Dictionary* and other contemporary works of lexicography.

The Liverpool
English Dictionary

A

Abbadabba (n.): nonsense; meaningless language. 'I couldn' make 'ead ner tail o' that feller, e guv me a lotter abbadabba' (Lane 1966: 1). *NR; the nonsensical form mimics the meaning.

Abnabs (n.): sandwiches. 'Sarneys, abnabs. *Sandwiches*' (Shaw et al. 1966: 39). '"Abnabs" are sandwiches' (Channon 1970: 102). '*Abnabs* Sandwiches (juvenile, now rare)' (Spiegl 2000b: 123). *NR; derivation unknown.

Ace (adj.): excellent, outstanding; good man. 'It was really ace the way the place burnt' (Murari 1975: 126). 'All right, ace' (Bleasdale 1985: 250). 'Think about how ace the day will be' (Griffiths 2003: 6). Recorded as an e.20c. Americanism; from the high value of the 'ace' in cards; 'ace', 'important or outstanding person', was the slightly earlier usage.

Ackers (n.): money, cash. 'Ackers, money' (Shaw 1963a: 6). '*Money*: Readies, Poke, Bran Mash, Ackers' (Minard 1972: 89). 'It brings in the ackers' (Graham 1988: 38). Recorded as First World War Forces' usage; from Arabic 'akka', 'Egyptian piastre' (a small coin).

Act soft and I'll buy you a coal yard (phr.): directed to someone pretending to be less intelligent than they are; a warning that being silly will gain nothing. 'Liverpudlians sarcastically say to someone pretending to be "thick" – "G'wan, act soft and I'll buy yuh a coal-yard"' (Shaw 1959a: 40). There were other versions of this saying: 'act soft and I'll buy you a tin whistle/drag you to the grotto/you can have a ride on my back step' (Lane 1966: 1).

Afeared/feared (adj.): afraid. 'But, oh, I'm so afeard' (Hocking 1966 [1879]: 90). 'He beat her senseless then cos he was a-feared' (Hanley 2009 [1958]: 51). 'You mustn't lose him because you're feared' (Bainbridge 1973: 89). Recorded from Old English; glossed as 'chiefly regional and non-standard'.

After (adj.): later, shortly. 'I'll see you after' (Tirebuck 1891: 306). 'We'll 'ave a dekko at the till after' (Cross 1951: 155). 'We could go to the pictures after' (Owen 1961: 37). 'We went to the Crack for a change and the Phil after for a change' (Hignett 1966: 189). 'I've just come back early … to make some sandwiches for after' (Bleasdale 1975: 166). 'I weren't at the match … but I was there after' (Sampson 2002: 67). 'After' can mean 'later in time; afterwards; subsequently', but the Liverpool usage is more specifically 'later on but within a short time'.

Again (adv.): another time. 'Don't worry – we'll see yer again' (Sinclair 1999 [1930s–e.40s]: 62). '*Ile pay yer again*. "Again" is here used in a peculiarly Scouse (maybe Lancashire) way, meaning not a repetition but a promise' (Spiegl 2000b: 26). Recorded from e.19c.; Irish English, possibly from the Irish 'arís', 'again, at some future time'.

Agate, get (v.): to begin. 'Mrs. K's child was very restless, and got agate of crying' (Shimmin 1863: 15). Recorded from 15c.; 'agate', 'on the way to', became Scottish and northern dialectal 'get agate', 'get going, start'; from 'gate', 'way, road, path'.

Agony (n.): difficulty. '*Agony*. Difficulty, particularly used in the "Conway" and Mersey ships' (Bowen 1929: 2). *NR; see *Conway*; the derivation of this specific, weakened sense is unknown.

Ah eh (int.): exclamation of protest. 'Arr hey Mam, what about me?' (Bleasdale 1975: 30). 'Ar eh Mam' (Brown 1989: 10). 'Arr eh, girl!' (Bryan 2003 [1940s–50s]: 190). 'Ah, eh, sir' (Simpson 2011: 296). Recorded from m.20c.; simple combination of interjections 'ah' and 'eh'.

Ahl (adj.): old; see *ould*.

Aintree Iron (n.): unknown meaning. '"Thank U very much for the Aintree Iron" sang The Scaffold' (Channon 1970: 201). *NR; *The Aintree Iron* featured in The Scaffold's 'Thank U Very Much' (1967); despite much speculation, the reference is obscure and Mike McGear, the songwriter, refuses to disclose the origin of the phrase.

Airyated (adj.): very excited, irate. 'Don't you get aireated with me' (Owen 1961: 56). 'Don' get airyated. *Keep calm*' (Shaw et al. 1966: 73) 'I don't see what he's getting so aeriated about' (Sampson 2002: 195). Recorded from e.20c.; an extension of l.18c. 'aeration', a chemical compounding process with carbonic acid that produces bubbles.

Alaira (n.): skipping game. '*Alaira*: a children's skipping game based on the recital of *one, two, three, alaira!*' (Lane 1966: 2). 'Aye, and One-Two-

Three-A-ler-ah-/*Auntie Sarah* I did see,/ Sitting on her bum-de-ler-ah-/*Come and play a game with me*' (Hallowell 1972: n.p.). Recorded in m.20c.; the origin and precise sense are unclear and there are many variants; possibly from Old English 'lima lyre' (effectively 'lost limb').

Albert (n.): watch chain. 'The man went into the shop and produced a gold albert' (Anon. 1929b: 5). 'Respectable in good broadcloth and heavy gold Albert' (Cross 1951: 112). 'Exhibiting huge heavy gold "Alberts" as they were called' (Clerk 1971 [*c.*1900]: 75). Recorded from m.19c.; from the kind of heavy watch chain worn by Prince Albert.

Ale (n.): beer; alcohol. 'Fine old ale; yes, English ale, ale brewed in England!' (Melville 1849: 266). 'Ale, that happy escape, that Nirvanna of the slummies' (O'Mara 1934: 192). 'Beer is always "ale"' (Shaw 1959a: 36). 'All tanked up with ale' (Hignett 1966: 247). 'He's been drinking since half-past six, and has consumed about nine pints of ale' (McClure 1980: 244). 'I can stand my round, hold my ale' (Simpson 1990: 40). 'Can of ale an a line of beak back in me own gaff' (Griffiths 2003: 95). Recorded from e.OE; still a common word for 'beer' in Liverpool (and in the North more generally).

Ale-house (n.): pub. 'Nightly in the ale-houses' (Shaw 1959a: 36). 'We'd all go straight to the ale house' (Parker 1974: 70). 'While youse is in the ale-house with the lady' (Brown 1989: 6). 'Some alehouse in Chinatown' (Griffiths 2003: 49). 'There's four men in the alehouse' (Sanders and Sanders

2009 [1960s]: 41). Recorded in l.OE; still in common use in Liverpool.

Ale it (v.): to drink (alcohol). 'His Mam and Dad went out aleing it at the Labour Club' (Bleasdale 1975: 106). *NR; see *ale*.

Alica (n.): vinegar. '*Alica*, vinegar (from alicate on a ship's medicine chest?)' (Shaw 1962a: 10). *NR; possibly from 'Alicant', a type of wine made at Alicante in Spain.

Alley-apples (n.): stones. 'We wuz chuckin alley-apples. *We were throwing stones*' (Shaw et al. 1966: 44). *NR; derivation is clear.

Alley-oh (n.): see *Relalio*.

Allotment/allowance (n.): money paid to wives from the wages of merchant seaman or Forces personnel. 'They said when a man met with an accident at sea his allotment note was cancelled' (Hanley 1935: 306). '"Will you get an allotment?" asked the pawnbroker' (Forrester 1974 [1930s]: 99). 'Got yer dad's allowance terday' (Sinclair 1999 [1930s–e.40s]: 75). 'You would leave an allotment to your wife or mother, and she could draw so much every week out of your wages' (Dudgeon 2010: 84). Recorded from m.18c.; a practice initiated by statute in the Royal Navy, later extended to the other services and the merchant navy.

Alright? (adv.): common greeting: hello; how are you? '"All right, Dave?" each of them asked in ritual greeting' (Murari 1975: 10). 'Alright, son?' (Sinclair 1999 [1930s–e.40s]: 165). '"Alright?" "Sound, yeh"' (Griffiths 2003: 81). Recorded from l.19c.; an abbreviation of 'are you alright?', from 'all right', 'satisfactory, in good order'.

Anny-ur-gar (phr.): any old rags. '*Anny-ur-GAR*? A street cry meaning *any old rags*' (Lane 1966: 2). *NR; one of the cries of the rag and bone men; 'gar' was a variant of *gear*.

Antwacky (adj.): old fashioned, out of date. 'Some of this gear looks right Ann Twack' (Jacques 1975: n.p.). 'Gross antwacky foreign things' (Simpson 1990: 102). 'She looked like a fucking orphan. Antwacky clothes, bunches, white socks' (Sampson 2002: 60). Recorded from l.20c.; possibly from 'antique' and 'wacky', or rhyming slang 'Ann Twack', 'crap'.

Anyroad (adv.): anyway. 'Anyroad, forget your work' (Owen 1961: 15). '*Anyroad*, anyway' (Williams and Shaw 1967: xxiv). 'Santini's sell blinkin' good ice-cream any road' (Sinclair 1999 [1930s–e.40s]: 86). 'Any road, getting back to what I was saying' (Fagan 2007 [1950s]: 225). Recorded from 19c.; primarily northern dialectal; derivation is clear.

April Noddy (n.): April Fool. 'April Fool for Liverpool children is April Noddy (Lancashire)' (Shaw 1960a: 41). '*Noddy*, a fool – an April noddy. Mawdesley, Liverpool' (Howarth 1985: n.p.). 'Noddy', 'simpleton, fool', dates from 16c.; now rare, though retained dialectally in Lancashire.

Arab/street Arab (n.): homeless child; child living on the street. 'Our Liverpool arabs and London needle-women' (Anon. 1868b: 7). 'As a rule those street Arabs have the crudest notions of right and wrong' (Hocking 1966 [1879]: 181). 'After the detective suddenly turned into a schoolmaster and his street arab assistant Nipper into a Fourth form boy' (Shaw 1960a: 42). *Arab. A Liverpool Street Kid Remembers (The Autobiography of an Early Century Street Arab* (Clerk 1971 [*c.*1900]: title). 'The courage and initiative of the little street arabs' (Forrester 1974 [1930s]: 81). 'Come here boy, you filthy arab' (Elliott 2006 [1940s–70s]: 47). Recorded from m.19c.; now regarded as offensive; an extension of the slightly earlier 'Arab of the city/city Arab'.

Ardy Alligan (n.): old timer. 'An Ardy Alligan. *An old-timer*' (Shaw et al. 1966: 587). '*E's a Ardy Alligan* He is an experienced old-timer' (Spiegl 2000b: 104). *NR; derivation unknown.

Are yew werkin'? (phr.): are you in work/ do you know where there is work? Glossed as 'a Liverpool catch phrase of "the Hungry Twenties" and in frequent use until ca. 1940; occasionally used for some ten years longer' (Beale 1984 *s.v. are yew werkin'?*).

Argify (v.): to argue for the sake of it. 'I can't stay to argify' (Hocking 1966 [1879]: 77). '*E'd argify the 'ind leg offer donkey*' (Lane 1966: 3). 'I'll stop this argifying' (Jacques 1975: n.p.). Recorded from e.18c.; from 'argue', though with the connotation of petty argumentativeness.

Argufier (n.): petty disputant. 'And Lonnigan, the champion argufier, obeyed' (O'Mara 1934: 112). See *argify*.

Argy-bargy (n.): quarrel, argument. '*Argy-bargy*: A silly dispute; a quarrel' (Lane 1966: 3). 'So there's no argy-bargy' (McClure 1980: 97). 'Aloof from the argie-bargie that was going on' (Graham 1988: 127). Recorded from 19c.; from Scottish 'argle-bargle',

originally 16c. 'argle', a confusion of 'argue' and 'haggle'.

Arse (n.): audacity, confidence. 'Arse: bottle (r[hyming] s[lang]: "bottle and glass")' (Spiegl 1989: 18). 'Having the arse to come in when others are hesitant' (Sampson 2001: 53). 'Tommy hasn't got the fuckin arse to bounce in on the Chinks' (Griffiths 2003: 49). Recorded from l.20c.; possibly from 'arse', 'cheek'.

Arsed (adj.): bothered, concerned. 'I weren't that arsed' (Sampson 2002: 20). 'He didn't notice me, or if he did, he wasn't arsed' (Griffiths 2003: 1). Recorded from l.20c.; derivation unclear.

Arseholed (adj.): drunk. 'How much money have we got … Cos I'm going to get arseholed' (Bleasdale 1985: 261). Recorded from e.20c.; an abbreviation of 'pissed as arseholes'; derivation unclear.

As/As how (conj.): that. 'I'm glad as how they're lighting the lamps' (Hocking 1966 [1879]: 11). 'Sue Wilkinson as married Chick Riley!' (Cross 1951: 67). 'We must be the only people left round here as owns their own house' (Forrester 1974: 43). 'I'm not sure as a audition for all kinds of tasty grumble is the best way for my good self to recuperate' (Sampson 2002: 130). Recorded from 14c.; glossed as 'now regional'.

Aul fella/aul man (n.): see *old feller*.

Auld girl/auls lady (n.): see *old lady*.

Aussie white/White (n.): fortified Australian white wine. 'Laahj wite! *A double portion of Australian White Mountain wine, please*' (Minard 1972: 48). 'He'd got a bottle of Aussie whites' (McClure 1980: 172). 'A couple of small whites in Yates Wine Lodge' (Fagan 2007 [1950s]: 279). *NR; Yates's Wine Lodges, of which there were a number in Liverpool, sold sweet Australian white wine fortified with brandy; its effects were predictable and notorious.

Avo (n.): afternoon. 'Kids matinées on a Saturday avo' (Owen 1961: 16). See *avvy*.

Avvy (n.): afternoon. 'School children refer to "this afternoon" as "savvy" or "issavvy"' (Farrell 1950a: 4). 'Casual and lazy articulation produce dese (these), hospiddle (hospital), savvy or isavvy (afternoon or this afternoon)' (Whittington-Egan 1955a: 6). '"Eh yew ahr Nellie, werdye purrahr kid's cozzy? Shiz goin' to New Brighton the savvy"' (Hodgkinson 1960: 11). '"Avvy" is afternoon' (Channon 1970: 103). 'You can take it back thisavvy' (Graham 1988: 37). '*Disavvy* This afternoon' (Spiegl 2000b: 25). 'They're quiet this avvie' (Fagan 2007 [1950s]: 136). Recorded from m.20c.; an abbreviated elision of 'this afternoon'.

Away for slates, to be (phr.): to leave in a hurry. '"To be away for slates" (to depart in great haste)' (Farrell 1950b: 4). 'E wus away fer slates up the cooey' (Shaw 1959a: 40). Recorded as 'departing hastily: Liverpool: C 20' (Partridge *s.v. away for slates*); derivation unclear.

Away games/aways (n.): games played away from a club's home ground. 'The away games were the worst' (Murari 1975: 112). 'Some lad from over the water that used to go the aways' (Sampson 2001: 42). *NR; derivation is clear.

Aye (int.): affirmative expression (with variety of uses). 'Ay, to be sure' (Hocking 1966 [1879]: 82). 'I have noticed the following in speech and in the local press: Aye! As the affirmative particle' (Collinson 1927: 121). 'Aye, that's right' (Owen 1961: 16). 'Oh aye?' (Owen 1961: 100). '*Aye*: The affirmative with a slight emphasis. As in *aye, I've had a few jars*' (Lane 1966:4). '"Oh, aye", he replied, smiling' (Forrester 1979: 12). 'Oh aye, yeh' (Griffiths 2003: 110). Recorded from l.16c.; possibly related to 'ay', 'always'. Lane describes this as 'easily the most flexible word in Scouse' and notes that 'there is the *aye*-incredulous, the *aye*-sympathetic, the *aye*-sardonic, the *aye*-assertive and twenty or more other versions. Two Scousers can conduct a long conversation with one of them saying nothing but *aye* with various inflexions' (Lane 1966: 4).

Aye aye (int.): a greeting or warning. 'Aye! Aye! A Salutation' (Price: 1950: 4). 'He should have heard the varieties of "Ay, ay" in a dockside pub, a bus queue or on Spion Kop. It can mean yes, I'm watching you, don't try to fool me, hello, and a variety of other things' (Shaw 1961: 6). 'Just knock and shout "Aye, aye"' (Jacques 1979: n.p.). 'Aye, aye Chrissie, no need to shout' (Bleasdale 1985: 160). 'Aye-aye. See Eck-eck' (Spiegl 1989: 12). 'Aye-aye! What's our Stephen doing out?' (Sampson 2002: 134). '"Ay ey" for "I say there"' (Lees 2013: 136). Recorded from l.16c.; see *aye*.

B

Babsky (n.): William Brown Street around the Wellington column. 'The place where the arch was erected is about the most exposed part of the town when the wind is high, and in consequence is generally styled the Babsky' (Ware 1909: 13). *NR; a l.19c. nickname for a wind-swept part of Liverpool city centre; a corruption of 'Bay o' Biscay', referenced in Haigh's *Sir Galahad of the Slums*: 'The triangular piece of ground on which the great Wellington Column stands … the space known locally as the "Bay of Biscay"' (Haigh 1907: 437).

Bacalhoa (n.): salt fish. 'Salted codfish, known in the Park Lane area by the Portuguese word bacalhao' (Lees 2013: 133). See *salt fish*.

Back/back up/bank (v.): to arrange a fire, usually at night, so that it would burn slowly. 'For the first time ever since he could remember, the fire had not been backed up' (Hanley 2009 [1936]: 367). 'He banked up the fire' (Hanley 2009 [1950]: 75). 'I've left a *Hot Pot* cookin' slow/For I've backed up the fire' (Hallowell 1972: n.p.). 'A banked-up fire that smouldered' (Simpson 1990: 81). 'This was ideal for "backing" the fire' (Elliott 2006 [1940s–70s]: 62). *NR; a fire would be 'backed up' with *slack* and cinders in order to keep it just alight.

Back door job (n.): anal sex. '*Back door job*. Buggery' (Spiegl 1989: 13). Recorded from l.20c.; an extension of l.16c. 'backdoor', 'anus'.

Back-end (n.): latter part of a year; end of a season. '*Last back-end*. The latter part of the previous year' (Lane 1966: 61). Recorded from 19c.; Scottish and northern dialectal; derivation is clear.

Back-hander[1] *(n.)*: blow, smack with the back of the hand. 'Keep still, son, if you don't want a back-hander' (Baird 1957: 24). 'The only answer's a fuckin' back-hander' (Parker 1974: 97). 'A backhander to shut him up' (Sampson 2002: 186). 'The lad was now within striking distance of a back-hander' (Fagan 2007 [1950s]: 183). Recorded from e.19c.; derivation is clear.

Back-hander[2] *(n.)*: bribe. 'Captains of the ships did not mind the quality of the goods so long as they got their backhander' (Hall 2004 [1939]: 16). 'There'll be dozens of fellers after that job, dropping backhanders' (Parker 1974: 123). 'A backhander bottle of/ Bacardi rum for him' (Simpson 1990: 48). 'This sort of work is known in the building trade as a "foreigner" and is always paid with a "back-hander"' (Kelly 2006 [1930s–40s]: 91). Recorded from m.20c. though the Liverpool use is slightly earlier; a payment made with the back of the hand.

Backstop (n.): wicketkeeper. 'Backstop. *Wicketkeeper*' (Shaw et al. 1966: 44). Recorded from e.20c.; a variation on 'backstop', 'longstop' (a fielder who stands a way behind the wicketkeeper).

Backwards, the way Molly went to church (phr.): backwards, reluctantly. 'Phrases like *Backwards, the way Molly went to church*' (Shaw 1950b: 4). Recorded from 20c.; Irish English; derivation unknown.

Bad[1] *(adj.)*: ill. 'You were telling me some time back she was bad' (Hanley 2009 [1940]: 574). 'When a man is absent from work through illness he is said to be "off bad"' (Farrell 1950b: 4). Recorded from 14c.; the sense 'in ill health, unwell, poorly, sick', is glossed as now 'regional and nonstandard'. In Liverpool *bad* is used phrasally to refer to varying degrees of health: 'not so bad', 'in good health'; 'off bad', 'absent through illness'; 'taken bad', 'fallen ill; 'very bad', 'very ill indeed'.

Bad[2] *(adj.)*: dangerous, nasty, very unpleasant. 'West Africans in Anson Square. West Africans bad men' (Jerome 1948: 146). 'A bad man' (Shaw 1957a: 17). 'The judge will just say you're a bad man' (Parker 1974: 177). 'They were real bad men, both armed robbery merchants' (McClure 1980: 203). 'Bad, bad scallies' (Griffiths 2003: 31). Recorded from m.20c.; usually used in the phrase 'bad man', from 19c. African American 'bad', 'dangerous and menacing'.

Bad breath (n.): Welsh fruit loaf. '*Bad breath*: A spicy fruit loaf properly called by its Welsh name of *bara brith*' (Lane 1966: 5). '*Bad breath* Bara brith, a kind of fruit bread' (Spiegl 2000b: 117). *NR in this sense; a corruption of Welsh 'bara brith', 'speckled bread'.

Bad news (n.): something seriously bad, unacceptable, dangerous. 'I reckon it's bad news, smacking birds' (Parker 1974: 95). 'Fuckin hell, man. Bad news' (Griffiths 2003: 140). 'Going to be bad news tonight, lah' (Cornelius 2001 [1982]: 117). Recorded from m.20c.; an extension of an e.20c. Americanism, 'bad news', 'restaurant bill'.

Baddie (n.): nefarious, vicious person. 'In the mornin' the baddies were all signin' on' (Jacques 1975: n.p.). 'Even with the real baddies …' (McClure 1980: 115). 'Driving the "baddies" out of town' (Maddox 2008 [1930s–40s]: 135). Recorded from m.20c.; from American film discourse, though often a strong term of disapproval. See *bad*[2].

Badge-porter (n.): Officially endorsed porter. 'Badge-porter … Liverpool porters are licensed and controlled by the police and wear a little red badge' (Shaw 1959a: 34). 'Badge-porter. A Liverpool market porter' (Howarth 1985: n.p.). *NR; derivation is clear.

Bag[1] *(n.)*: insulting term for a woman. '*Bag*: In theory, a prostitute, but more often used as a term of abuse' (Lane 1966: 5). 'They wair right in the agency, this one *is* a fussy bag' (Griffiths 2000: 242). Recorded as an e.20c. Americanism; an extension of 17c. 'baggage', 'good-for nothing woman, of disreputable or immoral life'.

Bag[2] *(n.)*: wrap of heroin; heroin. 'BAG. Heroin in wrap form' (Spiegl 1989: 13). 'Bit of crack to make them high, bit of bag to lull them down' (Sampson 2001: 77). Recorded from m.20c.; an Americanism; derivation is clear.

Bag off (v.): to pair up for sex. 'Am goan firra baggoff. *I am going to pay a call on the local brothel*' (Minard 1972: 91). 'Ah, y' wouldn't stand a chance, the butler's bagged off with her' (Bleasdale 1985: 116). 'Al get yer rat-arsed and bagged off with some buxom

25

dairymaid called Rhiannon' (Griffiths 2000: 352). Recorded from m.20c.; derivation unclear.

Bags of (n.): a lot of, plenty. 'There's bags full of tarts here' (Hanley 2009 [1940]: 430). '*Bags a scoff*: plenty of food' (Lane 1966: 5). 'Yes, you get bags of scuffles' (McClure 1980: 53). 'As well as bags of booze, they all brought up crisps and stuff' (Griffiths 2000: 9). Recorded from e.19c.; sporting jargon, from 'bag', 'the day's kill'.

Bagsy (v.): to claim. 'Bagsy ferst shot on the syringe' (Griffiths 2000: 143). Recorded from m.19c.; originally 'bags I'; derivation unclear.

Bail out/bail (v.): to depart; leave quickly. 'He would take it rough, very rough, most likely, if he did bale out one day' (Cross 1951: 107). 'I baled out, and quick' (Owen 1961: 56). 'They've bailed out on us, Dave' (Russell 1996 [1976]: 267). 'We all baled out then' (Graham 1988: 40). 'Am bailin' out of 'ere' (Sanders and Sanders 2009 [1960s]: 5). Recorded from m.20c.; an extension of the slightly earlier 'bail out', 'the emergency exiting of a plane by parachute'; derivation is clear.

Baksheesh (n.): tip. 'A little "baksheesh" – which usually came forth in the pleasing jingle of small scattering copper coins' (Whittaker 1934: 30). 'The defences gave way, and backsheesh was forthcoming' (Ash 1954: 19). Recorded from 17c.; a borrowing from Persian 'bakhshīsh', 'present, gratuity'.

Balloon/balloonhead (n.): insult; idiot. 'You blew up that balloon till he burst' (Smith 1998 [1971]: 163). 'Make a fucking balloon out of any cunt' (Sampson 2002: 48). 'Ikey fucking balloonhead. Nutter' (Griffiths 2003: 85). Recorded from m.20c.; an extension of 17c. 'balloon', 'empty, hollow' person.

Band of Hope Street (n.): Royal Liverpool Philharmonic Orchestra. '*Band of Hope Street*: The Royal Liverpool Philharmonic Orchestra' (Lane 1966: 6). *NR; the RLPO is resident at the Philharmonic Hall, Hope Street; the Band of Hope was the most influential Temperance Society of the l.19–e.20c.

Bangeroo (n.): pig. '*Bangers*: Sausages. Hence *bangeroo*: a pig' (Lane 1966: 6). *NR; from e.20c. Australian *banger*, 'sausage'.

Banner-socket (n.): navel. '*Banner-socket*: A navel' (Lane 1966: 6). *NR; during sectarian marches in Liverpool, participants carried banners upon poles which were held in a socket in a girdle around the midriff.

Bannymug (n.): see *panmug*.

Bap (adj.): empty. 'An emmy oggie. A bap ossie. *An empty house*' (Shaw et al. 1966: 47). *NR; derivation unknown.

Bar (n.): one pound. 'A £1 note is generally known as a "nicker" or "bar"' ('Postman' 1937a: 6). 'Bar; nicker. *One pound note*' (Shaw et al. 1966: 34). 'The unit of currency was the "bar"' (Lees 2013: 32). Recorded from l.19c.; from the Romani 'bar', 'pound'.

Barley (int.): claim to be exempted from a game; safe. '"You're it", "No, I'm barley" (untouchable, having performed a certain right)' (Shaw 1960a: 40). '(In) Barley. In children's games a safe place, for scallies a safe house' (Spielgl 1989: 14). Recorded from e.19c., but much older; glossed as Scottish and northern dialectal and found in 14c. *Sir Gawain and the Green Knight* (written in north-west midland dialect); probably a corruption of 'parley', 'truce', from French 'parler/parlez'. In chasing games such as 'tick' or 'tag', a child could opt out by reaching a specific area, or crossing fingers, and shouting *barley*.

Barm cake (n.): type of bread roll. '*Barm cakes* (whose "barmy" association gave this as a name for a stupid person)' (Shaw 1958d: 19). 'Barmcake. A round cake made of flour and yeast' (Howarth 1985: n.p.). Recorded from l.19c.; northern dialectal; see *barmy*.

Barm-pot (n.): fool, idiot. 'He's a barmpot. He killed a policeman' (Martin 1963: 12). 'Barm-pot. A fool, a stupid person' (Howarth 1985: n.p.). Recorded from m.20c.; see *barmy*.

Barmaid's apron, sniff the (v.): to be particularly susceptible to the effects of alcohol. '*I'll just sniff dee barmaid's apron* I am a moderate drinker' (Spiegl 2000b: 88). *NR; derivation is clear.

Barmy (adj.): foolish, silly, crazy. 'Fanny must be going balmy' (Hanley 1935: 419). 'Worse than barmy!' (Cross 1951: 113). '*Barmisod*: A term of abuse, as in *I wooden be seen dead wit' that barmisod* (Lane 1966: 6). 'Pharoah would go barmy' (Jacques 1973: n.p.). 'She's barmy about organic chemistry' (McClure 1980: 174). 'He's bloody barmy' (Fagan 2007 [1950s]: 45). Recorded from l.16c.; originally 'full of ferment, excitedly active, flighty', hence 'foolish or insane'; from 'barm', 'the froth on the top of fermenting liquors'.

Barney (n.): fight, argument. 'Should she have a "barney" (quarrel) with him which results in him being "chucked"

(jilted) …' (Farrell 1950b: 4). '"If you're going to have a barney", said John, "I'll hold your coats"' (Burke 1964: 20). 'Then he has a barney with me mam' (Russell 1996 [1976]: 121). 'Just after we have our barney' (Brown 1989: 9). 'They're always half having a barney' (Sampson 2001: 27). Recorded from l.19c.; an Australian extension of m.19c. 'to raise a barney', 'to gather a mob'; derivation unknown.

Barrio (n.): neighbourhood (often deprived). 'Windsor Street. Tocky proper. The Holylands was sweet suburbia compared with that barrio' (Sampson 2001: 25). 'Don't come into someone else's barrio an start shoutin the fuckin odds' (Griffiths 2003: 114). Recorded from l.20c.; from contemporary American English; ultimately Spanish 'barrio', 'district, suburb'.

Baseball (adj.): small, insignificant. 'He evinced some nervousness, and stroked a "baseball" moustache faintly perceptible on his upper lip' (Ware 1909: 20). Recorded from l.19c.; an Americanism 'sometimes heard in Liverpool' (Ware); possibly rhyming slang.

Bash[1] (n.): try, attempt. '*Have a bash*: have a go' (Lane 1966: 6). 'A great friend of mine joined and I thought I'd give it a bash' (McClure 1980: 81). 'Nocker is special keen to have a bash' (Brown 1989: 32). Recorded as e.20c. Forces' usage; probably from 'bash', 'to hit hard'.

Bash[2] (n.): sexual intercourse. 'A quick bash behind the bushes of a Saturday night' (Bleasdale 1979: 23). Recorded from m.20c.; from the slightly earlier 'on the bash', 'working as a prostitute'.

27

Bash, on the (phr.): looking for sex; on a drinking bout. 'Glory, o glory, we'll go on the bash' (Kelly 1964: 8). '*On ther bash*: on a sexual spree' (Lane 1966: 6). See *bash*².

Basil (n.): fat man; policeman. 'The arrival of Basil the policeman' (Shaw 1960a: 38). 'Basil belly. *A fat man*' (Shaw et al. 1966: 28). 'Basil. Slang name for a fat man. Liverpool' (Howarth 1985: n.p.). Recorded as 'Liverpool: from before 1952' (Partridge *s.v. Basil*); derivation unknown.

Batter (v.): to hit, smack, beat. 'John said his dad would "batter" him' (Mays 1954: 84). '*Batter*: To smack or slap' (Lane 1966: 7). 'Me mam would batter me if she caught me in the boozer' (Parker 1974: 126). 'You'd have to batter him up so much you'd have to inflict quite bad injuries' (McClure 1980: 97). 'Move smartish, or he will batter him' (Brown 1989: 8). 'He'd've battered all three of the cunts' (Sampson 2002: 201). 'Stevie Gerrard sprints up from midfield and batters the net with a screamin thirty yarder' (Griffiths 2003: 216). 'Her husband used to batter her' (Dudgeon 2010: 118). Recorded from 14c.; from 'to batter', 'to strike repeatedly'.

Battle (v.): to fight. 'He'd been battling them one night' (Murari 1975: 10). 'Yer've gorrer chance of leggin it or battling em' (Griffiths 2003: 183). Recorded from 14c.; the Liverpool use retains the early, narrow sense of 'battle', which later broadened to 'engage in war, conflict'.

Battle-taxi (n.): police jeep. 'Blackie ... Also called a "paddy wagon"; or "battle taxi"' (Lane 1966: 9). 'The "'urry-up cart" is the Black Maria (also called "de battle-taxi")' (Channon 1970: 102). 'The bucks had called them "battle taxis", and the bobbies just "jeeps"' (McClure 1980: 36). '*Battle taxi, battle wagon, meat wagon* Police riot van' (Spiegl 2000b: 149). *NR; derivation is clear.

Bawley (n.): rag and bone collector. 'You sold your mam's old bedstead to that bawley with the handcart' (Hignett 1966: 48). *NR; the rag and bone collectors walked the streets bawling for *anny-ur-gar*.

Bayonet practice (n.): sexual intercourse. '*Bayonet practice*: sexual intercourse' (Lane 1966: 7). *NR; from l.19c. 'bayonet', 'penis'.

Bayos/bayoes (n.): public baths. 'There is even a peculiar unnecessary lengthening of words, as in Park-y Lane and in *bayos*, for baths' (Shaw 1962a: 9). '*Bayoes*: Public Baths' (Lane 1966: 7). *NR; derivation is clear.

*Beak*¹ *(n.)*: magistrate. 'You are a-calling for beaks and law-sharks' (Maginn 1844: 1.241). 'No fear of a summons to appear before any "beak"' (Roberts 1893: 27). 'When you get into court, the beak looks at your black face la' (Murari 1975: 78). 'Up before the beak for being drunk and disorderly' (Unwin 1984 [1920s–30s]: 65). 'The periwigged beak with his mallet and posh words' (Simpson 2011 [1998]: 239). 'Put before the beak on Monday morning' (Maddox 2008 [1930s–40s]: 60). Recorded from l.16c.; originally cant, possibly from 'beak', 'nose'.

*Beak*² *(n.)*: cocaine. 'Moving the beak and the smack' (Sampson 2002: 103). 'Can of ale an a line of beak back in me own gaff' (Griffiths 2003: 95). Recorded from l.20c.; probably from 'beak', 'nose'.

Beams (n.): eyes. 'Them scanning us but nothing behind the beams' (Sampson 2001: 146). 'Can't take yer friggin beams away from her, lar' (Griffiths 2002: 147). Recorded from l.20c.; probably from 'beams of light'.

Beaut (n.): something or someone unpleasant. 'Gave me a beaut right across the ear' (Parker 1974: 164). 'Take care of these beauts that's bothering our Stephen' (Sampson 2002: 199). Recorded from l.20c.; ironic reversal of 'beaut', 'something or someone desirable'.

Bed-mates (n.): fleas. *'E were fair crawlin' wit' bed-mates*: he had a lot of fleas' (Lane 1966: 7). *NR; derivation is clear.

Bed-wetter (n.): someone who gets up early. 'Bed-wetter: an early riser' (Lane 1966: 7). *NR; derivation is clear.

Beer for dogs (phr.): more than enough beer or drink. 'The was gear dos in them days, jars out, beer for dogs' (Shaw 1957a: 1). 'Let's ave a do at are ouse; dur's beer for dogs. *Let us have a party at home; there is plenty of beer*' (Shaw et al. 1966: 71). *'Dur's beer fer dogs* There is plenty of beer' (Spiegl 2000b: 84). *NR; derivation is clear.

Beetle-crushers (n.): feet or boots. 'He called his feet "beetle crushers" and his hands "maulers"' (Haigh [1907]: 89). 'Boots are now Beetle Crushers' (Shaw 1959a: 34). 'Purra beetlecrushers. *Pair of boots*' (Shaw et al. 1966: 37). '"If yer don't fok aff, I'll put me beetle crushers on you!"' (McClure 1980: 197). *'Beetle-crushers* Men's boots with Victorian pointed toes' (Spiegl 2000b:

72). Recorded from m.19c.; derivation unclear since 'beetle' is both the class name for coleopterous insects and the term for an instrument with a heavy head used to crush or flatten.

Bellows to mend (phr.): out of breath. *'Bellers ter mend*: Short of breath' (Lane 1966: 7). *NR; derivation is clear.

Bells (n.): o'clock. 'I'm here, matey. '"Eight bells, skipper" ... "Eight o'clock! Good heavens"' (Hall 2004 [1939]: 257). 'Eleven bells, you said' (Sampson 1999: 111). Recorded from e.19c.; bells rang on a ship each half hour to mark the progress of a watch (eight bells meant four hours, the period of a watch); the extension to hourly time was a l.19c. development.

Belt¹/belting (n.): hit, blow; beating. 'Give her a few belts now and again and knock some sense into her' (Hanley 2009 [1936]: 319). 'He would collect some belting for being out so late' (Cross 1951: 38). 'When he hears the things you did, You'll get a belt from your dad' (Kelly 1964: 5). 'Joe gave him a belt' (Jacques 1975: n.p.). 'A belt over the ear with a wet, smelly hand' (Robinson 1986 [1920s–30s]: 48). 'Just let me give 'er one good belt' (Bryan 2003 [1940s–50s]: 115). *NR in the sense of 'effort'; from 'belt', 'strip of leather'.

Belt² (n.): effort; sex. 'Belt: An effort: a blow. Also sexual intercourse' (Lane 1966: 8). *NR; an extension of *belt¹*.

Belt³ (n.): drink, swig. 'They both leave the shop and open the whisky and take alternate belts at it' (Griffiths 2001: 184). Recorded from l.20c.; an extension of m.20c. 'to belt', 'to drink heavily'.

Belt[1] *(v.)*: to hit, beat. 'When me dad comes homesir, he belts me' (Russell 1996 [1976]: 121). 'You'll get five years … for belting an officer' (Stamper 2010: 101). Recorded from m.19c.; from 'belt', 'strip of leather'.

Belt[2] *(v.)*: to rush. 'Before me dad could come in, the taxi drew up outside, and me Mam was belting down the path' (Bleasdale 1975: 181). 'They belt up the corridor' (Brown 1989: 8). Recorded from l.19c.; from dialectal 'belt', 'to bustle about'.

Belter (n.): something excellent or exceptional. 'Our boxer dog … was a belter' (McClure 1980: 333). 'You, my derlin, are a liddle fucken belter' (Sampson 1999: 25). Recorded from l.19c.; northern dialectal; derivation unclear.

Belting (adj.): excellent; superlative. 'Beltin' judies' (Shaw 1957a: 20). 'There was a belting piece in the next room to Sammy's' (Hignett 1966: 35). 'Next minute a beltin' cob of stuff came down' (Jacques 1975: n.p.). 'Eve bein' a beltin' cob of stuff' (McGovern 1995: 12). Recorded from m.20c.; probably an extension of *belter*.

Bender (n.): suspended sentence. '(A) Bender! Exclaimed with joy and relief: a suspended sentence' (Spiegl 1989: 13). Recorded from l.20c.; from rhyming slang.

Bent[1] *(adj.)*: spoiled, broken beyond repair. '*Bent*: Broken; smashed; completely destroyed. A smashed shop-window or a wrecked car are said to have been "bent"' (Lane 1966: 8). Recorded as e.20c. Forces' usage; derivation is clear.

Bent[2] *(adj.)*: corrupt; stolen. 'The sales assistant … is "bent"' (Parker 1974: 149). 'BENT. Stolen articles' (Spiegl 1989: 15). 'The checker they entrusted them to was bent' (Burnett 2011: 54). Recorded as an e.20c. Americanism; probably by analogy with 'crooked'.

Bevvied (adj.): drunk. 'All de talint was dere an' ev'body wus bevvied' (Shaw 1959a: 34). 'We was so bloody bevvied' (Hignett 1966: 116). 'Yeh, he was really bevvied' (Parker 1974: 93). '"Oh, you were bevvied" – to sort of excuse it' (McClure 1980: 357). 'Bevvied. Drunk, but like lushed and other words, now used nationally' (Spiegl 1989: 15). 'When she'd get bevvied' (Griffiths 2003: 112). 'Bevvied are we?' (Burnett 2011: 135). Recorded from m.20c.; see *bevvy*.

Bevvy (n.): alcoholic drink. '*Bevvy* which we borrowed from the Cockney who says "bivvy"' (Shaw 1950: 4). 'A drink is a bevvy' (Armstrong 1966: 6). 'I mean, wot's wrong in 'avin' a bevvy?' (McClure 1980: 306). 'We'll stop in for a bevvy at the Nook' (Grant 1996: 50). 'Let me go for a bevvy or two' (Burnett 2011: 131). Recorded from l.19c.; popularised in e.20c. Forces' usage; an abbreviation of 'beverage'.

Bevvy (v.): to drink (alcohol). 'Soon as he gets a coupla wins or a deuce he's down at the ale-'ouse bevvyin' (Shaw 1957a: 7). 'We're bevvyin' in Liverpool' (Jacques 1975: n.p.). 'After arl the swigging and the bevvyin' (Simpson 1995: 23). 'One of your committee members was seen bevvyin' with the gaffer' (Fagan 2007 [1950s]: 103). See *bevvy (n.)*.

Bevvy ken (n.): alehouse, pub. 'Bevvy ken. *Alehouse*' (Shaw et al. 1966: 67). *NR in this sense; see *bevvy*, *ken*.

Bezzie (n.): best friend. 'Elvis? Yeah. He's me bezzie' (Sampson 1998: 48). 'She's me bezzie mate' (Jolliffe 2005: 2). Recorded from l.20c.; derivation is clear.

Bezzies (n.): best clothes. 'Dese are me bezzies. *These are my best clothes*' (Shaw et al. 1966: 36). 'Best clothes are "bezzies"' (Channon 1970: 102). 'Wait for your ma to lay your "bezzies" out' (Jacques 1979: n.p.). '*Me bezzies* My best clothes' (Spiegl 2000b: 75). Recorded from l.20c.; probably a contraction of 'Sunday best' (clothes).

Biddy¹ (n.): old woman. '*Biddy*: An elderly woman of scruffy appearance. *Owd biddy*: old woman' (Lane 1966: 9). 'Six old biddies, all smoking away and giggling to each other' (Bleasdale 1975: 42). 'Just a few ahl biddies' (Griffiths 2003: 71). 'Some old biddy' (Callaghan 2011 [1910s–30s]: 18). Recorded from l.19c.; an Irish English diminutive of 'Bridget'.

Biddy² (n.): louse, nit. 'One of the very few genuine, undiluted Scouse words appears to be "biddies", meaning lice' (Anon. 1963b: 8). 'Teacher sent me 'ome; she sez me 'ead's full of biddies' (Lane 1966: 8). 'She combs out his hair looking for biddies' (Brown 1989: 7). 'Nitty Nora, the Biddy Explorer' (Dodd 2007: 53). Recorded from l.19c.; northern (mainly Lancashire) dialectal; derivation unclear.

Bifter (n.): cigarette; joint. 'Bifter. "Gorra bifter?" hand-rolled cigarette, especially in prison' (Spiegl 1989: 15). Recorded as l.20c.; 'originally and chiefly Liverpool' (*OED s.v. bifter* n); derivation unknown.

Big blow (n.): arrogant boaster. '*Big blow*: A braggart; a bombastic person. *That feller's jus' a big blow*' (Lane 1966: 9). Recorded from m.20c.; an extension of e.20c. American dialectal 'blow-hard', from earlier 'to blow', 'to bluster' hence 'boast, brag'.

Big ears (n.): nosey person. '*Big-ears*: An inquisitive person; a nosey parker. As in *yer mind yer own sufrance (sufferance) big ears!*' (Lane 1966: 9). 'Never you mind, big ears, I wasn't talking to you' (Parker 1974: 137). 'Like some beady-eyed/bastid big-ears luckin fer a barney' (Simpson 1995: 21). *NR; derivation is clear.

Big-head (n.): arrogant person. '*Big-'ead*: A term of abuse' (Lane 1966: 9). 'He was a sarcastic big-head' (Robinson 1986 [1920s–30s]: 144). Recorded from m.19c.; see *big-headed*.

Big headed (adj.): conceited, arrogant. 'Such people are described as "big-headed"' (Mays 1954: 74). You are the most arrogant big-headed …' (Russell 1996 [1976]: 252). 'I know it sounds big-headed an' that' (Sampson 1999: 105). Recorded from m.19c.; an Americanism; derivation is clear.

Big House, The (n.): The Vines pub, Lime Street; Liverpool Crown Court. 'De Big Ouse. *The Vines Public House*' (Shaw et al. 1966: 30). '(THE) BIG 'OUSE. Liverpool Crown Court. Also still used for The Vines public house in Lime Street' (Spiegl 1989: 15). 'Outside the "Big House" in Lime Street' (Elliott 2006 [1940s–70s]: 89). *NR; *The Vines* is a baroque Edwardian pub on Lime Street.

Billy Boys/Billies (n.): members of the Orange Order; Protestants in general. 'Curious people those Postlethwaites. Of course they were Billies' (Hanley

1935: 57). 'Something in its solidity led Billy Boys (Orangemen) to call a Priest Fr. Bunloaf' (Shaw 1958d: 19). Recorded from e.20c.; probably borrowed from Scotland; refers to King William of Orange, Protestant Conqueror of Ireland in 1690.

Binlid (n.): kid. 'Rear a few "bin lids"' (McGovern 1995: 29). 'It's just for his missus and binlids' (Sampson 2001: 305). 'When I was a binlid she lost one of her beams' (Griffiths 2003: 111). Recorded from l.20c.; from rhyming slang.

Binman (n.): refuse collector. 'The bin-feller is also known as, and calls himself, the *Muck-man* or *Midden-man*' (Shaw 1958d: 15). 'De binnie … The binman' (Shaw et al. 1966: 23). 'Ran off with a bin-man in the end' (Bleasdale 1975: 119). 'Beaten at Trivial Pursuit by a binman and his wife' (Graham 1988: 74). Recorded from m.20c.; the northern version of 'dustman'; derivation is clear.

Binnie (n.): binman. 'De binnie … The binman' (Shaw et al. 1966: 23). 'Completely ignoring the three binnies' (Graham 1988: 42). *NR; see *binman*.

Bint (n.): girl, young woman; girlfriend. '*Bint* A girl' (Spiegl 2000b: 40). 'That mad fuckin bint causin me this pain' (Griffiths 2002: 101). Recorded from l.19c.; popularised in Forces' usage; one account gives an accurate sense of both the etymology of the word and its derogatory nuance: '*Bint.*– A young female. The Arabic *bint*: daughter: a woman, as distinct from a lady' (Brophy and Partridge *s.v. Bint*).

Bird (n.): woman; girlfriend, wife. 'There were other men as well as other birds' (Hignett 1966: 182). 'Birds, tarts, wimmin' (Jacques 1973: n.p.). 'BAIRD: Standard Scouse for "bird" = girlfriend' (Spiegl 1989: 13). 'It's fuckin Victor with that bird from Magnet' (Griffiths 2002: 85). Recorded from l.19c.; in e.14c. *bird* meant both 'young man' and 'maiden, girl', though by 16c. it had narrowed to both 'a prostitute, a promiscuous woman' and 'a young woman, a girlfriend, a mistress'. The familiar, derogatory Liverpool sense, 'girl or woman', is a revival, probably an Americanism.

Bit of fluff (n.): woman, girlfriend. 'Martin was in love with his grandad's maid, a little bit of fluff called Mary' (Bleasdale 1975: 200). 'In the hope of picking up a "bit of fluff"' (Melly 1984 [30s–40s]: 39). 'He's latched on to a bit of fluff' (Fagan 2007 [1950s]: 287). Recorded from e.20c.; a derogatory extension of l.18c. 'fluff', 'light, feathery stuff', hence 'insubstantial and unimportant'.

Bit of meat (n.): woman. '[He] legged it to America with his bit of meat dressed up as a lad' (Bleasdale 1975: 85). Recorded from l.20c.; a 20c. derogatory extension (also used to mean 'vagina' and 'sexual intercourse') of 16c. 'meat', 'a woman's body'.

Bit of skirt (n.): woman. 'A nice juicy bit of skirt, eh?' (Brophy 1934: 42). 'Ditched her for/a plumper bit of skirt' (Simpson 1990: 94). 'I'm not a tart, I'm not a bit of skirt' (Sinclair 1999 [1930s–e.40s]: 54). 'Talkin' about bits of skirt; about birds' (Fagan 2007 [1950s]: 218). Recorded from e.20c.; a derogatory extension of l.19c. *skirt*, 'woman'.

Bit of stuff (n.): woman; girlfriend. 'Look at that bit of stuff over there. She's hot stuff!' (Hanley 2009 [1936]: 556). 'He usually drinks with his bit of stuff' (Bleasdale 1975: 66). 'All gone/to younger-looking bits of stuff' (Simpson 1990: 103). 'Stoppin' out all night with bits of stuff' (Fagan 2007 [1950s]: 261). Recorded from e.20c.; a derogatory extension of l.19c. 'stuff', 'attractive woman', and *bit of fluff*.

Bits (n.): scraps of meat at a butcher; scraps of potato or batter at a *chippy*. 'She can give the butcher full change ... fumbling in her pocket for the few coppers to pay for her "plate of bits"' (Shimmin 1863: 36). '*Bits*: Small pieces and left-over ends of meat used for making cheap stew, including *lobscouse* (scouse). Also over-cooked fragments of potato and batter sold as a by-product by some fish-and-chip shops' (Lane 1966: 9). 'Coopers for "three penn'orth of bits of bacon"' (Unwin 1984 [1920s–30s]: 39). *NR in this specific sense; ultimately from Old English 'bita', 'morsel' (a 'biteful, mouthful').

Bizzies/Busies/Busys (n.): the police. 'Policemen. Busys, Muskers, Mingees' (Minard 1972: 89). '"Jesus look at the busies!" Police officers are appearing from nowhere' (McClure 1980: 28). 'The busies warn us' (Brown 1989: 14). 'When the bizzies moved in' (Sampson 2002: 233). 'The thrill of victory over the "bizzies"' (Lees 2013: 171). Recorded from e.20c.; probably from 'busy' or 'busybody'.

Black and tan (n.): mixed beer drink (stout and mild). 'The mixture, beer and stout, "black and tan", is also much in demand' (Shaw 1959a: 37). 'Same again and a black and tan' (Hignett 1966: 43). 'It was as if a moonman had

walked into The Boundary and ordered a Black and Tan' (Bleasdale 1975: 204). '"Black 'n' Tan" is a mixture of Guinness and pale ale' (Lees 2013: 137). *NR; from the colour of the constituent beers.

Black-balling (n.): stealing, pilfering; cruelty. Recorded as 'a sailor's word' that 'originated amongst the employees of the old Black Ball line of steamers between New York and Liverpool' (Farmer and Henley 1890–1904 *s.v black-balling*). The scandalous conduct of officers towards the men, and sailors to each other, made the Black Ball line synonymous with cruelty and thieving.

Black Maria (n.): police van. 'No one became alarmed until the ambulance or the Black Maria pulled up to the door' (O'Mara 1934: 128). 'The police cars on the old tram lines and a Black Maria' (Bleasdale 1975: 71). 'Black Marias to cart the men to the cells' (Robinson 1986 [1920s–30s]: 18). 'Busies are swarming everywhere, nicking every likely head and lobbing them in the Maria' (Sampson 1998: 110). 'The police van, more commonly known as the "Black Maria"' (Stamper 2010: 25). Recorded from m.19c.; an Americanism; derivation unknown.

Blackheads (n.): car keys. 'Black 'eads. Not enlarged pores but a nickname for car keys' (Spiegl 1989: 16). *NR in this sense; from the black rubber tops to car keys.

Blackie (n.): police van. '*Blackie*: A police van. Derived from *Black Maria*' (Lane 1966: 9). *NR; see *Black Maria*.

Blacklead (n.): pencil. 'I have noticed the following in speech and in the local press: ... blacklead for "*pencil*"' (Collinson

1927: 121). Recorded from 17c.; glossed as obsolete; derivation is clear.

Blad (n.): newspaper. '*Newspaper*. Linenn, Blad' (Minard 1972: 90). *NR in this sense; 'blad' was a 20c. technical term in the book trade for a sheaf of specimen pages.

Bladdered (adj.): very drunk. 'Bladdered. Same as Bevvied' (Spiegl 1989: 17). 'Bladdered by the way, fucking *steaming* drunk' (Sampson 2002: 147). 'Bladdered lads grope sunbed blondes' (Lees 2013: 253). Recorded from l.20c.; probably from association with a full bladder.

Blag (n.): robbery; criminality. 'Our most famous blag was the transporter with all the Mercs on it' (Sampson 2001: 16). Recorded from l.19c.; an extension of the sense of deception in *blag¹ (v.)*.

Blag¹ (v.): to lie, pretend, deceive. 'Blag. To tell a fib, exaggerate' (Spiegl 1989: 17). 'I've … always blagged it that it's only a little VAT sting' (Sampson 2001: 100). Recorded from l.19c.; an Anglicisation of the French 'blaguer', 'to tell lies'.

Blag² (v.): to beg; to get for free (usually by deception). 'I'm going to need to blag a ride to school or I'll be late' (Sampson 2001: 86). 'Itchin to get ar hands on temazzy scripts or other stuff we could blag' (Griffiths 2003: 64). Recorded from m.20c.; an extension of *blag¹ (v.)*.

Blagger¹ (n.): purse or watch-snatcher; later robber. 'Pete was a blagger and very good at it' (Clerk 1971 [c.1900]: 69). 'A copper and a blagger – so what?' (Sampson 2001: 224). Recorded as e.20c. 'Liverpool street arabs' (Beale (1984) *s.v. blagger* 1); see *blag (n.)*.

Blagger² (n.): story-teller; liar. 'BLAGGER To tell a fib, to exaggerate' (Spiegl 1989: 17). Recorded from m.20c.; see *blag¹ (v.)*.

Blammo (n.): Racist term for black person. 'Blammo. *A negro*' (Shaw et al. 1966: 28). 'Most poor whites hated "blammos" (Blacks)' (Lees 2013: 124). *NR; an offensive 20c. coinage; possibly an abbreviation of 'blackamoor' or a combination of 'black' and 'Sambo'.

Blert (n.): idiot, fool. 'You BLERT! You fucking soft cunt!' (Sampson 2002: 118). 'The fuck's wrong with these blerts?' (Griffiths 2003: 92). Recorded as l.20c. 'Liverpool usage' (Dalzell and Victor (2006) *s.v. blert* n.); an extension of m.20c. 'blert', 'vagina'.

Blimp (n.): look, glance. 'Dijja gerra blimp. *Did you manage to peek up that girl's skirt?*' (Minard 1972: 65). 'Let's go down the precinct on the blimp then' (Redmond 1982: 99). 'So's I could get a blimp of those massive big tits' (Sampson 2002: 86). 'Chinkie blimped a girl' (Fagan 2007 [1950s]: 77). Recorded from m.20c.; usually with sexual connotations; derivation unclear.

Blind (adj.): used for negative emphasis, not one; not the slightest. 'Wooden say a blind werd to you' (Shaw 1957a: 12). 'E wooden take a blind bit er notice of me' (Lane 1966: 9). 'Don't believe a blind word of it' (Brown 1989: 30). ''Asn't done yer a blind bit of good' (Bryan 2003 [1940s–50s]: 183). Recorded from 20c.; derivation unclear but possibly an extension of 'blind', 'completely, totally' (from 18c. 'blind drunk').

Blind man/blinder/blindy (n.): alcoholic. '*Blind man/blinder/blindy*: A person addicted to the drinking of wood alcohol, surgical or methylated spirits' (Lane 1966: 10). *NR; a m.20c. revival of 17c. 'blind' meaning 'drunk'. See *blind*.

Blind O'Reilly (int.): a gentle expletive. 'Good Blind O'Reilly!' (Kersh 1942: 87). Recorded from e.20c.; Forces' usage; O'Reilly was supposedly 'a Liverpool docker trade unionist ca. 1910' (Beale (1984) *s.v. Blind O'Reilly!*).

Blind Scouse (n.): scouse without meat. 'Sometimes funds were low and did not suffice for the purchase of meat. On these occasions we made "blind scouse"' (Anon. 1939b: 4). 'It was almost like "blind scouse" – no meat in it' (Anon. 1945c: 3). 'When you are absolutely on the rocks, blind scouse, a concoction of any available vegetables containing no meat whatsoever' (Whittington-Egan 1955a: 6). 'Sometimes with meat, and sometimes without, when it was known as "blind scouse"' (Harrison 1964: 2). '"Blind Scouse" was the humorous term for [Scouse] without any meat' (Unwin 1984 [1920s–30s]: 31). 'Blind scouse, a stew with no meat' (Elliott 2006 [1940s–70s]: 8). *NR; an e.20c. coinage, from the general early sense of 'blind' meaning 'deficient'.

Block (v.): to have sex. '*Block*: To have sexual intercourse' (Lane 1966: 10). Recorded from l.19c.; probably an abbreviation of the Americanism 'to put the blocks to', by way of Irish English.

Block, do your (v.): to become angry, excited, worried. '*I done me block*; I went off my head; I lost my temper' (Lane 1966: 10). Recorded as an e.20c. Australian coinage; from 17c. 'block', 'head'.

Blocker (n.): bowler hat, worn by foremen on Liverpool docks. 'The "blocker" (bowler hat) was of the ordinary kind' (Owen 1921: 77). 'She seemed to remember him in a bowler hat. He'd worn one at the wedding, the first "blocker" he'd ever had' (Brophy 1934: 204). 'New blocker, new tie' (Hanley 2009 [1940]: 422). 'The Blocker is a bowler hat and signified with a blue-serge suit the utmost respectability. Liverpool had a peculiar-shaped bowler with a rocking horse brim' (Shaw 1959a: 32). '*Blocker*: A bowler or derby hat. Also called a *funeral* or *burial* hat. Less frequently a *plug-hat*' (Lane 1966: 10). 'Boys with their dads' bowler hats, or "blockers"' (Unwin 1984 [1920s–30s]: 79). *NR in this sense; recorded from e.20c.; from 'block', 'mould for a hat'.

Blocker-man (n.): foreman; supervisor. 'The "Blocker Man" (a Blocker is a bowler hat, ensign of the overseer) or "Cod boss" still denotes the foreman' (Whittington-Egan 1955a: 6). 'Blocker Men for supervisors of any kind' (Shaw 1959a: 32). 'Der blockerman. *The foreman*' (Shaw et al. 1966: 57). 'I'll show yez the Blocker Man' (Jacques 1975: n.p.). 'Bawl of blockermen doling out day's work' (Simpson 1995: 27). 'Blocker man – Foreman' (Callaghan 2011 [1910s–30s]: vii). *NR; see *blocker*.

Blocks (n.): cheap coal. '*Blocks*: Compressed cubes of coal-dust, sawdust and cement used to keep household fires going' (Lane 1966: 10). *NR; *blocks* were cheap fuel when coal fires were the main source of heating.

Blood (n.): passenger on a ship. 'Dthe bludz on yeah? *Have the passengers begun to embark*' (Minard 1972: 92). Recorded from e.19c.; a term used by the crew, usually stewards, on liners; derivation unclear.

Blood olly (n.): red *olly*, marble. '*Blood-olly*: An olley or marble made of red-streaked stone' (Lane 1966: 10). *NR; from the colour of the marble.

Bloody bucket (n.): an insult. 'I turned and challenged him, "Come on yer bloody bucket", I said' (Clerk 1971 [*c*.1900]: 27). Attributed to 'Liverpool street arabs and other lower-class Liverpudlians: late C.19–earlyish 20' (Beale (1984) *s.v. bloody bucket*); from the 'blood bucket', used in an abattoir to store blood (for black puddings), hence dirty and unclean.

Bloody Forty (n.): gang name from the 1850s. '*Bloody Forty*. A criminal gang in the Liverpool Docks in the 'fifties' (Bowen 1929: 14). 'Bloody Forty … forty seamen who together would ship as a crew aboard hell-ships, in order to turn the tables on rough bucko mates and masters' (Hughill 1967: 89). 'A gang of feared Liverpool seamen who went by the name of "The Bloody Forty"' (Lees 2013: 74). Recorded from m.19c.; derivation is clear.

Blosh (v.): to ejaculate. 'An can I blosh on yer fuckin chin, by the way' (Griffiths 2003: 12). Recorded from e.21c.; probably echoic, from 'splosh', 'splash'.

Blow (n.): rest, breather. '*Rest period*. Welt, Blow' (Minard 1972: 90). 'You can't stop and have a blow under a tree' (Bleasdale 1975: 105). Recorded as a m.19c. Americanism; from 'blow', 'breathe'.

Blow out (n.): large meal or drinking session. 'A good blow out like wot you 'ave jus' gived me' (Roberts 1893: 208). 'A good blow-out at the shipbuilders' expense' (Hall 2004 [1939]: 131). 'He felt tempered to stooge into some café and stand himself a blow-out but refrained' (Cross 1951: 195). Recorded from e.19c.; derivation unclear.

Blow through (n.): sex. '*Blow-through*: Sexual intercourse' (Lane 1966: 11). 'I yad a cup of tea anna blowthrough. I slept with an unknown lady' (Minard 1972: 68). Recorded from l.19c.; supposedly from the process of blowing steam through an engine's cylinders.

Blow up (v.): to inform on, betray. 'He was one of the people that Blazes, when he was drunk, was blowing up as a pirate' (Maginn 1844: 2.43). 'Someone's blown you up, Freda' (Bleasdale 1985: 98). 'He wouldn't hesitate to blow you up if he saw you misbehaving' (Burnett 2011: 68). Recorded from 16c.; current from l.16c.–18c. but retained in northern dialectal use; derivation unclear.

Blower (n.): phone; public address system in a bookie. 'The general noise and the crackle from the blower' (Hignett 1966: 271). 'We'll 'ave ter gerron the blower' (Jacques 1975: n.p.). 'Up to Basher's room for a free use of his blower' (Brown 1989: 66). Recorded from e.20c.; originally 'phone', but the more specialised use of the term is m.20c.; from the 'blowers', 'speaking tubes', used in shops and factories.

Blowing for tugs (phr.): out of breath, wheezy. '"I'm blowin fer tugs" ("I am short of breath")' ('Postman' 1966a: 6). '"Yer blowin' fer tugs", the old dear remarks sympathetically' (McClure 1980: 377). 'Anyone who had overexerted himself and was out of breath would describe himself as "Blowin' for tugs"' (Sanders and Sanders 2009 [1960s]: 12). *NR; possibly from ships signalling ('blowing') the need for help (the 'tug').

Blue frightener (n.): debt collection letter. 'I have lost count of the "blue frighteners"' (Whittaker 1934: 288). *NR; see *blue paper*.

Blue paper (with a duck on it) (n.): a summons. 'A policeman standing at the door, a blue paper in his hands' (Hanley 1932: 169). '[What is] "a blue paper with a duck on it"?' (Shaw 1962g: 6). '*Summings*: A summons ... Also a *blue paper*' (Lane 1966: 104). 'Blue-paper. A summons, Liverpool' (Howarth 1985: n.p.). 'I gorra blue paper wid a duck on. I have received a summons from court' (Spiegl 2000b: 153). *NR; official notices, such as debt collection letters or summonses, were written on blue paper; summonses from Liverpool City Magistrates' courts bore the emblem of the Liver Bird (the duck).

Blue Pig (n.): Whisky. '*Blue Pig*. Maine is a temperance state, therefore liquor has to be asked for under various strange names ... as in this instance' (Ware 1909: 38). *NR; a l.19c. Americanism recorded as 'common in Liverpool' (Ware *s.v. Blue Pig*).

Blues, the (n.): Everton F.C. 'The Blues became slovenly in passing and clearing' (Anon. 1945f: 3). 'Up the blues, up the reds' (Hignett 1966: 224). 'Dthe blooz lost' (Minard 1972: 23). 'Devotees of the reds or the blues' (Fagan 2007 [1950s]: 76). *NR; nickname based on the colour of Everton's home kit.

Bob (n.): shilling. See *few bob*.

Bobber (n.): champion *cherrywob*. 'How a "bobber" (the champion cherry-stone in a certain game) was made' (Shaw 1960a: 37). 'Bobber. A champion cherry-stone used in children's games. Liverpool' (Howarth 1985: n.p.). *NR; see *cherrywobs*.

Bobbing (n.): taking time off. '"Bobbing" is the same as skiving' (Spiegl 1989: 84). *NR in this sense; probably from 14c. 'to bob', 'cheat, deceive'.

Bobby/Bobbies (n.): the police. 'The bobbies'll 'ave their eyes on yer' (Hocking 1966 [1879]: 133). 'Very soon after I seed a bobby sent fur' (Roberts 1893: 209). 'The bobbies walk up here in pairs' (O'Mara 1934: 5). 'A curious but slow country bobby' (Cross 1951: 226). 'The bobbies (known as scuffers in Liverpool, Paddy Rileys on the waterfront), would have to be watched' (Anon. 1955: 6). 'Cover her up before the bloody bobbies let her move' (Hignett 1966: 116). 'Things get accentuated in bobbies' minds' (McClure 1980: 20). 'I'll get the bobbies on yer!' (Sinclair 1999 [1930s–e.40s]: 24). 'The docker, the bobby, the teacher' (Callaghan 2011 [1910s–30s]: 7). Recorded from e.19c.; usually explained by reference to Sir Robert Peel, the Home Secretary responsible for the Metropolitan Police Act in 1828, but it may be an older allusion to the official square-keeper whose role was to keep the poor away from wealthier areas: 'Bobby the beadle'.

Bobby dazzler (n.): something exceptional;

an attractive woman. '*Bobby dazzler*:
Anything considered good-looking,
attractive, especially a girl' (Lane 1966:
11). 'We do look a bobby dazzler'
(Bainbridge 1973: 25). 'Mind you
some bobby-dazzlers too!' (Simpson
1995: 22). Recorded as m.19c.; north-
western dialectal; 'bobby' is probably
an extension of 'bobbish', 'well, in
good spirits'.

Bog (n.): toilet. 'Eh laz, wurz dthe bog?
*Excuse me, sir, would you direct me
to the toilet?*' (Minard 1972: 49). 'A
quiet ciggy in the bog' (Brown 1989:
6). 'Gonner have to make a bog stop
soon, I'm burstin' (Griffiths 2003: 151).
Recorded from m.19c.; an abbreviation
of 17c. 'bog-house', from 'to bog', 'to
evacuate the bowels'.

Bog-eyed (adj.): bleary-eyed. 'I was still
usually bog-eyed till about half way
through the round' (Bleasdale 1975:
57). 'Bog-eyed. Sleepy, half-asleep'
(Howarth 1985: n.p.). Recorded from
l.20c.; derivation unknown.

Bogies (n.): type of *ollies*. '*Bogies*. Large
pottery marbles' (Lane 1966: 11). *NR;
derivation unknown.

Bogtrotter/boghopper (n.): Irish person.
'*Bog-trotter* or *bog-hopper*: An Irishman,
usually not from Cork or Dublin' (Lane
1966:11). Recorded from 17c.; though
used to refer to the Irish, the term was
dated in this general derogatory sense
by 20c.; the specificity of the Liverpool
usage suggests a borrowing from 20c.
Irish English in which *bogtrotter* meant
'a person with awkward manners'
rather than an Irish person in general.

Boilermaker (n.): a half of draught
mild added to a half of bottled
brown ale. 'Another mixed drink is a
BOILERMAKER'. Recorded from
20c.; from the 'boiling' appearance of
the drink when mixed.

Boiling piece (n.): insulting term for
woman. '*Boiling piece*: Used to describe
a fat, ugly woman' (Sanders and Sanders
2009 [1960s]: 184). *NR; probably an
abbreviation of 'boiling piece of meat';
see *bit of meat*.

Bollocky Fifth (n.): Fifth Rifles, The
King's (Liverpool) Regiment. '*Bollicky
Fifth, Ther: The 5th (Rifle) Battalion,
The King's (Liverpool) Regiment*' (Lane
1966: 11). *NR; the nickname was
derived from a marching song.

Bomb (n.): lot of money. 'Making you pay
a bomb for it'. (Smith 1998 [1971]: 12).
'Me and Mooey did a bomb with the
trees' (Bleasdale 1975: 36). Recorded
from m.20c.; the precise derivation is
unclear.

Bomb (v.): to move very quickly. 'There's
no traffic on the roads. Y'll bomb
along, no messin'' (Bleasdale 1975:
114). Recorded from m.20c.; derivation
is clear.

Bombed church/Bombed out church (n.):
St. Luke's Church. 'Right at the back
of the bombed church' (Hignett
1966: 147). 'The ugly beauty of the
bombed-out church' (Lees 2013: 252).
*NR; St. Luke's Church (1832), in
Liverpool city centre, was destroyed
during the Liverpool Blitz in May 1941
but is preserved as a war memorial.

Bommy[1]/bombdie (n.): bombed site;
derelict area. 'A debbie, bommie A
derelict (bombed) house' (Spiegl 2000b:
133). *NR; Second World War bombing
raids, and the urban regeneration
schemes of the 1960s, created many
derelict sites; derivation is clear.

Bommy²/bonny (n.): Bonfire, usually with reference to Bonfire Night. 'Then the was Bonfire night wid all sorts a bonnies and bangolits' (Shaw 1957a: 4). 'A "bonny" is made from contributions of inflammable material levied on all houses, each street having its own' (Shaw 1960a: 41). 'One favourite activity is "bonnies in the oller"' (Parker 1974: 47). 'I wonder what he'll say when we burn it down next Bommie Night' (Bleasdale 1975: 22). 'There's something/for your bommy' (Simpson 1990: 64). *NR; derivation is clear.

Bonce (n.): head. 'He knocks the box right on the rentman's bonce' (Brown 1989: 44). 'It was good to feel the sun on the back of my bonce again' (Sampson 2001: 4). Recorded from l.19c.; derivation unknown.

Bonzer (adj.): excellent, outstandingly good. '*Bonzer*: very good; excellent. Less used than *ther gear*' (Lane 1966: 11). Recorded from m.20c.; an Australian variant of 'bonanza'.

Boodle (n.): money. 'He always treats the boys after he receives "the boodle" from the Sheriff for sending an unfortunate to the other side' (Ware 1909: 42). Recorded from l.19c.; an Americanism recorded as 'Boodle (Liverpool). One of the New York terms for money' (Ware *s.v. boodle*); from Dutch, 'boedel', 'possession, inheritance, stock'.

Booze (n.): alcohol. 'Sam was such a beggar for the booze' (Hall 2004 [1939]: 131). 'The devising of phonetic equivalents without recourse to the symbols which look like the alphabet has been on the booze' (Shaw 1962f: 12). 'An ancient Irish woman full of booze and goodness' (Murari 1975: 101). 'Made

sure he had money for booze' (Flame 1984: 8). 'That early-hours tingle of nicotine and booze and possibility' (Sampson 1999: 460). 'After he had had his booze' (Stamper 2010: 113). Recorded from 14c.; originally 'bouse', 'to drink' (alcohol), but popularised through l.16c. cant; from Middle Dutch 'bûsen', 'to drink to excess'.

Booze-hound (n.): a drunk. '*Booze-hound*: A persistent drunkard' (Lane 1966: 11). Recorded from e.20c.; an Americanism; derivation is clear.

Booze-jerk/booze-jerker (n.): bartender. '*Booze-jerk* or *jerker*: bartender' (Lane 1966: 11). *NR; recorded from m.20c.; from 'jerk', 'pull' (pints); see *booze*.

Booze-moke (n.): dray horse. '*Booze-moke*: A brewery horse' (Lane 1966: 12). *NR; see *moke*.

Booze-mopper (n.): heavy drinker. 'Many a Scouser considers it flattering to be known as a bloody good booze-mopper' (Lane 1966: 71). *NR; see *mop*.

Booze up (n.): drinking session. 'Evr'y Satdy night we 'ad a bloody good booze up' (Lane 1966:12). Recorded from l.19c.; see *booze*.

Boozer (n.): pub. 'She does spend all her time in the boozer' (Hanley 1932: 100). 'Some lovely boozers up here and all!' (Owen 1961: 16). 'The boozer on the corner' (Moloney 1966: 38). 'Just fucked off to the boozer' (Parker 1974: 94). 'This boozer, yer mean?' (McClure 1980: 339). 'After midnight boozers' (McGovern 1995: 22). 'Fin a boozer an get wrecked there' (Griffiths 2002: 51). Recorded from l.19c.; see *booze*.

Boozery (n.): brewery. '*Boozery*: A brewery' (Lane 1966: 11). *NR in this sense; see *booze*.

Boozing with the bugs (phr.): drinking at home. '*Boozin' wit' ther bugs*: solitary drinking at home' (Lane 1966: 12). *NR; derivation is clear.

Boss[1] *(n.)*: familiar term of address. 'Come, old boss, we ain't a-blamin' yer' (Hocking 1966 [1879]: 125). 'You haven't had it long, boss?' (Haigh 1907: 89). 'If the term "boss" is used it will be in a casual, non-sycophantic manner … "Boss" as we give it, or get it, has none of the subservience I find in the Cockney "guv" or "guv'nor"' (Shaw 1963e: 4). '"Whurr's we goin' boss" asks the taxi-driver' (Channon 1970: 104). 'Wot's this boss? Somethin' op?' (McClure 1980: 313). 'There y'are, boss' (Maddox 2008 [1930s–40s]: 217). Recorded from m.19c.; an Americanism; an extension of 17c. 'boss', 'master' (also American usage); from Dutch 'baas', 'master'.

Boss[2] *(adj.)*: excellent. 'It was boss la' (Murari 1975: 53). 'Considering that it's nearly Christmas and that, it's a boss fucking day' (Sampson 2001: 3). 'Fuckin boss it was' (Griffiths 2003: 112). Recorded from m.19c.; an American extension of *boss*[1].

Boss-eyed (adj.): cross-eyed, squinty. 'If it's "no" y'tell him he's a boss-eyed bastard an y' run off' (Bleasdale 1975: 122). Recorded from m.19c.; originally 'a person with one eye, or one eye injured'; 'to boss' was dialectal, 'to miss an aim, make a mistake', though this may be a back-formation from *boss-eyed*.

Bothered (adj.): deaf. 'The vocabulary of the Irish area [of Liverpool] contains several genuine Anglo-Irish and Irish (= Gaelic) words, such as "skallan" (young onion) "caubeen" (hat), "bothered"

– deaf (ear)' (Oakes Hirst 1951: 4). Recorded from e.18c.; from dialectal, 'to deafen'; probably a borrowing from Irish English, ultimately Gaelic 'bodhar', 'deaf'.

Bottle (n.): courage. 'Lot lost his bottle an' left' (Jacques 1975: n.p.). 'Thought yer bottle was goin' to go there for a second like!' (McClure 1980: 62). 'He lost his bottle' (Spiegl 1989: 18). 'They bottled it' (Sampson 1999: 419). 'You had to possess a little bottle' (Burnett 2011: 26). Recorded from m.20c.; possibly from m.19c. 'no bottle', 'no good, useless'.

Bottle (v.): hit with a bottle. 'The "bottling" of the glass thrower' (Parker 1974: 141). 'You get bottled, you get stoned' (McClure 1980: 100) 'Big mad fights, lads getting bottled' (Sampson 2002: 241). Recorded from m.19c.; derivation is clear.

Bottle-nose (n.): ugly, swollen, aged nose. Recorded from 16c.; glossed as the 'scornful designation of the aged nose … Heard in Liverpool' (Ware *s.v. bottle nose*).

Bowyanks (n.): bands worn around trousers to keep them up. 'The bits of string navvies still wear around their moleskins are called Bowyanks' (Shaw 1959a: 34). 'Bow-yank. Cord tied round the trouser leg. Liverpool' (Howarth 1985: n.p.). Recorded from l.19c.; an Australian coinage, derivation unknown.

Boxed[1] *(adj.)*: placed in a coffin or buried. '*Boxed*. Boxed in one's coffin or actually buried' (Lane 1966: 12). *NR in this sense; from 'box', e.19c. 'coffin'.

Boxed[2] *(adj.)*: very drunk or intoxicated. 'Wrecked. Totally ruined by excesses, usually drugs and/or alcohol. Also Boxed' (Spiegl 1989: 84). Recorded from m.20c.; an Americanism; probably from 'box', 'head' (hence 'out of one's box').

Boxed off (adj.): looked after, taken care of. 'Barrie Wells has the kids boxed off for smiles at Liverpool FC' (Hilton 2012: 4). Recorded from l.20c.; derivation unknown.

Boxer (n.): coffin-maker, undertaker. '*Boxer*: A coffin-maker. Sometimes applied to an undertaker' (Lane 1966: 12). *NR in this sense; see *boxed*[1].

Boys call 'meal' after her (phr.): sexually attractive woman. Recorded as '1950–75: perhaps mostly Liverpudlian' (Beale (1985) *s.v. boys call 'meal' after her*); derivation is clear.

Boys' Pen (n.): section of Anfield and Goodison football grounds reserved for boys. 'Admitting boys to the "Boys' Pen", where they are well away from the influence of Spion Kop' (Anon. 1939c: 8). 'Stay in the boy's pen as long as you can, it's cheaper' (Hignett 1966: 202). 'I thought y'was banned from the Boys' Pen' (Bleasdale 1975: 15). 'The Boys' pen at Anfield or Goodison Park' (Unwin 1984 [1920s–30s]: 36). 'There was a "Boy's Pen" at one corner of the ground' (Maddox 2008 [1930s–40s]: 100). *NR; until the late 1970s, at the back of the Kop and the Gwladys Street End, there was a small, fenced-off section of the terrace reserved for boys; from 'pen', 'animal enclosure'.

Brass[1] *(n.)*: prostitute. '*Promiscuous woman*. Brass, Pallyass, Good thing, Cert, Charva' (Minard 1972: 89). 'I'd scoured these streets, this city, relentlessly in pursuit of brass on many a drug-fuelled bender' (Walsh 2004: 2). 'Local brasses lured the foolhardy' (Lees 2013: 78). Recorded from e.20c.; from rhyming slang, 'brass nail', 'tail' (l.18c. term for 'prostitute').

Brass[2] *(n.)*: money. 'As true as you are here, that nagur of mine just comes home, pitches the brass on the table, and cuts away to his cronies' (Shimmin 1863: 2). 'No brass, no ship' (Hall 2004 [1939] 133). 'Fucking brass la … fucking leather chairs' (Murari 1975: 20). Recorded from 16c.; from the earlier 'brass', 'bronze or copper coin'.

Brass (v.): to pay. 'He wanted us, but "bras us fust", Rhuie told him' (Clerk 1971 [c.1900]: 16). Recorded as 'Liverpool proletarian, esp, street arabs: since ca. 1880' (Beale (1984) *s.v. brass v.* 3).

Brassed off (adj.): annoyed, fed up. 'I could tell they was brassed off' (Bleasdale 1975: 119). 'I'm getting brassed off with me dad' (McGovern 1995: 8). Recorded from e.20c.; an extension of e.20c. Forces' usage 'to brass off', 'to grumble'; derivation unknown.

Brassic (adj.): broke, penniless. 'Ah'd spent enough poke to sink the Mint/Full to the tonsils an' Brassick Lint' (Jacques 1972: n.p.). 'Ee's flush like, which is fine by me cos I'm fuckin brassic' (Griffiths 2000: 94). Recorded from m.20c.; from rhyming slang; 'boracic lint', 'skint'.

Brawn (n.): pig-meat. 'The cold brawn sandwich he had made for himself' (Cross 1951: 135). 'Then there was brawn, a red-coloured meaty product' (Kelly 2006 [1930s–40s]: 104). 'Corned beef; delicious brawn' (Callaghan 2011 [1910s–30s]: 17). Recorded from 14c.; *brawn* was a cheap cut in m.20c. Britain, though when taken from the pig's head, it is a gourmet delicacy (known in France as 'fromage de tête').

Bread and spit (n.): dry bread; bread with a lick of margarine. '*Bread 'n' spit* Bread and margarine' (Spiegl 2000b: 124). *NR; the threatened diet of disobedient Liverpool schoolchildren (supposedly based on the diet of prisoners); derivation is clear.

Break eleven (v.): to get caught, found out. '*Break eleven*: To be caught in a nefarious act' (Lane 1966: 12). *NR; recorded from l.19c.; a reference to the 'Eleventh Commandment': 'Thou shalt not be found out'.

Breaks (n.): broken biscuits. '*Breaks*: Broken, defective or damaged biscuits sold cheaply, usually from a crate or barrel' (Lane 1966: 12). *NR in this sense; derivation is clear.

Breck/Brekkie (n.): breakfast. 'BRECK: A prisoner's last meal, i.e. breakfast at 8am, on the last day of his sentence' (Spiegl 1989: 19). 'A bite of brekkie with Sandy' (Sampson 1999: 111). 'That bag of Sayer's doughnuts yer ad for yer brekkie' (Griffiths 2003: 75). Recorded from e.20c.; derivation is clear.

Brew¹/brue/broo (n.): hill or slope. '"Brue", meaning hill' (Griffith 1950: 2). 'Follow the fellers from the boozer up the *broo* (hill)' (Shaw 1959a: 35). '*Brew*: A slope, rise or hill. *Oop ther brew*: Up the slope' (Lane 1966: 12). 'I was comin' down the brew towards our house' (Bleasdale 1977: 44). 'Brow. A hill or incline on a road' (Howarth 1985: n.p.). 'Gazing down the headlong brew at the great/business of the river' (Simpson 2011 [2001]: 282). Recorded from l.19c.; not the more common top

or 'brow' of a hill, but its slope; from Scots and Northern dialectal 'brae', 'slope, steep bank'.

Brew² (n.): tea; cup of tea. 'They'd do all their proper feeding in restaurants, and just keep a brew in the flat' (Cross 1951: 138). '*Tea, Sugar and Milk. A Brew*' (Minard 1972: 90). 'Get a brew on Loggo, will you, we won't be long' (Bleasdale 1985: 44). 'Be right when I've 'ad me brew' (Sinclair 1999 [1930s–e.40s]: 97). 'Get the brew on' (Fagan 2007 [1950s]: 54). Recorded from e.20c.; Forces' usage; a narrowing of 'to brew' (from Old English).

Brew up (v.): to make tea. '*Brew up*: To make a pot or can of tea' (Lane 1966: 12). 'They go to brew up' (Brown 1989: 62). 'They use it to brew up' (Sampson 2002: 160). Recorded as e.20c. Forces' usage; see *brew*.

Brewster's (n.): a lot of money. 'Costing us Brewster's by the way' (Sampson 2001: 84). See *brewstered*.

Brewstered (adj.): rich. 'Place's friggin screaming to be screwed. We'll be brewstered' (Griffiths 2003: 59). Recorded from l.20c.; from the title of a film, *Brewster's Millions* (1985), about inheriting a large amount of money.

Bridewell (n.): jail, lock-up. 'He and Terence went to the bridewell' (Haigh 1907: 472). 'I have noticed the following in speech and in the local press: … bridewell for "*prison*"' (Collinson 1927: 121). 'At a certain bridewell in another part of the city' (Mays 1954: 181). 'Why is it called the Bridewell?' (Shaw 1962g: 6). 'Three hours sleep in a cell at the main bridewell' (Smith 1998 [1971]: 172). 'The Main Bridewell, central lock-up for the Liverpool Petty Sessions area' (McClure 1980: 141). 'You'll all end up in the Bridewell' (Robinson 1986 [1920s–30s]: 50). 'Member them two that gave yis a kickin in the Copperas Hill bridewell?' (Griffiths 2003: 31). 'Essex Street Bridewell' (Stamper 2010: 25). Recorded from l.16c.; originally a 'house of correction' near St. Bride's holy well in London; retained as the common term for police lock-ups in Liverpool.

Briffen (n.): bread with anything on it. Recorded as 'Liverpool street arabs' and tramps' since ca 1900' (Beale (1984) *s.v. briffen* 1); possibly an abbreviation of 'bread an' anyfin'.

Bright, not too (adj.): well, healthy. *'I'm not too bright today'* (Lane 1966: 12). *NR in this exclusively negative formulation; derivation is clear.

Bristlers (n.): breasts. 'Er bristlers. *Her bosom'* (Shaw et al. 1966: 20). 'Get back to the bristlers on page three' (Graham 1988: 60). *NR; a Liverpool variant of 'bristols', 'breasts', from rhyming slang, 'Bristol Cities', 'titties'.

Bronzy (n.): suntan. *'Suntan:* Bronzy' (Minard 1972: 89). 'One thing that all Judies like is a boss bronzie' (Sampson 2002: 167). 'Not your bronzie merchants' (Fagan 2007 [1950s]: 224). *NR; derivation is clear.

Brown (n.): a copper coin; farthing or halfpenny. 'Down with the browns and don't be stingy' (Shimmin 1863: 79). 'Can't You Spare a Brown/ For the Echo Poor Kids Christmas Treat' (Clerk 1971 [*c.*1900]: 82). Recorded from e19c.; from the colour of the coin.

Brownie (n.): male prostitute. '"Brownie!" shouted a voice' (Hanley 1935: 331).

'Brownie: A male prostitute. Also called a *joy-boy, ship's Mary, etc'* (Lane 1966: 13). Recorded from m.20c.; a derogatory extension of the slightly earlier Americanism 'brownie', 'anus'.

Bubble (v.): inform on. 'Me ould lady bubbled me to Molly, so now she's talkin' about packin' me in' (Fagan 2007 [1950s]: 107). *NR; derivation unknown.

Buck (old) (n.): cheek, impudence. 'The buck she gives the old lady' (Hanley 1932: 90). 'If you gave him any ould buck' (Shaw 1957a: 15). Recorded from e.20c.; Forces' usage; from Hindi 'bak', 'exaggeration', 'buk buk', 'bragging talk, insolence'.

Buck/bucko (n.): a rough, sometimes criminal, man. 'You, my bucks, have here, in the course of the last couple of years, done me out of perhaps five or six thousand pounds' (Maginn 1844: 1.148). *'Bucko.* A hard case under sail, particularly a mate' (Bowen 1929: 19). 'As we stood in the crowd a couple of bucks walked in, ordered up some chips and fish and refused to pay' (O'Mara 1934: 232). 'Next time I'm in Belfast I'll tell the buckos' (Jerome 1948: 144). 'Me I'll alwis be a bucko I know dat' (Shaw 1957a: 7). 'I'm a Liverpool Bucko from Huyton' (Anon. 1965: 4). 'Now gather round buckoes' (Jacques 1972: n.p.). 'A typical Liverpool "buck" with his breathtaking contempt for authority' (McClure 1980: 16). 'Buck. Any young male, not necessarily criminal' (Spiegl 1989: 19). 'I used to think I was a bit of a buck back in them days' (Sampson 2001: 124). 'Young black bucks' (Lees 2013: 166). Recorded as 'a rough fellow; a criminal: Liverpool: since the 1920's' (Beale (1984) *s.v. buck*), and 'originally Liverpool use, where it survives' (Dalzell and Victor (2006) *s.v. buck*). An extension of the nautical 'bucko mate'; probably from 'buck', 'the male of several types of animal', but possibly Irish English, from Gaelic 'buachaill', 'boy'.

Buckess (n.): female *buck*. 'Bucks and buckesses! That's a good police phrase all right' (McClure 1980: 469). *NR; see *buck*.

Bucket (n.): toilet. '*Toilet*. Carzy, Bog, Bucket' (Minard 1972: 87). *NR; derivation is clear.

Bucks/Buckos (n.): the underworld; gangsters. 'This underworld is described as *Rowdies, Bucks, Buckos*, and (rarely now) *Prigs*' (Shaw 1958d: 16). *NR in this specific plural sense; see *buck/bucko*.

Buckshee (adj.): free; extra, surplus. 'Goin the match is buckshee a tree quarter time' (Shaw 1957a: 16). 'A couple of buckshee hours isn't goin' to bankrupt them' (Fagan 2007 [1950s]: 133). Recorded from e.20c.; Forces' usage; an extension of *baksheesh*, from the 17c. borrowing from Persian 'bakhshīsh', 'present, gratuity'; see *baksheesh*.

Buggered (adj.): tired out, exhausted. 'She had two jobs, one in the daytime and one at night, so she was always buggered' (Bleasdale 1975: 201). Recorded from e.20c.; a weakened sense of 'bugger'.

Bugle (n.): cocaine. '"Djer bring any with you?" — "Bugle? Nah. Ad be fuckin snortin it if I ad've done" (Griffiths 2003: 11). A l.20c. coinage; possibly from m.19c. 'bugle', 'nose'.

Bulk (adj.): see *in bulk*.

Bullamacow (n.): corned beef. '*Bullamacow*: Corned beef' (Lane 1966: 14). '*Bullamacow (also corned dog)* Corned beef' (Spiegl 2000b: 113). Recorded from l.19c.; from Fijian pidgin; originally referred both to cattle and meat.

Bulls eye lanterns/Bulls eyes (n.): police lights. 'It was only a policeman; nevertheless, Dorrie's heart jumped as his bull's-eye shed a light through the narrow space' (Tirebuck 1891: 174). 'A policeman came along and swung his bull's eye in her face' (Hanley 1932: 161). 'The police then had oil lamps, known as bulls eye lanterns' (Clerk 1971 [c.1900]: 42). Recorded from m.19c.; from the slightly earlier sense of a piece of glass inserted into the side or deck of a ship to allow light in.

Bully (n.): Princes Road Boulevard. '"Bully", Princes-road boulevard' (Jones 1935: 5). 'Princes Park Boulevard soon became "The Bully"' (Unwin 1984 [1920s–30s]: 78). *NR; derivation is clear.

Bum (n.): general insult; disreputable person; scrounger. 'Ain't you content to be a bum?' (Maginn 1844: II, 84) 'Working ashore – ah, it's a bum's life' (Hanley 2009 [1936]: 526). 'They're a right shower of bums down there' (Parker 1974: 11). 'He is a no-god drunken bum' (Brown 1989: 81). 'The bum would be drinking very slowly' (Maddox 2008 [1930s–40s]: 35). Recorded from l.19c.; an abbreviation of 'bummer', 'loafer, idler'.

Bum (v.) to beg, borrow, cadge. 'They're trying to bum money from their old ladies' (Hanley 1932: 17). 'Can I bum a cupfulla sugar fer ther time bean' (Lane 1966: 14). 'He bummed a cigarette off Sue' (Murari 1975: 24) 'Trying to bum a free ride' (Brown 1989: 66). 'He said, "sorry Mary", bummed a cup of tea' (Stamper 2010: 27). Recorded from l.19c.; an Americanism; from *bum (n.)*.

Bum boys/chum (n.): male homosexual partner. 'Where all the bum boys come from, the Wallasey bum boys' (Hignett 1966: 195). 'I'm not a bum boy' (Robinson 1986 [1920s–30s]: 80). 'Bum chum. Homosexual friend' (Spiegl 1989: 19). Recorded from m.20c.; a derogatory term; derivation is clear.

Bum-droops (n.): the effect of short legs. '*Bum-droops*: Condition attributed to person long in the trunk and short in the legs. Also called *duck's disease*' (Lane 1966: 14). *NR; derivation is clear.

Bumfluff (n.): thin facial hair (especially that of an adolescent boy). 'I'll kick your bum-fluffed face in' (Hignett 1966: 272). 'After whisking the bum fluff from my pimpled chin' (Fagan 2007 [1950s]: 73). Recorded from m.20c.; derivation is clear.

Bum's rush (n.): forceful ejection. 'Gives us the bum's rush back to the bus' (Brown 1989: 30). 'Some fussy engine rating on duty gave you the bum's rush' (Burnett 2011: 35). Recorded from e.20c.; derivation is clear.

Bumstarver (n.): short, badly fitting jacket. '*Bumstarver*: A short, ill-cut jacket' (Lane 1966: 14). *NR; derivation is clear.

Bumsuck (n.): to creep, toady. 'If you bumsuck the teachers they give you another couple of years' (Bleasdale 1975: 45). Derived by back-formation; see *bumsucker*.

Bumsucker (n.): creep, sycophant. '*Bumsucker*: A person who curries favour; a toady' (Lane 1966: 15). Recorded from l.19c.; university usage; derivation unclear.

Bun-oven (n.): top hat. 'It were a rill posh wedd'n' – 'e were wearin' stripey kecks an' a bun-oven' (Lane 1966: 15). *NR; derivation unclear.

Bunce (n.): bonus, extra money. 'You clean up a bit of bunce and your manager collars nearly half of it for himself' (Jerome 1948: 99). 'Wenever he gor good extry, a bunce for sugar say' (Shaw 1957a: 7). '*Bunce*: extra pay, bonus' (Lane 1966: 13). '*Bunce* Extra pay' (Spiegl 2000b: 103). Recorded from c.19c.; probably a simple corruption of 'bonus'.

Bundook (n.): rifle or firearm; umbrella. '*Bundook*: A rifle, shotgun or airgun. Applied ironically to an umbrella, especially when neatly folded' (Lane 1966: 15). Recorded from l.19c.; from Hindi 'bandūq', 'filbert nut', hence by extension 'musket ball' and later firearm (later still, 'umbrella').

Bung/bungole (n.): cheese. '*Bung* or *bungole*: Cheese'. (Lane 1966: 14). Recorded from e.20c.; First World War Forces' usage; supposedly from costive effects of cheese; derivation is clear.

Bunk, do a/the bunk (v.): to leave, often hurriedly or surreptitiously. 'She'd done a bunk with him back to Gelton' (Hanley 2009 [1940]: 310). 'Now she wanted him to do a bunk with her right away' (Cross 1951: 135). 'If he keeps on at me, I'm goin' t'do a bunk' (Bleasdale 1975: 80). 'Her mother did the bunk years ago' (Cornelius 2001 [1982]: 140). 'Bunk it if yer have to, but just fuckin disappear' (Griffiths 2003: 141). Recorded from l.19c.; an extension of English dialectal 'bunk', 'to escape, run off under pressure'; derivation unknown.

Bunk in/on (v.): to do something without paying for it. '"Bunking in", ie, getting into a cinema without paying' (Mays 1954: 196). 'Less bunk inter de pictures. *Let us see a film without paying*' (Shaw et al. 1966: 46). 'We'll have to bunk in the ground first, never mind slip anyone a quid' (Bleasdale 1975: 136). 'BUNK ON (E.g on buses) riding without paying' (Spiegl 1989: 19). 'I kept bunking off school, bunking the train out to Aughton' (Sampson 2001: 34). 'We'd walk over, bunk in' (Dudgeon 2010: 135). Recorded from m.20c.; an extension of the l.19c. Americanism 'bunk', 'to cheat, deceive', ultimately from 'bunkum', 'nonsense, flattery'.

Bunk off (v.): to leave; specifically to play truant. 'He let's you bunk off as well if it's important' (Bleasdale 1975: 46). 'Zammo was puzzled to see no sign of Jonah. He was beginning to wonder if he'd decided to bunk off' (Redmond 1982: 61). 'BUNK OFF (I.e. school) Playing truant, i.e. SAGG OFF' (Spiegl 1989: 19). 'I kept bunking off school' (Sampson 2001: 34). Recorded from m.20c.; see *bunk, do a*.

Bunko (adj.): dubious, deceptive. Recorded as 'from S. America. Heard in Liverpool' (Ware 1909 *s.v. bunko*) from l.19c.; originally used to refer to a card-swindle or swindler; possibly from the Spanish card game 'banca'.

Bunloaf (n.): rich currant cake. 'Bunloaf was what southrons called Christmas Cake' (Shaw 1958d: 19). Recorded from m.20c.; from Lancashire dialectal 'bunloaf', 'plum or currant cake'.

Burgoo (n.): porridge. 'Bur goo. *Porridge*' (Shaw et al. 1966: 41). '*Bur goo* Porridge' (Spiegl 2000b: 121). Recorded from 18c.; a nautical term for porridge or a sort of gruel (also known as 'loblolly'); from Arabic 'būrgūl', 'cooked, dried and crushed wheat', by way of Turkish 'bulgur'.

Burial hat (n.): see *blocker*.

Burial suit (n.): see *funeral suit*.

Burst (n.): pee. '(A) berst. Urination' (Spiegl 1989: 15). *NR in this sense; see *bursting*.

Burst (v.): attack; beat up, hit. 'I'll burst you if you're going to sit here letting me buy you coffee and watching every bird that comes in' (Hignett 1966: 168). 'I got up to burst a couple of them straight off' (Bleasdale 1975: 95). '"I'll bairst yer!" Usually said to a child, meaning "I shall strike you very hard"' (Spiegl 1989: 41). 'Outside now, you prick, if you don't want your kids to see you get burst!' (Sampson 2002: 202). Recorded from l.20c.; common in Liverpool and Irish English; an extension of the earliest sense of 'burst', 'to break, snap suddenly under pressure'.

Bursting (adj.): in urgent need of a pee. 'He's bursting to go to the lavvy' (Brown 1989: 25). 'Gonner have to make a bog stop soon, I'm burstin' (Griffiths 2003: 153). See *burst*.

Bury (v.): to do violence to. 'Come on. Who said it? I'll bury them' (Bleasdale 1975: 165). Recorded from m.20c.; derivation is clear.

Bush (n.): lodging house, pub. 'Bush. A lodging house. Liverpool' (Howarth 1985: n.p.).

Bush Baptist (n.): religious fundamentalist. 'Ah – gerron with you, y'bush Baptist!' (Owen 1961: 31). Recorded from e.20c.; Australian usage; presumably from Protestant evangelism in rural areas.

Bushed (adj.): lost, confused. '*Bushed*: Lost, bewildered' (Lane 1966: 13). Recorded from l.19c.; Australian usage; from 'being lost in the bush', hence 'confused'.

Bushwa (n.): nonsense, rubbish. '*Bushwa*: Nonsense; idle talk; a foolish rumour' (Lane 1966: 13). Recorded from e.20c.; an American euphemism for 'bullshit'.

Business girl (n.): prostitute. 'COW A prostitute or BUSINESS GIRL' (Spiegl 1989: 23). Recorded from e.20c.; an Americanism; an extension of 17c. 'business', 'sexual intercourse'.

Bust a gut (v.): become angry; exert great effort. 'To get very angry, as in *I could a bust a gut*. Also to work extremely hard, as in *I 'ad ter slog at it until I could a bust a gut*' (Lane 1966: 14). *NR in the sense of 'angry'; derivation is clear.

Busy Lizzie (n.): busybody. '*Bizzy Lizzie*: A busybody; a persistent interferer in other people's affairs' (Lane 1966: 14). *NR; a rhyming double.

Buttons¹ (n.): small amount of money. 'We got paid buttons fer that ship' (Jacques 1972: n.p.). 'Here's us workin for friggin buttons' (Griffiths 2003: 170) 'I wen there once and it paid buttons' (Burnett 2011: 132). Recorded from 14c.; from 'button', 'something of small value'.

Buttons² (n.): children's game (played with buttons). 'As for Buttons the was all sorts of rules – ow to fang, ow to make a delly – all sorts' (Shaw 1957a: 1). 'Buttons. *Marble substitutes*' (Shaw et al. 1966: 43). *NR; *buttons* was a sort of cross between *ollies* (marbles) and pitch-and-toss, with its own terms and complex rules.

Butty (n.): piece of bread spread with butter or margarine; sandwich. 'I have noticed the following in speech and in the local press: ... buttie, general in North for a piece of "*bread and butter*" (together with jam-buttie)' (Collinson 1927: 121). 'The word "butty" is age-old in Liverpool ... in my young days it was understood to be an ellipsis for "sugar butty" ('Postman' 1931b: 5). '*Butty* (piece of bread even if not buttered) (Shaw 1952: n.p). 'Margarine butties and bugger all else' (Hignett 1966: 146). 'He was reading a book an' eatin' his butties' (Bleasdale 1975: 195). He unwrapped his butties' (Graham 1988: 20). 'He tucked into his butty' (Sinclair 1999 [1930s–e.40s]: 7). 'I sit on the step and eat a ketchup buttie' (Jolliffe 2005: 1). Recorded from m.19c.; northern dialectal; an abbreviation of 'butter'. A *butty* might have neither butter nor margarine (children were often threatened with a '*bread and spit butty*'), and the variants were many. Lane notes: 'batty butty' ('an unidentifiable paste'); 'chip butty'; 'dip butty' (dripping); 'dog butty' (corned beef); 'dry butty' or 'gerk-butty' (plain bread – probably by association with *Joe Gerks* – 'jail'); 'gip-butty' (dipped in gravy); 'jam-butty'; 'tripe butty';

'Welsh-butty' (cheese and raw onion) (Lane 1966: 15).

Buy a book ref! (phr.): learn the rules. 'Buy a bewk, ref! *The referee appears to have forgotten the rules of the game*' (Shaw 1965: 51). Recorded as 'a common Liverpool catch phrase' of m.20c. (Beale (1985) *s.v. Liverpool Catch Phrases*); derivation is clear.

C

Cabbage Hall Yank (n.): would-be American. '*Cabbage Hall Yank*: A Youth who tries to behave like, or pretends to be, an American. Also called a *Wells Farthole type*' (Lane 1966: 16). *NR; the Cabbage Hall Picture House stood on Lower Breck Road, but derivation is unclear.

Cabbaged (adj.): exhausted; intoxicated; confused. 'Me ead's cabbaged. Very confused' (Spiegl 1989: 53). 'Half fucking cabbaged from zero sleep and endless nightmares' (Sampson 2001: 266). 'Ploddin along without words, absolutely cabbaged' (Griffiths 2002: 174). Recorded from l.20c.; an extension of m.20c. 'cabbaged', 'mentally incapacitated', from m.19c. 'human cabbage', 'a dull-witted or unambitious person'.

Cabbaging (n.): stealing. 'Cabbaging. Pilfering' (Spiegl 1989: 20). Recorded from e.18c.; drapers' usage referring to the pilfering of off-cuts; derivation unknown.

Cack (n.): excrement. 'I'll get me grandson t' come an' kick the cack out of yer' (Bleasdale 1975: 26). 'My First Morning with cacked kecks' (Simpson 1990: 33). 'We've got the fucking cack all over ourselves' (Sampson 2002: 132). Recorded from 16c.; retained in its original sense in Liverpool, though categorised as obsolete elsewhere except in the extensions 'nonsense' or 'worthless, useless'; from Latin 'cacāre', 'to void excrement'.

Cack (v.): to defecate. 'Cack. To defecate. Liverpool' (Howarth 1985: n.p.). 'How many cacked their knickers' (Sinclair 1999 [1930s–e.40s]: 75). Recorded from 15c.; glossed as obsolete or dialectal; see *cack (n.)*.

Cack-handed (adj.): clumsy, awkward; left-handed. 'Winnick, if yes ask me, cack-'anded' (Shaw 1957a: 12). 'Gammy-anded; cack-anded. A *left-handed person*' (Shaw et al. 1966: 29). 'That may strike one as a right cack-handed way of doing it, but it works!' (McClure 1980: 385). 'Saws, planes/that I'm cack-handed with' (Simpson 1990: 100). Recorded from m.19c.; dialectal, probably from 'kay', as in 'kay-fisted', 'left-handed' (coined too early for the extended sense of *cack*, 'worthless, useless').

Cadge (v.): to borrow, beg. 'The old codgers, cadging from us, encouraged this vanity' (O'Mara 1934: 220). 'I had to turn from the kids who cadge pennies' (Naughton 1945: 16). 'A tap-room loafer cadging drinks' (Mays 1954: 201). 'Dey've cadged der last latch-lifter out a me' (Shaw et al. 1966: 77). 'After cadging a match from a passer-by' (Unwin 1984 [1920s–30s]: 47). 'Then go and cadge a match somewhere' (Dudgeon 2010: 212). Recorded from e.19c.; an extension of e.16c. 'cadge', 'itinerant dealer'; from 'cadge', 'to tie'.

Cady/caidy (n.): hat or cap. 'I would add "straw-cady" for the straw hat or boater' (J.A.S. 1950: 2). 'Where did you get that hat, where did you get that cady' (Shaw 1959a: 32). '*Caidy* or *straw caidy*: A straw boater hat. Also called a *cheese cutter*' (Lane 1966: 16). '*Hat.* Caydee' (Minard 1972: 46). 'Straw hats which we in our part of Merseyside called "Straw Cadies" or "Straw Gussies"' (Unwin 1984 [1920s–30s]: 47). Recorded from m.19c.; derivation unknown.

Cakehole (n.): mouth. 'The mouth … *Cakehole*' (Minard 1972: 43). Recorded from m.20c.; Forces' usage; derivation is clear.

Can-lad (n.): apprentice, junior employee. 'The sailor's peaked cap which apprentice engineers (or CAN-LADS) used to wear' (Shaw 1959a: 32). '*Jer take me fer a bloody can-lad?*' (Lane 1966: 16). 'How about giving me a job as a can lad?' (Bleasdale 1985: 46). 'I'm more y can-lad' (Simpson 1995: 23). 'Lowest of all occupations, can lad with the Army or the Navy' (Callaghan 2011 [1910s–30s]: 78). *NR; the lad who does menial tasks (like fetching the can).

Cane¹ (v.): to beat severely. 'Some pal Louis had turned out to be tonight, letting Doonan cane him like that' (Cross 1951: 126). Recorded from m.20c.; an extension of 17c. 'to cane', 'to hit with a cane'.

Cane²/give a caning (v.): drink excessively; over-use. 'The Jerries … had been giving some bottles of vino no end of a caning' (Cross 1951: 109). 'The cunt must've been caning the steggies' (Sampson 2002: 154). Recorded from m.20c.; an extension of *cane¹*.

Caper (n.): dubious, often illict, affair. 'I

know your caper. The kidney punch and the rabbit clout' (Burke 1964: 104). 'The catseyes [car radios] caper spread' (Parker 1974: 77). 'This whole caper ain't for my good self' (Sampson 2002: 222). 'Those capers and the pranks he got up to' (Fagan 2007 [1950s]: 334). Recorded from e.20c.; an extension of 17c. 'caper', 'dodge, trick'.

Car (n.): tram. 'I have noticed the following in speech and in the local press … car where in London we usually said "*tram*"' (Collinson 1927: 121). 'She almost ran across the road and boarded a car' (Hanley 1935: 9). '"Cars" (that is to say "trams"), will be applied to buses' (Farrell 1950: 4). 'Der car (now obsolete). *An electric tramcar*' (Shaw et al. 1966: 66). 'Liverpool people never called a tram a tram. It was either a tram-car, or, more commonly, the car' (Melly 1984 [1930s–40s]: 8). Recorded from e.20c.; probably an Americanism; an abbreviation of 'tramcar'.

Cards (n.): employment documents. 'The overseer willingly gave me "my cards" … so that I might look for work elsewhere' (Whittaker 1934: 220). 'Give us me caardz: *I have no desire to work here any longer*' (Minard 1972: 19). 'They give them their cards otherwise' (Brown 1989: 39). 'I'll sort out your money and cards' (Kelly 2006 [1930s–40s]: 88). Recorded from e.20c.; used phrasally in 'ask for one's cards' (voluntarily leave a job), 'get given one's cards' (get sacked); employers retained workers' documents during the period of employment.

Carnival ribbons (n.): toilet rolls. '*Carnival ribbons*: toilet rolls (Lane 1966: 16). *NR; from the practice of throwing toilet rolls onto the pitch at football matches.

Carpenter's Day (n.): 12th July. 'For a while the 12th July procession became known as "Carpenter's Day"' (Neal 1988: 40). 'The 12th July became known as "Carpenter's Day" in Liverpool' (Lees 2013: 93). *NR; from the preponderance of ships' carpenters in the m.19c. Orange Lodges in Liverpool.

Carpet (n.): three-month prison sentence. 'You'll get a carpet if they lumber you!' (Steen 1932: 107). '*Tzonygorra caahrpet. Anthony was sentenced to three months imprisonment*' (Minard 1972: 57). Recorded from e.20c.; an abbreviation of 'carpet-bag', rhyming slang for l.18c. 'drag', 'three-month sentence'.

Carry on (v.): to make a fuss, behave badly; engage in sexual impropriety. 'The earlier meaning, as in "Yes, me old girl carried on something cruel!", was "made no end of a fuss"' (Anon. 1954: 2). 'If that's how she wants to carry on' (Sampson 2002: 225). 'They were carrying on behind his back' (Burnett 2011: 120). Recorded as an e.19c. Americanism from l.17c. 'carryings-on', 'outlandish behaviour'; the sexual connotation is a l.19c. development.

Carry on (n.): misbehaviour, nonsense. 'Nowadays I aven' no times for the likes a dat carry-on' (Shaw 1957a:1). 'Me and Nocker enjoy all this carry-on' (Brown 1989: 12). 'Sheila, what a carry-on!' (Bryan 2003 [1940s–50s]: 142). Recorded from l.19c.; an extension of *carry on (v.)*.

Carrying (v.): in possession of money or, later, drugs. 'I'm carryin. *I am fairly affluent at present*' (Shaw et al. 1966: 34). '"Are you carrying?" – "How many do you need?"' (Grant 1996: 52). '*I'll mug yer when I'm carryin*' I will treat you when I have some funds' (Spiegl 2000b: 126). Recorded from m.20c.; an Americanism; derivation is clear.

Carrying out (n.): the midday meal (dinner). 'Sandwiches intended to be eaten at midday are called either "dinner" or "carrying out"' (Farrell 1950b: 4). 'His judy gives him a lunch to eat at work (*Carrying Out)*' (Shaw 1958d: 19). 'It's fer my feller's carryin-out. *It is for my husband's packed lunch*' (Shaw et al. 1966: 39). 'When they asked him how it got there, he said it was his carrying out' (Bleasdale 1975: 28). 'Many a workman's favourite "carrying out" was a package of chip butties' (Unwin 1984 [1920s–30s]: 32). 'His carryin' out, always cheese' (McGovern 1995: 5). 'I set out for work with my carrying-out tucked under my arm' (Callaghan 2011 [1910s–30s]: 89). *NR; probably from an e.20c. Americanism, 'carry out', 'prepared food and drink sold for consumption away from the premises of sale'.

Carzy (n.): toilet. '*Toilet*. Carzy, Bog, Bucket' (Minard 1972: 87). Recorded from m.20c.; Polari, from Italian 'casa', 'house'.

Case (n.): person who is interesting; unusual; amusing; dangerous. 'Eez a case 'im: *That bloke is really amusing*' (Minard 1972: 31). 'Youse are fokkin' cases' (McClure 1980: 306). 'Madcap Cliff, a "case"' (Simpson 1990: 14). 'Fucking case, she is' (Sampson 2002: 233). Recorded from m.19c.; an

Americanism, from e.18c. 'case', 'a condition of disease in a person', hence 'an instance or example of disease', and by extension 'an exemplary or interesting patient'.

Casey (n.): football. '"Casey" for football' (Shaw 1955a: 18). '*Football*. Casey' (Minard 1972: 87). 'Must 'ave a bladder like a casey (football)' (Sinclair 1999 [1930s–e.40s]: 131). 'Hoofing a leather casie all over the place' (Fagan 2007 [1950s]: 75). *NR; from the ball's leather casing.

Cassie/Cazzy (n.): the Cast iron shore. 'Cazzy, Cast iron shore' (Jones 1935: 5). 'We went swimmin' in the Scaldie or up at the Cassie' (Shaw 1957a: 4). '*Cast Iron Shore, Ther* or *Ther Cazzy*: A rocky riverside shore at the southern end of Liverpool' (Lane 1966: 17). '"The Cassie", needless to say, was the Cast Iron Shore' (Unwin 1984 [1920s–30s]: 78). 'Syb on the Cazzy. The cast iron shore' (Grant 1996: 355). 'This was the cassey (cast iron river shore)' (Stamper 2010: 11). *NR; see *Cast iron shore*.

Cassoona (n.): figure of mischief. '*Cassoona*: A mythical individual alleged to have teeth in his backside and blamed for biting buttons off railway carriage seats' (Lane 1966: 17). *NR; derivation unknown.

Cast iron shore (n.): Cast iron shore. 'Well here's another clue for you all/The walrus is Paul/Standing on the cast iron shore' (The Beatles, 'Glass Onion', *The White Album*, 1968). 'Summer holidays were spent on the Cast Iron Shore' (Unwin 1984 [1920s–30s]: 75). 'The Cast Iron Shore (a particular part of the beach that was a favourite with the lads)' (Sinclair 1999 [1930s–e.40s]:

16). 'The Cast Iron Shore at Aigburth' (Elliott 2006 [1940s–70s]: 67). *NR; near the Dingle, the Mersey shore was studded with the detritus from the 19c. Mersey Steel and Iron Works.

Cat/Cat'lick (n.): Catholic. 'Cats – all Catholics were *Cats* – suffered more than Protestants' (Hanley 2009 [1940]: 202). '*Cat'licks*: Roman Catholics' (Lane 1966: 17). 'Proddydogs Catterlicks' (Jacques 1973: n.p.). 'Catslicks and Prodidogs' (Robinson 1986 [1920s–30s]: 7). *NR; recorded from m.20c.; from a pronunciation of 'Catholic' and by contrast with *proddy-dog*.

Catch-on (n.): dupe, fool. 'The public houses where he could ply his baiting of sailors or other available "catch-ons"' (O'Mara 1934: 37). *NR; the Liverpool dockside was replete with fraudsters and tricksters seeking to waylay recently paid-off sailors.

Caubeen (n.): hat or cap. 'The vocabulary of the Irish area [of Liverpool] contains several genuine Anglo-Irish and Irish (= Gaelic) words, such as "skallan" (young onion) "caubeen" (hat), "bothered" – ear, deaf (ear)' (Oakes Hirst 1951: 4). 'Caubeen. Hat. Liverpool' (Howarth 1985: n.p.). Recorded from m.19c.; Irish English; a transliteration of Gaelic 'cáibín', 'old hat'.

Cental (n.): weight of one hundred pounds. 'Some years ago the corn trade of Liverpool became convinced that a great improvement would be effected by the adoption of one common measure. The result was that the cental of 100 lb. avoirdupois was unanimously agreed to in that town' (Anon. 1870: 470). The term and measure were introduced in the Liverpool Cornmarket in 1859 and legalised in 1879; from Latin 'centum', 'one hundred'.

Champion (adj.): excellent. '*Champion* or *proper champion*: Very good, first class, excellent. This is part of Lancashire dialect and less used than *ther gear*' (Lane 1966: 17). Recorded from l.19c.; a Lancashire dialectal extension of 'champion' (noun).

'Change (n.): Exchange Flags. 'He went upon 'Change, to transact affairs with his brother merchants' (Maginn 1844: 1.16). 'On 'Change the great sugar merchant could say ...' (Powys 1857: 52). 'Young John Belstock ... made himself quite quickly a popular figure on 'Change' (Owen 1921: 21). *NR; an abbreviation of 'Exchange Flags', the large flag-stoned space behind the Town Hall that was used for trading.

Chant (v.): to sing. 'She caahnaahf chant: *That female is a remarkably good singer*' (Minard 1972: 14). Recorded from 15c.; glossed as archaic or poetic but retained in its original sense in Liverpool; probably from *chanty/shanty*.

Chanty/Shanty man (n.): a singing sailor. 'The sing-song tone, which has long made Dicky Sam in demand on sailing ships as "chanty-man"' (Shaw 1950c: 4). 'The chantyman, or leader of the singing' (Shaw 1957c: 6). 'Mick Stanley, a real live shanty' (Jacques 1972: n.p.). 'We sing a song of Liverpool/A chanty rolling free' (Simpson 2011 [2001]: 280). Recorded from l.19c.; an extension of m.19c. 'shanty'/'chanty', 'sailor's song', from the French 'chantez'.

Char[1] (n.): tea. 'Soldiers or other Servicemen were responsible for many Hindustani phrases, the most popular, of course, being "char" for tea' (Holbrow 1964: 6). '*Char*: Tea. *Cuppachar*: A cup of tea' (Lane 1966: 17). 'A mug of strong char' (Graham 1988: 75). Recorded from 20c.; a version of the Chinese (Mandarin) 'ch'a', 'tea', first recorded in English in 17c.; popularised through Forces' usage.

Char[2] (n.): charwoman. 'Hard-nosed chars' (Simpson 1990: 67). See *charwoman[1] (n.)*.

Charabang (n.): coach. 'She went for a charabang drive with her club' (Kerr 1958: 106). 'A bloody great enormous white Jaguar like a charabang' (Hignett 1966: 143). 'Charabang trips were immensely popular in the 20s and 30s' (Unwin 1984 [1920s 30s]: 119). See *sharrer*.

Charva (n.): sexually active woman (derogatory). '*Promiscuous woman*. Brass, Pallyass, Good thing, Cert, Charva' (Minard 1972: 89). Recorded from m.19c.; an extension of 17c. cant 'charver', 'to have sex'; possibly from Italian 'chiavare', 'to fuck'.

Charwoman (n.): woman employed to do cleaning work. 'All such yonge Wemen and others called Charr Wemen in this towne as are in noe service' (Picton 1883 [1596] 1.116). 'My wife is a good charwoman' (Haigh 1907: 228). 'Mother was still slaving as charwoman down in the Chicago Building in Paradise Street' (O'Mara 1934: 270). First recorded in Liverpool Municipal Records in 1596; from 'char', 'occasional work, odd job' ('chore').

Charwoman (adj.): menial. 'The war was on and even we "charwomen" sailors, being Britishers, were initiated into its mysteries' (O'Mara 1934: 263). *NR in this adjectival sense; an extension of *charwoman*[1].

Chatty (adj.): lousy. 'Did the Army or Navy give us, say, *jack*, for detective, *chatty, have a cob on, whack* (to share)?' (Shaw 1950b:4). Recorded from e.20c.; an extension of l.17c. cant 'chat', 'louse'; derivation unknown.

Chav/chavvy (n.): child; kid. '*Baby. Chavvy*' (Minard 1972: 88). Recorded from l.19c.; from Romani 'chavvi' 'baby'; displaced by the e.21c. pejorative sense of 'chav'.

Cheese cutter (n.): straw boater. See *cady*.

Cheesed off/cheesed (adj.): annoyed, upset, exasperated. 'He wuz cheesed off an' nearly beat' (Jacques 1975: 19). 'Nocker goes to his first sex lesson and is feeling very cheesed' (Brown 1989: 7). Recorded as 'Disgruntled: Liverpool boys' – 1914; Liverpool troops (1914–18)', the term was popularised in Forces' usage; possibly from l.19c. 'Liverpool boys' cheese off!, run away and don't be a nuisance' (Beale 1984 *s.v. cheesed(-off)*).

Cheque/check/cheque on the knocker (n.): credit issued by a particular store. 'Cheques are a hire-purchase system' (Kerr 1958: 91). 'Dad … would get a cheque on the knocker (a permit to trade on credit) and take him to a store' (Shaw 1959a: 32). 'Certain stores issued "checks" to needy people' (Unwin 1984 [1920s–30s]: 106). 'Colliers took cheques which allowed you to purchase goods on the weekly (credit/tic)' (Elliott 2006 [1940s–70s]: 28). *NR in this sense; before personal bank accounts became

common, the only *cheque* a working-class Liverpudlian was likely to see would have been issued by stores such as T.J. Hughes, Freeman Hardy Willis, Sturlas and so on; *cheques* were repayable weekly (with interest).

Cherrywobs/cherrybobs/cherrywogs/ cherrywags (n.): cherry stones used to play marbles. 'Cherrywobs (cherrystones)' (Farrell 1950b: 4). 'Cherry stones in my time, were Cherrybobs not wobs' (Carter 1955: 4). 'The term for cherry stones in my boyhood days was about fifty–fifty cherrybobs and cherrywogs' (Bidston 1955: 4). 'Cherrystones in my day were called Cherrywags, and Cherrywags – "up the spout" was a favourite pastime – another juvenile gambling game' (Jones 1955: 4). '*Cherry-bobs* or *cherry-wobs*: A children's game in which cherry stones are flipped at a rainwater-spout, or used as marbles substitutes' (Lane 1966: 17). 'Hop Scotch and Cherry Wobs were played by both boys and girls too' (Unwin 1984 [1920s–30s]: 19). 'Cherry stones were cherrywobs to us' (Callaghan 2011 [1910s–30s]: 14). *NR; the use of cherry stones as children's marbles was common in Liverpool; the derivation of 'wob', 'bob' and so on is unclear.

Chief (n.): familiar term of address. 'I think the use of "Chief" indiscriminately by the tip-seeking class should not be taken seriously!' (Shaw 1963e: 4). 'Come on, chief, we've been in ten minutes' (Shute 1971: 124). '"Hey, lads, pack it in!" … "A'right chief …"' (McClure 1980: 295). Recorded from e.20c.; a weakening of nautical 'chief', 'Chief Engineer', 'Commander'.

Childer (n.): children. 'Now you childer, be off out and play' (Shimmin 1863: 32). 'Childer is drowned' (Hocking 1966 [1879]: 52). 'Let Janie get you a job and you can lave the childer here' (O'Mara 1934: 46). 'There are other Gaelicisms … "childer" for "children" – especially among the older folk' (Shaw 1955a: 6). 'Childer. Children. Everton' (Howarth 1985: n.p.). 'Drinkin' again and the childers without a crust' (Maddox 2008 [1930s–40s]: 137). Recorded from 17c.; from Irish English.

Chin (v.): to hit someone on the chin. 'Achindim' (Minard 1972: 82). 'Run over there and chin one of the coppers' (Sampson 2002: 234). Recorded from c.20c.; the derivation is clear.

Chinaman (n.): Chinese man. 'The same thing occurred among the Chinamen in Pitt Street (Chinatown)' (O'Mara 1934: 13). 'The word "Chinaman" was a nightmare to him … it signified the condescending approach of colonial rulers in the Far East' (Jerome 1948: 122). '*Chinee*: A Chinaman' (Lane 1966: 18). 'The police car, with a Chinaman sitting next to the driver' (Murari 1975: 134). 'Lascars, Chinamen … Coolies' (Robinson 1986 [1920s–30s]: 102). 'I think it was a Chinaman' (Dudgeon 2010: 197). Recorded from l.19c.; an Americanism; derivation is clear.

Chinee (n.): Chinese person (singular). '*Chinee*: A Chinaman. Chinese being considered already plural' (Lane 1966: 18). 'The wild Chinee' (Jacques 1972: n.p.). Recorded from m.19c.; a derogatory term, possibly from the belief that if 'Chinese' meant a number

of Chinese people, then one Chinese person must be a 'Chinee'.

Ching (n.): five pounds. 'A Handful, a Ching, a Fiver' (Minard 1972: 86). Recorded from m.20c.; derivation unknown.

Chink/Chinky (n.): offensive term for a Chinese person; Chinese restaurant. '"Do's" there were outside every other house – in Sparling Street, with its Negroes, Pitt Street, with its Chinks, and Frederick Street (Flukey Alley) with its Flukes' (O'Mara 1934: 275). 'They trust me, these Chinks, and I trust them' (Jerome 1948: 54). 'Al be in dthe chinx. *I can be located at the Chinese restaurant*' (Minard 1972: 50). 'Chinky, paki, wog and so on and so on' (Redmond 1982: 35). 'Tommy hasn't got the fuckin arse to bounce in on the Chinks' (Griffiths 2003: 49). Recorded from l.19c. to refer to people; probably Australian in origin; the reference to restaurants and food is a l.20c. development.

Chinky chuck (n.): Chinese food. '*Chinky chuck*: Chinese food' (Lane 1966: 18). *NR; see *Chink*, *chuck*.

Chip (n.): one shilling. '1/-. A Chip' (Minard 1972: 86). Recorded in m.20c.; 'chip' for money dates to m.19c.; probably from gambling discourse.

Chip-chopper/chip girl (n.): wood chip seller. 'Have you seen the chip-girls using saw and axe, seated on the cold stones of court and alley?' (Haigh 1907: 327). '"Gentle Annie", a chip-chopper with twelve children' (O'Mara 1934: 58). *NR; chip-chopping was a job for the poorest in working-class areas when coal fires were standard.

Chippy (n.): fish and chip shop. 'Already hangin' round herbies and workin' as a lad in a chippie' (Shaw 1957a: 16). 'De chippy. *The fish and chip shop*' (Shaw et al. 1966: 42). 'Marko standing outside the chippy' (Murari 1975: 11). '*Dee chippy* The fish-and-chips takeaway' (Spiegl 2000b: 115–16). 'Searching for a late night chippie' (Fagan 2007 [1950s]: 289). Recorded from m.20c.; a Liverpool coinage; fish and chips were part of the working-class diet from m.19c. ('chipped potatoes and fried fish' [Haigh 1907: 504]).

Chocker¹/chocka (adj.): cram-full. 'I heard Liverpool was chocka with GIs' (Grant 1996: 75). 'The castle grounds're chocka with all the people on their dinner hour' (Griffiths 2003: 86). Recorded from m.20c.; an extension of 18c. nautical 'chock-a-block' (when the 'chock' and 'block' of hoisting tackle are tightly drawn together).

Chocker² (adj.): disappointed; upset. 'Peter and Keith an' 'at'll be chocker if we don't go down!' (Sampson 1999: 288). 'He'll be chocker if I pay him off in front of the lads' (Sampson 2001: 62). Recorded from m.20c.; Forces' usage; derivation unclear.

Chocolate port (n.): port that offers cheap amusements for sailors. 'I remember the place [Liverpool] being referred to by them as a "chocolate port"' (Cornelius 2001 [1982]: 68). 'Liverpool was a "chocolate port" and a twilight zone' (Lees 2013: 144). *NR; the derivation is clear.

Choker (n.): muffler, scarf. 'His splendid choker, now soiled and greasy' (Cross 1951: 166). '*Choker*: A muffler; a working scarf' (Lane 1966: 18). Recorded from e.20c.; an extension of m.19c. 'choker', 'neckerchief worn with evening dress'.

Choss (n.): chaos. '*It were absolutely berluddy choss*' (Lane 1966: 18). *NR; the Liverpool version of Sean O'Casey's Irish English 'chassis'.

Chow (n.): food. 'To see what kind of bloody chow this lousy bastard … was going to give us' (O'Mara 1934: 158). 'The hunger got the better of her and she ordered a plate of "Chow"' (Jerome 1948: 10). Recorded from m.19c.; possibly from Anglo-Chinese pidgin, 'chow', 'mixture', hence 'food'.

Chuck¹ (n.): bread, food. 'A *cob of chuck* (chuck is the very old word once generally used for food or bread)' (Shaw 1950b: 4). 'I can wait for me – (*Searches for a Liverpool word*) – chuck!' (Owen 1961: 49). 'Chuck. Bread' (Shaw et al. 1966: 38). 'Chuck. Food. Liverpool' (Howarth 1985: n.p.). 'A kipper and a couple of chucks of bread' (Kelly 2006 [1930s–40s]: 93). Recorded from m.19c.; nautical usage, 'chuck', 'bread, meat, food in general'.

Chuck² (n.): familiar term of address. 'What's the matter, Maury, me chuck?' (Hanley 2009 [1940]: 78). 'If, on one day, you are cordially hailed as "mate", "sis" (sister), "la" (lad), "Mac" (favoured by bus conductors), "chuck", "wack" or even simply "yew" (plural "youse") do not be annoyed' (Shaw 1963e: 4). 'Chuck. A term of endearment. Liverpool' (Howarth 1985: n.p.). "'Ow 'ave yer been keepin', chuck?' (Sinclair 1999 [1930s–e.40s]: 84). Recorded from l.16c.; now northern dialectal; possibly from 'chicken'.

Chuck[1] *(v.)*: to give, pass. 'Chuck us a cigarette, Keeg' (Hignett 1966: 294). 'Chuck the exact amount through the window' (Bainbridge 1989: 10). '*Chuck us* Please be so good as to pass' (Spiegl 2000b: 119). Recorded from m.20c.; an extension of 'chuck', 'throw'.

Chuck[2] *(v.)*: to stop doing something. 'The usual life of a dock labourer of that period, seeking work when he liked and chucking it when he liked' (O'Mara 1934: 36). '"Chuck it", he growled' (Hanley 2009 [1940]: 61). 'She would have liked to have broken with Sue and chuck this cheap-jack, divorce-lawyer capering' (Cross 1951: 131). 'I suppose when we saw kids about dressed up we were discouraged. Anyway we chucked it' (Clerk 1971 [*c*.1900]: 46). Recorded from 19c.; an extension of 'chuck up', a boxing phrase meaning 'to surrender, give in' by throwing in the towel.

Chuck[3] *(v.)*: end a relationship. 'What's wrong, she chucked you, what's her address?' (Hignett 1966: 257). 'He might chuck her' (Russell 1996 [1976]: 132). 'Chuck. To give the brush off. "I've chucked the girlfriend"' (Howarth 1985: n.p.). See *chuck*[2] *(v.)*.

Chuck box (n.): a food container. '*Chuck box*: a food container' (Lane 1966: 19). See *chuck*[1] *(n.)*.

Chucked, get/be (v.): jilted; rejected. 'Should she have a "barney" (quarrel) with him which results in his being "chucked" (jilted)' (Farrell 1950b: 4). '*To get chucked*: to have one's friendship or engagement abruptly terminated' (Lane 1966: 19). See *chuck*[2].

Chuffed (adj.): happy, pleased, satisfied. '"So you were in it", he said, all chuffed with himself' (Bleasdale 1975: 13). 'Jimmy rode off to his house, looking dead chuffed' (Flame 1984: 32). 'Chuffed at seeing Lily again' (Sinclair 1999 [1930s–e.40s]: 124). 'Billy seemed rather chuffed' (Fagan 2007 [1950s]: 16). Recorded from m.20c.; an extension of m.19c. dialectal 'chuff', 'pleased, elated', from 16c. 'chuff', a 'cheek swollen or puffed with fat'.

Chump, off one's (adj.): crazy. 'Sheez offer chump. *The lady is slightly deranged*' (Minard 1972: 42). Recorded from m.19c.; from 'chump', 'head, face', an extension of 17c. 'chump', 'block of wood'.

Churchyard luck (n.): bitter comment on child mortality. 'The "good fortune"' which the mother of a large family experiences by the death of one or more of her children: e.g., "Yes, mum, I hev brought 'em all up ten boys, and no churchyard luck with it." Said by a Liverpool woman to a district-visitor' (Ware 1909: 77). *NR; derivation is clear.

Ciggie/ciggy/cig (n.): cigarette. 'I don wan any ciggies' (Shaw 1951: 5). 'CIGGY, of course, is cigarette, the cheap kind being a WOODY' (Shaw 1959a: 39). 'Anyone want a camera for ten ciggies?' (Hignett 1966: 230). 'She gave him a packet of ciggies' (Murari 1975: 7). 'The wife's had a ciggie pushed in her hair' (McClure 1980: 101). 'He chuckled to himself and stubbed out his ciggie' (Sampson 1999: 26). 'Ciggies an lighter an wallet an keys' (Griffiths 2003: 6). 'She sold everything, veg, meat, cigs' (Stamper 2010: 27). Recorded from m.20c.; the *Scottish Daily Mail* (1968) claimed that 'what had been "fags" became "ciggies" because The Beatles always talked of ciggies' (*OED s.v. ciggy n.*).

Cinder Walk (n.): a pathway in South Liverpool. '"Cinder Walk", overlooking Herculanaeum dock' (Jones 1935: 5). 'There was a path overlooking Herculaneum Dock known as "The Cinder Walk"' (Unwin 1984 [1920s– 30s]: 78). *NR; derivation is clear.

Clanger (n.): artwork on Drury Lane. 'What many Liverpudlians call "The Contraption" or "The Clanger" (Channon 1970: 150). *NR; a gift from the Civic Society, this public sculpture featured water cascading from various buckets; it was much derided.

Clarence Mbongo (n.): offensive racist epithet. '*Clarence Mbongo*: Applied to a Negro, especially if young and dressy' (Lane 1966: 19). *NR; one of a number of terms belonging to the discourse of racism.

Clat/Clat-tale (n.): tell-tale, informer. '"Clat", a tell-tale, or a gossip' (Jones 1935: 5). 'The informer would be called a *clat* ("Clat tale tit") and accused of snitching' (Shaw 1950: 4). 'Clatting is tale-telling' (Armstrong 1966: 6). '*Clat tale tit* You are an informer' (Spiegl 2000b: 131). Recorded from l.19c.; northern dialectal; possibly from 16c. 'clatter', 'noisy talk, gossip'.

Clean the pan (v.): to urinate to effect. '*Clean ther pan*: a primitive superstition … only practiced by males' (Lane 1966: 19). *NR; derivation is clear.

Clever, not too (adj.): unhealthy, not well. '*I'm not too clever jus' now*' (Lane 1966: 19). Recorded from l.19c.; a dialectal example of litotes (affirmation by negation) based on the slightly earlier 'clever', 'well, in good health, physically strong, active'.

Clew (n.): slap, blow. 'He gives you a clew on the lug' (Hanley 1932: 32). 'A child will get a clew on the ear for being "too 'ard faced"' (Shaw 1959a: 36). 'Clew. A slap or blow. Liverpool' (Howarth 1985: n.p.). Recorded from m.20c.; possibly a variant of m.19c. dialectal 'claw', 'to hit'.

Clew (v.): to hit. 'A coupla stones in he's white gloves to clew you wid as soon as look at you' (Shaw 1957a: 15). See *clew (n.)*.

Click with (v.): to meet; to get on well with. 'I realised I should have to be a bit of a swank if I wanted to "click" with a girl' (Whittaker 1934: 216). 'Noted promenades, to the joy of Liverpool's youth, as a means to "click" or "cop on", in other words to get acquainted' (O'Hanri 1950a: 2). 'He'd clicked with the lead in *Rose Marie*' (Bainbridge 1989: 30). 'He hasn't won the pools or clicked with one of the cleaners, has he?' (Fagan 2007 [1950s]: 40). Recorded from e.20c.; Forces' usage; probably from e.19c. Scots 'cleek, cleik, click', in the phrasal verb 'to cleik in (or up) wi(th)', 'to associate with, be intimate with'.

Climp (adj.): very good, excellent. '"Climp" … it is years since I met anyone using or even able to recall this widely used current superlative expression, roughly equivalent to the modern monstrosity "smashing"' (J.A.S. 1950: 2). 'The much older "It's climp"' (Whittington-Egan 1955a: 6). '*The gear* … once ousted *climp* (pre-1914)' (Shaw 1962a: 9). *NR; derivation unknown.

Clobber[1] *(n.)*: clothes. 'Fling my old clobber overboard' (Bower 2015 [1936]: 166). 'One silk hankerchief what was all the clobber he had by him' (Hanley 2009 [1958]: 51). 'We all bought a load of clobber (clothes)' (Parker 1974: 70). 'All good, sound, sensible clobber' (Cornelius 2001 [1982]: 54). 'I look shite in that kind of clobber' (Sampson 2001: 13). 'A new suit an' some clobber' (Fagan 2007 [1950s]: 76). Recorded from l.19c.; derivation unknown.

Clobber[2] *(n.)*: general term for things. '*Clobber*: A generic term similar to "gear"' (Parker 1974: 212). 'The scran in this place looks all right. Simple enough clobber' (Sampson 2002: 57). Recorded from l.19c.; derivation unknown.

Clock (n.): face. 'De clock. *The face* (Shaw et al. 1966: 19). Recorded from e.20c.; derivation is clear.

Clock[1] *(v.)*: to hit someone, usually in the face. 'He would have to clock her before she brought all the neighbours in' (Cross 1951: 136). 'I'll clock yew in a minit' (Shaw 1959a: 40). 'Yor'll punish em more dat way den if yer clocked em' (Anon. 1967b: 4). 'If I was a man I'd clock yer one' (Bryan 2003 [1940s–50s]: 60). Recorded from e.20c.; probably from *clock (n.)*.

Clock[2] *(v.)*: to see, look at, stare; notice, recognise. 'Clock: To catch sight of' (Parker 1974: 212). 'We'd better go back and get this van changed … they're sure to have clocked us in this' (Bleasdale 1985: 44). '*E wuz clockin me!* He was looking at me' (Spiegl 2000b: 146). 'To get out of the way before the bobby clocked him' (Sanders and Sanders 2009 [1960s]: 77). Recorded

from m.20c.; an Americanism; probably an extension of *clock (n.)*.

Clock, to have a hard (v.): to be cheeky. 'I had a 'ard clock' (Shaw 1957a: 15). *NR; this m.20c. term derived from *clock* by analogy with *hard-faced*; see *hard clock*.

Clod (n.): one penny. '1d. A Clod' (Minard 1972: 85). Recorded from e.20c.; Forces' usage; derivation unknown.

Cloggie (n.): clog-wearer. '*Cloggie*: A person who wears wooden clogs' (Lane 1966: 20). *NR; derivation is clear.

Clonkers (n.): wooden clogs or heavy hobnailed boots; clog-fighting. '*I belted 'im wi' me clonkers*: I kicked him'. *Clonkers* is also a contest in which opponents grip hands and kick each other with clogs until one admits defeat' (Lane 1966: 20). *NR; derivation unclear, possibly from the 'clonking' sound of the clogs.

Clout (n.): blow, hard smack. 'A hefty clout sent him reeling' (Cross 1951: 17). 'She landed them both a clout or two' (Hallowell 1972: n.p.). 'A clout round the earhole was the more usual reward' (Sexton 1996: 11). Recorded from e.15c.; glossed as now 'dialectal or vulgar'; derivation unknown.

Clout (v.): to hit. 'He clouted them viciously' (Hanley 1932: 29). 'She clouts a kid' (Russell 1996 [1976]: 129). See *clout (n.)*.

Club (n.): insurance association or money lender. 'It was no use talking to the poor fellow then about putting the child in a burial club' (Shimmin 1863: 77); 'I wonder if the club will allow anything. He's paid up' (Tirebuck 1891: 102). 'I've paid my penny a week into the club for forty years, because I shuddered at the thought of a pauper's burial' (Haigh 1907: 184). 'Club. Money put aside each week for Burial Clubs and Insurance schemes etc.' (Howarth 1985: n.p.). ''Ere's Mrs Parry, the money-lender, ter get me mam's club' (Sinclair 1999 [1930s–e.40s]: 76). Recorded from m.19c.; an abbreviation of 'benefit club', a voluntary mutual assurance association whose members paid in small sums regularly and received benefits that covered sickness, old age or death; the *club* played an integral and essential role in working-class life.

Club, in the (adj.): pregnant. 'Putting women in the club' (Hignett 1966: 255). 'You got our Betty in the club before y' were married' (Russell 1996 [1975]: 64). ''*I tink I'm in der club, doctor /I'm up de duff* I think I may be pregnant' (Spiegl 2000b: 109). Recorded from l.19c.; an abbreviation of 'pudding club', from 'a bellyful of marrow-pudding'.

Club money (n.): savings, insurance. 'He had to call and pay his club-money' (Shimmin 1863: 16). 'Death and club-money are almost synonymous' (Haigh 1907: 118). 'She's bought the dress on "club money"' (Kerr 1958: 207). 'I've paid me digs and me club money' (Fagan 2007 [1950s]: 75). See *club*.

Clubman (n.): insurance agent or debt collector. 'Three School Board visitors, and half a dozen club-men, as they are called' (Haigh 1907: 11). 'The insurance man is usually given the name of his company, or is simply "the insurance feller", "the insurance", or

"the clubman"' (Farrell 1950b: 4). 'The insurance collector escapes "feller". He (hated and feared in poor areas) is *the* Clubman, the association being with the old burial clubs' (Shaw 1958d: 15). 'De clubman. *The insurance (or other) collector*' (Shaw et al. 1966: 24). 'An agent of the Friendly Society, known as the "clubman"' (Unwin 1984 [1920s–30s]: 63). 'The clubman would call to your house each week to collect an agreed amount of money off the loan' (Elliott 2006 [1940s–70s]: 30). Recorded from l.19c.; the agents who called to houses to collect dues for insurance policies or *cheques* were often known by the name of the *club* that issued the policy ('the Co-op man', 'the Provvy (Provident) man'). See *club*.

Clumb/clum (v.): past tense 'climb'. '*I clumb over ther wall*' (Lane 1966: 20). Recorded as archaic, this form of the past tense was retained in Liverpool.

Coat-puller (n.): a favourite; tell-tale. 'The cod bosses who listen too much to coat-pullers snitching' (Shaw 1957a: 7). 'To fool the eavesdropper ("earwigger") or the tale-carrier ("coat-puller")' (Shaw 1959c: 6). *NR; presumably from pulling the coat of the boss to gain attention.

Coats 'n' 'Ats (n.): the C&A department store. '*Coats 'n' 'Ats* A Liverpool departmental store properly called *C&A Modes Ltd.*' (Lane 1966: 20). '*Coats'n'ats* Nickname for C & A Modes' (Spiegl 2000b: 77). *NR; C&A opened in Church Street in the 1930s and closed in 2000; from the first names of the 19c. Dutch textile and retail magnates Clemens and August Brenninkmeijer.

Coats off (adj.): ready to fight. 'If they'd been in our road, they'd have been coats off and fighting long ago' (Bleasdale 1975: 157). *NR; derivation is clear.

Cob¹ (n.): a piece or lump of something. 'The word "cob" means a lump about the size of one's fist, as "a cob of coal", "a cob of chuck" (a hunk of bread)' (Farrell 1950b: 4). '*Cob* (piece, as in 'a cob er muck') (Shaw 1952: n.p.). 'If I don' go 'ome ther gaffer'll knock cobs off me' (Lane 1966: 20). 'Our dog bit a cob out of his knee' (Jacques 1979: n.p.). Recorded from e.19c.; northern dialectal, 'cob', 'lump or small round hard mass'; possibly related to 'cobble', but derivation unclear.

Cob² (n.): small round loaf or bun. '"I have a bit of a cob of a loaf with me"' (Tirebuck 1891: 142). 'The promise of a big fresh bread cob – *after* service' (O'Mara 1934: 9–10). 'A "cob" is a roll … I have heard a Liverpool councillor confounding the waiter in a high-class London hotel by demanding his "cob"' (Shaw 1958d: 18). 'Kewins an' a cob o' chuck' (Anon. 1961b: 3). 'Cob-o-chuck. A piece of bread. Liverpool' (Howarth 1985: n.p.). '*A cob a chuck* A piece of bread' (Spiegl 2000b: 119). Recorded from e.19c.; Lancashire dialectal; see *cob¹*.

Cob (v.): to throw. 'Make sure they don't come back and cob half a brick through the window' (Brown 1989: 69). Recorded from e.19c.; Lancashire dialectal; probably from *cob¹*.

Cob Hall (n.): Evangelical Mission Hall. 'The purpose of Cob Hall was to save the Irish Catholic slummy children from a life-long devotion to the Pope' (O'Mara 1934: 82). 'Many will recall Cob's Hall where a famous evangelist gave poor people large pieces of meat' (Shaw 1950b: 4). 'The Mission "Cob" Hall was close by' (Lees 2013: 88). *Cob Hall* was an evangelical Mission, run by the Methodist 'Gypsy' Smith, which operated from premises at the corner of Slater and Leece streets; long after it had gone, it was used to threaten Catholic children.

Cob on, have a/get a (v.): to be annoyed, angry, moody. '"The queer feller had a right cob on this morning" means "That moody fellow, whom nobody can trust, was very irritated about something or other this morning"' (Farrell 1950b: 4). 'Yer gorra cob on'. *You are in a bad* mood' (Shaw et al. 1966: 22). 'I don't know why Dixie's got a cob on with us for' (Bleasdale 1985: 39). 'Still got a cob on, Da?' (Griffiths 2003: 73). Recorded from m.20c.; derivation unclear but probably from the Lancashire-Cheshire adjective 'cob', 'comical, queer', which may be related to 18c. Cumberland dialectal 'cobby', 'headstrong, tyrannical'.

Cock (n.): familiar term of address. 'The old cock'll be all right' (Hanley 2009 [1940]: 78). 'The same "wotcher, cock" from the same workmates' (Cross 1951: 14). 'Am goin' 'ome for a read. Fetch us a good luv story, cock' (Hodgkinson 1960: 11). 'When we "did the messages" for our parents, shopkeepers called us "cock" which has died out. From them you'll get "luv" here too' (Shaw 1963e: 4). Recorded from e.19c.; northern dialectal, 'a brisk, smart fellow; a familiar term of address'; obsolete in Liverpool by l.20c.

Cockwood (n.): waste wood. 'All I got is some cockwood fer are ouse. *All I have is some waste wood for my home*' (Shaw et al. 1966: 64). 'There would be plenty of cock (waste) wood' (Stamper 2010: 62). *NR; probably from 'cock', 'a heap of produce or material' (dung, turf, wood).

Cocky-watchman (n.): see *coggy*.

Cocoa-room (n.): café, eating place. 'I slept in model lodging-houses and got what I wanted to eat in cocoa rooms' (Haigh 1907: 71). 'All took their meals I the same cocoa-rooms' (Fury 1932: 14). 'The worker will probably go to a coffee-house ("dining rooms", "cocoa-rooms") to have tea with his sandwiches' (Farrell 1950b: 4). 'If there was no work at seven-thirty you'd go to the Cocoa Rooms' (Lane 1987: 90). 'The Cocoa Room was a warm and welcome refuge' (Callaghan 2011 [1910s–30s]: 83). Recorded from l.19c.; institutions originally set up for temperance purposes to sell cocoa to the working class.

Cod¹ (n.): fool; nonsense. 'Don't you ever think you were a cod to give up the sea?' (Hanley 1935: 57). 'Cod. Rubbish, nonsense' (Howarth 1985: n.p.). Recorded from l.17c.; derivation unknown.

Cod² (n.): a joke; a hoax, fraud; a parody; someone who pretends. 'Now I find it's all a bloody cod. A bloody cod. She was only playing the fool with me' (Hanley 2009 [1936]: 488). 'Cod (a pretender)' (Shaw 1950b: 4). 'Cod: Deceit; leg-pulling; tomfoolery' (Lane 1966: 20). Recorded from l.19c.; Scots, Irish English and northern dialectal, an extension of *cod¹*.

Cod boss (n.): foreman, usually on the docks. 'The "Blocker Man" (a Blocker is a bowler hat, ensign of the overseer) or "Cod boss" still denotes the foreman' (Whittington-Egan 1955a: 6). 'The cod bosses who listen too much to coat-pullers snitching' (Shaw 1957a: 7). 'Cod-boss. A foreman. Liverpool Docks' (Howarth 1985: n.p.). *NR; possibly from *cod¹* but derivation unclear.

Cod on¹/cod (v.): to pretend, joke with, fool someone. 'Cod on yer don't know!' (O'Hanri 1950a: 2). 'There are other Gaelicisms … including "[to] cod" for "[to] fool"' (Shaw 1955a: 6). 'Yer cod on yer don know. *You pretend you do not understand*' (Shaw et al. 1966: 72). 'When I'm not coddin meself' (Simpson 1995: 23). Recorded from m.19c.; originally 'to hoax, to take a "rise" out of'; an extension of *cod¹*.

Cod on² (v.): to acknowledge. ''E wooden cod on wen I waned mugging, aldo I was skint' (Whittington-Egan 1955c: 216). 'The authorities aren't codding on as they don't want no panic' (Brown 1989: 19). *NR; derivation unclear; apparently unrelated to *to cod on¹*.

Coddy's show (n.): Punch and Judy. '*Coddy's Show*: An old-established Punch and Judy show run by a Liverpool family named *Codman*' (Lane 1966: 21). *NR; 'Professor' Codman's Punch and Judy show, situated just outside Lime Street Station, ran in various forms from 1860 for more than a century.

Codology (n.): hoaxing, kidding. 'Your bluster, your codology' (Simpson 1990: 79). See *cod¹*.

Cod's head (n.): idiot; sometimes friendly. 'Nowd then cod's 'ead: *Greetings, my friend*' (Minard 1972: 27). Recorded from m.16c.; retained as an insult in Liverpool; derivation is clear.

Cogger/Coggy (n.): Catholic. 'Cogger; left-footer. *A Catholic*' (Shaw et al. 1966: 27). 'More Coggy than the friggin Pope, me' (Griffiths 2002: 51). 'Catholics were derogatorily referred to as "left-footers" or "coggers"' (Lees 2013: 96). *NR; sometimes derogatory; derivation unknown.

Cogger's Circus (n.): The Catholic Cathedral. 'Coiners of such nicknames as "Paddy's Wigwam" and "Cogger's Circus"' (Channon 1970: 183). *NR; from *cogger*, and the circular shape of the Cathedral interior.

Coggy/cocky/cocky watchman (n.): school caretaker or night watchman on a building site. '"Coggy watchmen's" huts were a common sight in the 20s' (Unwin 1984 [1920s–30s]: 55). 'Whistle like 'ell if Cocky, the watchman, comes' (Sinclair 1999 [1930s–e.40s]: 68). 'The cockey watchman guarding the site' (Elliott 2006 [1940s–70s]: 162). 'Cocky watchmen, arcane Scouse vernacular for a night watchman' (Lees 2013: 238). Recorded from m.20c.; possibly from 'cogy', 'nightwatchman on naval training ships from the late nineteenth century', but ultimately Middle English 'cock', 'watchman of the night'.

Coke (n.): a café, eating place; cocoa room. 'Restaurants are cokes. That name apparently derived from the philanthropists of the last century who opened temperance "pubs" where cocoa was the standard drink' (Smith 1955: 5). 'The cokes is itself a truly Liverpool institution' (Shaw 1959c: 6). 'De cokes. *The restaurant; the eating place*' (Shaw et al. 1966: 42). 'I was lookin' for the coker rooms' (Jacques 1979: n.p.). 'What is known in the Liverpool jargon as a "coke room"' (Kelly 2006 [1930s–40s]: 91). See *cocoa rooms*.

Coloured (adj.): historical term for black, Asian, mixed-race person, now usually offensive. 'I was surprised that a colored man should be treated as he is in this town' (Melville 1849: 256). 'There were others who had great pride in our colored neighbours' (O'Mara 1934: 12). 'The "coloured population" come mainly from West Africa and the West Indies, but there are also small numbers of Somalis, Indians, Arabs, Burmese and Malays' (Silberman and Spice 1950: 8). 'There were two coloured girls opposite' (Hignett 1966: 288). 'Nearly all my friends are coloured' (Murari 1975: 131). 'I reckon we've got more *bucks* in this job than coloured bobbies' (McClure 1980: 477). '"Coloured" meant black. You couldn't say "black" then, although you could say "white"' (Dudgeon 2010: 258). Recorded from 18c.; the dominant British usage until the 1970s; in the USA, 'colored' was a term of racial pride after the Civil War, though it was later displaced by 'black' and then 'African American'.

Colquitt Mountain (n.): area in Liverpool city centre. 'The top of Bold Street, Hardman Street and all there we knew as Colquitt Mountain' (Clerk 1971 [c.1900]: 46). *NR; the 'Colquitt Smoker' (in Colquitt Street) was a ventilation shaft which allowed the smoke from steam trains to escape from the underground tunnel.

Come (v.): past tense of 'come'. 'The verb "to come" is easy to conjugate: I cum, you cum, he/she/it cum, we cum, you(se) cum, they cum' (Spiegl 1989: 24). 'In fairness, I come straightaway' (Sampson 2002: 90). 'They come. Told us to stop' (Dudgeon 2010: 86). *NR; this irregular past tense is one of a number of much-stigmatised dialectal forms (see *done, drug, give, see*).

Come'head/'ed (imp.): Come ahead, come on. '"Come 'ead" is hurry up' (Channon 1970: 102). 'Come 'head. We've only got three seconds before the searchlights hit us' (Bleasdale 1985: 31). 'Come ed, Ally. Stay focused' (Griffiths 2003: 82). '"Cum 'ed" meaning "come on let's get going"' (Lees 2013: 137). *NR; a phrase that can vary from a friendly invitation to join in, to a challenge to a fight; derivation is clear.

Come-overs (n.): visitors to the Isle of Man. 'Come-overs: A Manx term for visiting holiday-makers, many of whom are from Merseyside. Also for immigrants to that island' (Lane 1966: 21). *NR; derivation is clear.

Common (adj.): vulgar, socially inferior. 'You are common and mean, and only fit to be my door mats' (Haigh 1907: 109). 'You look quite common when you wear your hair like that' (Hanley 2009 [1936]: 127). 'That would not have made her feel so common' (Cross 1951: 131). '"It's getting' orful common round 'ere"' (Hodgkinson 1960: 11). 'The chief hater of the Scouse lingo is a certain type of Liverpudlian who refers to our native mode of speech as common, and to be common in Liverpool is to be inferior or vulgar' (Hughes 1963: 4). 'They say what right

have we got to call them common!' (McClure 1980: 146). 'Shocked to hear a lady speaking so common' (Brown 1989: 36). 'I was prepared, for the moment, to ignore his common voice' (Grant 1996: 45). 'Lizzie's "common" behaviour' (Bryan 2003 [1940s–50s]: 104). There are two senses of *common*, both of which date from the early medieval period: something which is public and shared ('commonwealth', 'common sense'), and something which is of ordinary occurrence and quality, and hence mean or cheap ('common as muck'). The dominant Liverpool usage is a l.19c. extension of the pejorative sense and denotes a specific evaluation of people and their habits – particularly speech – as 'low class, vulgar, unrefined'.

Compo (n.): compensation claim. 'If anyone can get you the limit in compo, your daddy's the one all right' (O'Mara 1934: 271). 'You know the compo money? I was told by the shore captain when he came aboard that the case was finished' (Hanley 2009 [1936]: 414). 'I've worked out all the angles out, all the compo and that' (Sampson 2002: 192). 'Got three grand compo though, didn't I' (Griffiths 2003: 31). Recorded from e.20c.; glossed as an Australian coinage, though the Liverpool usage is earlier; derivation is clear.

Compost-flake (n.): herbal tobacco. 'Compost-flake: Herbal tobacco' (Lane 1966: 21). *NR; herbal (non-nicotine) tobacco was first marketed in Britain just after the Second World War; derivation is clear.

Congo patois (n.): pidgin or creole language used in African trade. 'The professor had, probably, been reading those shockingly poor books, the Grandissimes, Dr Sevier and the Creoles, in which Congo patois, as it is called, is ascribed to educated white people' (Ward 1909: 89). Recorded from l.19c.; an Americanism which became a 'slang term heard at Liverpool' (Ward *s.v. congo patois*); derivation is clear.

Conk (n.): nose; head. 'There was a wort on his hand – he used to rub it against his conk' (Owen 1921: 50). 'His nose was reddening … we're all turning our conks into bloody lighthouses' (Hignett 1966: 269). 'Keep yer conk out o' this' (Sinclair 1999 [1930s–e.40s]: 14). 'See the conk and know the rest' (Fagan 2007 [1950s]: 34). Recorded from e.19c.; derivation unclear.

Conny-onny (n.): condensed milk. 'The shortening of words, or apocope, as conny-onny (condensed milk)' (Whittington-Egan 1955a: 6). 'We stuckh it on with conny-onny, miss' (Hodginson 1960: 11). '*Conny-onny*: Condensed milk. Also called *stiff moo* and *stiff tit*' (Lane 1966: 21). 'A conny onny butty' (Jacques 1973: n.p.). 'The good old tin of "conny-onny"' (Robinson 1986 [1920s–30s]: 49). 'Delicious conny-onny butties' (Callaghan 2011 [1910s–30s]: 48). Recorded as 'Merseyside: since ca. 1920' (Partridge *s.v. conny-onny*); *conny-onny* butties are the stuff of legend; generations of Liverpool schoolchildren were allegedly brought up on them.

Contract (n.): season ticket. 'The first class "contract" (Westport [Liverpool] for railway season ticket)' (Owen 1921: 144). 'I have noticed the following in speech and in the local press … contract for "*season ticket*" on the railways' (Collinson 1927: 121). 'Dan, who had contracts for the Wallasey and Birkenhead ferryboats' (Dawson 1951: 4). '*Ave yera contract*? Have you a season ticket?' (Shaw et al. 1966: 66). 'Smoke from the Rile Iriss funnel. Contract ticket for the Tunnel' (Shaw 1971: 101). Recorded from l.19c.; a specialised use of 'contract' to mean a 'season railway-ticket', later extended to other forms of transport.

Conway, The (n.): training ship. 'The splendid frigate *Conway* lay down river from the *Indefatigable*' (Channon 1970: 139). 'Out in that beautiful river lay *The Conway* and *The Indefatigable* [two training ships for boys]' (Dudgeon 2010: 24). *HMS Conway* (founded 1859) and *TS Indefatigable* (1864) were training ships to prepare boys for a life at sea; the Mersey also hosted reform ships, *The Akbar* (for Protestant boys) and *The Clarence* (for Catholics).

Cooey (n.): back alley, any out of the way corner or place. '"Jigger", which in its turn, has been largely replaced by the description "Cooey"' (Whittington-Egan 1955b: 6). 'So der's dese wackers like, in dis cooey in Canning Dock last night' (Anon. 1961b: 3). '*Cooey*: A lover's lane or any dark alley in which amatory exercises can be performed. *Up ther cooee*: to be placed in a difficult or embarrassing position' (Lane 1966: 21–2). 'Cooey. A lane. Liverpool' (Howarth 1985: n.p.). *NR in this sense; derivation unknown but apparently unrelated to 'cooee', 'call, signal'.

Coolie (n.): Indian, later, in a general and derogatory sense, Asian, seaman; menial worker. 'Brazen female hawkers seated on the floor lure Coolies, Chinamen, African Negroes and other Empire Builders' (O'Mara 1934: 5). 'The bastards. It's bloody coolie work' (Hignett 1966: 187). 'Harmless Merchant sailor boys – the coolie type, you know' (Hallowell 1972: n.p.). 'Much of the stall-holders' trade was done with the coolies' (Unwin 1984 [1920s–30s]: 61). Recorded from 16c.; used in India to refer to hired labourers; probably from Gujarati 'Koḷī', 'Gujarati person'.

Coon (n.): offensive racist epithet, black person. 'The innumerable coon-songs, with their maddening rhythm' (Haigh 1907: 291). 'You've got no coon' (Bower 2015 [1936]: 124). 'Pretend you're not looking at that coon on the bed' (Hignett 1966: 226). 'He was a nig-nog's kid – some coon from down the Dingle' (Bleasdale 1975: 27). 'G.H. Elliott – the "chocolate coloured coon"' (Unwin 1984 [1920s–30s]: 184). 'Mongrel territory where a dynasty of socialists still call black men coons' (Sampson 1999: 73). 'Others preferred "coon"' (Lees 2013: 28). Recorded from m.19c.; an Americanism; an abbreviation of 'raccoon'.

Cop/Copper (n.): policeman. 'The bloody cops. I hate them' (Hanley 1932: 174). 'Bigger than the biggest cop who ever walked the dock road' (Cross 1951: 18). 'You don' a course get coppers the same neether' (Shaw 1957a: 15). 'The cops had stopped seeing the joke' (Hignett 1966: 33). 'Coppers see us writing on the walls sometimes' (Bleasdale 1975:

17). 'A boy was usually put on "douse" to watch out for an approaching "copper"' (Unwin 1984 [1920s–30s]: 105). 'Okay coppers, we'll come quietly' (Brown 1989: 49). 'Run out in front of a copper' (Sampson 2002: 233). 'The copper stopped him' (Stamper 2010: 76). Recorded from e.19c.; probably from northern dialectal 'to cop', 'to capture, catch, lay hold of'.

Cop for (v.): to meet. 'Copferracracker lass nite. *I met a delightful member of the opposite sex yesterday evening*' (Minard 1972: 65). 'They cop for a ticket collector' (Brown 1989: 9). See *cop on with*.

Cop, not much (adj.): of little or no value. 'This lot are not much cop' (Hignett 1966: 194). 'A couple of lads from down by the Ice Rink in Kensington, but they're not much cop' (Bleasdale 1975: 191). 'Cop. "She's not much cop"' (Howarth 1985: n.p.). Recorded from l.19c.; an Australian coinage; possibly from 'cop', 'capture, catch' and by extension 'acquisition, something worth having'.

Cop off with (v.): to pair up; seduce. 'He was tryin' t' cop off with her an' she wasn't havin' any' (Bleasdale 1977: 34). 'I don't want yer coppin' off with 'im!' (Bryan 2003 [1940s–50s]: 186). 'I copped off with the dark 'aired one last week' (Fagan 2007 [1950s]: 107). See *cop on with*.

Cop on with (v.): to meet; become acquainted with; become involved with. 'Noted promenades, to the joy of Liverpool's youth, as a means to "click" or "cop on", in other words to get acquainted' (O'Hanri 1950a: 2). 'Yew could cop on wid some gear fellas'

(Shaw 1957a: 12). Recorded from e.20c.; mostly replaced by the more sexually loaded *to cop off with*, *to get off with*; probably from to 'cop', 'capture, catch'.

Cop shop (n.): police station. 'Ee's gone to de cop shop. *He has gone to the police station*' (Shaw et al. 1966: 64). 'By the time he gets t' the cop shop, his evidence'll have melted' (Bleasdale 1975: 197). 'Take him to the cop shop' (Brown 1989: 20). 'The cop-shop on the landing stage' (Elliott 2006 [1940s–70s]: 121). Recorded from m.20c.; possibly Australian usage; a combination of *cop* and 'shop' ('place of bizziness' – see *bizzies*).

Copped, be/get (v.): to be caught. 'Think anyone got copped?' (Cross 1951: 161). 'He was copped by a Paddy Kelly nicking a bit a slummy' (Shaw 1957a: 7). 'You know you're copped lad' (Parker 1974: 164). 'Jimmy wondered if he'd been "copped"' (Sinclair 1999 [1930s–e.40s]: 29). 'If he turned back, he's copped' (Sanders and Sanders 2009 [1960s]: 41). See *cop/copper*.

Coppers (n.): money (a small amount); loose change; wages. 'To avoid payment of too liberal overtime coppers' (Powys 1857: 171). 'So we all gave some coppers each, and that was settled' (Shimmin 1863: 77). 'All of which she was robbing of coppers' (Tirebuck 1891: 245). 'Michael meant to take care of his coppers' (Haigh 1907: 504). 'If you talk to a Judy, she lets you spend your couple of coppers' (Hanley 1932: 32). 'The Liverpool youngsters were doing all this … and they were raking-in the coppers' ('Postman' 1945a: 2). '"To collect my

wages" is "to pick up money" or "to go for me coppers"' (Farrell 1950b: 4). 'He collected the bets, paid out, and drew the commission, giving me a few coppers from the shillings he received' (Shaw 1962b: 12). 'A few coppers a week' (Robinson 1986 [1920s–30s]: 23). 'We had no coppers for the phone' (Simpson 1995: 45). 'Whatever we made, even if it was coppers' (Sampson 2001: 13). Recorded from l.16c.; the plural usage is a 19c. development from 'copper', 'money'; from 'copper coin'.

Corky (n.): cricket ball. 'Wid de corky. With a real cricket ball' (Shaw et al. 1966: 44). 'I could carry me own corky 'ome' (Sinclair 1999 [1930s e.40s]: 119). '*Corky* A real, hard cricket-ball' (Spiegl 2000b: 129). *NR; from the cork used in the making of regulation cricket balls.

Corn-dog/corn-yak/corn jock (n.): corned beef. 'Corned dog. Corned beef' (Shaw et al. 1966: 38). 'Corn jock; fishpaste; beef; jam' (Fagan 2007 [1950s]: 184). Recorded as 'Merseyside: since c. 1930' (Partridge 1961); derivation unclear.

Corpy (n.): Liverpool City Corporation; a Corporation house. 'Corpy' (Shaw 1954: 4). '*Corpy*: a corporation house' (Lane 1966: 22). 'A Liverpool "Corpee" bus' (Jacques 1972: n.p.). 'They can't get the Corpy to move them' (McClure 1980: 101). '(De) Corpy. Liverpool Corporation' (Spiegl 1989: 23). 'To catch the "Corpy" bus' (Fagan 2007 [1950s]: 166). 'Two lads from a "corpy" in the Dingle' (Lees 2013: 18). Recorded from m.20c.; glossed as originating in Liverpool (Beale (1984) *s.v. corpy*), the term came to refer not just to the City Corporation, but specifically to the housing department; derivation is clear.

Cosher (n.): a supervisor; a street paper-seller. 'The newspaper lads had badges too, called a BELT and woe betide one if his Captain (the COSHER) found him without it' (Shaw 1959a: 34). '"Cosher" meaning a young fellow selling the *Echo* and *Express* in the streets' (Welsh 1964: 8). 'Cosher. Supervisor. Liverpool' (Howarth 1985: n.p.). 'Exy-cosher was our affectionate name for all paper lads' (Callaghan 2011 [1910s–30s]: 48). *NR; derivation unknown.

Count of Monte Cristo (n.): showy or well-dressed man. '*Count of Monte Cristo, Ther*: A dressy man; a show-off' (Lane 1966: 23). 'Orl decked up like the Cunt of Monty Cristo' (Simpson 1995: 22). *NR; from the title character of Alexandre Dumas' *The Count of Monte Cristo* (1845).

Couple, a good (n.): many, a lot. '"A good couple" (a fairly large number)' (Farrell 1950b: 4). '"A good few" like a "good couple" being plenty' (Shaw 1959a: 37). *NR; usually used with reference to numbers of drinks (compare *few*). See *couple of*.

Couple of (n.): either a few or many. '*Coupler bob*: Very cheap; a bargain, as in *it only cost me a coupler bob*' (Lane 1966: 22). 'The Bevvy, the lotion, coupler jars' (Jacques 1973: n.p.). 'What about a coupla bob?' (McClure 1980: 333). '(A) COUPLA. Convenient understatement' (Spiegl 1989: 23). 'An a coupla rolls if thee've got any' (Griffiths 2003: 78). *NR; the various senses of this phrase are highly contextual; it hardly ever means 'two'.

Court (n.): block of houses enclosing a square; the poorest of poor housing. 'If one woman in a court or street is bent on keeping herself to herself' (Shimmin 1863: 33). 'Men with their hands in their pockets at court corners' (Tirebuck 1891: 7). 'To get into these pestilential rookeries you have to penetrate courts reeking with poisonous and malodorous gases' (Haigh 1907: 39). 'The term, of course, is ironic; what the "Court" represented was a narrow alley receding off the street to a larger areaway, like an unseen tooth cavity, and ending in a conglomeration of filthy shacks' (O'Mara 1934: 32). 'Courts leading off drably uniform streets' (Mays 1954: 39). 'Living in hovels in courts up Scotland Road' (Hignett 1966: 221). 'All round here were these old-fashioned courts of tiny houses' (McClure 1980: 163). 'It was better than living in the courts at the bottom of our street' (Stamper 2010: 1). Recorded from m.19c. in this sense; Liverpool's housing problem in the 1920s was notorious and the *courts* were amongst the worst of it; a 19c. extension of 'court', 'walled space', ultimately from Latin 'cohors', 'enclosed area'.

Courter (n.): inhabitant of the *courts*. 'The customary domestic procedure of the courters was to drink and fight' (O'Mara 1934: 32–3). *NR; derivation is clear.

Courting (n. and v.): engaging in a relationship. (Whittaker 1934: 228). 'It's a long time since I did any courting' (Hall 2004 [1939]: 168). 'Older members tried to get the courting males to dance with their girls' (Kerr

1958: 125). 'She was courting once' (Bainbridge 1973: 53). 'I didn't even know that you were courting' (Graham 1988: 108). 'Courting and marriage were very different things' (Jones 1999: 12). 'I started courting Eileen in 1958' (Stamper 2010: 149). Recorded from 16c.; a 20c. extension of 'to court', 'to pay court/courteous attention to'; ultimately from the practice of attending the royal court to win favour.

Cow (n.): derogatory term for prostitute. 'It's these old cows who do it in back parlors that put the risk in it' (Hignett 1966: 275). '"Beef" and "pussy". To our faces. It makes us feel like cows' (Murari 1975: 68). 'Uniformed policemen are laffin' and jokin' with the cows' (McClure 1981: 133). 'COW A prostitute or BUSINESS GIRL' (Spiegl 1989: 23). Recorded from e.17c.; from the slightly earlier 'cow', 'unattractive woman'.

Cow-head (n.): idiot, fool. 'Cow-'ead: A simpleton a yokel' (Lane 1966: 22). *NR; an e.20c. Lancashire dialectal term.

Cow juice (n.): milk. 'Wonna cowjooce. *A bottle of milk, please*' (Minard 1972: 37). '*Cowjuice* Fresh milk' (Spiegl 2000b: 111). Recorded from l.18c.; derivation is clear.

Cowboy (n.): outsider; unprofessional tradesperson; reckless person, idiot. 'A Cowboy. A rank outsider' (Shaw 1966: 56). 'Y'mean when me and Kevin got the sack because of you cowboys' (Bleasdale 1982: 38). 'COWBOYS. Fly-by-night tradesmen who do shoddy work, take the money and disappear' (Spiegl 1989: 23). 'Which cunt is backing this cowboy up?' (Sampson 2001: 69). 'A baldy 'eaded cowboy from the sausage factory' (Fagan 2007 [1950s]: 48). Recorded from m.20c.; an Americanism; an extension of 'cowboy', 'British loyalist in the American Revolutionary War'.

Cowie (n.): cowboy film. '"It's John Wayne", Mad Dog said, "in a cowie"' (Bleasdale 1975: 121). 'No proper Cowie! There was no singin' in it, la' (Simpson 1990: 57). *NR; derivation is clear.

Cozzy/cossie (n.): swimming costume. '"Eh yew ahr Nellie, werdye purrahr kid's cozzy?"' (Hodkinson 1960: 11). 'I got no bayden cozzie. *I have no swim-suit*' (Shaw et al. 1966: 44). 'A bathing costume is a "baydin' cozzie"' (Channon 1970: 102). 'Swingin' their wet "cossics" as they went' (Sinclair 1999 [1930s–e.40s]: 150). *NR; derivation is clear.

Crack¹ (n.): small place, alleyway. 'This meeting place in a back crack behind the Walker Art Gallery' (Shaw 1955c: 4). 'Back crack: A back alley' (Lane 1966: 5). 'You also knew every back crack and nook and cranny' (McClure 1980: 165). 'On the edge of the kerb in a back crack' (Brown 1989: 52). Recorded from l.19c.; from 'crack', 'a slight opening between a door and the door-post'.

Crack² (n.): sharp or mocking comment. 'One more crack like that an' I'll box your own bloody ears' (Bleasdale 1975: 30). 'Smart aleck, another crack like that an' yer'll break' (Bryan 2003 [1940s–50s]: 139). Recorded from l.19c.; an Americanism; an extension of the earliest sense of 'crack', 'sharp dry sound'.

Crack[3] *(n.)*: conversation, banter, chat. 'A couple of pints of good beer, maybe the first of the week, and the crack ... the crack ...' (Bleasdale 1985: 252). 'There's nothing comes close to the crack you have on the train down to a London match' (Sampson 2001: 161). 'There's no crack at all in our place' (Fagan 2007 [1950s]: 76). Recorded from m.20c.; Irish English; probably from the earlier Scottish and northern dialectal 'to crack', 'to converse briskly and sociably'.

Crack, Ye/The (n.): Ye Cracke pub. 'They'd all be in the Crack or the Phil at nine o'clock' (Hignett 1966: 17). 'Favoured by the male members of the Philharmonic Choir (for some years, indeed, "Ye Crack" was better known as "The Songsters")' (Channon 1970: 118). 'Fancy the Crack, or the Phil?' (Cornelius 2001 [1982]: 27). 'Above the urinal in Ye Cracke' (Lees 2013: 253). *NR; 'Ye Cracke' is a 19c. pub on Rice Street in central Liverpool; see *crack*[1] *(n.)*.

Crack[1] *(v.)*: to change money. Recorded as 'used, by seamen, of cashing advance notes: mostly a Liverpool word: C.20' (Partridge *s.v. crack*); from 'crack', 'break open, break apart'.

Crack[2] *(v.)*: to hit, slap. 'I'll crack your pepper-box for you' (Melville 1849: 166). '*Crackerjack!* Chastise her, John' (Minard 1972: 77). 'Landed 'im such a crack' (Jacques 1979: n.p.). Recorded from m.15c.; glossed as 'dialectal and colloquial'; from 'crack', 'to strike with a sharp noise'.

Crack on[1] *(v.)*: to acknowledge. 'Don't crack on to dat one, missus' (Shaw 1957a: 12). 'Ee won't crack on. *He is ignoring us*' (Shaw et al. 1966: 40).

'Thee just crack on to each other' (Griffiths 2003: 10). *NR; possibly from *crack*[3] but derivation unclear.

Crack on[2] *(v.)*: to pretend. 'Crack on. To reveal or pretend' (Howarth 1985: n.p.). 'Cracking on that that's her proper name' (Sampson 2002: 34). 'Just crack on to Tommy we couldn't find the cunt' (Griffiths 2003: 95). *NR; derivation unclear.

Crack on[3] *(v.)*: to inform, tell on. 'Steve came down the bus then and asked what was going on but nobody cracked on to him' (Bleasdale 1975: 197). *NR; derivation unclear.

Crack up (v.): to laugh; burst out laughing. 'I was that close to cracking up' (Sampson 2002: 5). Recorded from m.20c.; probably simply from 'crack', 'break'.

Crackers (adj.): crazy, stupid. 'He's crackers, I'm not kidding' (Bleasdale 1975: 16). 'Yer must've been crackers' (Bryan 2003 [1940s–50s]: 65). Recorded from e.20c.; an extension of e.17c. 'cracked (head)', 'crazy'.

Craggy (adj.): serious, grumpy. '*Craggy bastard*: A serious minded, somewhat severe person' (Lane 1966: 23). *NR in this sense; probably an extension of 'craggy', 'hard to get through or deal with; rough, rugged, difficult'.

Crapper (n.): toilet. '*Crapper* or *crappus*: A lavatory' (Lane 1966: 23). Recorded from e.20c.; an Americanism; from m.19c. 'crap, to ease oneself by evacuation', ultimately from Middle English 'crap', 'residue, dregs'.

Cream poof (n.): derogatory term for homosexual. '*Cream poof* or *poofter*: An effeminate male' (Lane 1966: 23). Recorded from e.20c.; see *puff*.

Crease (v.): to beat, punish. 'The ould masters used to crease me' (Shaw 1957a: 15). 'Crease for to beat' (Shaw 1962a: 10). 'Crease. Punish. Liverpool' (Howarth 1985: n.p.). Recorded from e.20c.; probably a weakening of an e.19c. hunting term, 'crease', 'to stun (an animal) by a shot in the "crest" or ridge of the neck'.

Creased (adj.): tired out. '*I'm dead creased*, I am very tired' (Shaw et al. 1966: 60). Recorded from e.20; probably an extension of *crease (v.)*.

Creep/creeper (n.): unpleasant, even nasty person. 'Hoping to be made use of, the lousy creepers' (Cross 1951: 61). '*Creep*: A worthless person; a slob' (Lane 1966: 23). 'He hasn't had time to tell anybody what a creep you are' (Parker 1974: 220). 'A creep if ever I saw one' (Callaghan 2011 [1910s–30s]: 88). Recorded from l.19c.; northern dialectal; an extension of 'creep', 'move stealthily'.

Creep (v.): to dance. '*C'mon kid, let's creep*: Invitation to the dance' (Lane 1966: 21). Recorded from m.20c.; probably from the dance 'the Creep'.

Creeping Jesus (n.): an ill or unlucky person who constantly seeks pity. '*Creepin' Jesus*: Applied to a person who enjoys bad health or constant misfortune; somebody who solicits sympathy by wearing an air of patient martyrdom' (Lane 1966: 23). '*E's a creepin Jeezus* He enjoys bad health, martyrdom' (Spiegl 2000b: 50). 'E's a creepin Jesus' (Lees 2013: 137). Recorded from m.20c.; an extension of William Blake's l.18c. coinage to refer to sycophancy and hypocritical piousness, though the Liverpool use incorporates the sense of manipulation by the ever-patient sufferer (compare 'bit of a saint').

Crimbo (n.): Christmas. 'Dick Crimbo = St. Nicholas' (Moloney 1966: 63). 'Crimbo = Christmas' (Minard 1972: 10). 'In the run-up to Chrimbo' (Sampson 2002: 9). Recorded from m.20c.; derivation is clear.

Cross-cut (n.): offensive racist term for a Chinese or Jewish woman. '*Crosscut. A Chinese woman*. Derived from a popular but entirely baseless superstition. Also used for Jewish woman' (Shaw et al. 1966: 28). Recorded as 'a [20c.] Liverpudlian term' (Dalzell and Victor (2007) *s.v. crosscut*); from the belief that the genitalia of Asian and Jewish women are distinctive in form.

Crown jewels (n.): head. '*Crown jewels*: injuries to the head' (Lane 1966: 23). *NR in this sense (the more usual m.20c. meaning is 'male genitals'); derivation is clear.

Crubeen (n.): pig's foot. 'A crubeen is a pig's foot (Irish)' (Shaw 1958d: 19). Boiled pig's trotters were a delicacy; Irish English; from the Gaelic 'crúibín', 'hoof'.

Crud (n.): shit; nonsense. '*Crud*: Rubbish; nonsense' (Lane 1966: 23). '*I got Bombay crud*, I am suffering from looseness of the bowels' (Shaw 1966: 56). 'There's crud all over the place' (Grant 2002: 175). Recorded from m.20c.; an Americanism; *crud* and 'curd' are variants for the substance formed when milk coagulates.

Cunard feet (n.): splay feet. '*'Im with ther Cunard feet*: The man with big splay feet' (Lane 1966: 52). *NR; presumably from the stance required to balance on a ship.

Cunard Yank (n.): Liverpool seaman influenced by American culture. 'Not for nothing did many of the young seamen going there become known locally as "Cunard Yanks"' (Lane 1987: 108). 'Cunard Yanks, the men who took pictures of American styles to Liverpool tailors to be copied' (Grant 1996: 49–50). 'Cunard Yanks returned in blue or red zoot suits, button down shirts and hand-painted ties' (Lees 2013: 180). *NR; Liverpool sailors on transatlantic routes were one of the conduits for the 20c. American cultural influence in Liverpool that was evident in clothes, music and language.

Cunt[1] (n.): nasty person, idiot; general term of abuse. (Murari 1975: 35) 'He's the world's number one cunt' (Parker 1974: 84). It doesn't cost much, you cunt' (Robinson 1986 [1920s–30s]: 40). 'Look at these cunts, Ally' (Griffiths 2003: 31). Recorded from e.20c.; from 13c. 'cunt', 'vagina'.

Cunt[2] (n.): person, usually male, non-pejorative. 'Any cunt might walk in' (Robinson 1986 [1920s–30s]: 146). 'She was one bird that every cunt was after' (Sampson 2002: 41). Recorded from l.20c.; a weakening of *cunt[1]*.

Curd (n.): lemon cheese. '*Curd*: Lemon cheese' (Lane 1966: 24). Recorded from m.20c.; an abbreviation of l.19c. 'lemon curd'.

Cushty/Custy (adj.): beautiful, excellent. '*Beautiful*. Custy' (Minard 1972: 88). 'Alright Aldo Sound as a pound/I'm cushty la but there's nothing down' (Johnson 1988). *NR; probably from Romani 'kushto' 'good'.

Cushy (adj.): easy, undemanding. 'They have the idea that it is quite "cushy" and without trouble' (Whittaker 1934: 266). 'During his last year he had a "cushy" time' (Mays 1954: 199). 'Jobs that were supposed to be going, all cushy numbers' (Hignett 1966: 124). 'Is it a cushy number?' (Parker 1974: 71). 'This was a "cushy number"' (Elliott 2006 [1940s–70s]: 147). 'Besides, it was a cushy number' (Burnett 2011: 41). Recorded from l.19c.; Forces' usage; from Urdu 'ku̱šī', 'pleasure' (ultimately Persian 'ku̱šī', 'pleasure, convenience').

Cut (n.): look, style. 'By the cut of you, you've never done anything else' (Hignett 1966: 36). Recorded from m.20c.; usually in the negative phrase 'look at the cut of you'; an extension of a 16c. coinage referring to clothes or hair.

Cut, the (n.): Leeds–Liverpool canal. 'It may have something to do with the banks of the canal (THE CUT)' (Shaw 1959a: 38). 'These same boys chose to swim "bare pelt in der cut up ter der scaldy end"' (Williams 1962: 12). '*A dip in ther cut*: a swim in the canal' (Lane 1966: 24). 'Cut. A canal' (Howarth 1985: n.p.). *NR in this sense; a specific m20c. extension of 16c. 'cut', 'a channel cut out'.

Cutty/cuddy (n.): bargeman; type of smoker's pipe. 'The men … smoked their cuddies, or chewed their plug' (Haigh 1907: 309). '*Cutty*: A bargee. Also a stubby type of clay pipe' (Lane 1966: 24). 'Cutty. Clay pipe' (Howarth 1985: n.p.). *NR in the sense of 'bargee' ('bargeman'); *cutty*, 'short clay tobacco-pipe', is e.18c. dialectal, from 'cut short, curtailed'.

Cutty shark (n.): small fish. '*Cutty shark*: A small fish; a tiddler or stickleback caught in a canal' (Lane 1966: 24). *NR; an ironic echo of 'Cutty Sark', one of the last (l.19c.) tea clippers.

Cuzzies (n.): H.M. Customs officers. 'De cuzzies. *The customs officers*' (Shaw et al. 1966: 73). '*Dee cuzzies* The customs officers' (Spiegl 2000b: 100). *NR; derivation is clear.

D

D, the (n.): detective. 'De dee. *The detective*' (Shaw et al. 1966: 64). 'The plain-clothes policemen, or "D"s' (Unwin 1984 [1920s–30s]: 100). '*De dee; dee jack* The detective' (Spiegl 2000b: 148). Recorded from m.19c.; an Australian coinage; by simple abbreviation.

D.R. (phr.): 'Declines to report'. 'Ee gimee a dee aah!' *A yelp often heard from one of the crew meaning: The Captain stamped a D.R. in my Seaman's Discharge Book*' (Minard 1972: 97). *NR; at the end of a voyage, the captain submitted a brief report in a seaman's discharge book on his ability and conduct; D.R. was effectively a negative comment.

Da (n.): father. 'If the kid didn't start yowling and calling me "da"' (Hanley 2009 [1940]: 193). 'A present for me da' (Owen 1961: 21). '"Mon Per" is yer da' (Jacques 1972: n.p.). 'Me da's suit' (Sinclair 1999 [1930s–e.40s]: 34). 'Da's family worshipped him' (Callaghan 2011 [1920s–30s]: 46). Recorded from m.19c.; a simple abbreviation, probably from Irish English.

Daddy Bunchy¹ (n.): Liverpool bogeyman. 'The gallery of Liverpool's characters with Dick Tutt, Hickey the Firebobby, Daddy Bunchy (a bogey for the children) …' (Shaw 1955a: 6).

Daddy Bunchy² (n.): children's game. '"Daddy Bunchy" reminds me that years ago the girls used to play a game with that name in the playground or streets' (Lovegreen 1955: 6). *NR; the name for

a game of snatch and a skipping song; presumably from *Daddy Bunchy*¹.

Daddy Bunchy³ (n.): dandelion. 'Daddy Bunchie. Dandelion when the flower heads have ripened. Everton' (Howarth 1985: n.p.). *NR; derivation unknown.

Damage (n.): cost, price; bill. 'Regie asked the young woman at the stall "what the damage was"' (Tirebuck 1891: 297). '*Wossa damage?* How much does it cost?' (Spiegl 2000b: 73). Recorded from 18c.; an extension of an earlier legal meaning: the monetary value of a loss or injury (modern English 'damages').

Dancers (n.): stairs. 'If instead of *up the dancers* you say up the apples and pears …' (Shaw 1950b: 2). 'Up duh dancers. – Upstairs' (Shaw 1962f: 12). '*Stairs*. Dancers' (Minard 1972: 87). 'Get up them dancers' (Sinclair 1999 [1930s–e.40s]: 69). 'I managed to stagger home and up the dancers' (Fagan 2007 [1950s]: 106). Recorded as l.17c. cant; derivation unclear.

Dandy (n.): see *delly*.

Darky/darkie (n.): offensive racist epithet. 'As I ate ravenously … the darky cursed the place roundly' (O'Mara 1934: 247). 'Blood was beginning to show on Darkie's silken lip' (Jerome 1948: 35). 'So will about two million others, darkies and all' (Hignett 1966: 123). 'I didn't want him to be ashamed of bein' a little darkie' (Bleasdale 1975: 186). 'This darkie jumped over the counter' (McClure 1980: 111). 'Dingle Berty, the darkie with one eye' (Fagan 2007 [1950s]: 241). Recorded from l.18c.; an Americanism; derivation is clear.

Dashing (n.): see *step-dashing*.

Day old chick (n.): new worker on the docks. 'The newcomer to the docks ("a day old chick")' (Shaw 1959c: 6). 'Day old chick. Newcomer to the docks. Liverpool' (Howarth 1985: n.p.). '*Day-old Chicks*: Young men just starting to work on the docks' (Sanders and Sanders 2009 [1960s]: 184). *NR; derivation is clear.

Dead (adv.): a general intensifier. 'When I came in this evening I was dead tired' (Hanley 1935: 52). '*Dead*: used for emphasis, as in *it's dead easy* or *she's dead nuts on 'im*' (Lane 1966: 25). 'You could see they was dead chuffed' (Bleasdale 1975: 61). 'DEAD. Very, extremely; as in "Dead good"' (Spiegl 1989: 25). 'It's dead easy' (Elliott 2006 [1940s–70s]: 124). Recorded from l.16c. in this sense; an extension, 'unrelieved, unbroken; absolute; complete; utmost', from earlier senses of 'dead' connoting 'absence of physical activity, motion, or sound; profoundly quiet or still'. Perhaps the best example of *dead* as an intensifier, which illustrates the senses of 'lacking motion' and thus 'absolutely', is 17c. 'dead drunk'.

Dead house (n.): mortuary. 'In the basement of the church is a Dead House, like the Morgue in Paris' (Melville 1849: 226). 'The dead body was … conveyed to the dead house' (Hocking 1966 [1879]: 41). 'There's someone alive in the dead-house!' (Tirebuck 1891: 169). Recorded from e.19c.; a room or building where dead bodies were stored (hence, later, a

nickname for a quiet pub); the original Liverpool *dead house* was the crypt beneath the city's parish church, Our Lady and St. Nicholas.

Dead scouse (n.): cold Scouse. '*Dead-scouse*: The same stew when cold' (Lane 1966: 93). See *scouse*[1].

Debby (n.): derelict piece of ground. 'De debbie. The derelict bombed site' (Shaw et al. 1966: 47). '*A debbie, bommie* A derelict (bombed) house' (Spiegl 2000b: 133). *NR; German bombing raids in the Second World War, and the urban regeneration schemes of the 1960s, left many derelict areas (also known as *bommies/bombdies*); from the French 'débris', 'broken remains' ('I went out and got a brick off the debris' Sanders and Sanders 2009 [1960s]: 161).

Deck (n.): floor. 'We hit the deck with him on top of me' (Jacques 1972: n.p.). 'He slides down the pipe and hits the deck' (Brown 1989: 70). 'The sound his head made when he hit the deck' (Sampson 2002: 236). 'Rioters began to hit the deck' (Lees 2013: 169). Recorded from e.20c.; Forces' usage, from e.19c. nautical 'deck' (on a ship).

Decker (n.): peaked cap. 'A likkle decker on he's big bald head' (Shaw 1957a: 7). 'Decker wid a lettin board. *A cap with a big peak*' (Shaw et al. 1966: 37). 'Decker. A peaked cap. Liverpool' (Howarth 1985: n.p.). Recorded from e.20c.; an Australian coinage; from 'deck', 'floor'.

Decko/Dekko (n.): a look. 'Take a dekko!' (Hanley 1932: 60). 'Decko. A look at something' (Price: 1950: 4) 'I wonder whether the Lascar seamen on their visits to "Paddy's Market" were invited to have a "Dekko"?' (Holbrow 1964: 6). 'I takes a little decko at him' (Sampson 2002: 194). 'Did you 'ave a decko at 'is arse end?' (Fagan 2007 [1950s]: 81). Recorded from m.19c.; possibly from Indian English (by way of e.20c. Forces' usage), 'deck', 'look or peep'; from Hindi 'dekho', the imperative of dekhnā, 'to see, look at'.

Deffo (int.): definitely, absolutely. '"Deffo, Snotty", I said'. (Bleasdale 1977: 217). 'Deffo. Afghani black' (Sampson 2002: 48). '"An arm or a leg?" "Me arm, deffo"' (Griffiths 2003: 110). Recorded from l.20c.; derivation is clear.

Deliver the luggage (n.): children's game. 'A dirty game, *Deliver the Luggage* in which an innocent has a bag of ordure thrown in his face' (Shaw 1960a: 40). *NR; derivation is clear.

Delly (n.): type of button used in children's game. 'Whether the name for a "delly" in the game of Buttons was not more properly a "dandy"' (Shaw 1960a: 37). *NR; a *delly* was a prize button, flattened on a tram-line and shaped square by grinding; derivation unknown.

Delly/Dellie, The (n.): Adelphi cinema; Adelphi hotel. 'Delly (Adelphi)' (Shaw 1954: 4). '"The Delly" originally referred to Liverpool's Old Adelphi Theatre. Nevertheless, it has now been inherited by the Adelphi Hotel' ('Postman' 1961b: 4). 'There was the Adelphi, the "Dellie" in Byrom Street, a flea box' (Clerk 1971 [c.1900]: 52). '"The Theatre Royal Adelphi" … inevitably with "scousers", who couldn't resist cutting a name down to size, it soon became the "Delly"' (Unwin 1984 [1920s–30s]: 176). 'The Adelphi (the Delly) in Christian Street' (Dudgeon 2010: 245). *NR; the *Delly* was one of more than one hundred cinemas in m.20c. Liverpool; the Adelphi hotel is one of Liverpool's landmarks.

Desert wellies (n.): sandals. 'Purra desert wellies. *Pair of sandals*' (Shaw et al. 1966: 37). '*Desert*-wellies? They turned out to be sandals' (Channon 1970: 103). 'Sandals, or desert wellies, as he called them' (Sinclair 1999 [1930s–e.40s]: 124). *NR; derivation is clear.

Deuce (n.): two pounds. 'Christ … A deuce' (Hanley 1932: 150). 'Soon as he gets a coupla wins or a deuce he's down at the ale-'ouse bevvyin'' (Shaw 1957a: 7). 'I've just made a duce [two pounds]' (Parker 1974: 73). Recorded in relation to money from 17c.; from French 'deux', 'two'.

Dewybar (n.): two pounds. '£2 A Deuce, a Dewybar' (Minard 1972: 86). See *bar, deuce*.

Dhobi (n.): washing. 'It's dhoby day with me. I'm washing the sins out of my clothes' (Hall 2004 [1939]: 29) 'Am doomee dhobi. *I am washing some clothes*' (Minard 1972: 102). *NR in this sense; an extension of e.19c. Indian English 'dhobi', 'washerman/woman', from Hindi 'dhōb', 'washing'.

Dibs (n.): Money. 'Dibs! Dibs! – In with the dibs for The Pet, that risked his life' (Shimmin 1863: 79). 'I'm a little too old to be spending my hard-earned dibs in the Duke of York' (Owen 1921: 197). 'All you think about is picking up your dibs on Friday' (Hanley 2009 [1936]: 538). Recorded from m.19c.; an extension, probably nautical, of 17c. children's game, 'dibstones', played with pebbles.

Dick (n.): detective. '*Dick*: A detective. *Sly dick*: a store detective' (Lane 1966: 26). 'JACK. C.I.D. Officer. Formerly DICK' (Spiegl 1989: 48). Recorded from e.20c.; an Americanism; probably an abbreviation of 'detective'.

Dick Tutt (n.): mythical Liverpool character. 'The gallery of Liverpool's characters with Dick Tutt, Hickey the Firebobby, Daddy Bunchy (a bogey for the children) and Donnelly' (Shaw 1955a: 6). *NR; derivation unknown.

Dickhead (n.): idiot, fool. 'What's that got to do with it, dickhead?' (Russell 1996 [1976]: 137). 'You pair of dickheads' (Brown 1989: 40). '*Dickhead!* Stupid, despicable fellow/Wanker!' (Spiegl 2000b: 38–9). 'Dickhead, you forgot to lock the hutch door' (Griffiths 2003: 218). Recorded from l.20c.; from 'dick', 'penis'.

Dickie-dyke (n.): toilet attendant. 'Dickie-dyke. Lavatory attendant. Liverpool' (Howarth 1985: n.p.). *NR; possibly from 'dicky', 'penis', and 'dyke', 'urinal'.

Dicky-docker (n.): Rabbi. '*Dicky-docker*: A Rabbi' (Lane 1966: 26). '*A dickie-docker* A rabbi' (Spiegl 2000b: 56). *NR; mocking, possibly derogatory term; from the fact that the rabbi 'docks' (trims) the 'dicky' (penis) during the Brit Milah ceremony.

Dicky Lewis (n.): statue over the door of Lewis's department store. *NR; Lewis's was one of Liverpool's premier department stores; to mark its centenary in 1956, a pioneering work of modern sculpture, Epstein's *Liverpool Resurgent*, was installed on the outside of the building. Known as *Dicky Lewis* (or *Moby Dick*), for anatomical reasons, its function as a meeting-place features in Pete McGovern's 'In My Liverpool Home' (1961): 'We speak with an accent exceedingly rare,/Meet under a statue exceedingly bare' (McGovern 1995 [1961]: 4).

Dicky Sam[1] (n.): Liverpudlian. 'We are not sufficiently skilled in Etymological Antiquity to explain to him the derivation of the term DICKY SAM, as applied to the good people of Liverpool' (Anon. 1821: 96). '*Dicky Sam*. – Whence this expression as applied to the inhabitants of the great commercial port of Liverpool?' (Anon. 1855: 226). 'A Liverpool man, or Dicky Sam, as we love to call our native-born inhabitants' (Picton 1888: 210). 'Born in Liverpool, and therefore entitled to the dignified cognomen of "Dicky Sam"' (Roberts 1893: 1). 'He found such a crowd of "Dicky Sams" that he could scarcely get in … "I was greeted with cries of 'I'd love a bowl of scouse'"' (Anon. 1943b: 3). 'Who was Dicky Sam?' (Ford 1957: 6). 'In Defence of Dicky Sam' (Anon. 1963c: 8). 'The genuine "Dicky Sam" was probably born within a mile of the Mersey wall and earned his living at sea or in the docks' (Channon 1970: 101). 'Dicky Sam used to run a pub on Mann Island' (Unwin 1984 [1920s–30s]: 103). 'Dickie sam's number one lookout' (Fagan 2007 [1950s]: 224). Recorded from e.19c.; the common term for a person from Liverpool in the 19c.; it may have originated in l.18c. as a Lancastrian insult, directed at the big city dwellers, combining 'dicky', 'dandy' or 'swell' and 'sam', from 'sammy', 'fool'.

Dicky Sam[2] *(n.)*: glass of beer. 'Dicky Sam. Small beer glass over a quarter less than half a pint. Liverpool' (Howarth 1985: n.p.). *NR; derivation unclear, presumably from *Dicky Sam*[1].

Diddy (adj.): small or tiny. 'The Song of the Diddymen/Doddy's Diddy Party (Dodd 1965a: title). '"Diddy" is little' (Channon 1970: 102). 'All these other places are just diddy little villages' (Griffiths 2003: 47). 'Diddy – Short' (Callaghan 2011 [1910s–30s]: vii). Recorded from m.20c.; often thought to have been coined by the Liverpool comedian Ken Dodd, whose 'Song of the Diddy Men' had the refrain: 'We are the Diddy Men, Doddy's little Diddy Men, We are the Diddy Men, who come from Knotty Ash'. In fact, the 'Diddy Men' and 'the Treacle and Jam Butty Mines' were invented by one of Dodd's influences, the Liverpool comedian Arthur Askey, though Dodd popularised them. Derivation unclear; possibly from dialectal 'tiddy', 'very small, tiny'.

Diddy-mise (v.): abbreviate. 'Liverpudlians like to "diddy-mise" words' (Channon 1970: 102). *NR; there is a notable Liverpool tendency to shorten words (technically 'hypocorism'); see *diddy*.

Diddys (n.): headlice. 'Diddys. Headlice. Liverpool' (Howarth 1985: n.p.). *NR; derivation unclear, but presumably from *diddy*.

Different ships, different long-splices (phr.): different countries, different cultures. Recorded from m.19c.; supposedly a saying of the notorious Liverpool crimp, Paddy West.

Dig (n.): blow, punch. 'Even the most timid of henpecks would have given the user a "dig in the chin"' (Shaw 1950: 4). 'If you're going to fuckin' dig me, go on then, dig me' (Parker 1974: 163). 'He used to box. Had a terrific dig on him' (Sampson 2001: 48). 'Duncan was as fit as a flea and had a good dig' (Sanders and Sanders 2009 [1960s]: 122). Recorded from e.19c.; 'dig', 'thrust, sharp poke'; an extension of 'to dig'.

Dimbo (n.): fool; idiot. 'DIMBO. The same as a DIVVIE' (Spiegl 1989: 25). Recorded from l.20c.; possibly a combination of 'dim' and 'dumbo'.

Ding-dong, have/give (v.): to fight, row. 'Didn't they go at it ding-dong?' (Shimmin 1863: 190). 'I had a cob on so I gave him high ding-dong' (Shaw 1955b: 18). '*We ad a birrova barney/a dingdong* We had an altercation' (Spiegl 2000b: 144). Recorded from m.19c.; an extension of l.17c. 'ding dong', 'hammer away' (at a subject).

Dingle, the (n.): area of South Liverpool. 'Mr Roscoe resided fro some time in the vicinity of "the Dingle" in Toxteth park' (Roscoe 1853: 79). 'Dingle born and proud of it' (Hallowell 1972: title). 'She'd been lucky and managed to have herself moved to the Dingle' (Murari 1975: 43). 'The Dingle lads have our own way of talking' (Sampson 2001: 24) 'Aigburth and Toxteth, The Dingle, Bootle' (Simpson 2011: 279). *NR in this sense; like many of the commonly used place names of Liverpool, *The Dingle* refers to an ill-defined area, though one with a strong local identity (its inhabitants are known as 'Dingleites') (Hallowell 1972: n.p.); it was immortalised in William Roscoe's l.18c. 'Inscription' (a lament for the disappearance of Dingle Brook).

Dinner (n.): the midday meal. 'The regular dinner time in the country was, in those days, twelve o'clock' (Maginn 1844: 1.110). 'Till twelve o'clock when we went to dinner' (Melville 1849: 175). 'He arrived at dinner-time; at tea-time I was in Rochdale' (Whittaker 1934: 182). 'Sandwiches intended to be eaten at midday are called either "dinner" or "carrying out"' (Farrell 1950b: 4). '"Do you eat your lunch there?" "No, but I have me dinner!"' (Owen 1961: 122). '*Dinner = lunch. Tea = supper. Supper = a late night snack*' (Lane 1966: 26). 'Half a mild beer and a sandwich for dinner and chips or beans or bread and cheese, that sort of thing, at night' (Clerk 1971 [*c.*1900]: 36). 'I'd skip brekkie and just have an early dinner about half eleven' (Sampson 2002: 57). 'Gave them breakfast. Then dinner …[They] stayed for tea' (Burnett 2011: 80). Recorded from 13c.; as the *OED* definition (1896) indicates, the idea that the use of 'dinner' instead of 'lunch' to refer to the midday meal is somehow incorrect is a recent invention: 'the chief meal of the day, eaten originally, and still by the majority of people, about the middle of the day (cf. German *Mittagsessen*), but now, by the professional and fashionable classes, usually in the evening'.

Dip, on the (phr.): pickpocketing. 'Could earn fifty notes on the dip down Ally Dock' (Griffiths 2003: 11). See *dipper*.

Dipper (n.): pickpocket. 'DIPPER Pickpocket' (Spiegl 1989: 25). 'There's hardly no one who's totally legit. There's kites, dippers, dealers, spivs, all kinds' (Sampson 2001: 161). Recorded from m.19c.; underworld usage; derivation is clear.

Dirty (adv.): very, extremely. 'A *Dirty Big plateful*. (Big is commonly so "qualified" by Dirty)' (Shaw 1958d: 19). '*Dirty*: … used for emphasis, as in *a dairty big muck-up*' (Lane 1966: 27). 'Anna durty big French puff' (Jacques 1977: n.p.). 'A dirty big rush for it' (Brown 1989: 11). 'A dirty, big tide-mark all the way round!' (Sinclair 1999 [1930s–e.40s]: 56). Recorded from e.20c.; derivation unclear.

Dirty black Protestant lie (n.): complete untruth. '*Dat's a dairty black Protistant lie!*: The absolute ultimate in untruths, usually proclaimed as such in an hysterical shout' (Lane 1966: 25). *NR; an example of Liverpool's sectarian history finding its way into the vernacular; 'black Protestant' is a derogatory reference to a descendant of the Cromwellian Settlement in Ireland in 1652; from Irish English; see *dirty*.

Dirty when she's dollied (adj.): term of disapproval applied to women. 'Also from the wash-house, now superseded by the "laundryette": "That wan's dirty when she's dollied"' (Shaw 1955b: 18). 'Yewr dirty when yewr dollied (This refers to Moral dirt …)' (Shaw 1959a: 40). *NR; *dirty* as 'repugnant' dates from 17c.; 'dollied' is a variant of 'dolled' ('dolled up').

Div/divvy (n.): idiot, fool, general insult. 'Eez a birrova divvy. He isn't too intelligent' (Minard 1972: 34). 'The "divvy" is the antithesis of the smart, quick person' (Parker 1974: 150). 'If anyone goes too far with the divvies, the bucks will take their part' (McClure 1980: 295). 'She says not to be a divvy' (Brown 1989: 10). 'These divs, like, they're not usually any kind of menace'

(Sampson 1999: 379). 'Divvy. Don't know what he's missin' (Griffiths 2003: 37). 'Derided at school and called a divvie' (Lees 2013: 214). Recorded from l.20c.; possibly from 'individual', but the derivation is unclear.

Dive (n.): rough or unpleasant bar or pub. 'An underground drinking bar. Reached England through Liverpool from "diving under to reach it". Equivalent to the lost London word "Shades" from the underground darkness of these resorts' (Ware 1909: 110). 'You won't be safe in this dive' (Jerome 1948: 109). 'Finding his evening's diversion in a round of dockland dives' (Cross 1951: 120). 'These catchpennies abounded in dives along one part of Lime Street' (Channon 1970: 90). 'The clubs and dives of Liverpool 8' (Cornelius 2001 [1982]: 8). 'A dive down by the docks' (Lees 2013: 82). Recorded from l.19c.; an Americanism; possibly from 'diving' into a cellar or basement.

Dixie/keep dixie (v.): to keep watch, keep a lookout. 'Dixy: To keep look-out or "nicks"' (Parker 1974: 212). 'Dixie. To keep watch during job' (Howarth 1985: n.p.). 'Keepin' Dixie Keeping watch, or Dowse' (Spiegl 1989: 50). *NR; possibly from Romani *dik*, 'to look, to see'.

Do (n.): party, celebration. 'I have noticed the following in speech and in the local press ... a do for any "*festivity or treat*"' (Collinson 1927: 121). 'Just then Papa came up and said it had been a splendid do' (Duke 1939: 155). 'They're 'avin' a do at are kid's for he's lad's twenny-first' (Shaw 1957a: 1) 'We're having a do, come on up, it's jars out' (Hignett 1966: 290). 'And often we would have

"a do"' (Hallowell 1972: n.p.). 'He was pissed. He'd been to this do, y'see' (McClure 1980: 244). 'It's not that sort of a do' (Bainbridge 1989 155). 'Flowers, photos, cars, carriages, and the do' (Sampson 2001: 29). 'A "do" at the Archbishop's residence' (Callaghan 2011 [1910s–30s]: 28). Recorded from 19c.; an amelioration of the 16c. sense 'commotion, stir, trouble, fuss', as in 'a deal of do' (now obsolete), a corruption of 'ado'.

Do one (v.): to run away; leave. '"He did one", meaning "he escaped"' (Spiegl 1989: 26). 'I'm wondering whether it's all right just to do one' (Sampson 2002: 5). 'She did one a year or two ago' (Griffiths 2003: 19). Recorded from l.20c.; glossed as 'Brit. slang (orig. and chiefly Liverpool and Lancs.)' (*OED s.v. one* Phrases 5); possibly from l.20c. 'to do a runner'.

Dobber (n.): penis. 'Lad had a big mad hairy dobber on him' (Sampson 2001: 12). 'As long as I didn't have to lose me dobber I'm not bothered' (Griffiths 2003: 110). Recorded from l.20c.; probably from 'dab', 'strike, peck'.

Dock, in (phr.): in hospital; laid up. 'A girl cousin, who had started writing to me when I lay in "dock" at Aldershot' (Whittaker 1934: 273). 'Having trod on a wooden box-mine and landed hisself in dock' (Cross 1951: 109). Recorded from l.18c.; a nautical phrase; derivation is clear.

Dock walloper (n.): casual labourer at the docks; docker. 'No longer did ships in port work dock-wollopers overtime' (O'Mara 1934: 281). Recorded from m.19c.; an Americanism; derivation unclear.

Docker (n.): dock-labourer. 'The young dockers and carters and their friends' (Haigh 1907: 302). 'I'll give the dockers the word to go ahead' (Hall 2004 [1939]: 215). 'Dockers have permeated their working lives with pet expressions' (Shaw 1958c: 6). 'He'd had vast respect in those days when he was a docker' (Murari 1975: 44). 'Stevedore – Docker elected in the gang to tell the others what to do' (Burnett 2011: 13). Recorded from l.19c.; an extension of l.18c. 'docker', 'someone who lives near the docks' (specifically Devonport); *stevedore* is an older term.

Docker, docker's (adj.): unusually large in size. 'Next to a tin of Carnation and a big docker's mug' (Bleasdale 1975: 88). *NR in this adjectival sense (another example is a 'docker butty'); presumably from the characterisation of dockers as big, strong men.

Dockers' ABC (n.): Ale, baccy, cunt. 'The dockers' ABC is ale, baccy and cargoes' (Shaw 1959c: 6). Recorded as 'British docksides, mostly dockers' (esp. Liverpool): late C.19–20' (Partridge *s.v. dockers ABC*); Shaw's version was adapted to the standards of an evening newspaper column.

Dockers' Umbrella (n.): Liverpool Overhead Railway. 'The scrapped the good ould Over'ead, the Dockers Umberella an all' (Shaw 1957a: 15). 'De Dockers' Umberella. *The Overhead Railway*' (Shaw et al. 1966: 33). 'The clatter of the Overhead railway above – the "Dockers Umbrella"' (Unwin 1984 [1920s–30s]: 79). 'The Liverpool overhead railway ... known locally as the dockers' umbrella' (Elliott 2006 [1940s–70s]: 75). *NR; the world's first electrically operated raised railway, which opened in 1893 and closed to public dismay in 1956, ran alongside the Liverpool docks.

Dockology/doxology (n.): the lore and language of Liverpool dockers. 'We 'ad a proper good jangle about the Scouse language. Or as I call the lingo – doxology' (Anon. 1955: 6). 'A loose account of dockology' (Jacques 1973: n.p.). 'A banter called "dockology" emerged' (Lees 2013: 121). *NR in this sense; a play on Greek 'doxa', 'opinion, belief'.

Doddle (n.): easy task. 'It was a doddle. Everybody happy?' (Cross 1951: 39). 'It wuz a proper doddle. *We won easily*' (Shaw et al. 1966: 33). 'By the end of September it'll be a doddle' (Graham 1988: 83). 'It must be a doddle' (Smith 1998 [1971]: 53). 'A doddle of a job' (Fagan 2007 [1950s]: 258). Recorded from e.20c.; possibly a combination of 'dawdle' and 'toddle'.

Dodger[1] (n.): a glass of beer containing about a third of a pint. 'A "dodger" is a glass of beer containing less than a half-pint and more than a "pony" or quarter pint' ('Postman' 1931c: 5). 'A small glass which contains more than a quarter but rather less than a half-pint of beer. This has been christened locally a "Dodger" or "Peter Hudson"' (Whittington-Egan 1955a: 6). 'Dodger. A measure of ale less than half a pint' (Howarth 1985: n.p.). *NR in this sense, though m.19c. 'dodger' was a 'dram' (from 'dram glass', 1/8 of a fluid ounce); derivation unknown.

Dodger[2] (n.): eight-sided threepenny bit. 'Dodger. *Eight-sided Threepenny* piece' (Shaw et al. 1966: 34). *NR; the eight-sided threepenny bit was replaced by the bulkier twelve-sided piece in 1937; derivation unknown.

*Dodger*³ *(n.)*: bread, cake; sandwich. 'Dodger, bread or sometimes crude cake' (Lane 1966: 27). Recorded from e.19c.; an Americanism; possibly from Scots 'dodge', 'cut or slice of food'.

Dodgy (adj.): unreliable, poor quality; risky. 'Then questions would be asked. Dodgy, very dodgy' (Cross 1951: 39). 'Dodgy: Unreliable, doubtful, risky' (Lane 1966: 27). 'God help anyone with a dodgy ticker' (Cornelius 2001 [1982]: 157). 'Responsible for fitting the dodgy installation' (Fagan 2007 [1950s]: 306). Recorded from m.20c.; an extension of m.19c. 'dodgy', 'full of dodges', hence 'tricky, evasive'.

Dog (n.): corned beef. 'Dog: corned beef. *Dog wi' bite*: corned beef with mustard' (Lane 1966: 27). *NR; derivation unclear, though 'dog' is a m.19c. Americanism for 'sausage' ('hot dog').

Dog/dock end (n.): last part of a cigarette. 'She leaves more dog ends in a day than me Mam smokes all week' (Bleasdale 1975: 51). 'He sucked down on the last millimeter of nicotine and stubbed the dock end' (Sampson 1999: 399). Recorded from e.20c.; probably an abbreviation of 'docked end'.

Dogooder (n.): well-intentioned but misguided person. 'All the do-gooders in the hall inside' (Hignett 1966: 149). 'The leniency of the middle century, the travesties of the dogooders' (Clerk 1971 [c.1900]: 15). 'For the do-gooders The Boys are part of a "social problem"' (Parker 1974: 201). 'The judiciary takes far too much

notice of what "do-gooders" have to say' (McClure 1980: 493). Recorded as current 'among Liverpool street arabs of late C.19 earlyish 20' (Beale (1984) *s.v. do-gooder*); a l.19c. Americanism; derivation is clear.

Dogsbody (n.): person assigned to menial tasks. 'Can lad and dogsbody' (Bleasdale 1985: 113). 'I was the dog's body' (Stamper 2010: 60). Recorded from e.19c.; 'dogsbody' was a type of nautical stew (Melville lists it alongside *scouse* and 'lob-scouse'); the term was extended to a junior midshipman and hence to anyone of low standing given menial tasks.

Dole (n.): unemployment benefit. 'With the dole abject starvation was out of the question' (O'Mara 1934: 302). 'She had to appear at the Labour Exchange for her dole on Friday' (Naughton 1945: 17). 'They had just done three on the hook and three on the book, meaning three days at work and three on the dole' (Anon. 1955: 6). 'Relying on the dole and what his wife earned' (Hignett 1966: 23). 'He didn't want the dole, but he took it for a while' (Murari 1975: 45). 'Dole queues reached hundreds of yards' (Robinson 1986 [1920s–30s]: 109). 'Straight to the humiliation of the dole' (Griffiths 2003: 40). 'We joined the flat-capped, four-deep dole queue' (Callaghan 2011 [1910s–30s]: 101). Recorded from e.20c.; statutory state assistance to the unemployed dates from First World War; an extension of 14c. 'dole', 'money or food given charitably'.

Doll (n.): attractive woman. 'She's worth ten of that doll' (Hall 2004 [1939]: 213). 'A living doll stood there' (Smith

1998 [1971]: 83). 'She's a little doll' (Sampson 2002: 158). 'Where all the dolls used to go' (Dudgeon 2010: 262). Recorded from e.20c.; an extension of e.17c. 'doll', 'woman'; a short form of 'Dorothy'.

Dollar (n.): five shillings. 'I'll bet a dollar' (Hanley 2009 [1940]: 94). 'A level dollar each way he might get away with it' (Cross 1951: 196). 'Dollar. *Five shillings*' (Shaw et al. 1966: 34). 'Hope I get more than a dollar for today's work' (Graham 1988: 85). Recorded from the 1940s; the pound sterling was rated at around four dollars and thus a dollar at five shillings.

Dolly tub (n.): washing tub. 'The dolly tub which was standing in the backyard' (Hallowell 1972: n.p.). 'The galvanised dolly tub' (Unwin 1984 [1920s–30s]: 43). 'When the washing had been boiled it was transferred to a Dolly tub' (Kelly 2006 [1930s–40s]: 12). 'Dolly tub and Reckitt's blue' (Simpson 2011: 282). Recorded from e.19c.; northern dialectal, see *dollypeg*[1].

Dollypeg[1]/*dolly (n.)*: wooden instrument used to stir hand-washing. 'Large, wooden, peculiar-looking dolly pegs' (Unwin 1984 [1920s–30s]: 43). 'A dolly … a three-legged stool with a long vertical prop rising from its centre' (Kelly 2006 [1930s–40s]: 12). Recorded from l.18c.; *dollypegs* were small pieces of wood fixed to the bottom of the churning instrument, the *dolly*; northern dialectal, possibly rhyming slang 'peggy', from 'meggie', 'centipede' ('meggie-many-legs').

Dollypeg[2] *(n.)*: leg. 'Me dollypegs. *My legs*' (Shaw et al. 1966: 20). '*The Legs*. Dolly Pegs' (Minard 1972: 44). '*Me dollypegs.*

My legs' (Spiegl 2000b: 67). *NR in this sense; see *dollypeg*[1].

Done (v.): past tense of 'do'. 'She done us well' (Hanley 2009 [1940]: 200). '*E done it – I seen 'im*: He did it – I saw him' (Lane 1966: 28). 'We'll batter that nigger to death for what he done' (Murari 1975: 99). 'The verb to do is inflected "I done, you done, he/she/it done, we done, you(se) done, they done' (Spiegl 1989: 27). 'Fuck knows what's got into me, doing what I just done' (Sampson 2002: 81). *NR; see *come*.

Donkey's years (n.): a long time. 'Some damn fool joke he'd made donkey's years ago' (Duke 1939: 27). 'You haven't been inside a church for donkey's years' (Bainbridge 1973: 86). 'Here's me, too late by donkey's years' (Simpson 1995: 31). Recorded from e.20c.; derivation unknown.

Donkeystone (n.): cleaning stone. '*Donkeystone*: A soft stone, creamy or light grey, used for colouring doorsteps and window-ledges' (Lane 1966: 28). 'A Donkeystone, floor cloth and pail' (McGovern 1995: 33). *NR; the donkey, imprinted on the stone, was the trade mark of the manufacturer Edward Read; a clean step was a matter of pride.

Don't forget the diver (phr.): Liverpudlian catchphrase. '"Don't forget the diver"? [was] used by a one-legged diver at New Brighton and the Tommy Handley show, "Itma"' (Shaw 1963d: 4). '"Don't forget the diver! Penny for the diver!" he'd keep shouting' (Unwin 1984 [1920s–30s]: 81). 'Tommy Handley was always a favourite of Jimmy's … "Don't forget the diver"' (Sinclair 1999 [1930s–e.40s]: 164). ITMA was probably the most popular (and influential) of the BBC's Second World War radio comedy series and featured Tommy Handley, a Liverpudlian comedian who used various aspects of Liverpool's cultural life in the show. *Don't forget the diver* referred to a one-legged diver (a casualty of the First World War) who jumped into the Mersey at New Brighton and solicited money from the ferry crowds.

Doolally (adj.): mad, crazy. 'She's doolally, not elevenpence for a shillin'' (Shaw 1957a: 12). 'Do-Lally. Being driven towards, or instantly going mad' (Howarth 1985: n.p.). 'Fucking doolaly she is now' (Sampson 2001: 33). 'You'll 'ave me Mam goin' doolally' (Fagan 2007 [1950s]: 48). Recorded from e.20c.; an abbreviation of First World War Forces' usage 'doolally tap'; 'Deolali' was the location of a British Army transit camp near Mumbai, 'tap' was a form of malarial fever.

Doorstopper/doorstep/doorknocker (n.): big piece of bread; large sandwich. 'A tramstopper; doorstopper. *A large piece of bread*' (Shaw et al. 1966: 41). 'Gerra big soft loaf of bread an' cut us some real door-knockers' (Sinclair 1999 [1930s–e.40s]: 135). 'The latest set of cheese doorsteps' *(Fagan 2007 [1950s]: 254). *NR; derivation is clear.

Dosh (n.): money. 'Dosh. Money' (Howarth 1985: n.p.). 'Fucking weighed down with dosh' (Sampson 2002: 10). 'When they start flashin' the dosh' (Bryan 2003 [1940s–50s]: 139). Recorded from m.20c.; derivation unknown.

Doss (n.): bed, place of shelter. 'Shelter from the impending rain, a doss, tea and a butty in the morning' (O'Mara 1934: 9). 'I never reproached you when you made this house a doss for band boys and barrow spivs' (Melly 1965: 26). Recorded from l.18c.; from the French 'dos', 'back'.

Doss (v.): to sleep, lie down. 'An hour or two's kip at Charlie's when we get thro' Brum an 'e can doss down with me' (Cross 1951: 209). '*Doss*: to sleep. *Me ole man can't see yer now, 'e's 'avin' a doss*' (Lane 1966: 29). 'He dossed down in his pram' (Jacques 1975: n.p.). 'There'll be no kipping or dossing' (Fagan 2007 [1950s]: 63). Recorded from l.18c.; see *doss*.

Doss house (n.): cheap lodging house; second-rate pub. 'A "fourpenny doss" for a decent lad was hell upon earth' (Haigh 1907: 503). 'We had heard he was staying down at the fourpenny doss-house' (O'Mara 1934: 136). 'Doss houses like Paddy Doyle's' (McColl 1952: 3). 'Those bloody evacuee dosshouses in North Wales' (Hignett 1966: 147). 'He mentions the Salvation Army's Doss House where for sixpence a night you could sleep in something shaped like a coffin' (Clerk 1971 [c.1900]: 38). 'The most famous doss-house in the world' (Unwin 1984 [1920s–30s]: 62). 'In the doss ouse of Yatsiz Wine Loge' (Simpson 1995: 21). Recorded from e.19c.; an extension of *doss (n.)*; the derogatory reference to a pub is l.20c.

Dough (n.): money. 'It's his old lady's dough he's playing with' (Hanley 1932: 150). 'I haven't made much dough tonight' (Cornelius 2001 [1982]: 100) 'That's where the dough is these days' (Sampson 2002: 119). 'No dough comin' in at all' (Fagan 2007 [1950s]: 66). Recorded from m.19c.; an Americanism; derivation unknown.

Douse, keep (v.): A warning; to keep watch, lookout. '[We] talked and took turns in keeping douse again for our common enemy' (O'Mara 1934: 133). '"Keeping douse", meaning "Keeping a sharp lookout"' (Griffith 1950: 2). 'Ee's keepin douse. *He is keeping watch*' (Shaw et al. 1966: 63). 'A boy was usually put on "douse" to watch out for an approaching "copper"' (Unwin 1984 [1920s–30s]: 105). 'DOWSE Watch, as in "keepin' dowse"' (Spiegl 1989: 26). 'I'd a ha'penny to keep douse [look-out]' (Dudgeon 2010: 106). *NR; possibly from Romani 'dik', 'to look, to see'.

Douser/dowse/dowsey (n.): lookout. 'Now everyone had money. Result: no trustworthy "douser" (O'Mara 1934: 145). '"Douses" were posted back and front' (Callaghan 2011 [1910s–30s]: vii). See *douse*.

Down the banks (give someone) (v.): to scold, remonstrate, argue or even fight with someone. 'I do not know where "*down the banks*" came from' (Shaw 1950b: 4). 'E give er down duh banks' (Shaw 1959a: 38). 'To give me down the banks for being a bit of a reprobate' (Jacques 1979: n.p.). 'Giving this poor cunt of a night porter down the banks' (Sampson 2001: 185). 'The long-haired one comes back and gives me down the banks' (Simpson 2011: 415). Recorded from m.19c.; apparently from Irish English; derivation unknown.

Down the nick, let yourself go (v.): lose one's standards. 'Sometimes I think you're afraid ... You're letting yourself

go down the nick' (Hanley 2009 [1936]: 295). *NR; derivation unclear, possibly from 'nick' in the sense of 'state or condition'. See *nick*.

Down the road (phr.): sent to jail. 'For all I know I'll be up in court and down the road' (Bleasdale 1985: 133). Recorded from l.20c.; possibly from m.19c. Americanism 'to send down', 'to jail'.

Dozy arse (n.): idiot, stupid person. '*Dozy-arsed bastard*: a stupid person' (Lane 1966: 29). 'OK, so I'm a dosey-arsed bastid' (Simpson 1995: 22). 'Dozy arseholes' (Griffiths 2003: 10). Recorded from m.20c.; an extension of l.17c. 'dozy', 'drowsy, sleepy', from e.17c., 'doze', 'bewilder, confuse', and l.20c. 'arse', 'fool' or 'unpleasant person'.

Dream's out, me (phr.): said when someone appears unexpectedly. '*Me dream's out*, (talk of the devil)' (Shaw 1952: n.p.). 'ME DREAMS OUT, sarcastic. "I saw something lovely in my dream and now I see you"' (Shaw 1959a: 41). *NR; derivation unclear.

Drink out of a sweaty clog (phr.): To be rash; very thirsty. 'Ee'd drink out of a sweaty clog. *He is intemperate*' (Shaw et al. 1966: 67). '*I'd drink outa a sweaty clog* I am very thirsty' (Spiegl 2000b: 87). Recorded from m.20c.; derivation is clear.

Drom (n.): house. '*House*. Drom, Ken, Gaff' (Minard 1972: 87). *NR; possibly from Romani 'drom', 'way, road'.

Dropsy/dropsie (n.): bribe, tip; payment or loan. 'Give the doorman is dropsy. *Tip the commissionaire*' (Shaw et al. 1966: 62) 'Dropsy: A backhander, a tip, a pay-off' (Parker 1974: 212). 'Dropsy. A tip, a bribe' (Howarth 1985: n.p.).

'Dja reckon you can see us right for a bit of a dropsy. Just till after Chrimbo, like?' (Sampson 1998: 128). 'I just give the lad his dropsie at the end of the week' (Sampson 2001: 81). Recorded from 17c.; an e.20c. extension of 17c. 'dropsy', 'money' from 'to drop'.

Drownded (adj.): extremely wet. 'Charlie's just come home drownded. That's the second time he's been drownded this week' (Farrell 1950a: 4). 'Dey going 'ome starvin' ungry and drownded' (Shaw 1957a: 15). Recorded from 20c.; Liverpudlian hyperbole – a person can be *drownded* without being harmed.

Drug (v.): past tense of 'drag'. 'Ther scuffers drug 'im outer ther boozer' (Lane 1966: 30). Recorded from m.20c.; glossed as 'nonstandard and regional use', though possibly a confusion with 'drug', 'pull forcibly'. See *come*.

Dubs (n.): toilet. ''E luvs 'is dubs: he goes frequently to the lavatory' (Lane 1966: 30). *NR; an extension of 16c. 'dubs', 'stagnant pool'.

Duck (n.): search warrant. 'We were doing what we called a "duck", which was a search warrant under the local Corporation Act, and so it had a Liver bird at the top of it' (McClure 1980: 530). See *Blue paper (with a duck on it)*.

Duck's disease (n.): see *bum-droops*.

Duff (adj.): defective, broken. 'Yer flogged me a duff kettle' (Lane 1966: 30). 'I may have made it with some duff mayonnaise' (Fagan 2007 [1950s]: 94). Recorded from e.20c.; an extension of l.19c. 'duff', 'counterfeit money or jewellery'.

Duff, up the (phr.): pregnant. '*I'm up de duff* I think I may be pregnant' (Spiegl 2000b: 109). Recorded from e.20c.; an Australian coinage; possibly from 'duff' as a pronunciation of 'dough', thus 'pudding' ('plum duff'), hence 'in the pudding club', 'bun in the oven' and so on.

Dunnage (n.): waste material. 'Away from the dunnage pile' (Hanley 2009 [1940]: 566). 'Moving dunnage (odd pieces of timber)' (Sanders and Sanders 2009 [1960s]: 41). 'Lying among some dunnage on the deck' (Burnett 2011: 75). Recorded from 15c.; an extension of 'dunnage', 'material used to protect or balance cargo in a ship'.

Dunner (n.): debt-collector. 'They could have used each other's rooms for dossing from dunners and irate women' (Hignett 1966: 128). Recorded from 17c.; from 'to dun', 'to importune for money', probably cant.

Dunno (v.): don't know. 'Well, I dunno yet' (Hocking 1966 [1879]: 22). '"And what does she want?" asked Katherine. "Dunno"' (Tirebuck 1891: 400). 'A sed "Wharar thee wack?" "A dunno", she said back' (Moloney 1966: 22). '"Dunno", Paddy said' (Murari 1975: 109). 'I dunno ... something about her' (Griffiths 2002: 5). Recorded from m.19c.; an abbreviation of 'don't know'.

Dursent (v.) dare not. 'Naw, I dursent, me Mam sez I shouldn't oughter' (Lane 1966: 31). 'Ah dursent! I dare not!' (Spiegl 2000: 97). Recorded from l.19c.; a Lancashire dialectal variant of 'dare not'.

E

Each way (adj.): backing a horse for a win and (at reduced odds) a place. 'They were "threepence each way" or "a tanner to win"' (Hallowell 1972: n.p.). 'They'd accept threepence-each-way bets at that time' (Unwin 1984 [1920s–30s]: 100). 'I'll back it each way, three shillin' stake' (Sinclair 1999 [1930s–e40s]: 13). Recorded from m.19c.; the derivation is clear.

Ear-basher (n.): chatterbox; bore. '*Ear-basher*, one who talks too much; a garrulous person' (Lane 1966: 32). Recorded from m.20c.; an extension of the slightly earlier Australian 'to ear-bash'.

Earwig (v.): eavesdrop. 'Trying to puzzle the eavesdropper (EARWIGGER)' (Shaw 1959a: 33). '"Earwigging" is eavesdropping' (Channon 1970: 102). 'A spot of earwigging at the keyhole' (Brown 1989: 66). 'There was no denying I'd done more than enough ear-wigging' (Fagan 2007 [1950s]: 58). Recorded from m.19c.; an extension of late-medieval 'earwig', 'person who gains influence secretly, by whisper or insinuation'.

Easy six (n.): Sunday work (with extra pay) on the docks. 'What the young ones do not know, in these days of a guaranteed week, worked or not, and reasonable overtime pay (such as double pay, the Gold Nugget or the Easy Six), is how bad conditions once were' (Shaw 1959c: 6). 'I ad an easy six. *Sunday work (six hours: 8–11 a.m.,* *1–4 p.m.)*' (Shaw et al. 1966: 59). *NR; Sunday work on the docks was considered highly desirable because of the extra pay and the structure of the day.

Eat/get eaten (v.): to be beaten comprehensively – either physically or in sport. 'I thought she was going to eat me when I said that' (Hanley 1932: 182). 'Dishonor faces the captain whose side takes the field to the cries of "Yiz ge ret" ("You will be eaten")' (Farrell 1950b: 4). 'I stiffened 'im. I 'alf et 'im' (Shaw 1950a: 40). *NR; possibly from 'to eat up', 'to ruin or destroy'.

Echo Belt (n.): Echo seller's official belt and badge. 'The newspaper lads had badges too, called a BELT and woe betide one if his Captain (the COSHER) found him without it' (Shaw 1959a: 34). 'I have not seen an "Echo Belt" since long before the last war' (Welsh 1964: 8). *NR; derivation is clear.

Eck-eck/Ek, ek (int.): watch out! 'By this time the street was up, and everybody was yelling "Heck, heck"' (Haigh 1907: 22). 'Ek, ek, here's the bobby' ('Postman' 1931a: 5). '"Eck-eck" and "Hey-up"; both with similar meanings, "look out"' (Jones 1935: 5). 'Eck, eck, 'ere's the nightman' refers to an ignoble practice in poor areas of making an official visit to a house by night to detect overcrowding' (Shaw 1960a: 39–40). 'Eck, eck, ere's de parkie. *Beware, here comes the park attendant*' (Shaw et al. 1966: 63). 'ECK-ECK!

All-purpose exclamation of surprise, caution, threat or warning' (Spiegl 1989: 27). '"Eck-eck" for "hello" or "watch out"' (Lees 2013: 136). *NR; derivation unclear.

Edge Hill, get off at (phr.): coitus interruptus. 'I'll get off at Edge Ill. *I will resort to coitus interruptus*' (Shaw et al. 1966: 63). 'I'll get out at Edge Hill, I promise' (Grant 1996: 50). '"Getting off at Edge Hill" … is actually a reference to pulling out on time in the sexual act' (Dudgeon 2010: 101). Recorded from m.20c.; Edge Hill was the last station before Liverpool Lime Street, the terminus of mainline train services; there are variants (Gateshead–Newcastle, Haymarket–Edinburgh, Paisley–Glasgow), though the Liverpool usage seems to be the earliest.

Eenog (n.): back-alley. 'Jigger – jowler – entry – eenog: four words for the narrow passage-way between the backs of urban terrace-houses' (Spiegl 2000b: 47). *NR; derivation unknown.

Egg-bound (adj.): constipated. 'Aw cheese, I bin egg-bound fer a week' (Lane 1966: 33). Recorded from m.20c.; an extension of a l.19c. veterinary term meaning 'a diseased fowl unable to lay'.

Egg-shell blond (adj.): bald. '*Egg-shell blond*: bald' (Lane 1966: 33). Recorded from m.20c.; derivation is clear.

Eggy (adj.): irritated, annoyed. 'E wusn' arf eggy' (Shaw 1959a: 38). 'Don' get eggy. *Do not get agitated*' (Shaw et al. 1966: 73). 'Eggy. Annoyed. Liverpool' (Howarth 1985: n.p.). Recorded as 'Liverpool: 20C' (Beale (1984) *s.v. eggy*); from 19c. dialectal 'to egg', 'tease, irritate'.

End away, get your (v.): have sex. 'I don't think I'd get my end away now anyroad' (Simpson 1995: 23). 'If I can get my end away while I'm out' (Sampson 2001: 36). Recorded from m.20c.; from 16c. 'end', 'penis' and 'vagina'.

Endless belt (n.): prostitute. '*Endless belt*: A prostitute' (Lane 1966: 34). Recorded from e.20c.; see *belt*[1] *(n.)*.

Entry (n.): alleyway between houses. 'The men splashed him with cole water an left him in the entry' (Tirebuck 1891: 438). 'I always take entries in respectable neighbourhoods and leave the front for the milkmen' (Haigh 1907: 101). '"Jigger", an old word used in the south end of the town to denote a back-passage or entry between two rows of houses' ('Postman' 1945c: 5). 'Jigger. Back Entry or Alley' (Price 1950: 4). 'One day up our entry' (Jacques 1972: n.p.). '"Entry", the local name for those narrow high-walled alleys skirting the back-yards' (Melly 1984 [1930s–40s]: 8). 'Jigger – jowler – entry – eenog: four words for the narrow passage-way between the backs of urban terrace-houses' (Spiegl 2000b: 47). 'We ate them in the back entry' (Elliott 2006 [1940s–70s]: 63). Recorded from e.19c.; a dialectal extension of 16c. 'entry' 'approach to a house'.

Erny (n.): undertaker. '*Erny*: undertaker' (Lane 1966: 33). *NR; supposedly a pun on 'urn'.

Everton toffee (n.): mint toffee sweet associated with Everton Football Club. 'That luscious compound of sweets … under the name of Everton toffee' (Syers 1830: 53). 'Sam, in short, had been destined for the fat living of Everton-cum-Toffy' (Maginn 1844: 1.143). 'I wouldn't 'ave dis Eberdon doffee' (Tirebuck 1903: 184). 'Everton toffee … you know the old girl who was supposed to make it, years ago, Granny Noblett?' (Hignett 1966: 103). *Everton toffees* were invented by Molly Bushell and sold in her 'toffy shop' (established 1759). The sweet became associated with Everton Football Club from the proximity of 'Ye Anciente Everton Toffee House' and/or 'Mother Nobletts Toffee Shop' to Goodison Park after the club's move from Anfield in 1892.

Evertonian[1] *(n.)*: an inhabitant of Everton. '"An Evertonian" is informed that there is a law to prevent common beggars pursuing their vocation in Liverpool' (Anon. 1845: 8). 'He should claim the support of the Evertonians in the forthcoming contest' (Anon. 1872: 11). 'An old (now ex) Evertonian' (Anon. 1897: 8). '"Evertonian" (Liverpool 5). You are quite correct' (Anon. 1944a: 3). 'Their broad Evertonian accents' (Sinclair 1999 [1930s–e.40s]: 19). *NR;

the derivation of this mid-19c. coinage is clear.

Evertonian[2] *(n.)*: a supporter of Everton F.C. 'Right merrily did they reward the Evertonians for their kindness' (Anon. 1885: 7). 'Shall I have the customary challenge about my leanings to Liverpool from certain Evertonians, and to Everton from certain Liverpudlians?' (Anon. 1914b: 7). 'Evertonians and Liverpudlians will join in sending good wishes' (Anon. 1941c: 3). 'I'm a Liverpudlian, well he's an Evertonian' (Parker 1974: 197). 'My father was an Evertonian and his brother was a Liverpudlian' (Dudgeon 2010: 121). *NR; the derivation of this l.19c. coinage is clear.

Exchange (n.): a swop deal involving council houses. '"We can always get an exchange", he said' (Bleasdale 1975: 190). 'If you want an exchange, the Corpee remark' (Jacques 1979: n.p.). *NR in this sense; this specific usage refers to the system whereby a tenant could agree to swop to another council house.

F

Fades (n.): bruised, sub-standard fruit sold cheaply. 'A pennorth a fades' (Shaw 1957a: 2). 'Fades. Damaged, therefore cheap, apples' (Shaw et al. 1966: 39). 'See if he's got any fades left (old or bruised fruit)' (Sinclair 1999 [1930s–e.40s]: 44). 'We could now look for "fades" (damaged fruit which had been thrown in the tip)' (Elliott 2006 [1940s–70s]: 36). 'The "fades" went down to join the Togee, the locusts and the treacle' (Callaghan 2011 [1910s–30s]: 27). *NR; presumably from 'faded' quality.

Fag out (v.): to field (cricket). 'Street cricket with a lamp-post for a wicket, both sides "fagging out" at the same time' (Shaw 1966c: 4). 'Faggers out. Cricket fielders. Liverpool' (Howarth 1985: n.p.). Recorded from l.19c.; an extension of e.19c. public school 'to fag', 'to perform services for another'.

Faggots (n.): see *savoury ducks*.

Fallies (n.): bananas. '*Fallies*: bananas' (Lane 1966: 35). *NR; derivation unknown.

Fally (n.): type of beer. 'A popular drink is *fally*' (Shaw 1959a: 37). 'A pinta Fally's. *A pint of Falstaff ale*' (Shaw et al. 1966: 68). *NR; an abbreviation of 'Falstaff ale', brewed by Walker's of Warrington.

Falsies/falsie (n.): anything false (breasts, teeth, eye). 'Those knockers aren't real. They can't be. They're falsies' (Bleasdale 1975: 204). 'They gave her a falsie, y'know, like a glass one?' (Griffiths 2003: 111). Recorded from m.20c.; an Americanism; derivation is clear.

Fancy Dan (n.): dressy, fussy person; showy, pretentious. '*Fancy Dan*: A dressy person; a sartorial show-off' (Lane 1966: 35). '*Ere's Fancy Dan* Here is a dapperly-dressed man' (Spiegl 2000b: 76–7). Recorded from m.20c.; an Americanism; *Dan* is probably an abbreviation of l.18c. 'dandy', 'person excessively concerned with dress'.

Fancy feller/fancy man/fancy woman (n.): lover (usually adulterous). 'That fancy woman of yours' (Hall 2004 [1939]: 123). 'She's like the wink from a fancy woman' (Owen 1961: 15). 'This is just to make up for Norma's fancy men' (Hignett 1966: 84). 'She's got a fancy feller now, y'know' (Bleasdale 1975: 181). 'Her fancyman giving Mrs Whatsit one' (Simpson 1990: 62). 'Nellie seemed happy with her fancy-man' (Callaghan 2011 [1920s–30s]: 48). Recorded from l.18c.; 20c. extension 'fancy man', 'man kept by a woman lady for sexual purposes'; from 'fancy' (a contraction of 'fantasy'), 'amorous inclination'.

Fang (v.): to manoeuvre (in children's game of *buttons*). 'To "fang out" in Buttons … if your opponent's button could, at certain times, be reached by spanning, fingers stretched a whole octave, this fanning out meant you could take his button' (Shaw 1960a: 37–8). *NR: see *buttons*.

Fang farrier (n.): dentist. '*Fang farrier*: a dentist' (Lane 1966: 35). '*Dee fang-farrier* The dentist' (Spiegl

2000b: 66). Recorded from e.20c.; Forces' usage; an extension of 'farrier', 'someone who shoes or treats horses'.

Fangs (n.): teeth; false teeth. '*Whur's me fangs?*: Where have I put my dentures?' (Lane 1955: 35). '*Dee fangs* The teeth' (Spiegl 2000b: 65). 'Ratter's nickname is down to his fangs' (Sampson 2001: 12). Recorded from m.19c.; an extension of 16c. 'fang', 'canine teeth'.

Farting (adj.): small, piddling, inferior. 'He was down on his knees looking at this little farting dog' (Bleasdale 1975: 135). 'None of them farting tin efforts where the tea leaks all over the fucking table the moment you pour' (Sampson 2001: 227). Recorded as a m.20c. Americanism; derivation is clear.

Father Bunloaf (n.): Catholic priest. 'I thought you had to go and see Father Bunloaf' (Hanley 1932: 60). 'Bunloaf was what southrons called Christmas Cake and something in its solidity led Billy Boys (Orangemen) to call a Priest Fr. Bunloaf' (Shaw 1958d: 19). '*Farder Bunloaf.* Name usually applied to the local Roman Catholic Priest' (Lane 1966: 27). 'Gabbin away like Father Bunloaf' (Simpson 1995: 23). 'The sight of "Farder Bunloaf" knocking on the door' (Lees 2013: 124). *NR; a mocking, possibly derogatory, term; derivation unclear.

Father Christmas (n.): reluctant male sexual partner. '*Farder Christmas*: a reluctant husband or lover' (Lane 1966: 36). 'In Liverpool, the reluctant lover is called Father Christmas' (Redfern 1984: 3). *NR in this sense; 'Christmas comes but once a year'.

Fed up (adj.): very annoyed, irritated, bored. 'I'm fed up. Just fed up' (Hanley 1932: 172). 'Me dad's fed up with answerin' the door to them' (Bleasdale 1975: 212). 'They must've got fed up like with her comin in the bridewell, so they posted her' (McClure 1980: 416). Recorded from l.19c.; probably from 'fed to excess' ('to the back teeth') and hence 'had enough'.

Fella/feller (n.): fellow; man; father; husband/male partner. 'You fellers go amidships, the doctor's waiting there' (Hanley 2009 [1936]: 92). 'The term "feller" which some levels of society bless, and which some dictionaries elevate to a colloquialism, does service in many unexpected places' (Farrell 1950b: 4). 'A girl without a "fella" feels ashamed' (Mays 1954: 88). 'Which brings us to *Fellers* generally. It is a popular word in the *Pool* and is in no way insulting' (Shaw 1958d: 15). 'You're a Liverpool fella' (Owen 1961: 27). 'Me feller. *My man-friend; my escort (even temporary)*' (Shaw et al. 1966: 25). 'Jean thought Banner was her feller' (Murari 1975: 68) 'These fellas, y'see, they're half-wits' (McClure 1980: 95). 'ME FELLER My husband' (Spiegl 1989: 53). 'Yeh know that feller Flathead?' (Griffiths 2003: 178). 'Feller – Man, or boyfriend, husband' (Callaghan 2011 [1910s–30s]: vii). Recorded from e.19c.; a variant of 'fellow' and glossed as 'vulgar or affected' (though it is neither in Liverpool), this complex term has a multitude of uses. They range from the simple sense of 'man' ('I saw some fella'), to 'father' ('the old fella'), 'boyfriend, husband' ('my fella'), 'idiot, fool' ('the soft fella'), 'important person' ('the big fella') and a host of occupational roles ('the bread feller', 'the coal feller', 'the insurance feller', 'the rent feller', 'the pools feller' and so on).

Fellas/fellers, the (n.): regular set of male friends. 'But the fellers are a man's friends … "I'm goin to duh match with duh fellers"' (Shaw 1958d: 15). 'De fellers. *My colleagues*; my comrades' (Shaw et al. 1966: 25). 'I say we go an' see the fellers' (Russell 1996 [1976]: 240). See *fella*.

Fender ale (n.): beer drunk at home. 'A drop a fender ale and a sky at the telly' (Shaw 1957a: 1). '"Fender ale" is beer bought to consume at home' (Channon 1970: 102). 'Fender ale. Beer for consumption off licensed premises. Liverpool' (Howarth 1985: n.p.). *NR; from 'coal fender', hence 'in front of the fire'.

Fent (n.): cloth remnant. 'Fents: left-over oddments of the textile industry, often used for making cheap dresses' (Lane 1966: 36). 'Fent. The waste ends of cloth' (Howarth 1985: n.p.). 'Fents A Northern English word for cheap remnants of fabric' (Spiegl 2000b: 72). Recorded from m.19c.; a northern dialectal extension of 15c. 'fent', 'slit or opening' in a robe or dress. Hence 'Fent-man: a trader in such oddments' (Lane 1966: 36).

Few, a (adj.): a good number, a lot. 'I did get a few bob, y'know, we all did' (Shaw 1952: 6) 'A good jangle an' a few bevvies' (Anon. 1961b: 3). 'A *few* jars usually means a good many as in *aye, I've 'ad a few jars*, meaning more than enough' (Lane 1966: 55). '"A few", like A COUPLA, is relative' (Spiegl 1989: 37). The ironic sense of *few*, 'many', is unrecorded, though the nuanced use of 'few' relating to *booze*, 'to have a

few', 'to have several alcoholic drinks' is registered from m.20c.

Few bob, a (n.): anything from a small amount of money to significant wealth. 'This few bob kept coming' (Hanley 2009 [1940]: 194). 'I did get a few bob, y'know, we all did' (Shaw 1952: 6). 'We could go to any restaurant in Liverpool cos I've got a few bob' (Owen 1961: 37). 'Sending me mam home a few bob like' (Parker 1974: 69). 'Slavin' away fer a few bob a week' (Sinclair 1999 [1930s–e.40s]: 51). 'Lads who've got a few bob' (Sampson 2001: 38). 'The casket was worth a few bob' (Stamper 2010: 176). Recorded from m.19c.; 'bob is an abbreviation of 'bobstick', 'shilling', common from m.19c.; *a few bob* has been retained, despite the shift to decimal coinage in 1971.

Fid (n.): marline spike. 'Fid. A steel spike for "working" rope'. Liverpool Docks' (Howarth 1985: n.p.). *NR; an extension of 17c. 'fid', 'conical pin of hard wood used for splicing rope'.

Fiddle (n.): act of falsehood, deception; stealing. 'The stormproof mac he had bought out of that last little fiddle' (Cross 1951: 137). 'We'll be able to work the fiddle at the theatre' (Hignett 1966: 152). 'They were beginning to think he was working a fiddle' (Bleasdale 1975: 24). 'It's all a bit of a fiddle then?' (Graham 1988: 25). 'Having learned about the railway fiddle' (Fagan 2007 [1950s]: 68). Recorded from l.19c.; an extension of m.19c. 'fiddler', 'sharper or cheat'; derivation unclear.

Fiddle with (v.): to sexually abuse (usually children). 'Fuckin' sexual stuff, likes. Kiddie fiddling' (Griffiths 2001: 220). 'What they really want to do is to take us away in their cars and fiddle with us' (Jolliffe 2005: 2). Recorded from l.20c.; an extension of 17c. 'to fiddle', 'to take sexual advantage of a woman'.

Filth (n.): the police. 'FILTH Scallies name for DEE LAW' (Spiegl 1989: 30). Recorded from l.20c.; a revival of 'filth', 'vile person', an obsolete sense dating to 14c.

Filum (n.): film. 'The Liverpudlian, like the Dubliner, makes "film" the two-syllable "filum"' (Channon 1970: 101). 'They showed me a fillum' (Jacques 1975: n.p.). 'Oh no, kidder – in this filum I'm a lad that's got a tiny little dick' (Sampson 2002: 32). Recorded from e.20c.; the disyllabic pronunciation was widely used in Ireland, Scotland and northern England, 'particularly Liverpool' (Dalzell and Victor (2007) *s.v. filum*).

Finger (n.): person, often unpopular. 'Who's the finger? (Murari 1975: 139). 'Wid this finger from Kerby called John' (Jacques 1977: n.p.). Recorded from m.20c.; derivation unclear.

Finger pie (n.): fingering of female genitals. 'Penny Lane is in my ears and in my eyes/A four of fish and finger pie' (Beatles 1967: lyrics to 'Penny Lane'). 'I only gorra birra finger pie' (Minard 1972: 69). Recorded from m.20c.; derivation is clear.

Finick (n.): fussy, over-detailed person. '*I'm tellin' yer she's a rill finick*: she is a fusspot' (Lane 1966: 36). Recorded from l.18c.; effectively replaced by the adjective 'finicky'; from 16c. 'finical', 'over-particular', ultimately from 'fine'.

Finny Addy (n.): Finnan haddock (smoked haddock). '*Finny Addy* or what you will' (Shaw 1958d: 19). '*Finny-addy*. Finnan

haddock' (Lane 1966: 36). 'Fresh Finney 'addock!' (Robinson 1986 [1920s–30s]: 118). '*Finnyaddy* Finnan haddock' (Spiegl 2000b: 115). *NR; *Finny* was an abbreviation of either the river Findhorn or the place Findon in Scotland; haddock was popular and cheap.

Firebobby (n.): fire fighter. 'De firebobby. The Fireman' (Shaw et al. 1966: 28). 'No more headaches for the "fire-bobbies"' (Sexton 1996: 20). *NR; 'fireman' dates from 18c., but the use of *bobby* derives from the fact that the Liverpool Fire Service was instituted in 1833 as 'the Liverpool Fire Police'; once *bobby* had been adopted as the term for a policeman, the name also attached to members of the 'Fire Police'.

First wet! (n.): said to someone who has just had a haircut, accompanied by a smack to the head. 'Only men have the custom of banging a wet hand on a newly-cropped poll saying "First wet!"' (Shaw 1959a: 33). '"First wet, ha ha!" and she promptly spit on her hand and slapped her brother's head' (Sinclair 1999 [1930s–e.40s]: 120). *NR; variations included 'first lick' and 'first biscuits'; derivation unknown.

Fish and Money (n.): a type of extortionate lending. 'When the pawnshop betrayed you, you could always do business with the "Fish and Money" people, who relied less upon collateral than upon their reputation for administering physical beatings' (O'Mara 1934: 66). *NR; in working-class areas lenders would offer a loan of, for example, six shillings, constituted by four shillings in cash and two shillings' worth of (usually putrid) fish.

Fit (adj.): brilliant; good looking, attractive. 'Brilliant Magic Fit!' (Russell 1996 [1976]: 168). 'There's this young woman about twenty-eight, quite fit and all' (McClure 1980: 171). 'Fit Good-looking, e.g. a "fit Baird", or "fit lad"' (Spiegl 1989: 30). 'I mean fit as in sexy, attractive' (Griffiths 2003: 64). '"Fit" (attractive)' (Lees 2013: 137). Recorded from l.20c.; first found in British black usage; an extension of l.19c. 'fit', 'healthy', from horse racing discourse.

Flags, the (n.): short for 'Exchange Flags'. 'As we leave the "Flags" and pass through Exchange St. West' (Ward and Lock 1881: 40). 'The open space of the Exchange "flags" on the left' (Tirebuck 1891: 238). 'Those shadows of their own brief glory, who still encumber the outer places of "the Flags"' (Owen 1921: 48). 'I heard on the "Flags" last Friday that you'd turned speculator' (Hall 2004 [1939]: 45). *NR; the large flag-stoned space behind the Town Hall was used for trading for centuries; it was the site of the cotton exchange from l.18c.

Flapper (n.): derogatory term for young woman; prostitute. 'Barbed wire entanglements had to be put up around their quarters to keep the enthusiastic flappers away from them' (O'Mara 1934: 257). 'A blonde flapper lived next door' (Robinson 1986 [1920s–30s]: 19). 'The first Jewish flappers' (Grant 2002: 8). Recorded from l.19c.; probably from northern dialectal 'flap', 'young giddy girl; a hoyden'.

Flappers (n.): ears. 'The Ears. Flappers' (Minard 1972: 43). *NR; derivation is clear.

Flat (adj.): penniless. 'Skint, Broke, Flat' (Jacques 1972: n.p.). Recorded from e.19c.; an Americanism; an abbreviation of 'flat broke'.

Fleming's up the steps (n.): Paddy's Market. 'The expression "Fleming's up the steps" refers to Saint Martin's Market … in other words "Paddy's Market"' (O'Hanri 1950a: 2). *NR; anyone claiming to have bought quality clothing from W. H. Fleming's, an established tailor on Scotland Road, might have been met with the phrase 'You mean Fleming's up the steps' (Paddy's Market, which stood on the opposite side of Scotland Road to Fleming's).

Flemings (n.): a variation of pitch and toss played with metal buttons. 'Fleming's reminds me of the pitch and toss game we schoolboys used to play with metal buttons' (J.W. Jones 1955: 4). *NR; a 'Fleming' was a bright brass button with the name of Fleming the tailor embossed on it; *Flemings* (an alternative name was 'Bang Off') was a game in which players each 'banged off' a button from a wall and then used a special button, a 'Copper Lewie' or *delly* (flattened for the purpose on a tram line), to try to cover the opponent's button.

Flicks (n.): cinema; films. 'On the flicks they see a man like Clark Gable' (Jerome 1948: 118). 'Her taste for gin and a night at the flicks' (Cross 1951: 65). 'The flicks if it rains' (Owen 1961: 586). Recorded from e.20c.; from 'to flicker'.

Flies' cemeteries (n.): iced cakes or Eccles cakes. 'Flies' cemeteries are iced cakes' (Smith 1955: 5). 'Flies' symmetry. *Eccles cake*' (Shaw et al. 1966: 41). 'Fly's cemetery. Eccles cakes. Liverpool' (Howarth 1985: n.p.). *NR; an alternative name was '*fly pies*: derisory name for Eccles cakes' (Lane 1966: 37); derivation is clear.

Flinchers (n.): a handball game. 'No big walls for games like Flinchers for All in the big sub-burbs' (Shaw 1957a: 1). 'Flinchers requires a good warehouse wall against which to throw the ball with the cry of "Flinchers for All" or "Flinchers for X"' (Shaw 1960a: 36). 'Flinches. Children's ballgame. Liverpool' (Howarth 1985: n.p.). *NR, in a *Liverpool Echo* 'Scouser Quiz', Shaw described *Flinchers* as 'a game in which a ball is thrown against a wall to be "copped" by others whom the thrower names' (Shaw 1963: 4).

Flock (n.): bed. 'Eez inniz flock ... pist! *He is in bed, incapable*' (Minard 1972: 94). *NR; an abbreviation of 14c. 'flock-bed'; 'flock' was waste wool or cotton, often used for stuffing beds.

Flog (v.): to sell. '"I pinched it to flog it"' (Cross 1951: 35). 'I thought you were flogging vacuum cleaners these days' (Hignett 1966: 138). 'I flogged me dinner ticket and went home' (Bleasdale 1975: 178). 'We're flogging the slummy' (Graham 1988: 94). 'I flogged him a bike' (Griffiths 2003: 179). Recorded from e.20c.; Forces' usage for 'to sell something not the vendor's own to dispose of'; derivation unclear.

Floor (n.): ground. 'FLOOR Scouse for the ground' (Spiegl 1989: 30). Recorded as obsolete; a common usage in Liverpool.

Flophouse (n.): cheap lodging house. 'The doss-house was often known as the "flop-house"' (Unwin 1984 [1920s–30s]: 62). 'Flop-houses where they stole your money while you slept' (Grant 2002: 81). Recorded from e.20c.; an Americanism; from 'flop', 'rope', against which the tenants flopped.

Flopper (n.): roadsweeper. 'At Exchange Station there was a flopper who swept a way for likely plushbums' (Clerk 1971 [*c.*1900]: 66). Recorded from l.19c.; glossed as 'Liverpool street arabs' (Beale 1984 *s.v. flopper*); possibly from *flophouse*.

Fluff (n.): derogatory term for a woman. 'Fluff Alley. The section of the ship where ... female members of the crew live' (Minard 1972: 103). See *bit of fluff*.

Fluke (n.): offensive term for a Pacific Islander. '"Flukes" we used to call them on account of their flat faces. Hawaiians mostly' (O'Mara 1934: 14). *NR; probably from the 'fluke' (the common flounder), known as the 'flat fish'.

Footy/footee (n.): football. 'I to the footy game, she to the hell-hole we called home' (O'Mara 1934: 73). 'We played footee with any old ball' (Shaw 1957a: 1). 'A game a footee. *A game of football*' (Shaw et al. 1966: 47). 'They're alright though – especially when they're on your side playin' footie' (Bleasdale 1977: 27). 'We lose two footee periods' (Brown 1989: 6). '*Footee* Football, the game' (Spiegl 2000b: 128). 'Crucial footy results' (Fagan 2007 [1950s]: 199). Recorded from e.20c.; a Liverpool coinage, though used around the same time to refer to Australian Rules football or rugby; derivation is clear.

Foreigner (n.): unofficial and undeclared job or work. 'We just lost our life savin's doin' a foreigner for two con artists' (Bleasdale 1985: 39). 'FOREIGNER Work done by employees for cash in employers' hours' (Spiegl 1989: 31). 'Known in the building trade as a "foreigner" and always paid with a "back-hander"' (Kelly 2006 [1930s–40s]: 91). 'A foreigner (job on the side)' (Stamper 2010: 162). Recorded from e.20c.; popularised in Second World War Forces' usage; from the idea of something extraneous.

Foreskins and balls (n.): faggots and dumplings. '"O Mungarly Mungarly", Jim would say, "foreskins and balls!"' (Clerk 1971 [*c*.1900]: 75). Recorded as l.19c. 'Liverpool street arabs' (Beale 1984 *s.v. foreskins and balls*); derivation is clear.

Forties, one of the (n.): thief. 'Yewr one er duh Forties if dur ever wus one' (Shaw 1959a: 41). *NR; probably from 'Ali Baba and the forty thieves'.

Four-eyed (adj.): bespectacled. 'A four-eyed short-arse' (Melly 1965: 205). '*Four-eyed sod*: derisory term for a person who wears spectacles' (Lane 1966: 37). Recorded from m.19c.; derivation is clear.

Four mokes and a full belt (n.): the height of success. '*Four mokes an' a full belt*: the peak of success, namely, a ride in a four-horse (*mokes*) carriage after a heavy meal' (Lane 1966: 37). *NR; Lane's explanation is clear.

Frankie Vaughan (n.): porn. 'The Frankie Vaughan and the Viagra is worth more to me these days than a few keys of smack' (Sampson 2002: 76). Recorded from l.20c.; from rhyming slang (Frankie Vaughan was a Liverpool-born singer and actor).

Free and easy (n.): informal drinking and music session; pub. 'We must hear her husband, who is now at the *Goose Club*, where there is a "free and easy"' (Shimmin 1863: 90). 'In the window of the same public establishment a card with the words "Free and Easy every evening"' (Tirebuck 1891: 247). 'It was a very cheap free and easy, with a gallon of beer thrown in' (Haigh 1907: 20). 'He hid himself in the top room of "The Free and Easy"' (Hanley 2009 [1936]: 304). Recorded from l.18c.; the original sense, 'informal gathering', was extended in m.19c. to mean an organised (if notorious) establishment; from 'free and easy manner'.

Frig (v.): euphemism for 'fuck'. 'Frig off home now. Go on' (Bleasdale 1975: 121). 'I stood in that pub an' thought, just what the frig am I trying to do' (Russell 1996 [1980]: 329). 'Let's frig off!' (Robinson 1986 [1920s–30s]: 41). Recorded from m.20c.; a euphemism, though 'frig' itself meant 'to have sex', 'to masturbate' (self or other) from 16c.

Frig (someone) about (v.): waste someone's time; fool with someone. 'I'll tell them y' frigged me about' (Bleasdale 1975: 73). Recorded from m.20c.; see *frig*.

Frigging (adj.): euphemism for 'fucking'. 'Friggin' window cleaner an' the milkman earlier' (Bleasdale 1975: 41). 'Honey over his stupid frigging bigot boot' (Simpson 1990: 40). 'Friggin' 'ell' (Sanders and Sanders 2009 [1960s]: 29). See *frig*.

Frisby (n.): derogatory term for a lesbian. 'Frisby. A masculine lesbian woman' (Spiegl 1989: 32). *NR; an abbreviation of 'Frisby Dyke' ('dyke', 'lesbian') and a play on *Frisby Dyke*.

Frisby Dyke (n.): Liverpudlian. 'The universally recognised "Frisby Dyke" style' (Shaw 1950b: 4). 'Dicky Sam … has been lost because "I.T.M.A." and Tommy Handley replaced it with "Frisby Dyke"' (Smith 1955: 5). 'We Puds and Frisbies' (Shaw 1960b: 5). 'Frisby Dyke became a generic name for a Scouser (like Dicky Sam)' (Spiegl 1989: 32). *NR; the Liverpudlian comedians Tommy Handley and Derek Guyler (who played Frisby Dyke, a character named after a Liverpool department store bombed in the Blitz), were the first to bring Liverpool accents to a national audience in the Second World War BBC radio comedy 'It's That Man Again'.

Fuckwit (n.): idiot, fool; general insult. 'Every egomaniacal fuckwit of a boss' (Griffiths 2003: v). Recorded from l.20c.; Australian usage; probably based on 'dimwit'.

Fudge (n.): a farthing. '"Fudge", farthing' (Jones 1935: 5). '"Fudge" for a farthing, "meg" for a half-penny and "win" for a penny are no longer current coin' (Whittington-Egan 1955a: 6). '"Fudge" for a farthing, "meg" for a half-penny and "win" for a penny … flourished in the 1880s and 1890s' (Jones 1955: 4). 'Fudge.

Farthing. Liverpool' (Howarth 1985: n.p.). 'Fudge – Farthings' (Callaghan 2011 [1910s–30s]: ix). *NR; derivation unknown.

Fudge (v.): to mess something up. '*Fudge*: to spoil something; to make a mess of it' (Lane 1966: 38). Recorded from 17c.; a retention of the original sense, 'to fit together in a clumsy way' (later displaced by the sense of 'falsification, blurring'); possibly from 'fadge', 'to fit, suit'.

Funeral hat (n.): see *blocker*.

Funeral sugar (n.): lump or cube sugar. 'She thinks she's posh, she allus serves funeral sugar' (Lane 1966: 38). '*Funeral sugar* Lump sugar' (Spiegl 2000b: 112). *NR; probably from the use of cube sugar at catered funerals.

Funeral suit (n.): best suit. '*Funeral suit* or *burial suit*: A best suit' (Lane 1966: 38). '*It's me funeral suit* This is my best suit' (Spiegl 2000b: 75). *NR; either from the fact that suits are worn to attend funerals, or from the practice of dressing a dead man in his best suit for burial.

Fur coat and no knickers/drawers (adj.): pretentious; showy; deceptive. 'Fir coat an' no drawers' (Minard 1972: 79). 'I know der likes/fur coat an no nickers' (Simpson 1995: 22). '*Fur coat and no drawers*' (Spiegl 2000b: 58). *NR; derivation is clear.

G

Gab (v.): chat. 'If I go gabbing out of me, you can tell me to shut up' (Hanley 2009 [1950]: 161). 'Gabbin away like Father Bunloaf' (Simpson 1995: 23). 'We know you're workin' as fast as you're gabbin'' (Fagan 2007 [1950s]: 265). Recorded from l.18c.; probably from *gob*.

Gack (n.): cocaine. 'He took out a chubby wrap of gack … "I'm going to cover you in cocaine"' (Sampson 1999: 273). 'Could do with a bumper of that gack of Peter's, fuckin wake me up' (Griffiths 2003: 11). Recorded from l.20c.; possibly from Irish English 'gack', 'chatter idly'.

Gaff¹ (n.): house, flat; place, town. '"Me Gaff" meaning my flat, my house, etc.' (Minard 1972: 40). 'Risky gaff, Blackpool' (Sampson 1998: 81). 'A line of beak back in me own gaff' (Griffiths 2003: 95). Recorded from m.18c.; cant 'gaff', 'travelling fair', extended to a general sense of 'place' and then narrowed again to mean 'flat, house'; from the Romani 'gav', 'fair, market, village'.

Gaff² (adj.): first rate, excellent. 'A lot of other fellows in gaff top's 'ats' (Hall 2004 [1939]: 40). Recorded from m.20c.; derivation unknown.

Gaffer (n.): boss, head person; father. 'Was made a "gaffer" over a number of men' (Roberts 1893: 12). 'Run round the back and fetch the gaffer' (Hall 2004 [1939]: 26). 'Snubbing the wine-gaffer when he looked down his nose at them' (Cross 1951: 78). '*Gaffer*: a boss, foreman, overseer or even the father of a family' (Lane 1966: 39). 'You quiz/a gaffer about fishing in a lake' (Simpson 1995: 57). 'The gaffers are outside' (Fagan 2007 [1950s]: 50). Recorded from l.16c.; originally a rural term of respect for an older person; the sense of 'person in charge' is a m.19c. development; probably an abbreviation of 'godfather'.

Galosherman (n.): lamplighter; street worker. 'An elegy for the galosherman' (Simpson 1990: 13). 'Rag and bone men, midden men and knife grinders were galoshermen' (Lees 2013: 131). *NR; presumably from the fact that these workers wore 'galoshes', in the early sense of 'boots, protective shoes'.

Gam¹ (n.): leg. '"Will you tote the gams on that there judy?"' (Anon. 1958: 3). Recorded from l.18c.; originally 'thin, ill shaped legs'; probably from Italian 'gamba', 'leg', by way of Polari.

Gam² (n.): masturbation; fellatio. 'Puts her arms around us and slides her hand down me trackies and starts giving us a gam' (Sampson 2001: 217). Recorded from m.20c.; an extension of e.20c. 'to gam', an abbreviation of l.18c. borrowing from French, 'gamahucher', 'to practise fellatio or cunnilingus'.

Game/Gammy (adj.): broken, bad, left-handed. 'I'm all right but for my game arm' (Hocking 1966 [1879]: 171). '"Gammy." Left-handed person (gammy hand)' (O'Hanri 1950a: 2).

'Gammy-anded; cack-anded. *A left-handed person*' (Shaw et al. 1966: 29). 'I've got a game leg' (Cornelius 2001 [1982]: 4). Recorded from l.18c.; originally 'lame', it quickly extended to mean 'bad, inferior' ('gammy lowr' – 'bad coin'), 'unfavourable, poor-tempered' and, in widespread dialectal use, 'crooked, injured, sore, feeble'; possibly from Welsh 'cam', 'crooked, queer'.

Game/on the game (n.): prostitution. 'There were quite a number of girls there who carried on the game' (Whittaker 1934: 231). 'She was sent from Liverpool for a playing of the game' (McColl 1952: 8). 'On ther game: Engaged in prostitution' (Lane 1966: 78). '*Flame. A Life on the Game* (Flame 1984: title). 'She dropped out of classes and went on the game' (Sampson 2002: 210). Recorded from l.19c.; an extension of 'game', 'amusement, fun'.

Gansey (n.): jumper or pullover. 'De quare feller in de green gansey got lushed-up an wen in de cokes fer a wet-neller' (Whittington-Egan 1955c: 216). 'A jersey is a gansey' (Armstrong 1966: 6). 'Did you pull your ganzey o'er your head?' (Hallowell 1972: n.p.). '*Gansey* Jersey' (Spiegl 2000b: 71). 'We tucked our "gansies" (pullovers) into our trousers' (Elliott 2006 [1940s–70s]: 70). Recorded from l.19c.; an Irish English term (still current) that passed into English dialectal use; a variant of e.19c. 'guernsey', 'thick blue woollen shirt worn by seamen'. From the place name 'Guernsey'; fine worsted materials were products of the Channel Islands (compare 'Jersey', 'jumper, pullover').

Gate (n.): bicycle. '*Gate*: a bicycle. *Twin-gate*: a tandem bicycle' (Lane 1966: 39). *NR; derivation unknown.

Gazumped (adj.): tired out. 'Am gazumped. *I am extremely weary*' (Minard 1972: 71). *NR in this sense; this e.20c. coinage meant 'to swindle'; derivation unknown.

Gear/it's the gear/the gear (adj.): good, excellent. 'An adjective that seems to be applied wantonly to all pleasurable situations – "it's the gear" (or simply "de gear") holds a secure place' (Farrell 1950b: 4). 'An' dey all said it was de gear' (Anon. 1961b: 3). '*Gear*, ther: Very good, excellent, splendid' (Lane 1966: 39). 'It looks the gear' (Jacques 1975: n.p.). 'Gear. All-purpose Scouse word, as in "de gear" (good, excellent)' (Spiegl 1989: 32). 'Good old Mr. Ingham – e's the gear' (Sinclair 1999 [1930s–e.40s]: 131). 'That's bad gear saying that' (Burnett 2011: 146). Recorded from e.20c.; possibly from Forces' usage to refer to personal equipment including uniform ('that's the gear'); see *gear*[1] *(n.)*.

Gear[1] *(n.)*: clothes. 'She'd be lusting after all the middle-class gear in the shops' (Hignett 1966: 277). 'Bought all sorts of secondhand gear in the markets' (Russell 1996 [1980]: 333). 'Ey, Victor, I'm wearin expensive gear' (Griffiths 2003: 142). 'Never did like getting dressed up with gear like that' (Burnett 2011: 149). Recorded from m.20c.; 'gear', meaning apparatus and items of clothing, dates to e.14c.

Gear[2] *(n.)*: equipment, stuff; stolen goods. 'Real high grade scratch. No bum gear' (Smith 1998 [1971]: 14). '*Gear*: Similar to "clobber". Usually refers to stolen objects' (Parker 1974: 212). 'You can get your hands on any fucking gear you want' (Sampson 2002: 249). 'Drop your gear down the hold' (Fagan 2007 [1950s]: 292). Recorded from m.20c.; see *gear*[1].

Gear[3] *(n.)*: drugs. 'He just wanted more gear [drugs]' (Parker 1974: 99). 'Gear. Cannabis (blow, weed, spliff)' (Spiegl 1989: 32). 'So we starts doin the rocks in. Good gear' (Griffiths 2003: 67). 'Still "on the gear"' (Lees 2013: 245). Recorded from m.20c.; an extension of *gear*[2].

Gee gee (n.): horse, usually race horse. 'Going to have a ride on the gee-gees?' (Hanley 2009 [1940]: 420). 'Picking the gee-gees for the three o' clock race' (Hignett 1966: 198). '"Three Pence Each Way" on a Gee Gee' (Hallowell 1972: n.p.). 'A few bob on the gee gees' (Fagan 2007 [1950s]: 137). Recorded from l.19c.; from 'gee (up)', 'command to animals'.

Gegs (n.): gear. '*Gegs*: ... a perverted form of *ther gear*' (Lane 1966: 39). *NR; see *gear*[1].

Gelton (n.): Liverpool. 'She had lived in Gelton for a number of years' (Hanley 2009 [1936]: 3). *NR; James Hanley's fictional name for Liverpool in his five-novel history of the Hanley family.

Gen (n.): information. 'I've been looking over the gen thisavvy' (Sampson 2002: 48). 'Of course, this is all second-hand "gen"' (Fagan 2007 [1950s]: 224). 'We were all genned up to it' (Dudgeon 2010: 85). Recorded from m.20c.; from Second World War RAF usage, 'general information for all ranks'.

Gentleman (n.): a Liverpudlian (as opposed to a Mancunian). 'Gentleman (Liverpool). There are no men in Liverpool; all are gentlemen' (Ware 1909: 140). '"Liverpool gentleman, Manchester man", used often at one time, is heard much less frequently these days' (Channon 1970: 124). *NR in this specific sense; from the m.19c. distinction between Manchester men, who were involved in the making of things, and Liverpool gentlemen, who traded them; it was a form of snobbery by the self-regarding Liverpool merchants.

George Wiser (n.): Protestant. 'Proddydogs Rednecks George Wisers' (Jacques 1973: n.p.). *NR; mocking, often derogatory; Pastor George Wise was a clergyman who formed the Liverpool Protestant Party in 1903 to contest local elections.

Gerk-butty (n.): see *butty*.

Get (n.): fool, idiot; general term of abuse. 'You big mouthed Orange get' (Shaw 1952: 6). 'The little get's only just come in' (Hignett 1966: 31). 'An' anyway, y' cheeky get' (Bleasdale 1975: 15). 'You stupid friggin' get!' (Robinson 1986 [1920s–30s]: 14) 'It's in English as well, yeh dozy get' (Griffiths 2003: 165). 'Ye drunken get' (Sanders and Sanders 2009 [1960s]: 67). Abusive in its own right, the term is more often used phrasally ('you stupid get', 'you big-mouthed get', 'you lazy get'). Recorded from 16c.; 'get' had the sense of 'brat' or 'bastard' in Scottish and northern dialects, though its use as a general term of abuse developed in 20c.; from 'to beget'.

Get off with (v.): to pair up with someone, usually for sexual purposes. 'Perhaps he was trying to get off with her'

(Hanley 2009 [1940]: 325). 'Did you get off with her?' (Russell 1996 [1976]: 219). 'I'd love to get off with Natasha' (Sampson 1998: 157) 'An now ere she is tellin me that she got off with Malcolm' (Griffiths 2000: 42). Recorded from e.20c.; First World War Forces' usage, the equivalent of *cop off with*.

Get one's hole (v.): have sex. 'Goes back to when I first had my hole' (Sampson 2002: 85). Recorded from l.20c.; a Scottish coinage, an extension of 'hole', 'vagina', from l.16c.

Gets on me tits (phr.): irritates me. '*Gets on me tits*: annoys me very much' (Lane 1966: 40). 'This Forster, honest to God, he doesn't half get on my tits' (Russell 1996 [1980]: 305). '*Yer get on me tits* You irritate me' (Spiegl 2000b: 40). Recorded from m.20c.; Australian usage; there are other Liverpool variants – 'gets on me bib', 'gets on me wick'.

Ghosting (n.): illicit time off from a job. 'Ghosting See Welting' (Spiegl 1989: 34). *NR in this sense; derivation is clear.

Gigs (n.): glasses. 'Yer fucking gigs? Anything yer fuckin *did* remember to bring?' (Griffiths 2003: 32). Recorded from l.20c.; possibly from e.20c. 'gig', 'eye' or 'look', or a variant of *gogs*.

Gill (n.): a measure of liquid; in Liverpool traditionally a half (as opposed to a quarter) pint; now general for any alcoholic drink. 'The sexton and his apparitor fought over his grave for a gill of beer' (Powys 1857: 225). 'I wasn't a teetotaller, so we sat down and had a gill of ale each' (Shimmin 1863: 77). 'As good a text for those who take a gill as it is for those who take a gallon' (Haigh

1907: 195). 'They go to have a gill of beer, [and] a quiet hour' (Whittaker 1934: 225). 'That boy should break training with a few gills' (Jerome 1948: 63). 'A half-pint (quaintly called a *gill*) is bourgeois, a glass less than a half pint ("a pony") being positively effeminate' (Shaw 1959a: 36). 'A gill. *Half a pint of bitter beer*' (Shaw et al. 1966: 68). 'Cob a chuck, a gill of ale. [Note: As elsewhere in the North a *half* pint is always a gill]' (Shaw 1971: 102). 'Gill. Half pint. Liverpool' (Howarth 1985: n.p.). 'It was the practice for the boys to receive a gill of fresh milk' (Sinclair 1999 [1930s–e.40s]: 172). 'The milkman would ladle a pint or a gill into your jug or basin' (Stamper 2010: 27). Recorded from l.13c.; originally a quarter pint; from medieval Latin 'gillo', 'gellus', a vessel or measure used for wine.

Ginchy (adj.): excellent, first-class. Glossed as used in 'the lower forms of Merseyside schools' in the early 1960s (Beale (1984) *s.v. ginchy*); possibly from m.20c. Americanism 'ginch', 'sexually attractive woman'.

Gink (n.): wrongdoer. 'One of my club boys, no gink, was taken up for some trivial matter' (Clerk 1971 [c.1900]: 37). Recorded as 'Liverpool street arabs: late C.19–mid-20' (Beale (1984) *s.v. gink*); derivation unknown.

Ginny/Jinny Greenteeth (n.): Liverpool version of ghastly woman of English folklore; duckweed. '*Jinny Greenteeth*: The ghost of a child-eating female said to haunt St. James's Cemetery' (Lane 1966: 56). 'Her nose and mouth became so thick with moss that she eventually became known as "Ginny

Green-teeth"' (Unwin 1984 [1920s–30s]: 14). Also known as 'Jeannie Greenteeth', 'Wicked Jenny' and 'Peg o' Nell', and related to 'Peg Powler' and 'Grindylow', this was the name of a 'river hag', originally used to scare children away from rivers, ponds and so on. The name was Lancashire dialectal, but in Liverpool it also referred to duckweed, the thin plant cover which often disguises stretches of water.

Gip (n.): felon, criminal. '"You're no sledder", he said, "you're a bloody gip and I'll learn yer something"' (Clerk 1971 [*c*.1900]: 37). Recorded from m.19c.; a derogatory abbreviation of 'gypsy'.

Gip-butty (n.): see *butty*.

Gippo (n.): gravy. '*Bags of gippo*: Lots of gravy' (Lane 1966: 40). 'Gippo. Gravy' (Howarth 1985: n.p.). '*Gippo* Gravy, or sometimes a thin stew' (Spiegl 2000b: 121). Recorded from e.20c.; Forces' usage; from l.19c. dialectal 'jipper', 'gravy, juice or syrup, as of a pie or pudding'.

Girl (n.): girl or woman (of any age); girlfriend, wife. 'We had a fish-girl who regularly visited "Our Terrace." We called her a girl, but she was a middle-aged woman' (Shimmin 1863: 206). 'Have you got a girl?' (Hanley 2009 [1940]: 548). 'The young man's lady friend is called "his girl" or "his judy"' (Farrell 1950b: 4). 'You'll find some girl' (Owen 1961: 97). 'Me judy, me tart, me gerl. *My lady-friend; my fiancée; my* wife' (Shaw et al. 1966: 25). 'Don't fret yerself girl!' (Hallowell 1972: n.p.). 'Come on, girl. I should have been on site half an hour ago'

(Bleasdale 1985: 26). 'See her fucking wince when I call her girl' (Sampson 2002: 226). 'Take no notice of him gerl' (Callaghan 2011 [1910s–30s]: 38). Recorded from 16c. to mean 'girlfriend' or 'wife'; as with *la* and *lad*, *girl* ranges from signalling genuine friendliness to outright hostility or condescension.

Girls, the (n.): regular set of female friends. '"The Girls" is used as the generic name for The Boys' female contemporaries' (Parker 1974: 131). 'Shall we start, girls?' (Bleasdale 1975: 42). See *girl, the fellas*.

Giss/giz (v.): give me. 'Giss … Please serve me with' (Shaw et al. 1966: 68). 'Gizza job, go on, gizzit, go 'head' (Bleasdale 1985: 50). 'Giz a piecer that fudge' (Griffiths 2003: 74). Recorded from m.20c.; this elision of 'give us' featured in one of the most famous lines of modern Liverpudlian writing: Yosser Hughes's plaintive appeal – 'gizza job' – in Alan Bleasdale's *Boys from the Blackstuff* (1982).

Give (v.): past tense or past participle of 'give'. '"I give you one yesterday"' (Cross 1951: 17). 'She give im de rounds uv de kitchen' (Shaw et al. 1966: 27). 'The Scouse conjugation of the verb "to give" is: I give, you give, he/she/it give, we give, you(se) give, they give – in all tenses' (Spiegl 1989: 34). 'He's give me no choice' (Sampson 2002: 186). *NR; see *come*.

Glannie (n.): ollie. 'If they see you playing glannies in the street' (Hanley 1932: 127). 'Glannies: Glass marbles' (Lane 1966: 41). *NR; derivation unknown.

Gnashers (n.): false teeth. '*Gnashers*: false teeth' (Lane 1966: 41). Recorded from m.20c.; used to mean 'teeth' and 'false teeth'; ultimately from l.15c. 'to gnash', 'to grind the teeth'.

Gnat's piss (n.): weak drink (usually alcoholic). '*Gnats' piss*: cider, near beer, weak tea or any drink considered to be lacking in strength' (Lane 1966: 41–2). 'It's like bloody gnat's piss' (Fagan 2007 [1950s]: 87). Recorded from e.20c.; derivation is clear.

Go (n.): fight. 'Not that he would mind having a go at one of them' (Cross 1951: 6). 'The Liverpudlian says "Come on I'll 'ave you a go" … or "I'll have you a scrap"' (Opie and Opie 1959: 197). '*A Fight*. A Scrap, a Lumber, a Go' (Minard 1972: 89). One hefty bruiser offered to have a go' (Unwin 1984 [1920s–30s]: 62). 'I half know that he can have a go' (Sampson 2002: 155). 'Does anyone else wanna go?' (Elliott 2006 [1940s–70s]: 110). Recorded from l.19c.; an Americanism; from the slightly earlier sense of 'go', 'turn, attempt'.

Go along (n.): a punitive blow. 'Not to mention a "go-along" or a "pug in the gob"' (Shaw 1957c: 6). 'The priest's uncoordinated attempts to inflict an effective "go-along" on them all' (Bryan 2003 [1940s–50s]: 203). *NR; presumably from an 'encouragement' to 'go along'.

Go 'way (int.): expression of incredulity. '"Go 'way." "Nah, it's true"' (Griffiths 2003: 113). 'Go way, Yer kiddin' me' (Fagan 2007 [1950s]: 92). *NR; an abbreviation of 'go away!'; commonly used to express everything from credulous belief ('really?') to dismissive disbelief ('no way').

Gob (n.): mouth; face. 'Sometimes you get tired of seeing people with their ugly, miserable gobs – I mean their faces, ma'am' (Hanley 2009 [1936]: 400). 'Certainly from Ireland we received *gob, gom, mam, the queer feller, webs, lug, moider*' (Shaw 1950b: 4). 'A darling look sat on her great gob' (Hanley 2009 [1958]: 54). 'Lissen ter 'er wit' ther gob' (Lane 1966: 62). 'Her old man's gob down on the floor' (Parker 1974: 94). 'Shove it down his fuckin' gob' (Robinson 1986 [1920s–30s]: 9). 'Listen to the gob on her' (Grant 1996: 60). 'A chin strap stuck in his gob' (Fagan 2007 [1950s]: 173). Recorded from 16c.; glossed as 'northern dialectal and slang'; probably from Irish English, ultimately Gaelic 'gob', 'mouth, beak'.

Gobby (adj.): cheeky; loudmouthed. 'We'd lost, cunt got gobby, I taught him a lesson' (Griffiths 2003: 114). 'Straight away gobby Frankie went for the jugular' (Fagan 2007 [1950s]: 262). Recorded from l.20c.; from *gob*.

Gobshakes, got the (phr.): chatterbox. '*Got ther gob-shakes*: said of a persistent talker' (Lane 1966: 45). *NR; derivation is clear.

Gobshite[1] *(n.)*: idiot, fool; general insult. 'I walk around the estate, which is full of gobshites – bloody idiots' (McClure 1980: 73). 'But he's a fucking gobshite Ged is. He's a class one prick' (Sampson 2001: 299). 'Thick, useless and a gobshite' (Lees 2013: 214). Recorded from m.20c.; Second World War Forces' usage, but probably an earlier import from Irish English; possibly from 'gobshell', 'a big spittle direct from the mouth' (from Gaelic 'gob', 'mouth' and 'seile', 'spit'), or simply *gob* and *shite*[2].

*Gobshite*² *(n.)*: nonsense, rubbish. 'All it sounded like t' me was five minutes of non-stop gobshite' (Bleasdale 1977: 167). See *gobshite*¹.

*Gogs*¹ *(n.)*: glasses. '*Gogs* or *goggles*: spectacles' (Lane 1966: 42). Recorded from e.19c.; an abbreviation of 'goggles', 'spectacles', ultimately from 14c. 'to goggle', 'to look obliquely, squint'.

*Gogs*² *(n.)*: North Welsh person. 'Hundreds of wild "Gogs" (North Walians)' (Sinclair 1999 [1930s–e.40s]: 126). *NR; from the Welsh 'gogledd', 'north' ('y gogledd', 'North Wales').

Golden (n.): half of lager, half of bitter. 'I want four bitters, a golden and a lager' (Bleasdale 1985: 269). *NR; from the colour of the drink.

Golden nugget (n.): Weekend work on the docks (which brought extra pay). 'What the young ones do not know, in these days of a guaranteed week, worked or not, and reasonable overtime pay (such as double pay, the Gold Nugget or the Easy Six), is how bad conditions once were' (Shaw 1959c: 6). 'I ad a gold nugget. *I had a profitable spell of Saturday work*' (Shaw et al. 1966: 59). 'They scramble for a nugget or clamour for nights' (Jacques 1979: n.p.). 'Working Sunday was known as the "golden nugget"' (Elliott 2006 [1940s–70s]: 77). 'The ship was working Saturday night. This is called the Golden Nugget' (Burnett 2011: 133). *NR; derivation is clear.

*Golly*¹ *(n.)*: spit. '*Golly*: a wad of phlegm. *To stick a golly on someone*: to spit on him' (Lane 1966: 43). 'Golly. To spit, or a quantity of saliva' (Howarth 1985: n.p.). Recorded from m.20c.; an Australian coinage, possibly by way of English dialectal 'golls', 'mucus'.

*Golly*² *(n.)*: tag. 'Let us have a game of "Golly" – /I'll touch you, then you'll be out' (Hallowell 1972: n.p.). *NR; derivation unknown.

*Gom*¹ *(n.)*: fool or idiot. 'Certainly from Ireland we received *gob, gom, mam, the queer feller, webs, lug, moider*' (Shaw 1950b: 4). 'The large number of Irish words which occur in Liverpool's dialect – Gom (a fool), Ould (Old, which is pure Dublin), Feller (fellow), and Youse (You)' (Whittington-Egan 1955a: 6). 'The citizens suffer fools (GOMS) gladly enough' (Shaw 1959a: 40). 'Goms. Fools. Liverpool' (Howarth 1985: n.p.). Recorded from m.19c.; Irish English, from the Gaelic 'gamal', 'idiot, dolt'.

*Gom*² *(n.)*: policeman. 'Two goms came in and threw a drunken lascar over the rope' (Clerk 1971 [*c*.1900]: v). Recorded as 'Liverpool street arabs': late C.19–early 20' (Beale (1984) *s.v. gom*); an extension of *gom*¹.

*Gom*³ *(v.)*: to report to the police. 'Uncle was an outlet though often getting things for nought by threatening to gom us' (Clerk 1971 [*c*.1900]: 69). *NR; probably an extension of *gom*².

Gong (n.): chamber pot. '*Gong*: a chamber pot' (Lane 1966: 43). Recorded from m.20c.; 'gong' was an Old English name for a privy which became obsolete, but the more likely derivation is the shape of a 'gong', 'musical instrument'.

Good style (adv.): well, emphatically. 'They're at it good style on Smithdown' (Cornelius 2001 [1982]: 127). 'We give it to them, good style' (Sampson 2001: 16). 'I'll set you up good style'

(Fagan 2007 [1950s]: 294). *NR; the derivation is clear.

Goolies (n.): testicles. 'Ow'd yer like a kick in ther goolies?' (Lane 1966: 43). '*The Testicles* … Goolies' (Minard 1972: 44). 'They came up behind Paul Dukes last week outside the cakeshop and got hold of him by his goolies' (Bleasdale 1975: 98). Recorded from m.20c.; possibly from Hindustani 'golī', 'bullet, ball, pill' or the English dialectal 'gully', 'marbles'.

Goose¹ (v.): to have sex with. 'Before we'll approve of your goosing each other' (Hignett 1966: 94). 'He's tryin' t' goose me Mam' (Bleasdale 1975: 173). 'When I first had my hole. First proper goose and that, the full monty' (Sampson 2002: 85). Recorded from m.20c.; possibly from l.19c. 'to goose', 'to pursue women, to womanise' ('goose', the female bird), though it may be rhyming slang, 'goose and duck'.

Goose² (v.): to mess something up or mess someone around. 'Yer properly goosed that job, didn't cher?' (Lane 1966: 43). 'All y' had to do, Malloy, was to stop goosin' me on the side and make an honest man out of me' (Bleasdale 1985: 133). Recorded from m.20c.; possibly from m.19c. 'goose', 'ruin or spoil', from 'goose', 'hiss a play'.

Goosed (adj.): in trouble; exhausted; spoiled. 'If that old lady or sister of yours finds out, then I'm goosed' (Hanley 1932: 110). '*Goosed*: Tired out, exhausted, also spoiled or messed up' (Lane 1966: 43). See *goose²*.

Gorm (n.): idiot, fool. 'What the devil does this ugly-looking gorm want here?' (Hanley 2009 [1936]: 311). Recorded from e.20c.; probably a variant of *gom¹*.

Goss-eyed (adj.): cross-eyed. 'So bloody goss-eyed he could never get hold of the bloody handle-bars' (Hignett 1966: 117). *NR; derivation unknown.

Gozzie (n.): condom. '*Gozzie*: a contraceptive named, for reasons not made clear, "Gossamer"' (Lane 1966: 45). *NR; from 'gossamer', the silk of spiders and hence fine material.

Gozzy (adj.): cross-eyed; with a squint. 'I went all gozzy and me knees gave way' (Bleasdale 1975: 49). 'Mouse-coloured hair, gozzy eyes' (Robinson 1986 [1920s–30s]: 7). 'Him with the gozzy eye' (Griffiths 2003: 10). *NR; derivation unknown.

Graft (n.): work; hard work. 'You feel like doing a bit of graft [work] don't cha?' (O'Mara 1934: 126). 'I don't like this 'ere job – it's too much 'ard graft' (Lane 1966: 46). '*Job*. Graft' (Minard 1972: 89). 'Someone's going to be grafting today' (Graham 1988: 160). 'Provided by yours truly by way of honest graft' (Sampson 2002: 115). Recorded from m.19c.; Lancashire dialectal; from 'graft', 'the depth of earth that may be thrown up at once with a spade' (the same root as 'grave').

Graft¹ (v.): to work. 'Aah yer graftin?' (Minard 1972: 24). 'I myself was still half-grafting' (Sampson 2002: 10). Recorded from m.19c.; see *graft*.

Graft² (v.): to beg, defraud. 'A group of alleged ex-servicemen grafting in Lime Street' (Unwin 1984 [1920s–30s]: 101). 'Grafting. Cheque-book/bank-card fraud' (Spiegl 1989: 35). Recorded from l.20c.; an extension of the m.19c. Americanism 'to graft', 'to acquire money through trickery, fraud'.

Grand (n.): one thousand. '£1000 A Grand, a Long One' (Minard 1972: 87). 'Get knocked over, get paid. Ten grand' (Sampson 2001: 24). Recorded from e.20c.; an Americanism, from 'grand', 'big'.

Grass/grasser (n.): informer. '*Grasser*, a police informant; a stool-pigeon' (Lane 1966: 46). 'GRASS A police informer' (Spiegl 1989: 35). 'It's not one of your elite crew up there that's the grass' (Fagan 2007 [1950s]: 102). Recorded from e20c.; possibly from 'grasser', an abbreviation of rhyming slang 'grasshopper', 'shopper' (someone who 'shops' another).

Grass (v.): to inform. 'Grass: To "stooley", to "split", to tell Authority of a misdemeanour' (Parker 1974: 213). Recorded from e.20c.; see *grass (n.)*.

Greasy Fields (n.): 'Greasy fields: Ullet Road recreation ground' (Jones 1935: 5). 'Ullet Road Recreation Ground was called "The Greasy Fields"' (Unwin 1984 [1920s–30s]: 78). *NR; derivation unknown.

Greaty (n.): Great Homer Street Market. 'We keep hoofing it along Greatie' (Brown 1989: 61). 'Me nin said she was takin' me ter Greaty' (Sinclair 1999 [1930s–e.40s]: 39). 'In its position on Great Homer Street, it is known as "Greaty"' (Dudgeon 2010: 379). *NR; derivation is clear.

Green (adj. n.): Catholic. 'The stumbling block was colour. Mrs Hanley's was green – Mrs Postlethwaite's orange' (Hanley 1935: 289). 'Endless battle between Orange and Green' (Ash 1954: 48). 'The Green and the Orange have battled for years' (McGovern 1995 [1961]: 4). 'Some people are Orange, others are Green' (Jacques 1972: n.p.). 'The front line between Orange and Green' (Lees 2013: 95). Recorded from e.20c.; sometimes derogatory; green is the colour of Irish nationalism and was therefore associated with Catholicism.

Green Goddess (n.): tram. 'A speedy and comfortable type of tram or street-car known locally as a *green goddess*' (Lane 1966: 82). 'In the late thirties the old red and cream trams were replaced by green streamlined models … "the Green Goddesses"' (Melly 1984 [1930s–40s]: 105). 'A "Green Goddess" – the most magnificent, chromium-plated, dazzlingly modern tramcar' (Robinson 1986 [1920s–30s]: 105). *NR in this sense; derivation is clear.

Grid (n.): face. 'Do I want to be pulling a fucking stocking over my grid on Christmas Eve?' (Sampson 2002: 9). 'She's seen ar fuckin grids now, hasn't she?' (Griffiths 2003: 61). Recorded from l.20c.; derivation unclear.

Grid, the (n.): Bankhall railway exchange. 'Grid, The': the railway sidings and marshalling yards at Bankhall, Liverpool' (Lane 1966: 46). *NR; Bankhall, to the north of the city, was an important railway exchange for the docks.

Griffin/griff (n.): news, warning, tip. 'Let's give de fellers de griffin. *Let us warn our colleagues*' (Shaw et al. 1966: 63). 'The inside griff on the story' (Jacques 1975: n.p.). 'Griff. A warning. Liverpool Docks' (Howarth 1985: n.p.). '*Less give dee fellers der griff* Let us warn our accomplices' (Spiegl 2000b: 149). Recorded 'in modern use mainly as Liverpool dial[ect]' (Green *s.v. griffin* n.³); from l.19c. 'griffin', horse racing 'tip'; derivation unknown.

Grisly Risley (n.): Risley remand prison. '"Grisly Risley" has a reputation for harsh treatment' (Parker 1974: 88). 'Grisly Risley. Remand-centre near Liverpool' (Spiegl 1989: 36). *NR; Risley, near Warrington, opened as a remand centre in 1964 and was notorious; now a category C adult male prison.

Grotty (adj.): nasty, dirty, generally inferior. '"I wouldn't be seen dead in them. They're dead grotty." Marshall stared. "Grotty?" "Yeah—grotesque"' (Burke 1964: 88). 'That grotty little shed' (Flame 1984: 39). '*Grotty* An Abbreviation that came into fashion during the early Beatle years and is a typical Liverpool formation' (Spiegl 2000b: 29). Recorded as 'Liverpool s[lang]: C.20. Popularised by the Beatles and, by 1962, fairly general' (Beale (1984) *s.v grotty* 2); an abbreviation of 'grotesque'.

Growl (n.): whinger, grumbler. 'Bloody old growl. You keep my father's name out of it' (Hanley 2009 [1936]: 538). Recorded from l.19c.; dialectal but probably nautical in origin.

*Growler*¹ *(n.)*: a tin for food used by dockers. 'The tin in which Liverpool dockers take their "carrying-out" they call a *growler* as does the New Yorker' (Shaw 1950b: 4). 'Growler. A docker's food tin. Liverpool' (Howarth 1985: n.p.). Recorded from 19c.; an Americanism; originally 'a container to carry home beer bought in a bar'; derivation unknown.

*Growler*² *(n.)*: sex-offender. 'Growler. A Nonce, usually a child-abuser' (Spiegl 1989: 36). *NR; derivation unknown.

*Growler*³ *(n.)*: food; sausage. '*Can't* have fresh toms with your morning growler, just is not the done thing' (Sampson 2001: 227). 'A couple of pork growlers, and burnt ones' (Fagan 2007 [1950s]: 183). Recorded from l.20c.; possibly related to *growler*¹.

Gump stew (n.): chicken broth. 'I began to pick up and was given gump stew' (Clerk 1971 [*c*.1900]: 14). *NR; 'gump' is a l.19c. Americanism, derivation unclear.

Gussie (n.): hat. 'It is well established with a straw gussie and a pair of kecks' (Shaw 1950c: 2). 'Straw hats which we in our part of Merseyside called "Straw Cadies" or "Straw Gussies"' (Unwin 1984 [1920s–30s]: 47). *NR; an extension of e.20c. 'to gussy up', 'to dress smartly'.

Guv (v.): past tense of 'give'. 'I guv 'im a kick in ther moosh' (Lane 1966: 47). Recorded as a northern dialectal variant, the preterite of 'give'.

H

Haddy (n.): haddock. 'With cockles and haddies at the door, and you only having to "pick 'em out"' (Shimmin 1863: 206). See *Finny Addy*.

Haines (int.): shout of retreat. 'Intimation of sudden retreat. Heard in Liverpool, whence it arrived from New York' (Ware 1909: 149). *NR; derivation unknown.

Half (adv.): intensifier, depending on context. 'I have to sail, though I don't mind telling you I don't half like it' (Hanley 2009 [1940]: 121). 'You aren't half mean, Mam' (Bleasdale 1975: 69). 'They're arf 'angin' out o' yer tunnel' [mouth] (Sinclair 1999 [1930s–e40s]: 126). 'Half would've sworn that' (Sampson 2002: 172). 'He'd be half: "Here y'are bollocks"' (Sampson 2002: 195). Recorded adverbially from Old English; this complicated term, common in l.20c. Liverpool speech, varies from meaning 'completely and utterly' to 'not at all'.

Half a dollar (n.): two shillings and sixpence. 'It'll cost you half a dollar to get one not a tenth as good' (Hanley 2009 [1936]: 537). '2/6d: A Tosheroon, Half a Dollar' (Minard 1972: 86). 'It's worth half a dollar to the winners' (Fagan 2007 [1950s]: 12). See *dollar*.

Half-bar (n.): ten shillings. 'A ten shilling note [is generally known] as a "half-bar"' ('Postman' 1937a: 6). 'Alf a bar. *Ten shillings*' (Shaw et al. 1966: 34). '10/-. Half a Quid, Half a Bar' (Minard 1972: 86). See *bar*.

Half-caste (n. and adj.): derogatory epithet meaning mixed-'race'. 'Negroes, Chinese, Mulattoes, Filipinos, almost every nationality under the sun, most of them boasting white wives and large half-caste families' (O'Mara 1934: 11). 'I'm a bastard and you're a half caste' (Jerome 1948: 138). 'Half-castes who seem to be despised by both their white and coloured neighbours' (Kerr 1958: 115). 'Marko was Liverpudlian and half-caste' (Murari 1975: 13). 'A West Indian? An African? A half-caste?' (McClure 1980: 113). '"Half castes" were backward, inferior, and incompetent' (Lees 2013: 164). Recorded from l.18c.; from 'caste', 'race, lineage', from Spanish 'casta', ultimately Latin 'castus', 'pure, unpolluted'.

Half seas over (adj.): drunk. 'Whether he's drunk or sober/Whether he's half seas over' (Kelly 1964: 19). 'Half seas Mr Ellison, tottering like a bull' (Simpson 1990: 64). Recorded as l.17c. cant; an extension of 'half seas over', 'halfway across the sea' ('when they be halfe the seas over' Picton 1883 [1551]: 1.107).

Half-time (n.): any interval during an event. 'Better 'ang on till arf-time, then we'll take a look' (Cross 1951: 119). *NR in this sense; 'half-time' was a 19c. coinage meaning the period between the two halves of a football game; extended to refer to 'a break in proceedings'.

Halfpenny/penny book, talk like a (phr.): talk rubbish. '*Talk like a penny book* (speak foolishly)' (Shaw 1952: n.p.). 'Yew talk like a ha'penny bewk. *Your remarks are foolish*' (Shaw et al. 1966: 71). Recorded as a 'l.19–m.20c. Liverpool catch phrase' (Beale (1984) *s.v. you talk like a halfpenny book*); derivation unknown.

Ham and Egg Parade (n.): cafés and restaurants in New Brighton. 'Well, the "Ham and Egg Parade." I know you like a tasty dish' (Haigh 1907: 486). 'Arriving at New Brighton, we repaired first to the sands where my mother went over to the Ham and Egg Parade' (O'Mara 1934: 122). '*Am 'n' Egg Parade, Ther*: Victoria Road, New Brighton' (Lane 1966: 48). 'The "Ham and Egg Parade" with its busy shops' (Unwin 1984 [1920s–30s]: 109). *NR; a row of cafés and restaurants serving day-trippers to New Brighton.

Hammer (v.): to beat severely. 'What's the good of you hammering us? You allus do a that road' (Shimmin 1863: 140). 'My father used to get drunk wen I wus a little un, and used to 'ammer my mother awful' (Roberts 1893: 207). 'When I got it, he hammered me' (Owen 1961: 30). Recorded from m.19c.; an extension of 'hammer', 'strike with a hammer'.

Hammering (n.): severe beating or punishment. 'I got a terrible hammering that day' (Whittaker 1934: 155). 'He wouldn't like the hammerin', but it wouldn't affect him a great deal' (McClure 1980: 97). 'There's hundreds more who get a quiet little hammerin' down a dark alley' (Bleasdale 1985: 40). See *hammer*.

Handball (v.): arrange cargo by hand on the docks. 'There's no more handball or graft' (Jacques 1979: n.p.). 'He also "handballed" everything. Thousands of sacks' (Elliott 2006 [1940s–70s]: 77). 'You had no mechanical gear. Everything was handballed' (Dudgeon 2010: 91). *NR; derivation unclear.

Handful (n.): five pounds. 'A Handful, a Ching, a Fiver' (Minard 1972: 86). Recorded from m.20c.; probably a reference to the five fingers.

Handy[1] *(adj.)*: close at hand, useful; convenient; advantageous. 'I suppose you find him very handy about the farm' (Hocking 1879: 170). 'Handy to know' (Hanley 2009 [1940]: 4). 'Leave some boiled milk, an' the cough medicine 'andy' (Cross 1951: 67). 'Only about a hundred yards from his own place. That would be very handy' (Hignett 1966: 55). 'That's dead Andy. *This is really most convenient*' (Minard 1972: 36). '"That'll be 'andy", said Kate, "yer'll be home then when the baby's due"' (Sinclair 1999 [1930s–e.40s]: 44). 'The lamp-post was also handy if you were playing cricket' (Stamper 2010: 17). The various senses are extensions of the 16c. original meaning of 'handy', 'clever with the hands, dexterous'.

Handy[2] *(adj.)*: able to fight. 'Lad lives round by theirs, meant to be a little bit handy' (Sampson 2002: 199). 'The vague pretence of being handy with the gloves' (Fagan 2007 [1950s]: 209). 'Her husband is a handy lad still and we could end up fightin' our way out' (Sanders and Sanders 2009 [1960s]: 151). Recorded from e.19c.; retains an element of the original meaning of 'handy'; see *handy*[1].

Handy[3] *(adj.)*: early, in good time. 'Give her a treat by getting back handy and taking her out for a nice scran' (Sampson 2002: 200). *NR in this sense; a 20c. extension of *handy*[1], 'convenient'.

Hang a monkey (v.): to buy a suit. Recorded as 'proletarian (?mostly Liverpool): C.20' (Beale (1984) *s.v. hang a monkey*); possibly from 'monkey suit', 'formal dress'.

Hanging (adj.): disgusting. 'Marmite? Eeee God. Pure fuckin hangin that shit' (Griffiths 2003: 13). Recorded from 21c.; derivation unclear.

Hanging the latch (phr.): outstaying your welcome. 'What would you be doing if you were … hanging the latch? Failing to go home after wearing your welcome out' (Shaw 1963d: 4). 'Hanging the latch is to overstay one's welcome' (Armstrong 1966: 4). 'Simplee angin the latch' (Simpson 1995: 22). *NR; from keeping the latch hanging so the door can't be closed.

Hansel money (n.): 'lucky' money exchanged on the first Monday of a New Year. 'Money changing hands on the first Monday of the New Year was thought to be lucky. [The shawlies] called it "Hansel Money" (Unwin 1984 [1920s–30s]: 82). Recorded from 15c.; varieties of this tradition date to the Middle Ages and were common in Scotland, Ireland and the North of England; from 'hand' and Old English 'selen', 'gift, granting'.

Happy Harry (n.): misery-guts. 'Happy Harry. A disconsolate soul. Liverpool' (Howarth 1985: n.p.). *NR; derivation is clear.

Hard (adj.): tough, violent. 'Their area was the toughest, their men the hardest' (Parker 1974: 31). 'I wish I was hard. I mean I wish I had a leather jacket like that to make me hard' (Bleasdale 1985: 146). 'He's never said he's hard' (Sampson 2002: 66). Recorded from e.19c.; an American extension of a number of the earliest meanings of 'hard': 'not easily impressed or moved; obdurate; unfeeling, callous', 'harsh or severe'.

Hard case (n.): difficult, often violent or threatening person. 'These city lads are sometimes hard cases' (Melville 1849: 29). '*Bucko*. A hard case under sail, particularly a mate' (Bowen 1929: 19). 'He was a queer case, and a hard case' (Whittaker 1934: 155). 'Finding crews for hard-case skippers' (McColl 1952: 3). 'Hard Skin (hard case)' (Shaw 1958d: 16). 'He could see I was no hardcase' (Smith 1998 [1971]: 117). 'I also know he's classed as a hard case' (McClure 1980: 424). 'They may well be fucking hard cases' (Sampson 2002: 148). 'Conrad was particularly complimentary about Liverpool sailors, considering them to be hard cases' (Lees 2013: 74). Recorded from m.19c.; an Americanism, originally nautical; derivation is clear.

Hard cheese (n.): bad luck. '*Aw cheese*: An expression of disappointment or dissatisfaction' (Lane 1966: 4). Recorded from l.19c.; derivation unclear.

Hard clock (adj.): cheeky. 'Ardfaced get! Ardclock! Impudent fellow!' (Shaw et al. 1966: 29). *NR; see *Clock, to have a hard*.

Hard-faced (adj.): cheeky, impudent. 'Hard-faced young bastards' (Hanley 1932: 113). 'Impudent children are also said to be *Hard-Faced*' (Shaw

1958d: 16). 'Tell a few hard-faced lies' (Hignett 1966: 84). 'Don't mention that hard-faced little faggot's name' (Bleasdale 1975: 81). 'This hard-faced Liverpool/which gave us all our cockiness/and guilt' (Simpson 1990: 100). 'It's the 'ard faced one that's comin' over' (Fagan 2007 [1950s]: 11). Recorded as 'impudent: Liverpool; half way between coll[oquial] and dial[ectal]: late C. 19–20' (Partridge *s.v. hard-faced*); an extension of l.16c. 'hard-faced', 'stern, mean-faced'.

Hard knock (n.): a tough person. 'I was born in Liverpool, down by the docks/ Me religion was Catholic, occupation hard-knock' (McGovern 1995 [1961]: 4). ''Ard knock: a tough case' (Lane 1966: 48). 'I became a bit of a hard knock and proud of it' (McClure 1980: 311). 'Hard knock talk' (Simpson 1990: 23). 'I am as hard as nails, "a hard knock" they would say in my home town of Liverpool' (Kelly 2006: vii). *NR; *hard knock* is not quite as threatening as *hard case*.

Hard lines (n.): bad luck. 'You never said "I'm sorry", or "It's hard lines." Not a word' (Hanley 1935: 52). 'Hard lines on the child to be so plain' (Duke 1939: 105). 'Should there be no joy, but only disappointment, then the ejaculation "Hard lines!" is a consolation' (Farrell 1950b: 4). Recorded from l.19c.; possibly nautical since 'hard line money' meant the compensation received by sailors for difficult duties.

Hard skin (n.): tough man. 'The was hard skins' (Shaw 1957a: 15). ''Ard skin: a person who is very tough' (Lane 1966: 48). *NR; see *hard case, skin*.

Hatches are off (phr.): pub opening time. ''Atches is off, de*: The pub is open' (Lane 1966: 4). *NR; ironic reference to dock work since the removal of the lids on a ship's hatches signalled the start of the unloading process.

Have a try? (phr.): invitation to fight. 'Immediately, as was the custom, he dared me to "have a try?" (The invitation to fight)' (O'Mara 1934: 77). *NR; superseded by 'have a go'.

Have it away/off (v.): to have sex. 'Godbolt was having it off with his girlfriend' (Melly 1965: 59). 'The Boys could, they argued, "have it off" with another available girl' (Parker 1974: 136). 'I think they expect us to jump into a desk with a tart and have it off between lessons' (Bleasdale 1975: 98). 'We had it away there' (Flame 1984: 39). Recorded from e.20c.; an extension of 'to have', 'to have sexual intercourse'.

Head down, get one's (v.): to sleep; rest. 'Samson in less than five minutes 'ad 'is 'ead down' (Jacques 1975: n.p.). 'Just getting his head down, was he?' (McClure 1980: 363). 'Gerrin is ed down' (Simpson 1995: 21). 'Get home and get my head down' (Burnett 2011: 106). Recorded from l.19c.; a nautical coinage.

Head serang (n.): boss, person in charge. ''Ead serang: a boss or foreman' (Lane 1966: 49). 'The Lascar's gift of "head serang" for "boss"' (Lees 2013: 136). *NR; see *serang*.

Head the ball (n.): idiot, crazy person, often violent. 'Not as old as Steve, but a right head the ball' (Bleasdale 1975: 97). 'Fucking head the ball, he is … He's a animal' (Sampson 2001: 164).

Recorded from m.20c.; Irish English, possibly from the damage inflicted by heading a football.

Headbanger (n.): crazy person. 'Four old women with four old dogs, three flashers, five million bloody joggers and two head-bangers' (Bleasdale 1985: 225). 'There's loads of head bangers on our job' (Fagan 2007 [1950s]: 76). Recorded from e.20c.; a reference to a pathological condition and the behaviour that went with it.

Heavy on Ton Weight (n.): children's game. ''Eavy on Ton Weight (Weak horse etc.)' (Shaw 1957a: 4). '"Ton weight heavy on" was a particular favourite' (Unwin 1984 [1920s–30s]: 18). 'Other games to be played such as Heavy On' (Stamper 2010: 16). *NR; a game in which a child leans against a wall while another leans into his/her abdomen and others jump on the first two until they can no longer bear the weight.

Herby/herbalist/herb shop (n.): herbal remedialist and/or shop which served non-alcoholic beer. 'All three entered the herb shop' '(Hanley 1932: 44). 'Some little-known herbalist in a back street' (Whittaker 1934: 205). 'Already hangin' round herbies and workin' as a lad in a chippie' (Shaw 1957a: 16). 'De erby. *The mineral water shop*' (Shaw 1966: 39). 'Dingle Herbal Stores, Park Road' (Hallowell 1972: n.p.). 'We used to go into the herb shop to buy a ha'penny glass of a liquid called Vantas' (Unwin 1984 [1920s–30s]: 23). 'It was probably a lot cheaper for the working class to visit the herbalist than to consult the doctor' (Kelly 2006 [1930s–40s]: 9). 'We used to like going

to the herbal beer shop' (Stamper 2010: 26). *NR in the Temperance sense; before the widespread availability of modern medicine, herbalists tended to the needs of the sick; selling 'herb beers' such as dandelion and burdock or *sass*, they became a common part of the Temperance scene (along with *cokes*).

Hi Rip Gang (n.): Liverpool teenage street gang of the 1880s and after. 'Pimps (Hi-Rip lads), whose speciality is waylaying foreign sailormen' (O'Mara 1934: 5). 'The lineal descendants of the Hi Rip Gangs' (Shaw 1958d: 16). 'The youths shouted "High Rip! High Rip", which identified them with one of Liverpool's notorious organised gangs' (Dudgeon 2010: 115). 'North End High Rip pimps, in their distinctive "bucco caps" and mufflers' (Lees 2013: 78). *NR; derivation unknown.

Hickey the Firebobby (n.): fictional Liverpool character. 'The gallery of Liverpool's characters with Dick Tutt, Hickey the Firebobby, Daddy Bunchy (a bogey for the children) and Donnelly' (Shaw 1955a: 6). '*Ickey, ther firebobby*: the fireman' (Lane 1966: 51). *NR; derivation unknown.

Hiding (n.): a beating. 'I'm going to give you the hiding you deserve' (Haigh 1907: 511). 'Although I had one or two hidings' (Whittaker 1934: 111). 'A hiding he'll never forget' (Hanley 2009 [1940]: 442). '*Unmerciful hiding* (a smack: typical hyperbole)' (Shaw 1952: n.p.). 'He'd've given Dave the hiding of his life' (Marenbon 1973 [1920s]: 27). 'A respectable type of man is walking down London Road tonight and he gets a bit of a hiding' (McClure 1980: 97). 'He would give him a hiding and then it was over' (Sanders and Sanders 2009 [1960s]: 26). Recorded from e.19c.; sporting usage, an extension of 'to hide', 'to remove the hide from; to flay'.

Highfalutin' (adj.): ridiculously pompous or bombastic. '*Highfalutin'* … American slang, now common in Liverpool and the East-End of London' (Hotten 1860: 191). 'They were full of high-faluting talk' (Hall 2004 [1939]: 113). Recorded from m.19c.; an Americanism, possibly from Yiddish 'hifelufelem', 'ostentatious, self-glorifying'.

Hokey pokey (n.): ice cream, lolly-ice. 'A thing everyone talked about called hoky poky (which turned out to be our first lolly ices)' (Jacques 1979: n.p.). 'Okey-pokey, penny a lump!' (Unwin 1984 [1920s–30s]: 15). Recorded from l.19c.; derivation unclear.

Hold one's ale (v.): to be able to drink capaciously. 'Come back when you can hold your ale' (Parker 1974: 148). 'You can't hold your ale, you get into a scuffle' (Grant 2002: 56). 'A blonde who likes a laugh, can hold her ale' (Fagan 2007 [1950s]: 153). *NR; an extension of 'hold', 'have capacity'.

Holy ground (n.): consecrated space on a ship; any prohibited area. 'The holy ground, where the church services and prayers are held' (Masefield 1933: 307). *NR in this specific sense; coined in l.19c. to refer to a portion of the main deck of the *Conway* consecrated for church services; later extended to designate areas of restricted access.

Holy Joe (n.): prudish, ostentatiously fastidious person. ''Oly Joe: a person who is prim and proper; one who advertises his piety' (Lane 1966: 49).

'All the suckholes and Holy Joes' (Sampson 2002: 85). Recorded from m.19c.; sailors' term for a religious minister; the sense of false piety was a l.19c. development.

Holy Land, the (n.): a small network of streets off Park Road in the Dingle. 'It's only a few auld streets, the Holylands – ours was Moses Street – but clean, always just so' (Sampson 2001: 25–6). 'The Holylands are a bunch of streets round the Dingle' (Grant 2002: 141). *NR; the Holy Land consists of Moses Street, Isaac Street, Jacob Street and David Street. The epithet supposedly derives not from the names of the streets, which were built in l.19c., but from the fact that the first inhabitants of the area – c.17c. Puritan refugees who were granted right of abode by the Catholic Sir Richard Molyneux – referred to it in this way. Other relics of this period include Jericho Lane, the River Jordan (Otterspool Brook) and a rock, 'David's Throne'.

Holy Show (n.): exhibition, spectacle, thus embarrassment. 'They were making a holy show of themselves' (Bainbridge 1973: 70). 'Well, he's made a holy show of me there' (Sampson 2002: 156). 'Makin' a holy show of us, an' in front of complete strangers' (Fagan 2007 [1950s]: 117). Recorded from m.19c.; Irish English; probably from the veneration of the Eucharist during Catholic Mass.

Holy-stone (v.): scour the deck of a ship. 'I did not mind soojy-moojying and painting and "holy-stoning" the decks' (O'Mara 1934: 263). 'The deck was holy-stoned white and smooth' (Hall 2004 [1939]: 172). 'They would holy-stone the [paving] flags!' (McClure 1980: 164). 'A doorstep scrubbed and holystoned' (Simpson 1990: 81). 'They were told to holystone the decks' (Stamper 2010: 136). Recorded from e.19c.; a nautical term, derivation unknown.

Hom (n.): homosexual. 'He's all right, by the way, Paul the Hom' (Sampson 2002: 66). 'Coupla fuckin homs' (Griffiths 2003: 210). Recorded from l.20c.; an abusive abbreviation.

Honest (adv.): honestly. '"Honest" Burns said' (Hanley 1932: 119). 'That's all I've got, Mam, a quid. Honest' (Bleasdale 1975: 67). 'Come on, honest, it's lovely' (Bryan 2003 [1940s–50s]: 9). 'Honest. He just didn't have enough' (Burnett 2011: 56). Recorded from m.19c.; an Americanism; short for 'honest to God' or 'honestly', as a way of emphasising the truth of a claim; can also be used to query a statement – 'honest?'

Honk[1] *(v.)*: to vomit. 'Young fellers of about sixteen honkin' up everywhere' (Bleasdale 1975: 71). 'Bring some plonk but don't honk' (Sayle 1984: 116). Recorded from l.20c.; possibly from the noise of vomiting (like a goose 'honking').

Honk[2] *(v.)*: to smell, stink. 'Yer pure rank, I'm tellin' yeh, it's that fuckin arm; it honks' (Griffiths 2003: 133). Recorded from m.20c.; an Australian coinage, possibly from the smell given off by a gaggle of geese.

Hook and book/on the hook and on the book (phr.): employed (on the docks) and unemployed. 'They had just done three on the hook and three on the book, meaning three days at work and three days on the dole' (Anon. 1955: 6). 'Tree on the 'ook and tree on the book' (Shaw 1957a: 7). *NR; a reference to the docker's hook and the unemployment register.

Hooley (n.): party; fight. 'Hooley for a party' (Shaw 1962a: 10). ''Ooley: a dispute, a fight or a riot' (Lane 1966: 50). 'Into town for their big Christmas hoolie' (Sampson 2001: 60). Recorded from l.19c.; Irish English, probably from Gaelic 'ceilidh', 'party, dance'.

Hop (n.): a dance. 'The Lime Street hop was a favourite resort of his' (Powys 1857: 56). 'Sought after for every shilling hop by every lad in the neighbourhood' (Cross 1951: 70). 'A 'Op wus a 'op when I went to them' (Shaw 1957a: 12). 'Somewhere to recover from a strenuous hop' (Bryan 2003 [1940s–50s]: 142). 'You saved a shilling for the hop' (Dudgeon 2010: 248). Recorded from 18c.; derivation unclear.

Hospital note (n.): a note allowing free medical treatment. 'No one could go in hospital who could not pay for it, unless they could raise some "hospital notes" as they were called' (Clerk 1971 [c.1900]: 81). *NR; before the introduction of the National Health Service, individuals, or institutions such as churches or charities, subscribed to hospitals and were given *notes* which allowed the bearer to gain access to medical treatment.

Hot kecks for (phr.): keen on; amorous. 'She's got 'ot kecks fer 'im: she fancies that man' (Lane 1966: 50). 'She got ot kecks fer im She feels attracted to that man' (Spiegl 2000b: 93). *NR; 'hot', 'aroused', dates to 14c.; see *kecks*.

Hummer (n.): home-made toy. "*Ummer*: a children's toy made from a perforated can-lid and a loop of string' (Lane 1966: 50). *NR; derivation is clear.

Hump, get/take/have the (v.): to be annoyed, upset. 'He really had the hump now. He was shouting and all' (Bleasdale 1975: 155). Recorded from m.19c.; an extension of 'to have one's hump up', 'to be cross or ill-tempered'; possibly from the stance of a cat when annoyed.

Hunnery, the (n.): nickname for the German department at Liverpool University during First World War. 'During the war the German department here was – quite good-temperedly – called by the students "the Hunnery"!' (Collinson 1927: 124). *NR; the German department at Liverpool became the focus of considerable attention in First World War because one of its erstwhile professors, Kuno Meyer, engaged in pro-German propaganda work amongst Irish Americans and German Americans. Meyer's image was painted out of a collective portrait of Liverpool professors, a subject treated in Donald Davie's 'A Liverpool Epistle' (Davie 1991: 337–8).

Hurry up van (n.): police van, Black Maria. 'Thought the hurry-up van was coming any minnit' (Shaw 1957a: 7). 'De urry-up cart. *The "Black Maria" van*' (Shaw et al. 1966: 64) 'The "urry-up cart" is the Black Maria (also called "de battle-taxi")' (Channon 1970: 102). '*The urry-up cart* A police car' (Spiegl 2000b: 149). *NR; 'Hurry up wagon' was a l.19c. Americanism.

I

I or O? (n.): Irish or Orange? (Catholic or Protestant). 'I or O (Irish or Orange; the challenge to strangers on St. Patrick's Day' (O'Mara 1934: 86). '"I or O?" Now we all know what that meant – "Irish or Orange?"' (Unwin 1984 [1920s–30s]: 76). '"I or O?" – I standing for Irish and therefore Catholic, and O for Orange' (Lees 2013: 96). *NR; derivation is clear.

If they had any brains they'd be dangerous (phr.): Recorded as a phrase used to refer to 'the clerks at the Social' (the Department of Social Security) in Liverpool in the early 1980s (Beale 1985 *s.v. brains*).

Ignorance (n.): bad manners. 'Bad manners is always described as *Ignorance* ("'E wuddin bid yuh duh time er day; its only 'is ignorance")' (Shaw 1958d: 16). 'I jes' can't stan' that feller, 'e's plain bloody 'iggerant' (Lane 1966: 49). Recorded from m.20c.; an extension of l.19c. dialectal 'ignorant', 'ill-mannered' ('she said of him, "he's ignorant"' Kerr 1958: 107).

Ikey (adj.): smartly dressed; cheeky, rude. 'Yer very ikey. *You are dandified*' (Shaw et al. 1966: 36). '*Yer very ikey!* You are somewhat over-dressed' (Spiegl 2000b: 76). 'Ikey fuckin balloonhead' (Griffiths 2003: 85). Recorded from m.19c.; an Americanism; used pejoratively to refer to a Jewish man; from 'Ikey' for 'Isaac'. The nuanced sense of 'smart dresser' was reinforced in Liverpool by the fact that tailoring and the rag trade were main occupations of the city's Jewish community.

Improver (n.): (modern) intern. 'Frankie Roza now an "improver" [one grade above an apprentice] engineer' (O'Mara 1934: 259). Recorded from m.19c.; someone who accepted an opportunity to 'improve' trade skills wholly or partly in lieu of wages.

In bits (adj.): very emotional or upset. 'It's damned hard … I feel all in bits myself' (Hanley 2009 [1940]: 347). '"All upset about Roger was he?" "In bits, yeh"' (Griffiths 2001: 191) 'Women and family in bits' (Sampson 2002: 4). Recorded from m.20c.; an extension of 'bit', 'piece' ('broken to bits').

In bulk¹ (adv.): laughing a lot. 'We was in bulk laughing' (Parker 1974: 128). 'We was in bulk though. Fucking killing ourselves we was' (Sampson 2001: 36). *NR; recorded as adverbial phrase from l.20c. (usually qualifying the verb 'laughing'); derivation unclear but probably from 'in bulk', 'large quantity'.

In bulk² (adj.): in pain; incapacitated, disabled. 'If a docker has a hangover, flu, bellyache or other ailment, he'll say "I'm in bulk"' (Jacques 1973: n.p.). 'Fuckin hurts as well. Me back's in bulk' (Griffiths 2002: 106). 'The two of them were in bulk on the path' (Sanders and Sanders 2009 [1960s]: 110). *NR; derivation unclear but probably from billiards in which a player can only play a ball 'in baulk' by striking at it indirectly (hence disadvantaged, incapacitated).

In the bag (adj.): settled, achieved. 'If half the members of a Talkie audience shudder every time a character on the screen says "It's in the bag", the other half make a mental note of the expression for future use' (Anon. 1929a: 9). '*It's in ther bag*: It is settled, arranged' (Lane 1966: 53). Recorded from e.20c.; an Americanism; an extension of the hunting phrase 'caught, bagged'.

In tucks (adv.): laughing. 'She has us all in tucks' (Simpson 1995: 13). *NR; from 'tuck', 'fold, pleat', hence 'in pleats laughing'.

Indefatigable, The (n.): see *The Conway*.

Island, the (n.): Isle of Man. '*Island, Ther*: Isle of Man' (Lane 1966: 52). *NR in this sense; the Isle of Man used to be a popular Liverpudlian holiday destination.

It'll be like a pig's foot in the morning (phr.): said when someone has received a blow likely to result in bruising. ''Iddle be a pig's foot in der morning' (Shaw et al. 1966: 75). 'A hammer slipping and a blister … "It'll be a pig's foot in the morning"' (Simpson 1990: 84). *NR; from the colours of a *pig's foot*.

It's the change before death (phr.): comment made when someone acts out of character (as when a mean person buys a round). Recorded as 'a Liverpool usage still' in l.20c. (Beale (1985) *s.v. it's the change before death*).

It's the price of her/him (phr.): just desserts. 'It's the price uv 'er' (Shaw 1957a: 12). Recorded from l.20c.; glossed as Irish English, though the Liverpool usage is earlier; derivation is clear.

J

Jack (n.): plainclothes policeman, detective. '"Jack", plain clothes policeman' (Jones 1935: 5). 'You just call in that jack that's lookin's after you and see what he's got to say' (Jerome 1948: 25). 'Dodging the *Jacks* (detectives), the *Scuffers* (Police, *Slops*, also being used) or their friends' (Shaw 1958d: 16). '*Detectives*. Jacks, Old Bill, Plainees' (Minard 1972: 89). 'Black and white, a lot of Uniform work is, not bloody grey like the jacks have to deal with' (McClure 1980: 83). 'Jack C.I.D. Officer' (Spiegl 1989: 48). 'Wrecked the few brain cells the fuckin jacks left intact' (Griffiths 2003: 31). 'Jack – policeman, man, fellow' (Callaghan 2011 [1920s–30s]: vii). Recorded from m.19c.; derivation unclear, though there is a long history of 'jack' being used in a derogatory or contemptuous sense.

Jack (something) in (v.): to give up, renounce, finish. 'Beer mannan Jack! *Stick to your principles! Damn the job!*' (Minard 1972: 36). 'The only real escape is to jack in yer job, walk out' (Griffiths 2003: 39). Recorded from m.20c.; an extension of m.19c. 'to jack (something) up', 'to give up suddenly'.

Jackie/jacksharp (n.): stickleback. 'Chasing poor little fellows, because they were watching the jack-sharps play' (Shimmin 1863: 118). 'They were going to fish for Jack Sharps' (Hanley 1932: 123). 'They are called jacksharps … Of course the word is cut down to "Jackie"' (Shaw 1960a: 41). 'We wen ter Sevvie ter ketch jackies. *We went to Sefton Park to catch small fish (Jack Sharps)*' (Shaw et al. 1966: 46). 'Jackies. Tiddlers. Cf Jacksharps. Liverpool' (Howarth 1985: n.p.). Recorded from e.19c.; 'still current in Liverpool, mid c.20' (Beale (1984) *s.v. jack sharp*); a northern dialect name for the stickleback.

Jam butty car (n.): police car. 'The department's "jam butty" cars are distinguished by the red stripe across their sides' (McClure 1980: 19). 'JAM-BUTTY CAR Old type of police car' (Spiegl 1989: 48). 'The "jam butty" patrol cars' (Lees 2013: 166). *NR; from the red horizontal stripe that ran along the side of the white car.

Jangle (v.): to chat, gossip. 'She will wander off into a neighbour's house to jangle' (Shimmin 1863: 33). 'Clat is just old English dialect connected with the clatter of tongues (as probably is our word for gossip, *jangle*)' (Shaw 1950c: 4). 'An dey 'ad a good jangle an' a few bevies an' dey all said it was de gear' (Anon. 1961b: 3). 'Jangling is gossiping' (Armstrong 1966: 6). 'Missis Moses had stopped to jangle to ould Ma Silverman' (Jacques 1975: n.p.). 'Ders diss posh do wid lah-di-dah judies/janglin about ow thee once knew John Lenin' (Simpson 1995: 21). 'The women, all neighbours, would sit together jangling' (Kelly 2006 [1930s–40s]: 49). Recorded from 14c.; originally 'talk excessively or noisily';

glossed as obsolete, though retained in Liverpool speech.

Jangler (n.): piano. '*Jangler*: piano' (Lane 1966: 55) *NR; probably from 'jangle', 'discordant or unmusical noise'.

Jannock (n.): the truth. '*Jannock*: The real truth. *I'm tellin' yer an' that's jannock*: I am telling the absolute truth' (Lane 1966: 55). 'Jannock. Frank, sincere, genuine, admirable' (Howarth 1985: n.p.). '*I tell yer it's dee jannock* It is the gospel truth' (Spiegl 2000b: 41). Recorded from m20c. in this sense; an extension of e.19c. Lancashire dialectal 'jonnok', 'fair, honest, straight-forward'; probably from 'jannock', 'a loaf of leavened oaten bread' (as simple and reliable as a loaf of bread).

Jar (n.): pint or half-pint of beer, alcoholic drink in general. 'Was he in here having a jar?' (Owen 1961: 39). '*Jar*: Half a pint. *Jar of ale*: A half-pint of beer' (Lane 1966: 55). 'He's a bit of a divvil when he's had a few jars' (Jacques 1975: n.p.). 'I'll mug yer to a jar if y'like' (Graham 1988: 44). 'I had me a jar in Flanagan's bar' (Griffiths 2002: 42). Recorded from e.20c.; probably an import from Irish English; derivation is clear.

Jarg (adj.): illegal, suspicious; fake. 'If there's any of that, anything jarg about this development' (Sampson 2002: 21). Recorded from l.20c.; probably an abbreviation of 'jargoon', 'fake jewelry' (jargoon is a form of zircon, used as a cheap diamond lookalike), though possibly *jark*.

Jark (n.): a trinket in the form of a seal which hung from a watch chain. 'Exhibiting huge heavy gold "Alberts" as they were called which carried innumerable jarks' (Clerk 1971 [c.1900]: 75). Recorded as having 'survived among Liverpool street arabs – and presumably vagrants and beggars – well into C.20' (Beale (1984) *s.v. jark* 1); a 16c. cant term for a false seal used to stamp counterfeit papers.

Jars out (n.): off-licence sales of alcohol; party time. 'The was gear dos in them days, jars out, beer for dogs' (Shaw 1957a: 1). 'We're having a do, come on up, it's jars out' (Hignett 1966: 290). '*Jars out* Beer to take away' (Spiegl 2000b: 84). 'You bought your beer in the pub … this was known as "jars out"' (Stamper 2010: 189). *NR; before the deregulation of the sale of alcohol, pubs were the principal place for 'off sales' in working-class areas; derivation is clear.

Jasper (n.): cockroach. 'Dthurz jaspers 'ere. *I have noticed cockroaches on the premises*' (Minard 1972: 37). 'Jaspers that look like big orange cockroaches' (Sanders and Sanders 2009 [1960s]: 28). Recorded from 19c.; an extension of a dialectal term for a louse; derivation unknown.

Jaxy/joxy (n.): female genitals. Recorded as 'female pudend. Prostitutes' (notably Liverpool): C.20' (Partridge *s.v. jaxy*); derivation unknown.

Jerkbump (v.): to make someone jump by whipping. '"Bin jerkbumpt", he said' (Clerk 1971 [c.1900]: 37). Recorded as 'Liverpool street arabs': late C.19–mid-20' (Beale (1984) *s.v. jerkbump*) and glossed as 'given a hot bottom'; probably from 16c. 'jerk', 'to strike with a whip'.

Jerry-builder (n.): speculative builder who uses cheap materials to produce shoddy houses. 'If the work is not well done, and the houses not well finished, we call that the Jerry style' (Anon. 1839: 6). 'Welsh builders, who were so often, in derision, called "jerry builders", were a very industrious and persevering lot of men' (Roberts 1893: 91). 'Jerry-builder. A rascally speculating builder. Jerry built, run up in the worst materials. [The use of the term arose in Liverpool circa 1830]' (Farmer 1905: 244). 'Jerry-built council flats' (Murari 1975: 58). 'In a scrag-end classroom, jerry-built/after the war' (Simpson 1990: 38). 'A perfect, jerry-built street' (Sampson 2002: 24). Recorded from m.19c.; one of a number of related terms that signify the building of houses designed to be sold fast but not to last: 'jerry-build', 'jerry-built', 'jerry-building', 'jerry walls' and *jerry-builder*; Liverpool was notorious for the practice. Derivation unclear; probably nautical, from 'jury', 'temporary, makeshift, inferior', from e.16c. 'jury-mast', temporary replacement mast.

Jesus-boots (n.): sandals. 'Purra Jesus boots. *Pair of sandals*' (Shaw et al. 1966: 37). 'Me mam calls dese Jesus boots' (Sinclair 1999 [1930s–e.40s]: 131). Recorded from m.20c.; an Americanism, probably Forces' usage; derivation is clear.

Jib (v.): refuse to proceed; stop doing something. 'Over the wall the yen said I'd go if I jibbed it' (Clerk 1971 [c.1900]: 18). 'Elvis suggests we jib the club and go back to his' (Sampson 1998: 128). Recorded from l.19c.; possibly from French 'giber', 'to kick' (as of a horse).

Jigger (n.): an alley between back-to-back houses. '"Jigger", an old word used in the south end of the town to denote a back-passage or entry between two rows of houses' ('Postman' 1945c: 5). 'Jigger. Back Entry or Alley' (Price 1950: 4). '"Jowler" was widely used at one time but it subsequently fell into decline in favour of "Jigger" which in its turn, has been largely replaced by the description "Cooey"' (Whittington-Egan 1955b: 6). 'A jigger was a back passage 4ft. 6in. wide, a jowler was 2ft. 3in. wide' (Henry 1964: 6). 'There were cats in our jigger' (Jacques 1973: n.p.). 'Like a startled fawn, he's away down a back jigger' (McClure 1980: 497). 'Jigger – jowler – entry – eenog: four words for the narrow passage-way between the backs of urban terrace-houses' (Spiegl 2000b: 47). 'I ran from the house and through the jigger (entry)' (Elliott 2006 [1940s–70s]: 11). 'The jigger between rows of tenements ... much wider than the ordinary back entry' (Callaghan 2011 [1920s–30s]: 14). Recorded from e.20c.; various suggestions have been made for its derivation, the most plausible is 16c. cant 'gygger', 'door', possibly from Welsh 'gwddor', 'gate'.

Jigger-jerker (n.): sex in a back alley. 'Jigger-jerker: someone who has or claims to have frequent amorous adventures in back alleys' (Lane 1966: 56). *NR; see *jigger*.

Jigger-rabbit (n.): stray cat. 'De jigger rabbit. *A stray cat* (Shaw et al. 1966: 27). 'The cats, or "jigger rabbits" of the neighbourhood' (Unwin 1984 [1920s–30s]: 79). 'Like sum jigger rabbit' (Simpson 1995: 21). *NR; see *jigger*.

Jiggered (adj.): tired out, exhausted. 'Jigger. Tired out' (Howarth 1985: n.p.). 'Absolutely jiggered from the flight and the non-stop partying' (Sampson 1999: 404). Recorded from l.19c.; northern dialectal; possibly from 'to jig', 'to dance in a rapid, jerky, lively fashion', hence to be exhausted.

Jigs (n.): children's game. 'Jigs (a combination of marbles and buttons)' (Shaw 1960a: 40). *NR; derivation unknown.

Jimmy/Jimmy riddle (n.): urination. '*Jimmy riddle, to have a*: To urinate. Said of a person with a weak bladder: *e's got ther jimmy riddles*' (Lane 1966: 56). Recorded from e.20c.; Forces' rhyming slang, 'piddle'.

Jink (n.): bringer of bad luck. '*Jink*: A Jonah, bringer of bad luck' (Lane 1966: 56). *NR; the derivation may be a back-formation, on the assumption that 'jinx' is the plural form.

Jip/gip/gyp (n.): pain, hurt. 'Me old corns givn me jip an all' (Shaw 1952: 5). 'But she fairly gave him gip' (Clerk 1971 [*c.*1900]: 21). 'She was wearing new shoes and they were giving her gyp' (Bainbridge 1989: 76). Recorded from e.20c.; from northern dialectal 'jip', 'to give a thing (or a person) jip, to punish', possibly from 'gee-up'.

Jirry/jerry (n.): chamber pot. *Jirry* or *jerry*: A chamber-pot' (Lane 1966: 56). Recorded from e.19c.; possibly an abbreviation of 'jeroboam', 'large bowl or vessel'.

Job and knock (n.): to get paid for a job, not the time it takes to complete it. 'I was on a "job and knock"' (Fagan 2007 [1950s]: 259). *NR; derivation unclear, possibly 'do the job and *knock off*'.

Jockey¹ (n.): small cake or piece of bread. 'Children liked to buy loaves too, for the baker usually placed on the loaf,

as on a horse, the Jockey. This was to make it up to legal weight' (Shaw 1958d: 19). 'Jockey. A make-weight added to a loaf. Liverpool' (Howarth 1985: n.p.). 'If the bread was underweight he gave you a jockey (a piece of cake) to make up the weight' (Stamper 2010: 26). Recorded from l.19c.; northern dialectal. Before the advent of standardised food production, the *jockey* was a make-weight put in with various goods (bread, tobacco and so on); when Liverpool children went to the baker, they expected a *jockey* as a small bonus.

Jockey² (n.): a small glass used to top up beer. '*Gis a jockey* Give me a small glass for the overflow' (Spiegl 2000b: 82–3). *NR; beers that need to settle require a top-up; a *jockey* would be demanded in order to avoid short measure; an extension of *jockey*¹.

Jockey³ (n.): bonus; extra pay. 'Jockey; bunce. *Extra pay*' (Shaw et al. 1966: 59). An extension of *jockey*¹.

Jockey-bar (adv.): see *living jockey-bar*.

Jockeys (n.): chips. 'A plater jockeys. A portion of French Fried potatoes' (Minard 1972: 52). 'Last thing I ate was that bag of jockeys' (Griffiths 2003: 75). Recorded from l.20c.; rhyming slang, 'jockey's whip', 'chip'.

Jocks (n.): testicles. '*Jocks*: Testicles' (Lane 1966: 56). '*Me jocks, me nuts* My testicles' (Spiegl 2000b: 69). Recorded from 18c.; from 16c. cant, 'jockum', 'penis'; 'jock', 'genitals', is retained in American English (and in the phrase 'jock-strap').

Joe (n.): taxi. See *Joe Baxi*.

Joe Baxi (n.): taxi. 'Less gerra Joe Baksi. *We will ride by cab*' (Minard 1972:

22). Recorded from l.20c.; rhyming slang ('Joe Baksi' was the name of an American boxer), often abbreviated to 'Joe'.

Joe Gerks (n.): jail, usually Walton prison. 'Meanwhile readers might like to trace the origins of … *Joe Gerks*' (Shaw 1950b: 4). 'He'll finish up in Joe Gerks, you mark my werds' (Shaw 1957a: 12). 'Why should Walton Gaol be Joe Gerk's?' (Armstrong 1966: 6). '*Prison*. Nick, Blue Brick, Joe Gerk's' (Minard 1972: 88). 'Joe Gerks. Walton Prison. Liverpool' (Howarth 1985: n.p.). *NR; derivation unclear, though 'Joe Gurr' is m.20c. rhyming slang for m.19c. 'stir', 'prison'.

Joey (n.): threepenny bit. '"Joey", threepenny piece' (Jones 1935: 5). '"Joey" is still a threepenny bit' (Whittington-Egan 1955a: 6). 'Joey. *Threepence*' (Shaw et al. 1966: 33). '3d. A Joey' (Minard 1972: 85). 'Hundreds of threepenny joeys' (Robinson 1986 [1920s–30s]: 13). 'Joeys – Threepenny bits' (Callaghan 2011 [1920s–30s]: ix). Recorded from m.19c.; originally a 'fourpenny bit'; possibly from the name of the M.P., Joseph Hume, who campaigned for its introduction; the shift to 'threepenny bit' took place in e.20c.

John Hughes won't save yer! (phr.): derisory shout addressed to men of eligible age for the armed services in First World War. Recorded as a Liverpool catchphrase of the period (Partridge and Beale 1985 *s.v. Liverpool catchphrases*); supposedly a reference to John Hughes, a shopkeeper who found ways of exempting his employees from conscription.

Johnnies: black and Asian seamen. 'I was afraid of *Johnnies* … Poor harmless Merchant Sailor boys – the coolie type' (Hallowell 1972: n.p.). 'Johnies. Lascar seamen. Everton' (Howarth 1985: n.p.). 'These coloured seamen were engagingly known as "Johnnies"' (Elliott 2006 [1940s–70s]: 27). 'Lascar sailors (Johnnies)' (Callaghan 2011 [1910s–30s]: 25). *NR; probably from 20c. Forces' usage, often derogatory, 'John', Indian soldier, 'johnny', 'Arab'.

Johnny Todd (n.): folksong. 'Johnny Todd is a child's rhyme and game, heard and seen played by Liverpool children' (Kidson 1891: 103). 'Johnny Todd he took a notion/For to cross the raging tide,/And he left his love behind him/Weeping on the Liverpool side' (Kelly 1964: 4). *NR; a 19c. folksong recorded in Liverpool, Glasgow and Belfast; the melody was arranged by Fritz Spiegl and Bridget Fry and used as the theme tune to the Liverpool police series *Z-Cars*; it was later adopted as a signature tune by Everton F.C.

Johnny's shirt houses (n.): back-to-back terraced house. 'Five-roomed yellow brick houses just off the County-road tram. "Johnny's shirt houses", as they were called' (Owen 1921: 80). *NR; supposedly from 'the idea that a lady occupant of one house standing at her back door could talk to the lady of the next house standing at her back door, while she explained that she was washing "Johnny's shirt"' (Owen 1921: 80–1).

Jollop (n.): medicine; laxative. 'It had been laced with "jollops", a very strong laxative' (Melly 1965: 233). 'If yer don't wallop yer jollop yer'll get the beezers in yer belly' (Lane 1966: 57). Recorded from l.19c.; from Spanish 'purga de jalap', a medicine from the plant Exogonium Purga found near Xalapan in Mexico.

Jowl, do a (v.): to run away. 'If a boy ran off hurriedly he "did a jowl"' ('Postman' 1931a: 5). 'Jowler. To run away' (Howarth 1985: n.p.). *NR; probably from *jowler*.

Jowler (n.): an alley between back-to-back houses. 'A ragman comes down our jowler' (Hanley 1932: 15). 'Back-entries in the Everton district used to be popularly known as "jiggers" … they were also known as "jowlers"' ('Postman' 1947b: 6). '"Jigger" or "jowler" (the passage giving access to the rear of terrace houses)' (Farrell 1950b: 4). '"Jowler" was widely used at one time but it subsequently fell into decline in favour of "Jigger" which in its turn, has been largely replaced by the description "Coocy"' (Whittington-Egan 1955b: 6). 'A jigger was a back passage 4ft. 6in. wide, a jowler was 2ft. 3in. wide' (Henry 1964: 6). 'Ruler of all the jowlers' (Jacques 1972: n.p.). 'Jowler. Back-entry. Liverpool' (Howarth 1985: n.p.). 'Sum jowler prowlers' (Simpson 1995: 21). 'Jigger – jowler – entry – eenog: four words for the narrow passage-way between the backs of urban terrace-houses' (Spiegl 2000b: 47). 'A "jowler" is a rather wider back alley than a "jigger"' (Lees 2013: 137). Recorded from e.20c.; derivation unclear, possibly 'cheek by jowl', 'side by side, very close'.

Jowler-yowler (n.): stray cat. 'Jowler-yowler: An alley cat' (Lane 1966: 57). *NR; derivation is clear. See *yowler*.

Judas burning (n.): in a very restricted area of the Dingle, an effigy of Judas was burnt in a bonfire early on Good Friday morning. 'I often wonder whether the south end of Liverpool was the only place where the ceremonial burning of Judas took place on Good Friday' (Unwin 1984 [1920s–30s]: 49). 'In the Protestant streets of the Dingle … children ran through the streets at dawn on Good Friday dragging burning effigies of Judas Escariot' (Lane 1987: 38). 'The custom of "Judas Burning" is in itself a mystery' (Sexton 1996: 14). 'A custom we had in the south of Liverpool in the thirties was burning Judas' (Stamper 2010: 34). *NR; at dawn or thereabout on Good Friday morning, in a very specific area of the Dingle in the *south end*, an effigy of Judas was burnt on a bonfire (in the days beforehand children would use the effigy to collect money – 'Judas, penny short of his breakfast'). The origins of the ritual are unclear, though it may have been brought to Liverpool by Portuguese sailors in the l.19c.; the practice continued till the mid-1960s.

Judy (n.): woman, girlfriend, wife. 'They looked like foreign Judies to me' (Hanley 1932: 15). 'The young man's lady friend is called "his girl" or "his judy"' (Farrell 1950b: 4). 'The Judy is a fiancée, or the female you "are knocking about with"' (Shaw 1958d: 14–15). 'Eh la! Ask dat judy out der to gerrus a cuppa tea, will yer?' (Frank 1966: 8). 'Judy. Wife (or any female other than a mother)' (Williams 1971: 179). 'Judy is scouse for a girl' (Flame 1984: 34). 'Ders diss posh do wid lah-di-dah judies' (Simpson 1995: 21).

'Judy – Woman, girlfriend (as in "me judy")' (Callaghan 2011 [1920s–30s]: viii). Recorded from e.19c.; probably a reference to Judy, Punch's wife (whose name, 'Joan', was changed to associate with 'Judy', l.18c. 'fool, simpleton'). Despite protestations that *judy* is neutral, it has pejorative connotations.

Judy scuffer (n.): policewoman. 'De judy-scuffer. *The woman police officer*' (Shaw et al. 1966: 64). '"Judy scuffer" is a policewoman' (Channon 1970: 102). 'Judy scuffer Woman police officer' (Spiegl 1989: 49). Recorded from m.20c.; see *judy*, *scuffer*.

Jump (v.): to board. 'There appears no sign that the verb "to jump", meaning "to board" with reference to "cars" (that is to say "trams"), will be applied to buses' (Farrell 1950a: 4). 'I was just gonna jump a taxi' (Bryan 2003 [1940s–50s]: 159). 'We'd jump the Overhead' (Dudgeon 2010: 89). Recorded from m.19c.; an Americanism; an abbreviation of 'to jump aboard', now used to refer to any form of transport.

Jump over back (n.): leapfrog. 'There is also leapfrog under the name of *Jump Over Back*' (Shaw 1960a: 40). 'How about the game "Reliev-oh"?/And "Jump Over Back" as well' (Hallowell 1972: n.p.). *NR; derivation is clear.

Jump Sunday (n.): 'Aintree on "Jump Sunday" had the fairground atmosphere of Epsom Downs on the eve of the Derby' (Channon 1970: 201). *NR; on the Sunday before the annual Grand National meeting at Aintree race course, the public used to be able to walk the course and inspect the 'jumps' (fences); the custom was discontinued in 1959.

Jump Sunday, once every (adv.): very infrequently. 'Said of a reluctant lover or inadequate husband: 'e saves it fer Jump Sunday' (Lane 1966: 57). *NR; A play on 'jump', 'sexual intercourse'.

Jungle juice (n.): African rum, later any cheap, strong spirits; (ironically) beer. 'Pilfered docks rum (Jungle Juice)' (Shaw 1959a: 39). 'Jungle juice. *Rum*' (Shaw et al. 1966: 64). 'Pinta jungul jooce! *I'll try a pint of your best bitter, sir*' (Minard 1972: 53). 'The local "jungle juice" and "merry-merry" should be avoided' (Melly 1977: 138). '*Jungle juice* Rum' (Spiegl 2000b: 85). '"Jungle juice" is rum' (Lees 2013: 137). Recorded as 'Liverpool: since ca. 1920' (Partridge *s.v. jungle juice*); derivation is clear.

K

Kathleen Mavourneen System (n.): hire purchase. '"On the Kathleen Mavourneen" system (i.e. HP)' (Anon. [L. Iver] 1957b: 4). Recorded from e.20c.; an Irish English phrase from the refrain of the song 'Kathleen Mavourneen': 'It may be for years and it may be for ever'. Another term for HP was 'on the glad and sorry'.

Kay-fisted (adj.): left-handed. '*Kay-fisted*: Left-handed' (Lane 1966: 58). 'Kay-fisted. Left-handed' (Howarth 1985: n.p.). Recorded in modern use from l.19c.; found in *Sir Gawain and the Green Knight*, written in the local dialect area in l.14c.; 'key/kay', 'left', survived in Lancashire and Cheshire dialects.

Kayley (n.): sing song; party. '*Kayley*: A sing song, or musical get-together' (Lane 1966: 58). *NR; transliteration of the Gaelic 'céilidh', 'social gathering'.

Kaylied (adj.): drunk. 'Verbally "lushed up", "kali'd", "bevvied"' (Shaw 1962e: 6). 'Father Murphy 'ad been so kaylied' (Jacques 1979: n.p.). '*Kaylied* Very, very drunk' (Spiegl 2000b: 78). '"Kaylied" and "lushed as the landlord's cat" are terms for drunkenness' (Lees 2013: 137). Recorded from e.20c.; probably from Irish 'céilidh'; see *Kayley*.

Kecks/kex (n.): trousers/underclothes. 'Perhaps we got from Wales *kecks* for trousers' (Shaw 1950b: 4). 'Before they shit their kecks' (Hignett 1966: 158). 'Those at the back were laughing so much they was weeing in their best

kecks' (Bleasdale 1975: 196). 'E's gorri's dad's kecks on!' (Robinson 1986 [1920s–30s]: 103). 'Juss you see me in me dago kecks' (Simpson 1995: 24). 'I tore the seat of my "kecks" (trousers)' (Elliott 2006 [1940s–70s]: 36) Recorded from e.20c.; a development of e.19c. 'kickseys', an extension of l.17c. cant 'kicks', 'breeches'.

Kekka (int.): don't! Stop! 'Kekka mush dtherz a musker ind thee 'aystack. *Say no more, my friend, there happens to be a policeman behind you*' (Minard 1972: 55). Recorded from m.20c.; a direct borrowing from Romani 'kekka', 'don't', 'no'.

Ken (n.): house. '*House*. Drom, Ken, Gaff' (Minard 1972: 87). 'KEN A house, perhaps to be burgled' (Spiegl 1989: 50). 'Marie's always doing something new to their ken' (Sampson 2001: 24). Recorded from 16c.; the derivation of this cant term is unclear; possibly from Hindi 'khan', 'room, house'.

Kettle (n.): watch. 'Me kettle's in dthe Mountains o' Morn. *My watch has been pledged to the pawnbroker*' (Minard 1972: 71). Recorded from m.19c.; derivation unclear.

Kewin (n.): a winkle. 'Meanwhile readers might like to trace the origins of ... kewins' (Shaw 1950b: 4). 'Kewins an' a cob o' chuck' (Anon. 1961b: 3). '*Kewins*: winkles' (Lane 1966: 59). '"Kewin" was a Liverpool name for the common winkle' (Unwin 1984 [1920s–30s]: 98). 'To collect "kewins" (periwinkles) and boil them in an old tin can' (Sinclair 1999 [1930s–e.40s]: 163). *NR; derivation unclear, but possibly from dialectal 'cuvvins', 'periwinkle', from Norwegian 'kuvung', 'sea-snail'.

Kick off (n.): the time something starts. 'I thought it was a two o'clock kick-off?' (Bleasdale 1975: 197). Recorded from l.19c.; an extension of 'kick-off', the start of a football match; 'for a kick off', means 'to begin with'.

Kick off (v.): start (a fight or argument). 'Because when it all kicked off' (Sampson 2002: 161). 'Don't kick off on her' (Bryan 2003 [1940s–50s]: 171). *NR; a l.20c. extension of *kick off (n.)*.

Kick the can (n.): a version of *Relalio*. 'A variant of Relievo, Kick the Can is not peculiar to Liverpool' (Shaw 1959a: 37). '*Kick-ther-can*. A form of street football, using old tin cans' (Lane 1966: 59). 'Kick-the-can was one I liked' (Murari 1975: 59). 'Another popular game was "Kick the Can"' (Unwin 1984 [1920s–30s]: 17). 'I played football and kick-the-can' (Russell 1996 [1976]: 271). See *Relalio*.

Kid (n.): friend (either gender). '"Now my sporting kids", says he' (Shimmin 1863: 79). 'Among girls themselves, a mutual form of address which seems invariable is Kid – "'onest, Kid, if me Mam 'ad known, she'd ave murdered me"' (Shaw 1958d: 15). 'Kid. Mutual form of address amongst girls. Liverpool' (Howarth 1985: n.p.). 'Thanks, kid' (Smith 1998 [1971]: 45). Recorded from e.20c.; possibly from the l.19c. Americanism, 'kid-brother/sister'.

Kid¹ (v.): to fool, deceive, hoax. 'Well, we'll see who's going to be kidded!' (O'Mara 1934: 180). 'The whole world is just kidding itself' (Hanley 2009 [1940]: 475). 'If you want to kid yourself, son, carry on' (Owen 1961: 908). 'You trying to kid us?' (Hignett 1966: 201). 'I kidded him on … that he needed a passport to go to Southampton' (Bleasdale 1975: 106). 'They kidded them that they'd been to their schools' (Unwin 1984 [1920s–30s]: 102). 'Who's kidding who?' (McGovern 1995: 12). 'Yer can't kid a kidder' (Bryan 2003 [1940s–50s]: 151). Recorded from e.19c.; from a con trick, the 'kid rig', which involved stopping a child ('kid') running an errand and fooling them into handing over their goods or money by means of a false story.

Kid² (v.): to tease, joke. 'The firemen and sailors off watch sat on the hatches watching the sailors working and kidding with those they knew' (O'Mara 1934: 207). 'I used to kid Nan about a box' (Naughton 1945: 47). '*More kid than a pregnant goat*: said of a leg-puller' (Lane 1966: 45). 'She's not kidding' (Brown 1989: 21). 'What? You're kiddin' (Fagan 2007 [1950s]: 56). Recorded from 19c.; an extension of *to kid¹*, though the senses often overlap.

Kidden (n.): places where children were enticed into crime. 'We knew, even at our age, that there were houses, kiddens I've mentioned, which if they'd put us up for nothing, were best kept out of' (Clerk 1971 [c.1900]: 86). Recorded as 'Liverpool street arabs': late C.19–mid 20' (Beale 1984 *s.v. kidden*); an e.19c. contraction of 'kid-ken' or 'kiddy-ken', with both terms used in specialised senses: 'kid', 'a boy who commences thieving at an early age' and 'ken', 'a house where thieves meet'.

Kidder[1] *(n.)*: joker; someone who pretends. 'A friend of mine,/a kidder on a brutal scale' (Simpson 1995: 19). 'Yer can't kid a kidder' (Bryan 2003 [1940s–50s]: 151). Recorded from l.19c.; an extension of *kid*[1] *(v.)*.

Kidder[2] *(n.)*: brother or sister, sometimes friend. 'Here you are, kidder' (Bleasdale 1979: 30). 'Oh no, kidder' (Sampson 2002: 32). 'Did yeh, kidder?' (Griffiths 2003: 31). Recorded from m.20c.; an extension of *kid (n.)*.

Kidology (n.): the art of kidding. 'But are these kidology or not?' (Shaw 1966a: 4). Recorded from m.20c.; an example gives the Liverpool provenance – 'a form of kidology which seems to come naturally to most Merseysiders' (*OED s.v. kidology* n.); from *to kid*[1], possibly by analogy with *codology* (with the same sense).

Kill (v.): hit, beat; hurt. 'Me mam'll kill 'im when 'e gets 'ome' (Sinclair 1999 [1930s–e.40s]: 79). 'These shoes are killin' me feet' (Bryan 2003 [1940s–50s]: 20). 'I'm gonna kill you Elliott' (Elliott 2006 [1940s–70s]: 109). Recorded from 13c.; often cited as an example of Liverpudlian hyperbole, but 'kill', 'strike, hit, beat' is the earliest recorded sense ('put to death' is a 14c. development); the sense of 'the infliction of pain' dates from 18c., though the specific sense of feet or shoes 'killing' is common from m.20c.

Kinell (int.): fucking hell. 'I used to say "kinell" thinking it was only an expression' (Robinson 1986 [1920s–30s]: 14). 'Kinell, la!' (Sampson 2002: 239). *NR; derivation is clear.

Kip[1]/*Kip house (n.)*: cheap lodging house, usually serving sailors. 'Deck-hand Jones' lodgings, or carpenter Robinson's "kip"' (Whittaker 1934: 112). 'He was a ship's runner, a man who earned his living partly from the kip houses' (Jerome 1948: 11). 'A Rope – a tuppeny kip, we kids knew them as Lascar Ropes' (Clerk 1971 [*c*.1900]: v). 'All night kips' (Jacques 1972: n.p.). Recorded from l.19c.; from 'kip', 'brothel, house of ill-repute', the equivalent of *doss house*; ultimately from Danish 'kippe', 'mean hut, low alehouse'.

Kip[2] *(n.)*: bed. 'Alone there in yer kip' (Jacques 1972: n.p.). Recorded from l.19c.; an extension of *kip*[1], popularised through Forces' usage.

Kip[3] *(n.)*: sleep. 'He's having a kip' (Owen 1961: 83). 'Get home fer some kip!' (Jacques 1972: n.p.). 'Bill said he was going home for some kip' (Cornelius 2001 [1982]: 175). 'A decent night's kip' (Fagan 2007 [1950s]: 264). Recorded from e.20c.; popularised through Forces' usage; an extension of *kip*[1].

Kip (v.): to sleep. 'If you are not going to kip tonight' (Hanley 1932: 79). 'He could crawl over and into that doorway and kip' (Hignett 1966: 186). 'I can't see Freddie Fletcher's Mam an' dad lettin' her an' Hovis kip in with Freddie' (Bleasdale 1975: 160). 'Don't fancy havin to kip out in *this*, do you?' (Griffiths 2003: 226). Recorded from l.19c.; an extension of *kip*[1].

Kipper/kip (n.): face. 'The face. *Boat Race, Kipper*' (Minard 1972: 11). 'I clocked 'im one in the kipper' (Jacques 1975: n.p.). 'Kip on him by the way – fucking made up' (Sampson 2002:

237). 'A bloody kipper on 'im like a smacked arse' (Fagan 2007 [1950s]: 117). Recorded from l.20c.; derivation unclear.

Kirkby Kiss (n.): headbutt; blow to the face. 'KIRKBY KISS Head-butting the face' (Spiegl 1989: 50). See *Liverpool Kiss*.

Kisser (n.): mouth, face. 'Stow that or I'll wipe your kisser' (Hanley 1932: 29). 'You've tripped over it, flat on your kisser' (Grant 2002: 56). Recorded from l.19c.; originally boxing usage, 'kisser', 'mouth'.

Kite² (n.): criminal, fraudster. 'A kite who goes to France, Belgium, Holland and Germany and comes back with splendid merchandise' (Sampson 1998: 177). 'There's hardly no one who's totally legit. There's kites, dippers, dealers, spivs, all kinds' (Sampson 2001: 161). Recorded from l.20c.; see *kiting*.

Kite³ (n.): face. 'He even had the hard kite to nod to my old lady' (Hanley 1932: 83). 'They do not care whether they can put a name to your kite' (Sampson 2001: 37). 'Big grin on his kite' (Griffiths 2003: 204). Recorded from 19c.; an Americanism; derivation unclear.

Kiting/kiter/kite (n.)¹: fraud, esp. cheque book or credit card. 'KITING (KITER) Cheque-book/bank-card frauds' (Spiegl 1989: 51). 'New batch of Visas was coming in. Pure kite it were – clean as a whistle, not signed or nothing' (Sampson 2001: 23). Recorded from l.20c.; an extension of e.19c. 'kite', 'dud cheque', from the slightly earlier 'kite', 'bill of exchange used for raising credit'.

Klondyke (n.): the Orrell area of Bootle. 'Klondike: the Orrell district of Bootle' (Lane 1966: 59). 'Many tales have circulated as to how Orrell received the name of Klondyke' (McDermott 1984: 9). *NR in this sense; derivation unclear; explanations include an ironic reference to the simultaneous opening of a brickworks and a tin-smelting factory in the area, or the nickname of William 'Klondyke' Jones, a wealthy Welsh builder who lived locally.

Knacker, in the (adj.): naked. 'There was a drawing on the back of a woman in her knacker' (Bleasdale 1975: 102). *NR; a corruption of 'naked'.

Knacker's yard (n.): a room in a state of disarray. 'Knacker's yard: said of a place that looks a complete mess' (Lane 1966: 59). *NR in this sense; an extension of *knackered*.

Knackered (adj.): tired out, exhausted; worn out. 'You don't hardly notice you're knackered till you are' (Bleasdale 1975: 151). 'By the time we shake them we are nackered' (Brown 1989: 46). 'We pile off at Liverpool, triumphant, knackered and completely pissed' (Sampson 1998: 87). 'We leave the bistro an climb back up into Quockie's knackered old Bedford van' (Griffiths 2002: 45). Recorded from m.20c.; from e.19c. 'knacker', 'someone who bought old or ill ('knackered') horses, to slaughter them for hide, meat and bones.

Knee-bender (n.): religious person. 'Knee-bender: A pious person' (Lane 1966: 60). *NR; derivation is clear.

Kneetrembler (n.): perpendicular sex. 'The canal tow-path and the surrounding fields were suitable for knee-tremblers' (Melly 1965: 31). 'E's gone with 'er on a kneetrembler' (Channon 1970: 104). '[He] had a knee-trembler in an outhouse or up against a tractor' (Griffiths 2001: 7). Recorded from m.19c.; derivation is clear.

Knife and fork tea (n.): full evening meal. '*Knife 'n' fork tea*: A substantial early-evening meal, or a meal in which the host has included some kind of meat' (Lane 1966: 60). *NR; derivation is clear.

Knob (n.): penis; general insult. 'Little knobs and big gobs all of them' (Parker 1974: 137). 'My knob is like a fucking steel rod' (Sampson 2002: 158) 'I *know* it's fuckin Welsh, yeh knob' (Griffiths 2003: 54). Recorded from l.19c.; from 'knob', 'small rounded lump or mass'.

Knobhead (n.): idiot, fool; general insult. 'What a fucking nob-headed, shit-faced, bollock-brained, turd-shaped, prick-arsed, wanker-faced cunt!' (Sayle 1984: 21). 'Fuckinell! Knobhead's coming over!' (Sampson 1999: 251). 'Knob'ed. Get the fuckin bus, lad' (Griffiths 2003: 12). Recorded from m.20c.; an Americanism; from *knob*, 'penis'.

Knock/batter/welly the shit/e out of (v.): beat severely. 'Batter the shite out of the boys who'd done it' (Murari 1975: 5). 'There's this buck wellying shite out of the wings of the car' (McClure 1980: 37). 'They're knockin' the shite an' stuffin' out of you' (Bleasdale 1985: 177). 'He said he knocked the shit out of him' (Stamper 2010: 121). Recorded from l.19c.; derivation unclear.

Knock back/KB (n.): refusal, rejection. 'He's giving his wife the old KB – you

know, the Knock Back' (Bleasdale 1975: 11). 'I'd get a knock-back if I tried it on' (Grant 1996: 324). 'Half sounds like a magistrate giving you a KB' (Sampson 2001: 57). 'After a couple of knock-backs' (Fagan 2007 [1950s]: 207). Recorded from l.19c.; northern dialectal, extended to form a verb in e.20c. Australian usage.

Knock back (v.): to refuse, reject. 'So fuckin what if she knocks me back?' (Griffiths 2002: 6). 'You're not knockin' me back are yer?' (Fagan 2007 [1950s]: 109). See *knock back (n.)*.

Knock fuck out of (v.): beat severely. 'They can knock fuck out of you and get away with it' (Parker 1974: 164). 'If four black lads knocked fuck out of us, there and then' (Sampson 2001: 105). Recorded from l.20c.; the derivation is unclear.

Knock off (n.): stolen goods. 'They are in the market for various types of "knock-off"' (Parker 1974: 39). '"Knock off" merchants' (Unwin 1984 [1920s–30s]: 69). 'Searchin' houses for knock-off gear' (Fagan 2007 [1950s]: 98). See *knock off² (v.)*.

Knock off¹ (v.): to stop, end. 'I wish it were knocking-off time' (Hanley 1932: 119). 'He was about to stop. "Wants me to knock off?" he asked' (Clerk 1971 [c.1900]: 56). 'Knock if off, I said!' (Sinclair 1999 [1930s–e.40s]: 14). 'Knocking off and coming back at three o'clock' (Grant 2002: 297). Recorded from l.17c.; derivation unclear.

Knock off² (v.): to steal, break into. 'Knock one off in the station maybe' (Cross 1951: 138). 'He'd have to do the adolescent thing and knock off that picture of her' (Hignett 1966:

200). 'To knock off me old gas meter' (Jacques 1975: n.p.). 'I'm going to knock some peanuts off' (Robinson 1986 [1920s–30s]: 41). 'It's alright – they're not knocked off' (Sinclair 1999 [1930s–e.40s]: 156). Recorded from e.20c.; popularised by Forces' usage; derivation unclear.

Knock off[3] *(v.)*: to have sex with. 'Chatting up the boss and knocking off the secretaries' (Bleasdale 1975: 28). 'He was knockin' off a few others at the same time, including our Josie' (Fagan 2007 [1950s]: 305). Recorded from e.20c.; an Americanism; an extension of l.16c. 'knock', 'to have sexual intercourse'.

Knock rotten (v.): to beat someone senseless. '*Knocked rotten*: To be knocked silly; to be beaten into a stupor' (Lane 1966: 60). Recorded from e.20c.; an Australian coinage; an extension of 'rotten', 'in a poor state'.

Knocked back, to be (v.): to be refused, rejected. 'Eez bin knocked back (*turned down*) by so menny birdz' (Minard 1972: 65). See *knock back (n.)*.

Knocked off, to be (v.): to be arrested, caught. 'You'll get knocked off' (Jacques 1973: n.p.). 'The scuffers knock her old man off' (Brown 1989: 33). Recorded from e.20c.; an Americanism; derivation unclear.

Know the score (v.): see *score*.

Knuckle (n.): violence, aggravation. 'Can we stay and talk to the birds after the knuckle?' (Sampson 1998: 138). Recorded from m.20c.; derivation is clear.

Knuckle buttie (n.): punch. 'A knuckle buttie' (Jacques 1972: n.p.). *NR; derivation is clear.

Knurr and spell (n.): children's game. 'Knur and spell. A game similar to peggy' (Howarth 1985: n.p.). Recorded from m.19c.; a version of *peggy* or *tip-cat*; derivation unclear.

Koff! (int.): go away; fuck off. 'Koff. Ample … fit three of you in here!' (Sampson 1999: 440). Recorded from l.20c.; an abbreviation of 'fuck off'.

Kop, The (n.): football terrace at Anfield, home to Liverpool Football Club. 'This huge wall of earth has been termed "Spion Kop", and no doubt this apt name will always be used in future in referring to this spot' (Anon. 1906: 3). 'The Spion Kop Army at Anfield' (Anon. 1914f: 3). 'The Club had decided to concentrate upon improving Spion Kop at the back of the Oakfield-Road goal' (Anon. 1926: 9). 'Could an Everton player have a more unenviable task than to pick the ball out of the net overlooked by Spion Kop?' (Anon. 1941a: 5). 'He should have heard the varieties of "Ay, ay" in a dockside pub, a bus queue or on Spion Kop' (Shaw 1961: 6). 'There is in Liverpool a school of indigenous verse – known as the Kop choir' (Moloney 1966: 56). 'When he's in the Kop, and Liverpool are playing Arsenal' (Parker 1974: 31). 'Like United fans thrown in the Kop' (McGovern 1995: 12). 'ICF tried to come round the Kop and got legged' (Sampson 2002: 144). 'Oh I am a Liverpudlian and I come from the Spion Kop' (Lees 2013: 148). Recorded from e.20c.; one of the most famous football terraces, *The Kop* was named after 'the Spion Kop', the Afrikaans name of a hill near Ladysmith in S. Africa which was the scene of a battle

(1900) during the Boer War in which a Lancashire regiment suffered heavy losses.

Kopite/Koppite (n.): someone who watches from *the Kop*; a Liverpool F.C. supporter. 'Koppite: English and Irish internationals receive £4' (Anon. 1914a: 7). 'The well-packed Kopites showed their disapproval with ironical hand-clapping' (Anon. 1939c: 8) 'He got a tremendous ovation from the generous Koppites at the finish' (Liddell 1960: 53). '"You'll never walk alone", the Koppites sing' (Moloney 1966: 58). 'The president of the Cambridge University Boat Club who comes from Birkenhead is also a loyal Kopite' (Anon. 1974: 16). 'The Kopites insisted Liverpool F.C. reflected their own credo' (Lees 2013: 149). See *Kop*.

Kru (n.): Liberian seamen. '*E's a Kru* He is a West African seaman' (Spiegl 2000b: 62). 'The Kru of present-day Liberia, had a tradition of seamanship' (Costello 2001: 17). 'The Kru boys being the indigenous Kru tribes of the Liberian coast' (Dudgeon 2010: 34). Recorded from e.19c.; the Kru are an ethnic group in Liberia and were famed as seamen; Liverpool's links with West Africa (Freetown in particular), meant that Kru sailors became an important part of Liverpool's black community from l.19c.

L

La/lah/lar (n.): lad, mate. 'Hey you la'
(Farrell 1950a: 4). 'Ah … shurrup,
la!' (Owen 1961: 21). 'There are many
cordial terms of address such as mate,
sis for sister, la for lad; then chuck,
wacker (abbreviated to wack) or just
yew or youse' (Armstrong 1966:
4). 'You know what Parky done, la'
(Murari 1975: 13). 'Not me. Must be
you lah' (Bleasdale 1985: 118). 'The
only Scot in me la, is I come from
Scotland Road' (Stamper 2010: 90).
Recorded from m.20c.; glossed as
'mainly Liverpool use' (Dalzell and
Victor (2006) *s.v. lar*); as with *lad* (of
which it is an abbreviation) and *girl*,
la ranges from signalling genuine
friendliness to outright hostility or
condescension.

Lad (n.): male of any age; sometimes used
to signal an occupation. 'My lad, you
surely can't be inquiring for Riddough's
hotel' (Melville 1849: 199). 'Ay, that's
true, lad' (Hocking 1966 [1879]: 126).
'It doesn't impress me, lad' (Hanley
2009 [1940]: 167). 'There are *milk-lads*,
bread-lads, *and-cart-lads* and *Echo-lads*
who sell papers' (Shaw 1958d: 16).
'Look lad, you've been coming here for
years' (Hignett 1966: 43). 'You can't
blame me, lad' (Russell 1996 [1976]:
211). 'All right, lad' (Robinson 1986
[1920s–30s]: 130). 'Got a lot of time for
the lad' (Sampson 2002: 60). Recorded
as 'young male' from 15c.; derivation
unknown; as with *girl* and *la*, the
uses range from signalling genuine
friendliness to outright hostility or
condescension.

Lads, the (n.): regular set of male friends.
'His male friends are simply "the lads"'
(Farrell 1950b: 4). 'Lads as well as fellers
are a man's friends ("I bin out wit duh
lads fer a few bevies")' (Shaw 1958d:
15). 'Stay here with the lads' (Hignett
1966: 51). 'What am I going to tell
the lads?' (Cornelius 2001 [1982]: 44)
'Jimmy offered the lads a lift' (Burnett
2011: 147). Recorded from m.20c. in
this sense; derivation is clear.

Lady Muck (n.): pretentious woman;
female equivalent of *Lord Muck*. 'Lady
Muck of Muck Hall: A woman who
puts on airs' (Lane 1966: 61). 'When
I told all my friends that we were
moving all the way to Sefton Park, they
didn't make fun and call me "Lady
Muck"' (Marenbon 1973 [1920s]: 76).
'Parading along Bond Street as if she
was Lady Muck' (Grant 1996: 347).
'Lady Muck left me a list' (Bryan 2003
[1940s–50s]: 154). See *Lord Muck*.

Lah-di-dah (adj.): affected, posh. 'A
French pirate called La-di-da' (Haigh
1907: 318). 'Ders diss posh do wid
lah-di-dah judies' (Simpson 1995: 21).
'Me Mam said it was all lah de dah'
(Bryan 2003 [1940s–50s]: 54). 'This
was lah-di-dah gloom-filled Leeds'
(Lees 2013: 131). Recorded from l.19c.;
supposedly echoic of the pronunciation
of people with affected manners.

Lam/lamp[1] *(v.)*: to hit, beat. 'I'm gonna
lam you, see, like you ain't never been

lammed in your life before' (Cross 1951: 53). 'I thought he was going to lamp him' (Stamper 2010: 101). Recorded from l.16c.; ultimately from Old English 'lęmian', 'lame'; *lamp* is an e.19c. northern dialectal variant of *lam*.

Lamp² (*v.*): to look. 'De quare feller's lampin. *The stranger is watching*' (Shaw et al. 1966: 63). 'Lamp. To look or lookout for. Liverpool' (Howarth 1985: n.p.). Recorded from e.20c.; an Americanism, possibly from 'lamps', 'eyes'.

Lanny (*n.*): Landing Stage. 'The Liverpool Landing Stage is called the "Lanny"' (Farrell 1950a: 4). 'The Lanny, the good ould Stick' (Shaw 1957a: 15). '"Lanny" is landing stage (Princes or Georges)' (Channon 1970: 103). 'The bus terminus on the Lanny' (Lees 2013: 28). *NR; the Liverpool Landing Stage was/is a series of floating platforms (the first of which was completed in 1847) designed to serve passenger ships (including the Mersey ferries).

Lascar (*n.*): Indian sailor. 'She was manned by forty or fifty Lascars, the native seamen of India' (Melville 1849: 216). 'Colonies of Chinese, Lascars, Africans sprang up' (Hall 2004 [1939]: 10). 'She would see the mixed throng below, Europeans, Lascars and Chinese' (Jerome 1948: 16). 'Did the Lascars bring the "gear" to Paddy's Market?' (Anon. 1964b: 6). 'Two goms came in and threw a drunken lascar over the rope … A Rope – a tuppeny kip, we kids knew them as Lascar Ropes' (Clerk 1971 [c.1900]: v). 'Lascars, Chinamen … Coolies' (Robinson 1986 [1920s–30s]:

102). 'A lascar seaman all the way from India' (Grant 1996: 46). 'Lascar sailors (Johnnies)' (Callaghan 2011 [1910s–30s]: 25). Recorded from e.17c.; used in nautical and colonial discourse to refer loosely to Indian sailors; a corruption of Urdu 'lashkar', 'army, camp'.

Lash (*v.*): discard; throw. 'The sooner I lash that South Village [project]' the better I'll feel' (Sampson 2002: 182). 'He lashed the remains of the soup at her' (Sanders and Sanders 2009 [1960s]: 103). Recorded from 21c.; an extension of 'lash', 'move swiftly'.

Lashings (*n.*): an abundance. 'There'll be lashings of fine things for you' (Hanley 2009 [1950]: 223). 'Beer for dogs, lashin's a chuck' (Shaw 1957a: 1). Recorded from e.19c.; usually used in reference to food or drink; probably from Irish English ('floods or abundance'); an extension of 14c. 'lash', 'to pour' ('lashing down with rain' Dudgeon 2010: 144), from French 'lâcher', 'to loose, let go' (hence 'on the lash').

Last¹ (*adj.*): inferior, poor, disappointing. 'That was fuckin' last' (Parker 1974: 50). 'The ale's last!' (Russell 1996 [1976]: 202). 'Things are last when we get there' (Brown 1989: 33). '"It's last" meaning "it's terrible"' (Lees 2013: 137). *NR in this sense; an extension of 'last', 'at the end of a series arranged in order of rank or estimation; lowest'.

Last² (*adj.*): sad, embarrassed; mean towards (when used with 'on'). 'I looks out the window so's he doesn't feel too last' (Sampson 2002: 135). 'I'm not going to apologise to the cunt, but I do feel last on him' (Sampson 2002: 236). *NR in this sense; see *last¹*.

Latchlifter (n.): the price of a drink. 'Didden you tap me for fourpence for a pint the other night to get into Cain's's? A latchlifter you called it' (Shaw 1952: n.p.). 'De latchlifter. *The price of half-a-pint of beer*' (Shaw et al. 1966: 35). Recorded from e.20c.; Forces' usage; the meaning is 'the price of a drink in the hope that others will treat you to more'.

Lately? (int.): had sex recently? Recorded as 'a raffish greeting, very common, especially in Merseyside, during the 1930s' (Beale (1984) *s.v lately?*); Forces' usage up to the 1970s; a contraction of 'had it in lately?'

Laughing (adj.): well off, happy. 'I'll give up ciggies and I'll be laughing' (Smith 1998 [1971]: 70). 'Two points an' they should be laughin'' (Bleasdale 1975: 55). 'A good lock-up, an you're laffin'' (McClure 1980: 54). Recorded from e.20c.; Forces' usage; derivation is clear.

Laughing bags (adj.): very well-off. 'Wid the fellas down thur you're laffin bags if you gorra latchlifter' (Shaw 1957a: 7). '*Laffin bags*, very happy' (Williams and Shaw 1967: xxvi). 'The Liverpool equivalent of "Bob's your uncle" has, since c.1920, been "you're laffin bags", where "bags" = "very much"' (Partridge and Beale 1985 s.v. Liverpool catchphrases). *NR; see *bags of*.

Lavo/lavvy (n.): toilet. 'He's always in the lavo' (Hanley 1932: 23). 'Writing poems upon the lavvo wall' (Jacques 1979: n.p.). 'Nobody minds when you smoke in the lavvy' (Brown 1989: 6). 'Over the top of the lavvie door' (Sinclair 1999 [1930s–e.40s]: 108). 'I'm going to the lavvy' (Simpson 2011:

415). Recorded from e.20c.; derivation is clear.

Lazzy (n.): elastic. 'I'm sure the strings he used were "lazzie" bands' (McGovern 1995: 5). *NR; derivation is clear.

Learn (v.): to teach. 'We'll soon learn yer what yer've done' (Owen 1921: 52). 'Takin' money for learnin' kids to draw' (Cross 1951: 122). '*Lern Yerself Scouse*' (Shaw 1966: title). 'You're a bloody gip and I'll learn yer something' (Clerk 1971 [c.1900]: 37). 'They don't learn none of us to read' (Brown 1989: 17). This transitive sense of *learn*, glossed as 'now vulgar', was established usage in English from the l.14c.–19c.

Leather (v.): beat. 'She proceeded to leather him with her open hand' (Hanley 1932: 114). Recorded from m.17c.; from 'leather', 'beat with leather thong'.

Leather Hats, the (n.): The (Liverpool) King's Regiment. '*Leather Hats, the*: The King's Regiment (Liverpool)' (Fraser and Gibbons 1925: 190). The nickname supposedly derived from the regiment's soldiers replacing their lost headgear with the leather hats of dead American rebels during the American War of Independence.

Leathering (n.): beating. 'He hammered me … he gave me a terrible leathering' (Owen 1961: 30). 'He got a leathering with the strap' (Sinclair 1999 [1930s–e40s]: 79). Recorded from l.18c.; an extension of *leather (v.)*.

Leave on (v.): to give a deposit. 'My mother went over to the Ham and Egg parade, left sixpence on a borrowed teapot, and came back with it full of delicious tea' (O'Mara 1934: 122).

*NR in this sense; probably an abbreviation of 'leave a deposit on'.

Leavenport (n.): Liverpool. 'Patrick was a common enough type in Leavenport' (Jerome 1948: 10). *NR; *Leavenport* was the name given to Liverpool in *China White*, J.A. Jerome's pioneering novel of inter-racial marriage in the city.

Leccy/lecky/lekkie[1] *(n.)*: electric tram. 'He skipped a leccy down Scottie Road to get to the Lanny' (Farrell 1950a: 4). 'Leckie (electric tram)' (Shaw 1955b: 18). '*Lecky*: Electricity. Formerly used for Liverpool trams, i.e. Electric Cars' (Lane 1966: 61). 'Leckies. Tram cars. Liverpool' (Howarth 1985: n.p.). 'Lekkies – (Electric) trams' (Callaghan 2011 [1910s–30s]: viii). Recorded from e.20c.; derivation is clear.

Lecky[2] *(n.)*: electricity supply; electric. 'De lecky man. *The electric meter reader*' (Shaw et al. 1966: 24). 'She got our her ould lecky shaver' (Jacques 1975: n.p.). 'Put fifty pee in the lecky meter' (Brown 1989: 19). '*Dee lecky man* The electricity-meter reader' (Spiegl 2000: 49). 'Playin' me Hofner blonde like, Lecky, ye know' (Sanders and Sanders 2009 [1960s]: 150). Recorded from m.20c.; an extension of *leccy/lecky*[1].

Leeirpooltonian (n.): native of Liverpool. 'Had I knowne yr inclinations to stay longer among those infidell Leeirpooltonians' (Bradshaigh 1670: n.p.). *NR; one of the first names for natives of the city; derivation is clear.

Left-footer (n.): Catholic. 'A Catholic. Also "Cogger" or "Left-footer" or "Ail Mury", "Rat Catcher" or "Crate Egg"' (Lane 1966: 89). 'Catterlicks Papes Leftfooters' (Jacques 1973: n.p.).

'Left-footer. A Roman catholic' (Howarth 1985: n.p.). '*E's a cogger, a left-footer* He is a Catholic' (Spiegl 2000b: 52). 'Catholics were derogatorily referred to as "left-footers" or "coggers"' (Lees 2013: 96). Recorded from e.20c.; a complex term historically since *left-footer* can be either Catholic or Protestant, depending on the norm in the area in which the phrase is used. In Northern Ireland where the majority population is Protestant, left-footer means Catholic; in the Republic of Ireland, where the majority is Catholic, *left-footer* traditionally meant Protestant. In Liverpool the dominant sense is 'Catholic'. The derivation is from the negative associations of 'left' (compare English 'sinister' [from Latin] and 'gauche' [from French]; 'digs with the wrong foot' means 'someone of a different religious persuasion' and thus varies with the religion of the speaker.

Leg (v.): to chase. 'The conductor jumped out and started legging us down the road' (Bleasdale 1975: 21). 'Got legged all around town by about ten thousand of the twats' (Sampson 1998: 81). Recorded from l.20c.; a transitive extension of *leg it*.

Leg it (v.): to run away, run fast. 'Legging it like a mad ass over her estate' (Hanley 2009 [1940]: 525). 'I had to leg it for the fourteen bus' (Smith 1998 [1971]: 27). 'She legged it down Heyworth Street' (Bryan 2003 [1940s–50s]: 58). 'We would leg it to Eboes Café' (Burnett 2011: 70). Recorded from e.20c.; an extension of m.19c. 'leg', 'run', from l.16c. 'leg', 'travel by foot'.

Leg over (n.): sex. 'She's a bit free with the old "leg over" when she's had a few' (Bleasdale 1975: 18). 'Christ, I hadn't ad me leg ova faw awlmowst two years' (Griffiths 2000: 471). 'He probably never got his leg over this morning, that's his problem' (Kelly 2006 [1930s–40s]: 89). Recorded from l.20c.; derivation is clear.

Legless (adj.): very drunk. 'Succeeded in gettin' legless' (Jacques 1973: n.p.). 'After he had had his booze, he was legless' (Stamper 2010: 113). Recorded from e.20c.; derivation is clear.

Let on[1] *(v.)*: reveal, divulge. 'It's no use letting on we're beat, is it?' (Hanley 2009 [1950]: 286). 'She doesn't let on much, on the surface, what she's feeling' (Bainbridge 1973: 40). 'People who don't let on' (Grant 2002: 208). 'We didn't let on what was going on' (Stamper 2010: 50). Recorded from e.18c.; probably Scottish in origin; derivation unclear.

Let on[2] *(v.)*: pretend. 'He had let on to the people at home that he was still working' (Hanley 1932: 79). 'Letting on he hasn't heard' (Brown 1989: 13). Recorded from e.19c.; a dialectal usage that became an Americanism; derivation unclear.

Let on (to) (v.): acknowledge someone; say hello. 'Don't be letting on' (Hanley 1932: 69). 'Watch them without letting on' (Hignett 1966: 227). 'Being civil and "letting on" when they saw me' (Parker 1974: 214). 'He would have listened to the man on his right without letting on' (McClure 1980: 497). 'They want to be able to let on to lads like us' (Sampson 2001: 22). 'Did she let on to you?' (Burnett 2011: 39). *NR in this sense; probably a m.20c. extension of *let on*[1].

Letting board (n.): a large peak on a cap. 'A large peak on a cap is called mockingly a Letting board, a phrase taken from pigeon-fancying' (Shaw 1959a: 32). 'Decker wid a lettin board. *A cap with a big* peak' (Shaw et al. 1966: 37). *NR; from 'let-board', a landing board outside a pigeon-loft.

Levy (n.): a shilling. 'Levy, a shilling. – *Liverpool*. Among labourers a LEVY is a sum obtained before it is due, something to keep a man going till Saturday night comes' (Hotten 1860: 215). 'Levy (Liverpool), a shilling' (Barrère and Leland 1889: 15). Recorded from e.19c.; an Americanism imported, as Barrère notes, by way of Liverpool's 'intimate commercial relations with New York'; derivation unclear.

Lezzy (n.): lesbian. '*Lezzy*: a lesbian woman' (Lane 1966: 62). Recorded from m.20c.; often derogatory; derivation is clear.

Liblab (n.): library. 'Sevvy Park Liblab. *Sefton Park Public Library*' (Shaw et al. 1966: 32). '"Liblab" is a library' (Channon 1970: 102). *NR; derivation by echoic doubling.

Lift (v.): to steal. 'Purses and minor articles he "lifted" daily' (Whittaker 1934: 156). 'They were just lifting the Chink's money' (Murari 1975: 48). 'Thuh bottle uv brandy that Malcolm lifted out uv the Spar' (Griffiths 2000: 17). Recorded from m.16c.; originally referred to the stealing of cattle, later extended to 'shoplifting'.

Lightcake man (n.): street seller of cakes. 'When the poor man was calling "Light Cakes" to sell' (Hallowell 1972: n.p.). 'The Lightcake Man …

was a very welcome street seller on Merseyside' (Unwin 1984 [1920s–30s]: 95). 'I remember the lightcake man, who would carry a basket on his head, touting his wares' (Stamper 2010: 24). *NR; a familiar figure, especially on Sunday afternoons, in poorer areas.

Like (adv.): a discourse marker, often used to qualify a preceding statement. 'Some people have to work, like, for their living' (Owen 1961: 15). 'I feel sorry for them like' (Russell 1996 [1976]: 227). 'Like. All-purpose prefix, suffix and filler-noise' (Spiegl 1989: 52). 'It comes natural like' (Sinclair 1999 [1930s–e.40s]: 9). 'Next left. Bypass that town, like' (Griffiths 2003: 115). *Like* is often used in imitations of Liverpool speech (and working-class speech in general) for the purpose of ridicule; it attracts a peculiar level of opprobrium. Fowler's guide to modern English describes it as 'a hated parenthetic use', 'now scorned by standard speakers as a vulgarism of the first order', whose occurrence by m.20c. 'as an incoherent and prevalent filler had reached the proportions of an epidemic' (Fowler 1996: 459). Such condemnation is little more than class-based linguistic prejudice. *Like* is a functional and perfectly comprehensible discourse marker (used to manage what we say), in phrases such as 'what do you mean, like?' or 'as if she cared, like' (Bleasdale 1975: 209). Its use as a tag word or filler is as objectionable as those 'uhms', 'ahs', 'ers' and 'erms' used commonly by, for example, Old Etonian Prime Ministers; the failure to stigmatise those tags and fillers is social rather than linguistic in origin.

Linen (n.): newspaper. 'Newspaper. Linenn, Blad' (Minard 1972: 90). Recorded from m.20c.; an abbreviation of e.18c. 'linen paper' (also called European paper), made from pulped linen.

Lippy (n.): lipstick. 'She came back early t' change her coat an' put some lippy on' (Bleasdale 1975: 41). 'She talks proper posh and don't plaster lippy all over her gob' (Brown 1989: 76). 'She had loads of make-up on, mad red lippy' (Sampson 2002: 124). Recorded from m.20c.; an Australian coinage; derivation is clear.

Little Rome (n.): Recorded as 'Liverpool (England): coll[oquial]. Ex the large number of Catholics there' (Beale (1984) *s.v. Little Rome*).

Liverpoldon (n.): native of Liverpool. 'It seems ye Liverpoldons attended you not to engage you but to keepe you uningaged' (Ireland 1670: n.p.). *NR; one of the first names for natives of the city (see *Leeirpooltonian*s); derivation is clear.

Liverpolitan (n.): native of Liverpool. 'The tables were almost turned by the brilliant efforts of the Liverpolitan' (Anon. 1866: 3). 'Liverpolitans shiver' (Anon. 1914d: 10). 'L.M.S. Merseyside trip for "exiled" Liverpolitans' (Anon. 1933: 9). 'Liverpudlian means an inhabitant of the pool of Liver, which, of course, is Liverpool. Liverpolitan, on the other hand, means an inhabitant of the city of Liver, or Liverpolis, which does not exist' ('Postman' 1950: 4). 'Is it not a political example for all the world that the descendants of the Normans, Anglo-Saxons, Irish, Welsh, Scots and Vikings who have peopled Liverpool are now united in a common pride in being Liverpolitans?' (Chandler 1957: 9). 'The Liverpolitans who had stayed put' (Lees 2013: 254). *NR; recorded from m.19c.; a genteel term for people from Liverpool; by analogy with 'metropolitan'.

Liverpolitana (n.): things Liverpudlian. 'I once had a talk on Liverpolitana' (Shaw 1964b: 6). '*Liverpolitana*' (Williams 1971: title). *NR; derivation is clear.

Liverpool[1] *(n.)*: delftware and porcelain manufactured in eighteenth-century Liverpool. 'You must mistake about Liverpool ware being 21/Sterling' (Beekman 1956 [1750]: 1.115). 'One of my Liverpool ware teapots was broken' (Drabble 1964: 56). Recorded from m.18c.; the first use of *Liverpool* as an attributive; Liverpool was the location of a number of distinguished potteries between *c.*1754 and 1840, the most famous of which was the Herculaneum Pottery (on the site of what was later to become the Herculaneum dock).

Liverpool[2] *(n.)*: the spoken language of Liverpool. 'Although all the characters, except F[r]. O'Toole, speak Liverpool' (Shaw 1952: n.p.). 'Mrs Gibbons fulminated in good thick Liverpoool you could have cut with a knife' (Ash 1954: 142). *NR; Shaw's coinage appeared in the stage directions for his play *The Scab*, the first dramatic text written entirely in a form intended to represent Liverpool speech.

Liverpool Blues (n.): 79th Regiment of Foot (The Royal Liverpool Volunteers). 'In 1778, a regiment of regular soldiers, called the Liverpool Blues, 1100 strong, was raised by the Corporation and inhabitants of the town' (Brooke 1853: 359). 'The Liverpool Blues, a regiment funded by public subscription' (Lees 2013: 92). *NR; the regiment fought in the Americas during the American War of Independence.

Liverpool button (n.): a makeshift button or toggle used by sailors. '*Liverpool-button*. A kind of toggle used by sailors when they lose a button' (Farmer 1905: 270). '*Liverpool Button*. The makeshift used by a sailor when buttons ran short, generally a piece of wood made fast to the garment with a length of rope yarn' (Bowen 1929: 84). Recorded from m.19c.; derivation unknown.

Liverpool clamp-down/wash (n.): washing the torso. 'A Liverpool clamp-down (or wash) is a bath that extends down to the top of the trousers only' (Ferguson 1944: 106). *NR; recorded from e.20c.; derivation unknown.

Liverpool head (n.): ship's ventilation device. '*Liverpool head*. A sheet-metal ventilation fixture comprising two drums, one inside the other, with staggered openings' (de Kerchove 1948: 422). *NR; recorded from m.19c.; derivation unknown.

Liverpool hook (n.): specific type of docker's hook. 'Swivel cargo hook (Liverpool hook)' (de Kerchove 1948: 422). *NR; recorded from e.20c.; there were many variants of the docker's hook that fastened to the end of the cargo whip; presumably from the use of this type of hook on the Liverpool docks.

Liverpool house (n.): accommodation structure built on the deck of a ship. '*Liverpool House*. The old sailing ship name for midship deckhouse, in which the "idlers" had their quarters' (Bowen 1929: 84). '*Liverpool house.* A superstructure extending from side to side and situated amidships in large (steel built) sailing vessels. It contained the accommodation for the master and the officers' (de Kerchove 1948: 422). Recorded from l.19c.; derivation unclear.

Liverpool Irish (n.): Liverpudlian descendants of Irish emigrants. 'Liverpool Irish – that's not *real* Irish, I know. Some Liverpool Irish all right!' (O'Mara 1934: 249). 'The Liverpool Irish constitute the major ethnic group in the dockside area' (Mays 1954: 40). 'Private Higgins A.H. of the Liverpool Irish' (Brown 1989: 78). 'His ancestors were all Liverpool Irish' (Bryan 2003 [1940s–50s]: 88). 'Liverpool Irish to the core' (Maddox 2008 [1930s–40s]: 173). *NR; though a significant proportion of Liverpool's population is of Irish descent, it is probable that the phrase 'the *Liverpool Irish*' originated as the name of a volunteer corps of the British Army raised in 1860.

Liverpool kiss (n.): headbutt; blow to the face. 'A Liverpool kiss is a kick in the chin' (Ferguson 1944: 106). Recorded from m.20c.; used by sailors, probably originally an Americanism; displaced by *Kirkby kiss*.

Liverpool Pals (n.): First World War soldiers recruited from the city. '*Pals, the*: The familiar name of the four "City" (Service) Battalions of the Liverpool and Manchester Regiments, raised in 1914' (Fraser and Gibbons 1925: 196). The *Liverpool Pals* were effectively the first of the Pals battalions raised in response to Lord Kitchener's call for volunteers in 1914.

Liverpool pantile (n.): very hard seafarer's biscuit. '*Pantiles.* Hard Tack, or ship's biscuits, particularly those carried by Liverpool ships' (Bowen 1929: 100). 'Anything you want from a Liverpool pantile to a bower anchor' (Hall 2004 [1939]: 11). Recorded from l.19c.; probably from 'pantile', 'roofing tile', a reference to the shape and hardness of the biscuit.

Liverpool Rules (n.): short for the rules of 'The Liverpool Underwriters' Registry for Iron Vessels'. 'The Liverpool Rules require the rivet points to be perfectly fair with the surface of the plating' (Reed 1869: 197). *NR; recorded from m.19c.; the exact rules for the building of ships were set either by Lloyd's of London or the underwriters of the Liverpool Exchange.

Liverpool sailor's walk (n.): Recorded as a 'splay-footed walk, with fallen arches: M[erchant] N[avy]: 1960s' (Beale (1984) *s.v. Liverpool sailor's walk*), though it was coined earlier.

Liverpool sound (n.): an alternative to *Mersey Beat*. 'It's been boys, boys, boys from Merseyside who have dominated pop music since the "Liverpool sound" started to carry all before it towards the end of last year' (Anon. 1963a: 10). 'The distinctive Liverpool sound has spread across the world in the past five decades' (Anon. 2007: 9). Recorded from 1960s; not commonly used in Liverpool.

Liverpool tailor (n.): itinerant worker. 'Liverpool Tailor. A tramping work-man, one who sits with his coat and hat on, ready for the road' (Farmer 1905:

270). Recorded from l.19c.; derivation unknown.

Liverpool technique (n.): a method of anaesthesia. 'The contribution made by group of anaesthetists in Liverpool to the development of the use of relaxant drugs and the development of a safe anaesthetic regime which could be used with them – the so-called "Liverpool Technique"' (Utting 1992: 551) *NR; recorded from l.20c.

Liverpool virus (n.): rat and mouse exterminant. '*Liverpool virus*. A bacillus used for the destruction of rats on board ship, in warehouses, and so on' (de Kerchove 1948: 422). *NR; recorded from e.20c.

Liverpool weather (n.): cold, windy, unpleasant weather. 'Merchants will see from this that Liverpool weather must not be taken as a standard by which to judge of the weather generally' (*Liverpool Mercury* 1848: 2). 'There was a sou'wester brewin' when we made the mouth o' the Mersey, a bitter cold morn wi' a grey-green sea an' a grey-green sky – Liverpool weather, as they say' (Kipling 1898: 97). '*Liverpool Weather*. In the Merchant Service, a special brand of dirty weather' (Beale 1984: 691). Recorded from e.19c.; derivation is clear.

Liverpoolese (n.): the language of Liverpool. 'A one-act play of Liverpool working-class life written, largely in Liverpoolese' (Shaw 1952: prefatory note). 'It seems fairly certain that Liverpoolese is of comparatively recent origin' (Whittington-Egan 1955a: 216). 'Some "Scouser" in the *Echo* office thought up the term Liverpoolese' (Anon. 1957b: 4). 'Liverpoolese will never die as long as the port has dockers' (Shaw 1959c: 6). 'Liverpoolese, Yes, But I Don't Like "Scouse"' (Shaw 1962c: 8). 'Even spacemen have trouble with Liverpoolese' (Frank 1966: 8). *NR; recorded from m.20c.; contemporaneous with the 'discovery' of *Scouse*[3].

Liverpoolism (n.): Liverpool word or pronunciation. 'He says that "b" is substituted for "m" but this is not only a Liverpoolism' (Carter 1955: 4). *NR; derivation is clear.

Liverpuddler (n.): a person from Liverpool. 'May I suggest that "Liverpudlian" or "Liverpuddler" is the correct and appropriate designation for an inhabitant of Liverpool?' (Gribble 1957: 4). *NR; see *Liverpudlian*.

Liverpudlian (adj.): from or of Liverpool. 'The recent performances of the French company have proved beyond the bounds of Liverpudlian comprehension' (Anon. 1854: 11). 'A student adds "scowing" as a Liverpudlian expression' (Opie and Opie 1959: 372). Recorded from e.19c., the dominant adjective pertaining to Liverpool; derivation is clear.

Liverpudlian[1] *(n.)*: a person from Liverpool. 'Terrible tidings for the Dicky Sams, alias Liverpudlians' (Anon. 1833a). 'A Liverpudlian' (pseud.) (Anon. 1845: 7). 'I like the Manchester people, of whom I have been seeing a little, better than the Liverpudlians' (Clough 1888: 143). 'A man who calls a pool a puddle, must have a mind of mix and muddle. Your city is called LiverPOOL. Your monthly review is The "Liverpolitan". Don't be a Liverpudlian – get your Jan. "LIVERPOLITAN" today' (Anon.

1939d: 1). '"Over the water", as every Liverpudlian referred to the Cheshire shore' (Ash 1954: 76). 'They were black Liverpudlians with no country to call their own' (Murari 1975: 30). '"Liverpudlian" plays self-mockingly on the idea of "pool"' (Redfern 1984: 1). 'Liverpudlians are known all over the world' (Dudgeon 2010: 203). Recorded from e.19c., the dominant term for people from Liverpool; derivation is clear.

Liverpudlian[2] *(n.)*: the language of Liverpool. 'The polished Liverpudlian of manager Smith' (Ash 1954: 164). Recorded from m.20c.; not commonly used in Liverpool, except jokingly.

Liverpudlian[3] *(n.)*: supporter of Liverpool F.C. 'Shall I have the customary challenge about my leanings to Liverpool from certain Evertonians, and to Everton from certain Liverpudlians?' (Anon. 1914b: 7). 'This day which all Liverpudlians will want to forget' (Anon. 1945d: 3). 'I'm a Liverpudlian, well he's an Evertonian' (Parker 1974: 197). 'My father was an Evertonian and his brother was a Liverpudlian' (Dudgeon 2010: 121). *NR; recorded from m.20c.; derivation is clear.

Liverpudlian English (n.): the language of Liverpool. 'Even Bridge Wright was addressed in a mingling of Elizabethan and Victorian Liverpudlian English' (Tirebuck 1891: 290). *NR; apparently the first recorded reference to the language of Liverpool as a distinct form.

Liverpudlianese (n.): the language of Liverpool. 'Every county has its dialect and I have just received my first lesson in Liverpudlianese' (Anon. 1958: 3). *NR; recorded from m.20c.; not commonly used in Liverpool.

Liverpudlianism (n.): a word or phrase found in Liverpool. 'Liverpudlianisms' (Collinson 1927: 133). 'Liverpudlianisms directed at miserly folk' (Minard 1972: 32). *NR; in *Contemporary English*, Collinson, the Professor of German at Liverpool University, recorded 'a few peculiarities with which I have become acquainted since taking up residence in Liverpool in 1913'; *Liverpudlianisms* appears in the index to the work.

Living jockey-bar (phr.): co-habiting in common law marriage. 'I'm livin tally, I'm livin jockey-bar, I'm livin over de brush. *I am living in sin*' (Shaw et al. 1966: 27). *NR; recorded from e.20c.; derivation unclear; 'jockey-bar' is northern dialectal, 'the flat bar at the top of a grate (used for boiling)'.

Living over the brush (phr.): co-habiting in common law marriage. 'I'm livin tally, I'm livin jockey-bar, I'm livin over de brush. *I am living in sin*' (Shaw et al. 1966: 27). 'Over the brush – Unmarried couple living together' (Callaghan 2011 [1910s–30s]: viii). *NR; recorded from l.18c.; probably a variant of 'to marry over the broomstick'; jumping over a broomstick together was part of the Romani marriage ceremony.

Living tally (phr.): co-habiting in common law marriage. 'I'm livin tally, I'm livin jockey-bar, I'm livin over de brush. *I am living in sin*' (Shaw et al. 1966: 27). 'You're goin' t' live tally with him?' (Russell 1996 [1975]: 68). 'Common law wife/husband Recent euphemism for Livin' tally' (Spiegl 1989: 22). *NR;

'tally wife', 'the woman with whom a man cohabits', is recorded from 18c.; possibly from 17c. 'tally', 'two corresponding parts that fit together'.

Lobbo (n.): confusion. 'It wuz a proper lobbo. *The situation was confused*' (Shaw et al. 1966: 74). 'We turn this place over good style – in there, lobbo!' (McClure 1980: 352). *NR; derivation unknown.

Lobscouse (n.): scouse. 'They called it "lob scouse" – you know, lob everything in the pan' (Dudgeon 2010: 173). Recorded from e.18c.; see *scouse*.

Locust beans/Locusts (n.): type of bean, popular with children. 'They "sag schule" … to dodge bobbies, and chew locust beans (or, at Garston, bananas)' (Shaw 1959b: 6). '*Locust beans*: Carob beans used in the manufacture of cattle-food. Considered a delicacy by children' (Lane 1966: 62). 'Sacks of brown sugar, nuts, and locust beans' (Unwin 1984 [1920s–30s]: 80). 'Sacks of dried locusts, dried wrinkled beans, incredibly sweet' (Callaghan 2011 [1910s–30s]: 27). Recorded from l.16c.; generally literary or biblical; the locust bean is the fruit of the Carob tree.

Lodge (n.): Orange Lodge. 'Mr. Postlethwaite beat the big drum for the local lodge band' (Hanley 1935: 56). 'She raises money for the Lodge with these activities' (Kerr 1958: 106). 'I had enjoyed my first encounter with the Lodge' (Maddox 2008: 37). Recorded from e.19c.; an abbreviation of *Orange Lodge*.

Long one (n.): one thousand. '£1000 A Grand, a Long One' (Minard 1972: 87). Recorded from m.20c.; 'long' has

meant 'large amount' in relation to money from 18c.

Longees (n.): long trousers. 'Where did you get the longees?' (Robinson 1986 [1920s–30s]: 103). 'Tuck the legs of your longies (long trousers) down them' (Elliott 2006 [1940s–70s]: 60). 'I stood at our wicket gate, one "longy" shewing tentatively to the outside world' (Callaghan 2011 [1910s–30s]: 15). *NR; recorded from e.20c.; derivation is clear.

Looking for Harry Freemans (phr.): looking for something for nothing; scrounging. 'I wuz lookin fer some Arry Freeman's I was looking for something for nothing' (Shaw 1966: 58). 'Harry Freeman's. Something which is stolen or "removed" from the docks. Liverpool' (Howarth 1985: n.p.). 'Lookin fer Arry Freemans. Looking for something for nothing, or for left-overs' (Spiegl 2000b: 100). Recorded from e.20c.; Forces' usage; an adaptation of 'drinking at Freeman's Quay'; in the m.19c. free drinks were provided to porters at this quay, situated near London Bridge.

Loony (n.): idiot, madperson, eccentric; mad, foolish. 'Wrong in his noddle, and was above a bit luny' (Hocking 1966 [1879]: 39). 'What was the matter with me – was I goin' loony?' (O'Mara 1934: 287). 'Nancified, grinning looney' (Cross 1951: 121). 'Half the time I think you're a looney!' (Russell 1996 [1976]: 211). 'Don't forget, these are loons aren't they?' (McClure 1980: 352). 'Pelting downstairs like a loony' (Bainbridge 1989: 99). 'He's a loony, Elvis, but that's all part of his appeal' (Sampson

1998: 6). Recorded from l.19c.; an abbreviation of 'lunatic' (person affected mentally by the different phases of the moon).

Loopy (adj.): crazy, cracked. 'What was wrong with you this morning, Furey? I thought you'd gone a bit loopy' (Hanley 2009 [1936]: 93). 'Like that loopy moke we saw at the fight last night?' (Cross 1951: 162). 'Down at the Lanny these days, you get fellas, a bit loopy perhaps, the're gates is down, but givin' the pay out' (Shaw 1957a: 15). Recorded from e.20c.; Forces' usage; derivation unclear.

Loosie (n.): cigarette sold singly. 'A coupla loosies. *Two loose cigarettes*' (Shaw et al. 1966: 70). 'Even when she was smoking loosies and that' (Sampson 2001: 206). Recorded from m.20c.; it used to be possible to buy single ('loose') cigarettes.

Loot, the (n.): the period of the Liverpool Police Strike 1919. 'Before the War they used to wear a clog' an boot/Now they're wearing all the fancy things from The Loot … that brief lawless period was forever referred to as "The Loot"' (Callaghan 2011 [1910s–30s]: 9). *NR; as part of a national dispute with the Government, the Liverpool Police Force took strike action in August 1919 and serious disorder ensued.

Lord Muck (n.): pompous person; undeservedly important; sometimes over-fussy or fastidious in dress. 'Lord Muck, a dressy person' (Shaw 1958d: 17). '*Lord Muck of Muck Hall*, a bombastic person; a swollen-headed man who likes to assert his authority' (Lane 1966: 33). 'Y' think y' the King of the Castle, Lord and Lady Muck, lookin' down on the rest of us' (Bleasdale 1977: 98). Recorded from l.19c.; the original, Australian, sense was someone 'unjustifiably important or esteemed'; an alternative was 'The Lord Mayor of Cork'.

Love (n.): familiar term of address. 'He never called her Jinnie. He called her "love"' (Hanley 2009 [1940]: 191). 'Are yer sure yer alright, luv?' (Ash 1954: 223). 'The lady who did not fancy being hailed as "luv" by the Manchester waitress would hardly be pleased if she spent a few days at our end of the canal' (Shaw 1963e: 4). 'Waitresses, conductresses, the flower ladies and barrow girls address customers of both sexes as "luv"' (Channon 1970: 104). 'Come on, luv' (McClure 1980: 146). 'Excuse me luv' (Simpson 1995: 22). 'How far have you got to go, luv' (Kelly 2006 [1930s–40s]: 55). Recorded from e.20c.; often used to complete strangers, and can range from affection to condescension; an extension (through weakening) of an older sense involving intimacy.

Lowie/lowey (n.): low feeling; depression. 'I always get a little bit of a lowie on when that happens, but today more than ever I pure do not want to be left on my tod' (Sampson 2001: 195). 'All of it an insight into the darkness of men. Put me in a bit of a lowey' (Griffiths 2002: 238). Recorded from l.20c.; from 'low mood, low spirits'.

Lug/lughole (n.): ear. 'He gives you a clew on the lug' (Hanley 1932: 32). 'Cold enough to freeze your lugs off' (Ash 1954: 46). 'A goalong in the lug' (Shaw 1957a: 15). 'Is lugole. *His ear*' (Shaw et al. 1966: 20). 'Pin yer lugholes back an lissen' (Jacques 1975: n.p.). 'Another clout – on the lughole this time' (Brown 1989: 11). '*Me lugholes* My ears' (Spiegl 2000b: 66). Recorded from e.16c.; derivation unknown.

Lugger (n.): eavesdropper. 'Lugger. An eavesdropper. Liverpool' (Howarth 1985: n.p.). *NR; see *lug*.

Lumber/in lumber (n., phr.): trouble, a fight; in trouble. '*A Fight*. A Scrap, a Lumber, a Go' (Minard 1972: 89). 'When the kids got "in lumber"' (Parker 1974: 196). 'There are thieves who have been in lumber before' (McClure 1980: 97). 'Watch it or youse is in dead lumber' (Brown 1989: 14). 'Might be one of the binlids in lumber' (Sampson 2002: 241). 'Only one of us'll gerr in lumber' (Fagan 2007 [1950s]: 136). Recorded from e.19c.; probably a corruption of 17c. 'Lombard', a money-lender or pawnbroker (hence *in lumber*, 'in debt, trouble').

Lunch (n.): mid-morning snack. 'The word "lunch" does not mean the meal at midday, but is applied to a packet of sandwiches prepared at home to be consumed round about mid-morning' (Farrell 1950b: 4). Recorded from e.20c.; from 17c. sense of 'luncheon',

'a snack taken between breakfast and mid-day dinner'.

Lurk/lerk (n.): job, way of making money. '*What's yer lerk?*: what do you do to make money?' (Lane 1966: 63). Recorded from e.20c.; an Australian coinage, with the sense 'scheme, plan'; an extension of e.19c. 'lurk', 'fraud', possibly from 'lurk', 'move furtively'.

Lush (n.): drink; a drunk. '*Lush* (drink)' (Shaw 1952: n.p.). '*Lush*, one of our words for drink, surely goes back in print to Mayhew, over a century ago' (Shaw 1962: 9). 'Bevvy; lush. *Drink*' (Shaw et al. 1966: 67). 'Lush. A drunk. Liverpool' (Howarth 1985: n.p.). Recorded from l.18c.; originally 'strong beer' and extended by e.19c. to mean 'drunk, intoxicated'; derivation unknown.

Lushed/lushed up (adj.): drunk. 'De quare feller in de green gansey got lushed-up en wen in de cokes fer a wet-neller' (Egan 1955: 6). 'It's a long time since I wus lushed up' (Shaw 1957a: 7). 'One may get "lushed up" by too much' (Armstrong 1966: 6). 'LUSHED Drunk. Now dated' (Spiegl 1989: 52). '"Kaylied" and "lushed as the landlord's cat" are terms for drunkenness' (Lees 2013: 137). See *lush*.

M

Ma (n.): mother. 'There's some fancy gents to see you, Ma' (Hall 2004 [1939]: 232). 'If yer wanna win go wid yer ma' (Jacques 1973: n.p.). 'Is it summat yer ma puts in yer tea?' (Sinclair 1999: 9). 'Me ma said' (Sanders and Sanders 2009 [1960s]: 32). Recorded from e.19c.; an abbreviation of 'mam'.

Mac (n.): familiar term of address. 'If, on one day, you are cordially hailed as "mate", "sis" (sister), "la" (lad), "Mac" (favoured by bus conductors), "chuck", "wack" or even simply "yew" (plural "youse") do not be annoyed' (Shaw 1963e: 4). 'Fuck you mack, out of my way' (Parker 1974: 104). Recorded from e.20c.; an Americanism; an extension of Gaelic 'mac', 'son'.

Maccyowler (n.): a cat; by extension, a fur coat. 'One nudged the other, pointed to my parent's fur coat, and defined the coat as "maccyowler"' (Wozyer 1950: 2). '"Maccyowler" means a "backyard moggy" – in other refined expressions "a cat"' (Wright 1951: 4). 'Maccyowler. A fur coat. Liverpool' (Howarth 1985: n.p.). *NR; from *moggy* and *yowler*.

Made up (adj.): very pleased, happy. '"He was made up" (satisfied)' (Shaw 1964a: 12). '*Made-up*: Happy, pleased' (Lane 1966: 65). 'Tony was made up with himself for about a week' (Bleasdale 1975: 28). 'Made up ... Pleased, delighted' (Brown 1989: 5). 'I was made up myself that *they* was so made up' (Sampson 2002: 233). 'We were made up to get cases all the same size'

(Burnett 2011: 54). Recorded from m.20c.; derivation unclear but probably from 16c. sense of 'made', 'assured of happiness' (compare 'made man'); the phrase appears in Irish English and Liverpool English at the same time.

Maggie Ann (n.): margarine. 'A scanty meal of bread, "Maggie Ann" and tea' (Whittaker 1934: 114). 'Many people who can't understand Merseyside slang would not know that Maggie Ann means margarine' (Smith 1955: 5). 'Maggy Ann – margarine' (Williams 1971: 179). 'Maggie-Ann. Margarine. Liverpool' (Howarth 1985: n.p.). *NR; derivation is clear.

Maggie May (n.): folksong. 'The famous Liverpool forebitter *Maggie May*' (Hughill 1967: 96). 'Well gather round you people, while I tell of Maggie May' (Jacques 1977: n.p.). '"Maggie May", about a Liverpool prostitute who robs a sailor' (Dudgeon 2010: 251). Recorded from m.19c., but popularised from the late 1950s; recorded among others by Stan Kelly, The Spinners and The Beatles.

Make up man (n.): supplementary member of a team. 'Make up man. A man to make up required number in another part of the docks. Liverpool Maritime Museum' (Howarth 1985: n.p.). 'Make up – A man sent to a gang to replace a man who is absent' (Burnett 2011: 14). *NR; the derivation is clear.

Make your name Walker (phr.): get out! 'They are asked to leave. "Make your name Walker"' (Shaw 1957a: 22). 'Make yer name Walker, wack. *Please go away*' (Shaw et al. 1966: 18). Recorded as a 'Merseyside catch phrase dating from the early 1920s' (Beale (1985) *s.v. make yer name Walker*); a play on 'walk'.

Malapudlianism (n.): Liverpool idiom/ malapropism. 'Have you heard any good Malapudlianisms lately? I claim that, during a short walk in Liverpool, you can hear more of those twisted remarks called "bulls" – it must be the Irish in us – or those misused words called malapropisms, than anywhere in the U.K.' (Shaw 1958c: 6). 'They're all there at the docks, the richest breeding ground for Malapudlianisms' (Shaw 1960b: 5). 'What Frank Shaw has called "the malapudlianisms"' (Channon 1970: 104). *NR; a creative use of language 'caused by a rush of Scouse to the head' (Shaw 1966b: 8), which had 'a sort of wild sense of its own', produced by 'the exuberant Liverpudlian who loves words, but [who], as often happens … is not as familiar with what he loves as he might be' (Shaw 1960b: 5). Examples included: 'alive with dead rats'; '99 times out of 10' 'if the Lord spares me I'll be buried at Ford Cemetery'; 'I hate the sight of his voice'; 'the horns of a diploma'; 'to run Bismarck'; 'too small to perform me absolutions'; 'a state of kiosk' (Shaw 1958c: 6).

Mam (n.): mum. 'How's yer dad an' yer mam?' (Hanley 1935: 508). 'But me mam …' (Cross 1951: 178). '*Whur's me Mam?* (Lane 1966: 66). 'Can I stay off again, Mam?' (Bleasdale 1975: 68). 'The little judies introduce us to their mam' (Brown 1989: 67). 'Ow's yer mam?' (Sinclair 1999 [1930s–e.40s]: 14). 'Asked my Mam' (Elliott 2006 [1940s–70s]: 60). Recorded from l.16c. (around the same time as 'mum'); from Latin 'mamma', 'mother, nurse, breast'.

Manc (n.): person from Manchester; a Manchester United fan. 'Manc. A Mancunian (worse, probably a Manchester United supporter)' (Spiegl 1989: 52). 'He was a clever cunt, this Manc' (Sampson 2001: 48). 'A barmaid I know, a Manc girl called Sadie' (Griffiths 2002: 170). Recorded from l.20c.; derivation is clear.

Mardy (adj.): spoilt; petulant, whining. 'Oh, you're mardy … sulking now' (Owen 1961: 142). 'She's got a rill mardy kid' (Lane 1966: 65). 'He never had such a temper … He's grown mardy' (Bainbridge 1979: 96). 'I've 'eard enough, mardy arse' (Sinclair 1999 [1930s–e.40s]: 52). Recorded from l.19c.; see *marred*.

Mark someone's card (v.): to warn, advise. 'Maahrk iz caahrd: *Enlighten him*' (Minard 1972: 32). 'She's wanting me to mark Moby's card over the way he's going' (Sampson 2002: 224). Recorded from m.20c.; from the practice of tipping at horse-racing by marking the race card with supposed winners.

Marmalise (v.): to beat comprehensively, destroy, punish, chastise. 'Of like force are the verbs "to paralyse", "to marmalise", and (a macabre touch) "to stiffen"' (Farrell 1950b: 4). 'To marmalise … a fearsome admixing of murder and paralyse' (Whittington-Egan 1955a: 6). 'I'll marmalise yer. *I will chastise you severely*' (Shaw et al. 1966: 73). 'I'll marmalise yer' (Graham 1988: 37). 'Go out an marmalise someone' (Simpson 1995: 21). 'Doddy the Marmaliser' (Moloney 2001: 66). 'Marmalize – beat' (Callaghan 2011 [1910s–30s]: viii). Recorded from m.20c.; popularised by the Liverpool comedian Ken Dodd, a combination of 'murder' and 'paralyse'.

Marred/mardy (adj.): spoilt, over-indulged. 'Yer a marred kid. *You are a spoilt child*' (Shaw et al. 1966: 45). '*Mardy*: petulant, whining' (Lane 1966: 65). Recorded from l.18c.; now classed as regional and dialectal; from 'to mar', 'to spoil (a child) by indulgence'.

Marshy Musketeers (n.): Salvation Army. '*Marshy Musketeers, The*': Salvation Army' (Lane 1966: 65). *NR; the Salvation Army Citadel in the north end of the city stood on Marsh Lane.

Martin 'Enries (n.): cheap suits or second-hand clothes. 'Cheap suits were Martin 'Enries. (From the peculiar cut introduced by a gentleman of that name, for I believe, workhouse suits)' (Shaw 1959a: 33). 'Dem's Martin Enries. *These are cheap clothes*' (Shaw et al. 1966: 36). 'Martin-Enries. Cheap suits. Liverpool' (Howarth 1985: n.p.). Recorded from l.19c.; from the name of a clothes manufacturer; charity clothes – for the poor, orphans, and so on – were cut distinctively to discourage pawning.

Mary Ann (n.): derogatory term for a man who does house work. 'Now a "Peggy", to the uninitiated, is the "Mary Ann", or "slavey"' (Bower 2015 [1936]: 161). 'The grocer wus a proper Mary Ann did all the werk for he's wife' (Shaw 1957a: 18). 'Mary-Ann. Someone who is behaving like an old woman'

(Howarth 1985: n.p.). Recorded from l.19c.; from 'Mary', a generic colonial term for woman, but particularly a female servant. The phrase contains a bundle of derogatory attitudes in its implicit link between housework, 'effeminacy' and masculinity.

Mary Ellen (n.): old, working-class woman; sometimes a market trader. 'If you are in Liverpool, stroll in the evening up the Scotland Road, and talk to the fascinating people you meet there, such as the "Mary Ellens" the picturesque women who wear shawls over their heads, carry babies in their arms, work in the markets all day, and always have a good "tip" for to-morrow's race' (Lynd 1947: 47). 'Me ould girl, a real Murry Ellen' (Shaw 1957a: 7). 'Mury Helen (Mary Ellen): a working-class Liverpool woman, usually elderly and of scruffy appearance. Once known as a *shawlie* from the Irish habit of wearing a shawl' (Lane 1966: 72). 'I've got enough to think about without you actin' like a Mary Ellen' (Bleasdale 1975: 165). '"Mary Ellen", the Liverpool name for those beshawled old women who were the matriarchs of the slums' (Melly 1984 [1930s–40s]: 78). '*A shawlie, a Mury Ellen* A Liverpool (Irish) woman' (Spiegl 2000b: 57). 'Women referred to contemptuously as handcart women, or Mary Ellens' (Callaghan 2011 [1920s–30s]: 46). Recorded from e.20c.; probably a nickname derived from Mary Ellen Grant, the "Connaught Nigger", a notorious Edwardian moneylender, born of an Irish mother and a West African father.

Match (the) (n.): football game, usually featuring Liverpool or Everton. 'He liked a football match, he liked a good pantomime, and he liked a good music-hall show' (Hanley 2009 [1936]: 414). 'They bought it at half-time at the match' (Hignett 1966: 45). 'When he goes to the match of a Saturday' (Bleasdale 1975: 28). 'Seen him around, at the match' (Sampson 2002: 101). 'I had now started "going to the match" on Saturdays' (Elliott 2006 [1940s–70s]: 161). Recorded from m.20c.; 'match', 'sporting contest', dates from e.16c., but in Liverpool it often has the very specific sense of a game featuring one of the city's two Premier League teams.

Matchie (n.): worker at matchworks. '*Matchie*: An employee of Bryant & May's matchworks' (Lane 1966: 66). *NR; Bryant and May had two factories in the north and south ends of Liverpool, both of which were also known as 'the matchy'.

Mate (n.): familiar term of address. 'Well, maties … let's splice the mainbrace' (Melville 1849: 386). 'Several voices in the crowd called out, "tell us what you know mate"' (Haigh 1907: 442). 'Any chance of this boat sailing, mate?' (Hanley 1935: 239). 'The "slaves" don't seem to be doing so badly, mate' (Liddell 1960: 12). 'There are many cordial terms of address such as mate, sis for sister, la for lad; then chuck, wacker (abbreviated to wack) or just yew or youse' (Armstrong 1966: 4). 'It wasn't me, mate, it wuz 'im' (Spiegl 1989: 44). 'Not bad, mate, yeh!' (Griffiths 2002: 6). Recorded from 15c.; the term has a particular resonance in Liverpool,

probably from the historical nautical connotation.

Maternity Home (n.): Section of naval headquarters in Liver Buildings during Second World War. Glossed as 'the war-time nickname for the Liverpool Naval Base, whose headquarters were in the Liver Buildings' (Partridge et al. 1948: xx); from the 'storks' (Liver Birds).

Me (adj.): my. 'She's me own child' (Hall 2004 [1939]: 233). 'Why, I haven't me bag' (Hanley 2009 [1950]: 216). 'When me mother beats us I run out on the street' (Kerr 1958: 40). 'is me shirt ironed? (Russell 1996 [1975]: 6). 'I'll get me mam to wash them' (Robinson 1986 [1920s–30s]: 135). 'He doesn't like me mates' (McGovern 1995: 8). 'I can't take me eyes off her' (Griffiths 2002: 5). "Me Dad'll be waiting' (Callaghan 2011 [1910s–30s]: 106). Recorded from 13c.; common in Midland and Northern dialects, and Welsh, Irish and Scottish English.

Me lad/Meladdo/miladdo (n.): a general, mildly negative form of 'my lad'. 'Not so fast, young feller me lad' (Hanley 2009 [1936]: 552). 'He'll after watch meladdo doesn't ger the chance to lay he's hooks on um' (Shaw 1957a: 7). 'Meladdo. *An unnamed, but known, person*' (Shaw et al. 1966: 27). 'We've got yez me laddo' (Jacques 1975: n.p.). 'Ey yew! Meladdo. Excuse me! (when speaking to a man not known to the speaker' (Spiegl 2000: 46). 'Here you are, young fella me lad' (Kelly 2006 [1930s–40s]: 50). *NR; a gently mocking phrase, though often with a sense close to 'the other fella'.

Measure your length in the river (phr.): commit suicide. 'You look as though you were going to measure your length in the river' (Hanley 2009 [1936]: 83). *NR in this sense; an extension of 14c. 'to measure one's length', 'to fall, lie prostrate'.

Meff (n.): term of abuse. 'Poelly smacked this grock, big fucken meff, really twatted him but would the cunt go down' (Sampson 1998: 83). 'Yer've just caught sight of yerself in the wing mirror so the word is "meff"' (Griffiths 2003: 151). *NR; derivation unknown.

Meg (n.): halfpenny. '"Meg", halfpenny' (Jones 1935: 5). 'Meg. Halfpenny' (Price: 1950: 4). '"Fudge" for a farthing, "meg" for a half-penny and "win" for a penny are no longer current coin' (Whittington-Egan 1955a: 6). 'Og; meg. *One halfpenny*. Two mcg. *One penny*' (Shaw et al. 1966: 33). '½d. A Meg' (Minard 1972: 85). 'I'm noreevin in the make-specs' (Simpson 1995: 23). 'Megs – Halfpennies' (Callaghan 2011 [1910s–30s]: ix). Recorded from e.19c.; a variant of e.19c. 'magg'/'mag', from 16c. 'make'; derivation unknown.

Mersey Beat (n.): Liverpool music from the late 1950s and 60s. 'The Beatles, undoubted monarchs of the Mersey Beat scene' (*Meet the Beatles* 1962: LP cover). 'A couple of rocker dockers reading from the *Merseybeat*' (Hignett 1966: 149). 'Where the legendary *This is Mersey Beat* albums were recorded' (Lees 2013: 168). *Mersey Beat* was originally the name of a Liverpool music paper; it covered the host of musicians who were active in Liverpool at the time and spanned the complexity and range of the music scene. By contrast, *Mersey Beat*, as a

term to reference the music produced in the city, is identified primarily, but reductively, with 'The Beatles'.

Mersey Funnel (n.): Liverpool's Catholic Cathedral. '*Mersey Funnel* ... A general nickname for the new Roman Catholic cathedral, Liverpool, which is funnel, or tent-shaped. Also *Paddy's Wigwam*' (Lane 1966: 66–7). 'Our Paddy's Wigwam, our Mersey Funnel' (Grant 2002: 240). *NR; the Metropolitan Cathedral of Christ the King was consecrated 14th May 1967; its unusual shape, and the echoic rhyme with 'Mersey Tunnel', explains the 'funnel' reference.

Merseyside[1] (n.): a geographic, political and cultural designation for the area on both sides of the Mersey. 'Dr. McNeile, who is considered by a considerable part of Liverpool as wanting only an apron and a pound of buttons to accredit him as the true Bishop of Merseyside' (Anon. 1865: 3). 'Liverpool revived the old practice on a scale worthy of the Mersey-side city' (Anon. 1886: 7). 'Many of the Mersey-side city's public-houses are suggestive of "Saloon's" in the Wild West' (Anon. 1898: 3). 'A conference of the Merseyside authorities should consider the extension of such a tunnel from Liverpool to the Cheshire side of the Mersey' (Anon. 1914a: 4). 'A thrilling Merseyside street chase' (Anon. 1929b: 4). *Bombers over Merseyside* (1943a: title). *A Scientific Survey of Merseyside* (Smith 1953: title). 'At present it is not in vogue to use the word "scouse" on Merseyside' (Jacques 1973: n.p.). Recorded from m.19c.; originally used outside Liverpool to refer to the city;

it lacked precision even in texts such as Smith's *Scientific Survey* (1953), the first comprehensive treatment of the area. Since 1972, *Merseyside* has been used to refer to a specific bureaucratic and political entity, brought into being by the Local Government Act of that year.

Merseyside[2] *(n.)*: relating to or characteristic of Merseyside. 'The findings were officially issued yesterday of the Electricity Commissioners who recently held an inquiry in Liverpool into the Merseyside electricity scheme' (Anon. 1921: 7). 'Many a time he has heard one seaman remark to a Merseyside man: "Oh, you come from the place of scouse"' ('Postman' 1942c: 2). 'Merseyside speech is as foreign to Lancashire as the Liffeyside accent is to the Ireland around, and the two are almost the same' (Phelan 1948: 201). 'His thick, adenoidal Merseyside speech' (Ash 1954: 220). 'Pop records, which may be genuine transatlantic, mid-Atlantic, Merseyside, Midland (but probably not RP)' (Strang 1970: 19). See *Merseyside*[1].

Merseyside[3] *(n.)*: the language of Merseyside. 'The translation of African Blues or American western idioms (in "Baby, it's you" ...) into tough, sensitive Merseyside' (Anon. 1963c: 4). 'The Beatles spoke Merseyside and sang Motown' (Critchfield 1990: 323). Recorded from m.20c.; glossed as 'the variety of English spoken on Merseyside, esp. in Liverpool; the accent associated with this variety of English' (*OED s.v. Merseyside* n.); not used in this sense in Liverpool. See *Merseyside*[1].

Merseysider (n.): native or inhabitant of Merseyside. 'It was spectacles of destruction ... that steeled the Merseysiders' resolution to defeat the Luftwaffe's brazen challenge' (Anon. 1943: 25). 'A Scouser is a Merseysider who conducts his ordinary, everyday conversations in Scouse' (Lane 1966: foreword). '[He] laughs at the rest of the world who has never known the magic of being a ... Merseysider' (Anon. 1973: 16). Recorded from e.20c.; see *Merseyside*[1].

Mess (v.): to joke, tease. 'OK, Fatch, I was only messin'' (Parker 1974: 48). 'Y'll bomb along, no messin'' (Bleasdale 1985: 114). 'Honest, Da, no messin'' (Griffiths 2003: 74). Recorded from l.20c.; an extension of m.19c. 'mess', 'to spend time in a non-serious way'.

Message(s) (n.): shopping; general business. 'One who ran messages on the Exchange' (Tirebuck 1903: xx). 'He had to go a message for his old lady' (Hanley 1932: 173). 'I could have taken her messages' (Duke 1939: 135). 'When we "did the messages" for our parents, shopkeepers called us "cock", which has died out' (Shaw 1963e: 4). 'We'd run messages for a sweet' (Murari 1975: 59). '"Going on the messages" to our friendly little shops' (Unwin 1984 [1920s–30s]: 30). 'Got one or two little messages to do, first' (Sampson 2002: 84) 'An unfailing duty for children was to "go messages"' (Callaghan 2011 [1910s–30s]: 17). Recorded from e.20c.; an extension of 'message', 'communication', that appeared in Irish and Scottish English; it remains in common use.

Mewksis mix (n.): version of the *Black and Tan*. '*Gis a Black 'n' tan … a Mewksis mix*' (Spiegl 2000b: 82). *NR; 'Mewks' was from 'Meux', the name of the brewer.

Mick/mickey (n.): pigeon. 'Many supposed Irish words, such as gab (garrulity), mick (pigeon), scuffer (policeman) are not Irish at all' (Oakes Hirst 1951: 4). *The Mickey-Hunters* (Baird 1957: title). 'De mickeys are letting on de roof' (Shaw et al. 1966: 23). '"Mickies" are pigeons' (Channon 1970: 102). 'We would pinch corn to feed our micks' (Elliott 2006 [1940s–70s]: 48). Recorded from m.20c.; northern dialectal; derivation unclear.

Mickey-snatcher (n.): someone who catches pigeons '*Mickey snatcher*: A person who steals municipal pigeons' (Lane 1966: 68). *NR; see *mick*.

Micky Dripping (n.): anyone; anonymous. '*Micky Drippin*': Whozit, Whatzisname?' (Lane 1966: 68). *NR; derivation unknown.

Midden (n.): communal bin; bin. 'Mrs. Golding was an elderly woman who eked out a living by picking rags and other stuff from middens (refuse cans)' (O'Mara 1934: 117). '*King o' ther midden*: A conceited person' (Lane 1966: 59). 'Our neighbourhood still had middens – ten foot brick wells for throwing muck into' (Robinson 1986 [1920s–30s]: 12). 'I would fork it from the wheelbarrow into the midden over a 3ft wall' (Kelly 2006 [1930s–40s]: 61). 'Midden – Rubbish tip' (Callaghan 2011 [1910s–30s]: viii). Recorded from l.19c. in this sense; a Scottish and northern dialectal extension of 15c. 'myding', 'dung-heap'.

Midden-man (n.): bin-man, refuse collector. 'The bin-feller is also known as, and calls himself, the *Muck-man* or *Midden-man*' (Shaw 1958d: 15). 'Midden man. Dustbin man. Liverpool' (Howarth 1985: n.p.). 'Rag and bone men, midden men and knife grinders were galoshermen' (Lees 2013: 131). See *midden*.

Mind your car? (phr.): request by children to look after a car while the owner attends an event. '*Mind yer car, mister?*: The war cry of a juvenile protection racket' (Lane 1966: 68). 'The mind-your-car kiddies round there are fucking horrible' (Sampson 2002: 246). *NR; if attending a *match*, or other public events, a car owner will be hailed by this cry as soon as s/he has parked.

Mind your own hindrance/sufferance (phr.): mind your own business. '*Mind yer own 'indrance*: Mind your own business. An alternative phrase is *mind yer own sufrance*' (Lane 1966: 68). *NR; derivation unknown.

Minesweeper (n.): someone who steals unattended food or drink. 'A minesweeper. *A stealer of food or drink*' (Shaw et al. 1966: 57). 'A minesweeper. *A person who steals drinks from the bar or table*' (Minard 1972: 48). *NR; derivation is clear.

Ming (v.): to smell badly. 'Stinkarse here! Christ, that fuckin *mings*' (Griffiths 2003: 154). Recorded from l.20c.; possibly from e.20c. Scottish 'meng', 'human excrement, bad smell'.

Minge (n.): vagina. 'See who can shave their minge' (Sampson 2001: 38). Recorded from e.20c.; from the Romani 'mindj', 'vagina'.

Minge bag (n.): term of abuse. 'It's her, the minge bag' (Bleasdale 1985: 34). 'The bloody mingebag's got no sense of humour' (Fagan 2007 [1950s]: 81). See *minge*.

Mingee (n.): policeman. '*Policemen*. Old Bill, Busys, Muskers, Mingees' (Minard 1972: 89). *NR; from the Romani 'mingri', 'policeman'.

Mingy (adj.): mean, miserly. 'I know you were never mingy' (Shaw 1957a: 21). '*Mingy-arsed bastard*, a miserly person' (Lane 1966: 68). 'Bit mingy in't she?' (Sinclair 1999 [1930s–e.40s]: 121). 'Come on now girls, don't be mingy' (Fagan 2007 [1950s]: 12). Recorded from e.20c.; possibly a combination of 'mean' and 'stingy'.

Minty (n.): scruffy, dirty; damaged. 'There weren't a minty family between us' (Sampson 2001: 26). 'That feeling of hot water on a minty an ravaged body' (Griffiths 2002: 189). Recorded from e.21c.; derivation unclear.

Miseried, to be (v.): 'To use the language of you ragamuffins, you'd all have been miseried' (Clerk 1971 [c.1900]: 22). *NR; glossed by Clerk as 'sent to reformatory school' (presumably a place of misery).

Misery-hole (n.): miserable person. 'The misery-hole sitting next to him in a fur coat' (Bleasdale 1975: 35). *NR; 'hole' in the sense of 'mouth'.

Misery moo (n.): teetotaller. '*Misery moo*: A teetotaller: a person who prefers soft drinks, especially milk' (Lane 1966: 68). *NR; presumably from the belief that a teetotaller must be miserable; see *moo*.

Mither/moider (v.): to bother, pester, annoy. 'I would advise you, Robat, not to moider your head with such stuff' (Roberts 1893: 14). 'Certainly from Ireland we received *gob, gom, mam, the queer feller, webs, lug, moider*' (Shaw 1950: 4). 'A hard-faced chil who has MOIDERED her all day long (i.e. annoyed her)' (Shaw 1959a: 39). 'He's miderin'/the life right out of me' (Hallowell 1972: n.p.). 'Mither. To be bothered, irritated, vexed' (Howarth 1985: n.p.). 'If you keep on mithering a dog' (Lees 2013: 170). Recorded from m.19c.; an extension of l.16c. 'moider', 'to confuse, bewilder; to exhaust, overcome, stupefy'; possibly from the Gaelic 'modartha', 'dark, gloomy, morose'.

Mitt/mitten (n.): hand. 'You keep your mitts off that typewriter of yours' (Jerome 1948: 55). 'Me mitts. *My hands*' (Shaw et al. 1966: 20). 'Gerrab me mitt' (Minard 1972: 62). She took one look at my dirty mitt' (Graham 1988: 139). 'A bit of time on his mitts' (Sampson 2002: 119). Recorded from l.19c.; an Americanism; an abbreviation of e.19c. 'mitten', 'hand'.

Mizzle (v.): to run away, disappear. '*Mizzle*: To flee or disappear, usually to avoid the police' (Lane 1966: 69). Recorded from l.18c.; derivation unknown.

Mizzy (n.): *The Mystery* (Wavertree playground) 'I asked where Liverpool Show was held and was informed "on the Mizzie"' (Channon 1970: 103). *NR; see *Mystery*.

Mob (n.): gang of football hooligans; gang. 'It was only about a month ago that we'd had murder with the Arsenal Mob up at Anfield' (Bleasdale 1975: 141). 'The Delly Mob from up Kirkdale way' (Brown 1989: 76). 'One of the undisputed leaders of one of the hardest mobs in football' (Sampson 1998: 68). Recorded from l.20c.; a specific extension of l.17c. 'mob', 'disorderly or riotous crowd', an abbreviation of Latin 'mōbile vulgus', 'the fickle common people'.

Moby/mobie (n.): mobile phone. 'If he just switched that fucking mobie off' (Sampson 2002: 45). 'Pass us that fuckin moby, will yer' (Griffiths 2003: 36). Recorded from l.20c.; derivation is clear.

Moby Dick (n.): statue over the door of Lewis's department store. '*Moby Dick*: A nude male statue by Jacob Epstein much admired for its generous proportions' (Lane 1966: 69). *NR in this sense; see *Dicky Lewis*.

Moey (n.): mouth. 'So I kep me moey shut an whipped out an up de jowler' (Whittington-Egan 1955a: 6). 'De moey, de gob. *The mouth*' (Shaw et al. 1966: 19). Recorded from m.19c.; from the Romany 'mui', 'mouth'.

Moggy/moggie¹ (n.): cat. 'A "backyard moggy"—in other refined expressions "a cat"' (Wright 1951: 4). 'It is Liverpool lingo for a backyard Moggy or cat!' (Whittington-Egan 1955a: 6). 'I give the moggy conny onny and put her out in the cooey' (Anon. 1961a: 4). 'Moggy for cat' (Armstrong 1966: 6). 'With breath like a dead moggy on a hot day' (Bleasdale 1975: 86). 'Tread softly, moggies' (Simpson 1990: 14). 'An occasional rat with a moggy in pursuit' (Fagan 2007 [1950s]: 72). Recorded from l.19c.; a variant of 17c. 'Maggie', 'girl or young woman', later 'untidily dressed young woman', and

by extension 'a scarecrow'; the semantic shift to 'cat' is unexplained.

Moggy/moggie² (n.): unpopular woman. 'He's given our class to one of those old moggies on the staff' (Bleasdale 1975: 93). Recorded from l.20c.; possibly a retention of the historical senses of *moggie¹*.

Mojo (n.): methylated spirits. 'Mojo. *Methylated spirits*' (Shaw et al. 1966: 67). '"Mojo" means methylated spirits' (Channon 1970: 102). '*Mojo* Methylated spirits bought for drinking or lacing legitimate drink' (Spiegl 2000b: 85). Recorded from m.20c.; probably an extension of the e.20c. Americanism 'mojo', 'any narcotic (especially morphine)'; possibly from 'mojo', 'magic powers, Voodoo, the casting of spells'.

Moke (n.): horse, donkey; often used as an insult. 'Wot's the trouble, Mick. These mokes pickin' on you?' (Cross 1951: 9). '*Moke*: Any kind of equine quadruped from a seaside donkey to a one-ton carthorse' (Lane 1966: 69). 'Moke. A donkey' (Howarth 1985: n.p.). 'Moke – Donkey' (Callaghan 2011 [1910s–30s]: viii). Recorded from e.19c.; a dialectal term for 'donkey' and 'fool'; derivation unknown.

Moke Street (n.): Lightbody Street. '*Moke Street*: Lightbody Street ... in bygone days replete with carthorses' (Lane 1966: 69). *NR; Lightbody Street, to the north of the city, was a stabling place for the horses that served the docks and the Liverpool–Leeds canal.

Money (n.): wages, pay. 'For wages, payments, fees and such like, the single word "money" often suffices' (Farrell 1950b: 4). '"Good money" means excellent pay' (Shaw 1959a: 38). 'I believe you owe me a day's money?' (Owen 1961: 151). 'It'll be easy. Y'getting' good money now' (Bleasdale 1975: 67). Recorded from l.19c.; there are various phrases involving this sense of *money*: 'pick up me money', 'good money', 'not bad money', 'poor money' and so on (Farrell 1950b: 4).

Money Street (n.): Old Ropery. '*Money Street*: A street in Liverpool properly called The Old Ropery' (Lane 1966: 70). *NR; 'Old Ropery', situated between Fennwick Street and Drury Lane, was once one of the city's most important ropewalks; *Money Street* was coined when the area became the heart of the financial quarter.

Monkey (n.): five hundred pounds. '£500. A Monkey' (Minard 1972: 87). Recorded from m.19c.; from gambling discourse; derivation unknown.

Monkey-boat (n.): small tender or tow-boat used in the docks. 'The Negroes, many of whom were firemen and trimmers on the Elder-Dempster "Monkey" boats' (O'Mara 1934: 11). 'A donkeyman from a "monkey-boat"' (Shaw 1959a: 35). 'Known throughout the port as the "monkey boats"' (Lane 1987: 37). Recorded from m.19c.; whereas other ships had cats, the Elder-Dempster boats (which worked the West Africa route) kept monkeys.

Monkey house (n.): Town Hall Council Chamber. '*Monkey 'ouse*: A monastery; also the Council Chamber' (Lane 1966: 70). *NR; presumably an allusion to the behaviour of the inmates.

Monkey rack/the rack (n.): '"Monkey Rack", the broad walk in Sefton Park' (Jones 1935: 5). 'Meanwhile readers might like to trace the origins of … The Rack' (Shaw 1950b: 4). '"The Monkey Rack" was the main path in Sefton Park, very popular with courting couples' (Unwin 1984 [1920s–30s]: 78). *NR; also known as *the rack*; derivation unknown.

Moo (n.): milk. '*Moo*: Milk. *Stiff moo*: condensed milk' (Lane 1966: 70). Recorded from m.20c.; an abbreviation of the Americanism 'moo juice'.

Mooch (v.): to cadge, scrounge. 'I was coming out of the Daulby Hall with Jackie Sanchez (having mooched the entrance fee from him)' (O'Mara 1934: 232). Recorded from m.19c.; apparently unrelated to, though contemporary with, 'mooch', 'skulk, loiter'; derivation unknown.

Moody, throw a (v.): to be sulky, bad-tempered. 'No we didn't talk about it – you threw a moody and went out there' (Bleasdale 1985: 135). Recorded from l.20c.; an extension of the adjective 'moody'.

Moosh (n.): see *mush*.

Mop (v.): to drink (alcohol). '*Mop*: To drink, especially beer' (Lane 1966: 71). Recorded from l.18c.; from 'to mop up', 'to drink up. To empty a glass or pot' (hence 'moppy' and 'mopsy', 'drunk'); derivation is clear.

Mopse (v.): to mope. 'Come on Fanny … don't sit mopsing there' (Hanley 1935: 48). Recorded from l.19c.; a variant of 'mope'.

Mopsed (adj.): drunk. 'To see her getting "mopsed" (half-drunk) was something we dreaded' (O'Mara 1934: 112). *NR; see *mop*.

Mopus (n.): farthing or halfpenny. 'They gave me a penny. I bought a large crust and dripping and with the mopus change went and paid the Rope' (Clerk 1971 [c.1900]: v). Recorded from 17c.; current to l.19c. and Beale notes its survival 'among Liverpool street arabs, well into C.20' (Beale (1984) *s.v. mopus* 2).

Mortal sin (n.): occasions of pleasure. ''Ad a good time on me 'olidays – I done a few mortal sins' (Lane 1966: 71). *NR; an ironic allusion to the doctrine of 'mortal sin' in Catholicism (sin so serious that it will condemn the sinner to Hell if unforgiven).

Mot (n.): woman, girlfriend, wife. 'Fuckin gob on yeh, Victor. That new mot, is it?' (Griffiths 2002: 109). Recorded from 18c.; originally meaning both 'wife' and 'prostitute', though 'girlfriend' or 'wife' in 19c. Irish English; possibly from 16c. cant 'mort', or Romani, 'mot', 'woman'.

Mother Superior (n.): female boss. '*Mother Superior*: Any kind of female boss' (Lane 1966: 71). *NR; ironic reference to the senior nun in a convent.

Mother's milk (n.): Guinness. '*Mother's milk*: Guinness, a popular brand of stout' (Lane 1966: 71). '*Gis a pinta Mother's Milk* Give me a pint of draught Guinness' (Spiegl 2000b: 81). *NR; ironic allusion to the creamy head at the top of the pint.

Mott (n.): female genitalia; female pubic hair. 'Girls by ours I've fingered, they've all had hairy motts' (Sampson 2002: 89). Recorded from l.19c.; possibly from *mot*.

Mousehole (n.): the (second) Mersey Tunnel. '*Mouse-'ole, Ther*: A two-lane, second "bottle-neck" road tunnel under the Mersey' (Lane 1966: 71). *NR; the 'Kingsway' tunnel between

Liverpool and Wallasey was completed in 1971.

Mrs woman (n.): general term for woman. 'Only in Liverpool have I heard men use "Mrs Woman" instead of "missus"' (Channon 1970: 104). 'Some Mrs-Woman gabbing on' (Simpson 2011 [2001]: 299). *NR; derivation is clear.

Muck cart/truck (n.): cart or truck for the collection of refuse. 'Dusty Miller's [dad], who wore specs and pushed a muck-cart around the streets' (Cross 1951: 18). '*Mook cart* (muck cart): A refuse truck' (Lane 1966: 70). 'The muck truck was a truck towed by a horse into Lime Street Station' (Clerk 1971 [c.1900]: 30). 'The corporation muck-cart' (Robinson 1986 [1920s–30s]: 12). 'You know what Thought did! He followed/a muck cart, thought it was a wedding' (Simpson 2011: 361). Recorded from e.20c.; derivation is clear.

Muck in! Yer at yer granny's (phr.): eat up, make yourself at home. 'Muck in, la, yer at yer grannie's. (Enjoy the meal, friend. *Bon appétit!*)' (Shaw 1962f: 12). '*Mook in*: Help yourself' (Lane 1966: 70). Recorded from m.20c.; from e.20c. Forces' usage, 'to muck in', 'to share rations'.

Mucker (n.): refuse collector. 'All the filth and litter between the platforms and between the rails was shoveled up by the muckers' (Clerk 1971 [c.1900]: 30). See *muckman*.

Muckman (n.): *binman*, refuse collector. 'The bin-feller is also known as, and calls himself, the *Muck-man* or *Midden-man*' (Shaw 1958d: 15). 'Der muckman; de binnie. *The refuse*

collector; the binman' (Shaw et al. 1966: 23). 'Her father was a muck-man' (Robinson 1986 [1920s–30s]: 12). Recorded from 16c.; a Scottish coinage from 13c. 'muck', 'dung, excrement'.

Muffler (n.): scarf. 'Around his head was a greasy muffler' (Haigh 1907: 312). 'A black silk muffler round each neck' (Hall 2004 [1939]: 60). 'An overcoat and a big muffler' (Hanley 2009 [1950]: 138). 'A jewdy along Brreckh Roadz withouts a muffler' (Hodkinson 1960: 11). 'You'd come to work in a muffler in dem days' (Hignett 1966: 118). 'A man with a white muffler' (Bainbridge 1989: 3). 'North End High Rip pimps, in their distinctive "bucco caps" and mufflers' (Lees 2013: 78). Recorded from 16c.; now rare, from 15c. 'muffle', 'wrap and cover'.

Mug (v.): to treat, pay for. "E wooden cod on wen I waned mugging, aldo I was skint' (Egan 1955: 216). 'Mug us dem on de house' (Moloney 1966: 23). 'I'll 'ave to ask me 'usband, if he'll mug me to the cash' (Hallowell 1972: n.p.). 'You'll find an insurance company will want to mug you' (McClure 1980: 95). 'I'll mug yer to a jar if y'like' (Graham 1988: 44). 'If yer gets mugged from yer ma, yer can split it' (Sinclair 1999 [1930s–e.40s]: 132). Recorded from m.20c.; an extension of 19c. 'mug', 'bribe with alcoholic drink; to supply with alcoholic drink; to buy a drink for', from 17c. 'mug', 'to drink alcoholic liquor; to get drunk'.

Muggen jug (n.): earthenware jug or pot. 'Neither had they heard of a muggen jug' (Price: 1950: 4). Recorded from l.19c.; a north-western dialectal extension of 17c. 'mug', 'drinking vessel'.

Mugs for rags (phr.): cry of the rag and bone man. '"Mugs for rags" is one of the cries of the TATTER who deals in rags and bones' (Shaw 1959a: 40). *NR; derivation unclear.

Mumtip (n.): warning. 'We wanted no mumtip. No matter what a yen did with us … we didn't split' (Clerk 1971 [c.1900]: 43). *NR; possibly a combination of 'mum', 'to stay silent', and 'tip', 'advice'.

Mungarly (n.): food. '"O Mungarly Mungarly", Jim would say, "foreskins and balls!"' (Clerk 1971 [c.1900]: 75). Recorded from m.19c.; from Parlyaree and retained in the use of 'Liverpool street arabs' (Beale 1984 *s.v. mungaree*); from Italian 'mangiare', 'to eat'.

Murder (n.): serious consequences; a fuss. 'If me Mam comes in … there'll be murder!' (Bryan 2003 [1940s–50s]: 124). 'There'll be murder if I don't get it' (Burnett 2011: 96). Recorded from e.19c.; see *murder (v.)*.

Murder (v.): to punish, beat someone. 'I'll murder you. Do you see what you've done. You've wakened the child' (Shimmin 1863: 3). 'Everybody was shouting "Oh, they're murdering a policeman in the cellar"' (Haigh 1907: 53). '"A good telling off" may inspire the speaker to box the culprit's ears, a process known as "murdering" or "half-murdering"' (Farrell 1950b: 4). *If yer kilts yerself I'll bloody well merder yer*: orthodox warning to a Scouser child of the wrath to come' (Lane 1966: 52). 'This jack (policeman) took me home and told me old girl, and she fuckin' murdered me' (Parker 1974: 51). Recorded from m.19c.; a weakening of 'murder', 'kill unlawfully'.

Murdered (v.): badly beaten, either physically or in sport. 'Incompetent teams are "murdered" on many a sporting Sunday afternoon' (Farrell 1950b: 4). 'MURDERED for hurt' (Shaw 1959a: 38). Recorded from m.20c.; an extension of *murder (v.)*.

Mush¹ (n.): police-station, Bridewell. 'Someone had said I was mushed' (Clerk 1971 [*c*.1900]: 43). Recorded as 'Liverpool street arabs': ca.1880–1930' (Beale (1984) *s.v. mush* 5); from l.19c. Forces' usage, 'guardroom or military prison'.

Mush² (n.): general term of address; man, mate. '"Understand, though, mush", he warned; "turn up late any more an' you've 'ad it"' (Cross 1951: 39). '*Mush*: a neutral term of address less used than *wack*' (Lane 1966: 72). 'Look, mush, I've already told yer' (Jacques 1979: n.p.) Recorded from e.20c.; from Romani 'mush, musha', 'man'.

Mush³ (n.): an outsider. ''Ee's a mush. *He is a stranger*' (Shaw et al. 1966: 29). Recorded from m.20c.; derivation unknown.

Mush⁴ (n.): mouth, lower face. 'I guv 'im a kick in ther moosh (mouth)' (Lane 1966: 47). 'Better than a smack in the mush' (Bryan 2003 [1940s–50s]: 78). Recorded from l.18c.; possibly from northern dialectal 'muss', 'mouth'.

Mush⁵ (n.): prostitute's client. 'She was fed up being pestered by the mooshes every time she went out' (McClure 1980: 133). 'MUSH A picker-up of COWS' (Spiegl 1989: 55). Recorded from l.20c.; glossed as used specifically in Liverpool (*OED s.v. mush* n⁸ 2); possibly an extension of *mush¹*.

Musher¹ (n.): man, person. 'In would pour a gang of freshly docked "mushers"' (Cornelius 2001 [1982]: 664) 'There's got to be one Macca in a platoon of fucking Kirkby mushers' (Sampson 2001: 62). 'I met this Yank musher who was lookin for it' (Griffiths 2003: 76). 'The groping opportunities for mushers in the midnight hour' (Lees 2013: 146). Recorded from l.20c.; a variant of *mush²*.

Musher² (n.): criminal. 'He knows everyone, the Dool does, knows all the mushers and what have you' (Sampson 2001: 122). 'Tommy said he'd chuck in another ton if we find that other musher' (Griffiths 2003: 52). Recorded from l.20c.; an extension of *mush²*.

Musker (n.): policeman. '*Policemen. Busys, Muskers, Mingees*' (Minard 1972: 89). 'Kekka mush dtherz a musker ind thee 'aystack. *Say no more, my friend, there happens to be a policeman behind you*' (Minard 1972: 55). *NR; from Romani 'muskra', 'policeman'.

Mutton dagger (n.): penis. 'Walk up waving his mutton dagger' (Hignett 1966: 36). '*Mutton dagger*: penis' (Lane 1966: 72). Recorded from l.20c.; a combination of 'mutton', 'women', 'female genitalia' and 'dagger', 'penis' (both from l.16c.).

Muzzied (adj.): drunk, confused. '*Muzzied*: Muddle-minded, witless, usually through drink' (Lane 1966: 72). Recorded from m.20c.; a northern dialectal extension of e.18c. 'muzzy, 'vague, befuddled'.

Muzzy (n.): moustache. 'A muzzy like two snots: A narrow, close-clipped moustache' (Lane 1966: 73). 'How could anyone ever think a muzzy looked cool?' (Sampson 1998: 67). Recorded from l.20c.; derivation is clear.

My arse (int.): exclamation expressing disbelief, dissent. '"Got icebreakers on them." "Icebreakers my arse"' (Lowry 1933: 236). *Celebrities My Arse!* (Tomlinson 2008: title). 'With a litany of "my arses"' (Lees 2013: 279). Recorded from e.20c.; popularised by the character Jim Royle in *The Royle Family*, this is a 20c. reworking of a phrase coined in Ben Jonson's *The Poetaster* (1602): 'Valiant? so is mine arse'.

My arse and your face (phr.): standard response to the question 'have you got a match?' '"Got a match?" … "Your face, my arse"' (Sampson 2002: 189). Recorded from l.20c.; glossed as the 'Liverpolitan reply to the question "Have you a match"?' (Beale (1985) *s.v. yes, my arse and your face*).

Mystery, The (n.): Wavertree Playground. 'De Mizzy. *Wavertree Park. The Mystery*, because of uncertainty of ownership before it became a public park' (Shaw et al. 1966: 32). 'Wavertree Playground – the "Mystery"' (Unwin 1984 [1920s–30s]: 127). 'At Wavertree, near the Mystery' (Grant 1996: 60). *NR in this sense; the mystery was the identity of the donor who gave what had been a private estate to the city in 1895 (the answer was the shipping magnate Alfred Holt).

N

Nagur (n.): harsh, thoughtless person; general term of abuse. 'That nagur of mine just comes home, pitches the brass on the table, and cuts away to his cronies' (Shimmin 1863: 2). Recorded from 19c.; a northern variant of 14c. 'niggardly', 'mean, stingy'.

Naller (v.): to catch. 'We wuz nallered. *We were captured*' (Shaw et al. 1966: 47). *NR; possibly from 'nailed' or 'nab' and 'collar'.

Nan (n.): grandmother. 'My nan saw me off' (Flame 1984: 108). 'I think I'll have words with me Nan' (McGovern 1995: 8). '*Me nan/nin* My grandmother' (Spiegl 2000b: 46). 'When she was a kid at her nan's' (Griffiths 2003: 28). Recorded as m.20c. in this sense; an abbreviation of the earlier 'nana' or a variant of *nin*.

Nance (n.): derogatory term for man characterised as 'effeminate'; homosexual. '*Nance*: An effeminate male' (Lane 1966: 74). 'Malcolm Baker, what a nance. Wears knix an stockings under his pants' (Griffiths 2000: 423). Recorded from e.20c.; abbreviation of l.19c. 'nancy', 'homosexual', from e.19c. 'nancy', 'buttocks'.

Nap (n.): a certainty. 'It's more or less a nap' (Jacques 1975: n.p.). 'It's a fucking nap, by the way' (Sampson 2002: 190). Recorded from l.20c.; an extension of l.19c. 'nap', 'tip'.

Nark¹ (n.): argumentative, annoying person. 'A little nark, who was called Sir Stanley Grouse' (Jacques 1977:

n.p.). 'An obvious nark, in everyone's eyes' (Fagan 2007 [1950s]: 103). Recorded from m.19c.; from l.19c. northern dialectal 'to nark', 'to vex, annoy, irritate'.

Nark² (n.): state of anger, irritation. 'Not hardened junkies, when deprived of dope,/Ere felt such anger, ere got such a nark/As a Scouseville driver seeking space to park' (Moloney 1966: 51). 'She must still have had the nark on' (Bleasdale 1975: 81). *NR in this sense; an extension of *nark¹*.

Nark³ (n.): argument. 'Nark: A dispute, a quarrel' (Lane 1966: 74). 'A family nark then was started' (Jacques 1975: n.p.). 'In the end we start having a nark' (Brown 1989: 9). 'Our Stephen's half having a nark with Shy' (Sampson 2002: 112). *NR; an extension of *nark¹*.

Nark⁴ (n.): informer. 'The person next door could think they were a copper's nark' (McClure 1980: 115). 'NARK See GRASS' (Spiegl 1989: 56). Recorded from m.19c.; from Romani 'nak', 'nose'.

Nark (v.): to argue. 'They did bugger all but nark about which tribe should let their sheep eat grass in Sefton park' (Jacques 1975: n.p.). *NR; an extension of *nark¹*.

Narked (adj.): annoyed, irritated. 'I wassen arf narked when I 'eard' (Shaw 1957a: 15). 'They got narked if someone went to sleep on their bit of the hall-long bench' (Hignett 1966: 150). 'You could see they was narked 'cos we'd got the front seat' (Bleasdale 1975: 200). 'Proper narked for showing them up' (Brown 1989: 14). 'Don't get narked lad' (Fagan 2007 [1950s]: 322). Recorded from l.19c.; see *nark*[1].

Narky (adj.): irritable. 'Liverpool is narky, and I'm the chief nark' (Grant 1996: 47). 'Yeh still narky? Still got thee arse?' (Griffiths 2003: 74). Recorded from l.19c.; see *nark*[1].

Nash (v.): to rush, leave hurriedly. 'We've gorrer nash, lar' (Griffiths 2003: 82). Recorded in e.19c. but glossed as obsolete; from Romani 'nash', 'run, escape'.

Natter (v.): to chat, gossip. 'Natter. To gossip or talk. Also to lecture or give lengthy reproof' (Lane 1966: 74). 'Stop natterin' an' let me read' (Sinclair 1999 [1930s–e.40s]: 20). Recorded from m.20c.; an extension of e.19c. dialectal 'natter', 'grumble, complain'.

Natterbag (n.): woman scold. 'Owd natterbag: a scolding woman' (Lane 1966: 74). *NR; see *natter* and *bag*.

Naughty (adj.): seriously wrong. 'Words like "naughty" are used in "A" Division, when stronger language would be excusable' (McClure 1980: 128). 'He's the really naughty boy, practically making a profession out of it. I don't mind prosecuting him' (Bleasdale 1985: 150). 'Each gang had a junior faction, of which the mini-Woodchurch were the most numerous and famously naughty' (Sampson 1998: 125). 'They were very naughty, the police in them days' (Dudgeon 2010: 339). Recorded from m.20c.; distinct from the weakened sense of 'naughty' and effectively a retention of 19c. sense of 'violence, corruption, or serious wrong-doing'.

Neck (v.): kiss, snog. 'Necking in the back row' (Smith 1998 [1971]: 86). 'Robbie, who is now necking with Carol' (Russell 1996 [1976]: 264). 'She would just like to neck with a girl' (Sampson 2002: 33). 'We'd jus started neckin' (Fagan 2007 [1950s]: 108). Recorded from m.19c.; derivation is clear.

Negro (n.): black person. 'One half of us are just as much slaves as the negroes were' (Haigh 1907: 164). 'Flukey Alley's Flukes, Sparling Street's Negroes, and the Chinamen of Pitt Street – even into these un-British sections tragedy and gloom had seeped' (O'Mara 1934: 221). 'He would batter his tiny fists against the hard heads of the little negroes' (Jerome 1948: 25). 'She didn't suggest that she was married to the negro' (Baird 1957: 41–2). The politer designation for black people in Britain from 16c.–l.20c., though given endemic racism, it usually carried negative connotations and is now considered offensive.

Nesh (adj.): timid, weak, lacking spirit. 'Damn! I'm getting quite nesh … What's come over me at all' (Hanley 2009 [1936]: 92). 'Nesh. Tender, soft' (Howarth 1985: n.p.). Recorded from e.19c.; northern dialectal; from Old English 'hnesce', 'soft, yielding'.

Netherfield Road Navy (n.): Orange Lodge band of Netherfield Road. 'Netherfield Road Navy: The bands of the Loyal Order of Orange Lodges' (Lane 1966: 74). *NR; derived from the military attire of the bands.

New Cathedral/Old Cathedral (n.): Catholic Cathedral/Anglican Cathedral. 'I walked down towards the New Cathedral' (Bleasdale 1975: 214).

'A three-sided tenement that faced the old cathedral' (Murari 1975: 5). *NR; a shorthand way of distinguishing between Liverpool's two cathedrals: the Catholic Metropolitan Cathedral of Christ the King (1967) and the Protestant Cathedral Church of Christ in Liverpool (1910–78). The Catholic Cathedral is known as the *New Cathedral* despite the fact that it was started and finished before the completion of the *Old Cathedral*.

Newsarab   (n.):   newspaper   boy. 'Newsarabs were licensed by the police' (Clerk 1971 [*c*.1900]: 68). *NR; see *arab*.

Nick (n.): police station; prison. 'The main nick in Hardman Street' (Smith 1998 [1971]: 172). (Parker 1974: 171). 'I wuz on me way to dee nick to 'and them in' (Spiegl 1989: 46). 'I've kept a bit of distance from Rico for a while now, but only because he's in and out of nick' (Sampson 1989: 162). Recorded from l.19c.; an Australian coinage; see *nicked*.

Nick, in good (adj.): in good condition. 'He's in good nick for a old feller too' (Sampson 2001: 200). Recorded from l.19c.; probably an extension of 15c. 'nick', 'score or tally'.

Nicked (v.): caught by the police. 'So I got nicked' (Jacques 1972: n.p.). 'There's also this greater awareness he's going to get nicked' (McClure 1980: 97). 'I get stuck in the swing doors and find myself nicked' (Brown 1989: 24). 'You'd get nicked for smoking on the quay' (Sanders and Sanders 2009 [1960s]: 39). Recorded from 17c.; originally 'catch unawares, apprehend', later narrowed to 'caught by police'.

Nicker[1] *(n.)*: one pound; plural *nicker*. 'A £1 note is generally known as a "nicker" or "bar"' ('Postman' 1937a: 6). 'Bar; nicker. *One pound note* Five nicker. *Five pounds; five pound note*' (Shaw et al. 1966: 34). 'Cornelius often picked up the odd nicker' (Jacques 1977: n.p.). '"How much?" "A nicker"' (Graham 1988: 51). 'Still fifty nicker if we don't' (Griffiths 2003: 52). 'A bloody good nicker's worth of ale' (Fagan 2007 [1950s]: 314). Recorded from m.19c.; derivation unclear.

Nicker[2] *(n.)*: cigarette end. 'A NICKER is the nicked-off end of a cigarette' (Shaw 1959a: 39). 'Nicker for cigarette end' (Armstrong 1966: 6). Recorded as 'Liverpool: since ca. 1930' (Partridge *s.v. nicker* 4); from 'nick', cut short, 'nip'.

Nig-nog (n.): racist term for black person. 'He was a nig-nog's kid – some coon from down the Dingle' (Bleasdale 1975: 27). Recorded from m.20c.; now considered highly offensive; an abbreviation of *nigger*.

Nigger (n.): racist term for black person; mixed-'race' person. 'Black as a nigger's hand' (Tirebuck 1891: 13). 'Someone would ask Roza, "Frankie, is your father a Nigger?"' (O'Mara 1934: 85). 'A nigger straight from Africa' (Hall 2004 [1939]: 20). 'Some nigger she'd been with' (Parker 1974: 95). 'Hey, nigger! Come 'ere!' (McClure 1980: 476). 'He's not a nigger' (Bainbridge 1989: 34). 'The moment the first "nigger" would have come' (Sampson 2002: 98). 'My white nigger' (Lees 2013: 189). Recorded from 16c.; the pernicious, racist connotations develop specifically from m.18c.; still common parlance in Liverpool a generation ago; now considered highly offensive; from Latin 'niger', 'black'.

Nin (n.): grandmother. 'The granny, or "nin", or "nanny", or "nanna" or "gran" as she is often called' (Kerr 1958: 48). 'Me nin. *My grandmother*' (Shaw et al. 1966: 26). 'Me Mam, me Nin, an me Auntie Mury' (Moloney 2001: 18). 'My Nin – that's me mother's side, Nan's me dad's side' (Dudgeon 2010: 143). Recorded as m.20c. 'Eng[lish] regional (Liverpool)' (*OED s.v. nin²*); from Welsh 'nain', 'grandmother'.

Nipper (n.): boy, child. 'Aye ... the kids is the nippers for keeping a man to it' (Shimmin 1863: 142). 'As for the little bare-footed nippers round here' (Haigh 1907: 69). 'He had been quite fond of the kid when he was a nipper' (Cross 1951: 14). 'The first "nippers" were bright boys, chosen to deal deftly with short bits of rope called nips' (Anon. 1954: 2). 'We sang when we was nippers areselfs' (Shaw 1957a: 5). 'She nods at the nippers' (Sampson 2002: 117). 'Nipper Hollerhead, the youngest apprentice' (Fagan 2007 [1950s]: 291). Recorded from 16c.; originally 'thief' but extended in 19c. to mean 'young helper' or 'young person' (usually male); probably an extension of nautical 'nipper', 'a short piece of rope used to bind one rope to another temporarily'.

Nix/to keep nix/nicks (v.): watch out/ to keep a look out. 'Nix, the bobby' ('Postman' 1931a: 5). 'Nicks or Nix! Quiet! Someone coming!' (Price 1950: 4). 'We adter ave someone keepin' nix for a scuffer' (Shaw 1957a: 2). 'An old skin doubling his dole, keeping nick at the top' (Hignett 1966: 148). 'Dixy: To keep look-out or "nicks"' (Parker 1974: 212). 'Some poor sod was always chosen to "keep nicks"' (Flame 1984: 34). Recorded from l.19c.; used in Irish English, possibly from Romani 'nisser', 'to avoid'.

No chance (phr.): no possibility; definitely not. 'Not in our house. Not to me Mam. No chance' (Bleasdale 1975: 169). 'He says No Chance' (Brown 1989: 22). 'Ha! No chance!' (Sampson 1999: 156). 'That's fucked it all, now. I've got no bleedin' chance' (Griffiths 2002: 8). 'No fuckin' chance' (Burnett 2011: 51). Recorded from e.20c.; an emphatic usage, derivation is clear.

No mark (n.): unimportant, inferior person. 'He's just a fuckin' nomark!' (Russell 1996 [1976]: 232). 'I suspect he's had me down as a bit of a no-mark' (Sampson 1998: 29). 'This nomark who attached himself to me' (Kelly 2006 [1930s–40s]: 116). Recorded from m.20c.; possibly from the idea of 'making a mark', 'leaving an impression/having an effect' (Melville describes a sailor as 'a person of no mark or influence' Melville 1849: 81).

Noak (v.): to keep watch, lookout. 'Rhuie was noaking and I knew I was "for it"' (Clerk 1971 [c.1900]: 18). Recorded as 'Liverpool street arabs' (and beggars?): ca. 1870–1930' (Beale (1984) *s.v. noak*); derivation unknown.

Nobber (n.): a favoured worker in the casual labour system on the docks. 'If you were not a "blue-eye" or a boss's favourite (a "nobber") you were wasting your time' (Shaw 1959c: 6). *NR; derivation unclear, possibly from *knob*.

Nonk (n.): large clay marble. '*Nonk*: A large clay marble' (Lane 1966: 75). *NR; belongs to the discourse of *ollies*, derivation unknown.

North End (n.): the North End of Liverpool. 'It was determined to open the shops at the North and South ends of the town' (Anon. 1850: 6). 'So far the South end of the town has been spoken of. We will now go to the North' (Shimmin 1863: 121). 'The dregs of our civilisation, in the East End of London, the North End of Liverpool' (Haigh 1907: 174). 'Crossford, on the other hand, lived in cheap rooms in the north end' (Owen 1921: 141). 'One of the fourteen tough lads from the North End had irritated the lanky radical South End A[ble] B[odied] Seaman]' (O'Mara 1934: 160). 'His native parish of St. Sylvester's in the North End' (Anon. 1945: 3). 'People in the North End try to say the Dingle lads have our own way of talking' (Sampson 2001: 24). 'The north end is traditionally working-class and poor. The south end is a bit posher' (Dudgeon 2010: 63). *NR; the *North End* originally meant the northern end of the city centre but came to mean the northern end of the city itself – effectively from the north side of the Pier Head to Everton, Walton and Bootle (though the boundaries are historically variable).

North Ender (n.): someone from the north end of the city. 'Now then you Bootleites and North Enders' (Anon. 1914b: 7). 'After the separation I found myself hemmed in among a crowd of mature North Enders' (O'Mara 1934: 149). 'The Vale: Walton Vale to Liverpool north-enders, Aigburth Vale

to south-enders, St. Domingo Vale to in-betweeners' (Lane 1966: 113). *NR; see *North End*.

Nosh (n.): food; fellatio. 'A real smashing bit of nosh' (Brown 1989: 69). 'I stepped in for a coffee and a nosh' (Grant 2002: 234). 'Sonia gets down and starts to suck me. A nosh from the Nosh Queen' (Sampson 1998: 78). Recorded from l.19c.; the sexual sense is l.20c.; see *nosh (v.)*.

Nosh (v.): to eat. 'Ee caahn aahf nosh. That boy has a healthy appetite' (Minard 1972: 73). 'He'd noshed all the rusk' (Jacques 1975: n.p.). Recorded from l.19c.; an Americanism, probably from Yiddish 'nashn', 'eat a snack'.

Not on (phr.): something (usually a form of behaviour) which is not acceptable. '"Yer not on, la!" ... "You shall not have your way, young man!"' ('Postman' 1966a: 6). 'We've even had people knocking at the door at home collecting for them – "You're not on!"' (McClure 1980: 69). 'Ah no, you're not on' (Bleasdale 1985: 85). 'Not on, by the way – not a fucking chance of it' (Sampson 2002: 97). Recorded from m.20c.; possibly the negative version of the phrase used to tell dockers that they had been chosen for work under the casual dock labour scheme by the 'putter on': 'the Bowler-Hatted Boss (The Blocker Man) stalking the circle to tap certain men on the shoulder indicating that they were "on", that is to say, taken on for work' (Callaghan 2011 [1910s–30s]: 42). If so, it was an abbreviation of the phrasal verbs 'taken on', 'got on': 'two or three men, who had been to the docks earlier in the day and had not succeeded in being "taken on"' (Haigh 1907: 18); 'who among the men had "got on" down the dock?' (O'Mara 1934: 66).

Nothing down for you (phr.): you have no possibility of success. 'Do somethin' stupid and you know there's nothin' down fer yer' (McClure 1980: 306). 'You know the score Chrisse, – there's nothin' down for y" (Bleasdale 1985: 52). 'There's nottun down for ya, girl' (Lees 2013: 121). *NR; derivation unclear.

Now hat! (int.): greeting to anyone wearing a hat. 'Now att. *A friendly remark to anyone in Liverpool wearing headgear*' (Minard 1972: 18). *NR; derivation is clear.

Nowse (n.): skill, practical know-how. '*Nowse*: Skill, flair, knowledge' (Lane 1966: 75). 'Cummon Scouse, use yer nouse' (Jacques 1977: n.p.). 'Burdened with all the prejudice and none of the nous of the street' (Sampson 1999: 73). 'He wouldn't have the bottle or the nouse' (Fagan 2007 [1950s]: 121). Recorded from e.18c.; from ancient Greek 'νοῦς', 'mind, intellect'.

Nowt (n.): nothing. 'I don't see nowt o' sort' (Hocking 1966 [1879]: 16). 'With these sort yer hev to know nowt and know it all the time' (Tirebuck 1891: 402). 'I didn't say nowt to you!' (O'Mara 1934: 161). 'I'm 'avin' nowt ter do wit' it' (Lane 1966: 76). 'I know the feller on the door … I'll get in for nowt' (Bleasdale 1975: 146). 'Prepared excuses/for reddened eyes, said nowt' (Simpson 1990: 83). 'Nowt fuckin in it' (Griffiths 2003: 4). Recorded from 18c.; common in northern dialectal, Scottish and Irish English; a variant of 'nought'.

Nudger[1] (n.): penis. '*Light-hearted Scousims for the penis*: Nudger …' (Minard 1972: 45). 'She … grabbed me nudger through me trousers' (Bleasdale 1977: 69). 'Avunt seen me feet fer years, never mind me fuckin nudger' (Griffiths 2000: 153). 'They cut the end of its nudger off – it's called "circumcision"' (Fagan 2007 [1950s]: 14). Recorded from m.20c.; probably from l.18c. 'to nudge', 'to have sex'.

Nudger[2] (n.): long sandwich. 'A nudger. *A long sandwich made from an elongated bread roll*' (Shaw et al. 1966: 41). '*Nudger* An elongated bread roll' (Spiegl 2000b: 124). 'A bowl of thick and a nudger … (Pea soup and a French loaf sandwich)' (Elliott 2006 [1940s–70s]: 77). *NR; possibly from *nudger[1]*.

Nuf ced (phr.): say no more. Recorded as a 'contraction of "enough said" absurdly spelt. Warning to say no more. Used in Liverpool chiefly' (Ware 1909: 184). Recorded from m.19c.; an Americanism in which form mirrors content.

Nugget (n.): Saturday night shift on the docks. 'Working a "nugget" … was big money – almost a week's wages for working a Saturday night' (Sanders and Sanders 2009 [1960s]: 111). 'They scramble for a nugget/Or clamour for nights' (Jacques 1972: n.p.). *NR; see *golden nugget*.

Nut (v.): to butt. '*To put in ther nut*: To butt someone with one's head' (Lane 1966: 75). 'Landed him one below the chin with his head. Nutted him one neat and proper' (Bleasdale 1975: 103). 'This little judy nuts the female busy' (Brown 1989: 48). Recorded from m.19c.; an extension from boxing discourse, 'nut', 'to hit someone on the head'; from the slightly earlier sense of 'nut', 'head'.

Nutcase (n.): crazy, mentally disturbed person; an eccentric. 'Remember the Salisbury nutcase caught at the grave?' (Martin 1963: 12). 'Ooweh, 'e's a nutcase' (Jacques 1979: n.p.). 'His mate is a nut case too' (Brown 1989: 30). 'He was a Jekyll and Hyde nut case' (Stamper 2010: 143). Recorded from m.20c.; m.19c. 'nut', 'head' became e.20c. Americanism 'nut', 'crazy person, eccentric' combined with 'case', 'example or instance of something'.

Nutpox (n.): ringworm. '*Nutpox*: ringworm' (Lane 1966: 76). *NR; from 'nuts', 'testicles' and 'pox', 'infectious disease producing pustules (pocks)'.

Nuts on (phr.): infatuated with. '*She's dead nuts on 'im*' (Lane 1966: 25). Recorded from l.18c.; from e.17c. 'nuts', 'a source of pleasure or delight'.

Nutter (n.): crazy person, often violent. 'Even if you're not a nutter' (Smith 1998 [1971]: 12). 'They start laughing like a pair of nutters' (Bleasdale 1975: 11). 'The fella isn't sure whether I'm a nutter or not' (Sampson 2002: 203). 'Some nutters had taken the horse out' (Stamper 2010: 84). Recorded as originating in m.20c. Liverpool (Beale (1984) *s.v. nutter*); see *nutcase*.

O

Oats (n.): sex. 'Instead of getting' y' oats y' get chicken biryani' (Russell 1996 [1976]: 203). 'Yer must be missin yer oats' (Jacques 1979: n.p.). 'Yer were getting' yer oats then?' (Bryan 2003 [1940s–50s]: 55). Recorded from e.20c.; derivation unclear.

Ocker (n.): one shilling piece. 'Ocker. *Shilling piece*' (Shaw et al. 1966: 34). *NR; recorded from m.19c.; from 'ochre', 'money in general'.

Of (prep.): during, on (referring to repeated action at a particular time). 'Dishwash of a day and write epics at night' (O'Mara 1934: 245). ''Bout ten to one of a Sunday' (Hignett 1966: 90). 'We go of a Tuesday an' a Thursday night' (Bleasdale 1975: 15). 'We don't come to school of a Sunday' (Brown 1989: 38). 'I'd play football of a night' (Dudgeon 2010: 100). Recorded from l.18c.; a replacement of the Old English genitive of time, this now dialectal use implies regularity or repetition at a given time or on a specific day.

Off, the (n.): the start; departure. 'Ready for the off?' (McClure 1980: 512). 'It's waterworks right from the off' (Sampson 2002: 204). Recorded from l.19c.; probably from racing usage, 'they're off'.

Off one's onion (adj.): crazy, mad. 'When a fellow starts going off his onion like that about socialism' (Hanley 1935: 510). Recorded from l.19c.; from the slightly earlier 'onion', 'head'.

Offy (n.): off-licence. 'While yer there skank us a bottle from thee offy' (Griffiths 2003: 135). Recorded from l.20c.; derivation is clear.

Og (n.): halfpenny; shilling. 'Clutchin' your og or thrippenny joey or sproweser, or whatever it wus, to the grocer' (Shaw 1957a: 18). '2? – Two og' (Minard 1972: 86). 'Og; meg. *One halfpenny*' (Shaw et al. 1966: 33). *NR; derivation unknown.

Oggen (n.): sea. 'We were taking bets that he would go in the "oggen" (sea)' (Stamper 2010: 113). *NR; derivation unclear, probably a variant of 'ocean'.

Oggie/ossie (n.): house. 'An emmy oggie. A bap ossie. *An empty house*' (Shaw et al. 1966: 47). *NR; derivation unknown.

Old (owl/owld) one (n.): mother (less respectful). '"The old one" (or "owld one" or "owl one") is regarded as disrespectful' (Farrell 1950b: 4). 'You could bet the ould one's pension' (Jacques 1973: n.p.). See *old girl*.

Old/ahl/auld girl (n.): older woman, sometimes mother. 'In speaking of his mother a man will say "the old lady", or "the old woman", or "the old girl"' (Farrell 1950b: 4). 'With no lack of respect, his mother is called *The Old Lady* (pronounced *Ould* and accented on the adjective rather than on the noun), and even *The Old One* or the *Old Girl*' (Shaw 1958d: 14). 'I went to this old girl round the corner' (Hignett 1966: 179). 'Tell y'old girls they fell off a supermarket' (Bleasdale 1975: 61). 'She's a good auld girl' (Sampson 2001: 33). Recorded from l.19c. in this sense; derivation is clear.

Old/aul/ould/owl/owld feller (n.): father. 'Father is "the old feller" (or "owld feller" or "owl feller")' (Farrell 1950a: 4). 'When the smoke and dust had all cleared from the air/"Thank God" said the auld fella, "The Pier Head's still there"' (McGovern 1961: 'In My Liverpool Home'). 'De owl feller. Me owl man. *My father*' (Shaw et al. 1966: 26). 'They asked him where his old man was' (Bleasdale 1975: 62). '"Yer ol' fella's dead!"' (McClure 1980: 278). 'He's Mikey's aul' fella' (Sampson 2002: 3). Recorded from e.20c.; Irish English; derivation is clear.

Old Cathedral (n.): Anglican Cathedral, see *New Cathedral*.

Old lady (n.): mother (respectful). 'Trying to bum money from their old ladies' (Hanley 1932: 17). 'In speaking of his mother a man will say "the old lady", or "the old woman", or "the old girl"' (Farrell 1950b: 4). 'With no lack of respect, his mother is called The Old Lady (pronounced Ould and accented on the adjective rather than on the noun), and even The Old One or the Old Girl' (Shaw 1958d: 14). 'According to my old lady' (Brown 1989: 9). 'George had come to Liverpool to see the old lady' (Elliott 2006 [1940s–70s]: 124). Recorded from 16c.; derivation is clear.

Old man (n.): father. 'Your old man's seen you talking to her' (Hanley 1932: 32). 'De owl feller. Me owl man. My father' (Shaw et al. 1966: 26). 'They asked him where his old man was' (Bleasdale 1975:

62). 'My old man told me' (Robinson 1986 [1920s–30s]: 152). Recorded from l.17c.; derivation is clear.

Old Mary (n.): old woman. 'All these old Marys were scrambling in the gutter for his silver' (Bleasdale 1975: 21). *NR; possibly from *Mary Ellen*.

Old oil (n.): persuasive but untrue tale. '*I guv 'im the owd oil*: I tried to cajole him' (Lane 1966: 79). Recorded from e.20c.; from 'oil', 'glib or misleading talk used to persuade'.

Old quilt/quilt (n.): an 'effeminate' man. 'Dad never does owt in the house lest he be termed a Mary Ann or OLD QUILT' (Shaw 1959a: 32). 'I argue that those teams have got so many quilts that you'd never get to their boys' (Sampson 1998: 29). Recorded from m.20c.; from the l.19c. Americanism 'quilt', 'wife'.

Old Shawl (n.): man who does housework (used as an insult to suggest 'effeminacy'). 'A man who does housework is called an *Old Shawl* or a *Mary Ann*' (Shaw 1950b: 4). *NR; see *shawlie*.

Old woman (n.): see *old girl*.

Oldster (n.): older person. 'In the two back rooms was old Kitty Daugherty, "the professional witness", and a sooty oldster named "Scrogy"' (O'Mara 1934: 116). 'Oldsters Will Remember Them: Street Characters of a Bygone Day' (Dawson 1951: 4). Recorded from m.19c. in this general sense; originally a technical nautical term, 'a midshipman who had served for more than four years'.

Olla/oller (n.): waste ground; *debby*. 'This lumberron dthee olla. *There is a brawl on the waste ground*' (Minard 1972:

53). ''Oller: From hollow, a piece of waste ground' (Parker 1974: 213). 'A piece of sandstone obtained from the "olla" (waste ground)' (Elliott 2006 [1940s–70s]: 7). 'The oller – Patch of wasteland where children played games or men played "toss"' (Callaghan 2011 [1910s–30s]: viii). *NR; possibly from 'hollow'.

Ollies[1] *(n.)*: marbles. 'No gutters for a proper game a Ollies' (Shaw 1957a: 1). 'This is the only place, I think, where grown-up men play marbles called ollies' (Shaw 1966c: 4). 'Unemployed men playing one of their endless games of ollies, a form of marbles' (Forrester 1974 [1930s]: 133). 'Playing "ollies" in the gutters' (Unwin 1984 [1920s–30s]: 11). '*Ollies* Marbles' (Spiegl 2000b: 127). 'Ollies, marbles if you wanted to be posh' (Callaghan 2011 [1910s–30s]: 15). *NR; probably from e.18c. 'alley', 'marble', possibly an abbreviation of 'alabaster'. *Ollies* – often played with *cherrywobs* – was a serious game in Liverpool and featured in the pioneering BBC documentary *Morning in the Streets* (1959), partly shot in the Liverpool docklands. The game had its own vocabulary: 'bloody alley', 'jacks', 'lassies/lazzies', 'nunks', 'parrots', 'segs', 'stonies', 'steelies' 'ups' (Shaw 1960a: 37). By extension, 'yer ollie's down the grid' (Shaw 1957a: 16) meant that you were in a hopeless position.

Ollies[2] *(n.)*: testicles. 'What about that shot Pele hit from way behind the half-way line, eh? Made that goalie drop his ollies' (Smith 1971: 61). ''She would 'ave gripped your ollies so hard' (Fagan 2007 [1950s]: 35). *NR; an extension of *ollies*[1].

Omadhaun (n.): fool, idiot. 'He turns around and picks up with another bloody omadhaun and takes her into the pictures' (O'Mara 1934: 258). 'Anyone out of favour with Pat was an "omathuan!" I have never heard the word since' (Anon. 1959: 4). Recorded from e.19c.; a direct import from Irish English, from Gaelic 'amadán', 'fool'.

On the ale (phr.): out drinking. 'Going "on the ale", "doing the clubs"' (Parker 1974: 152). ''E's on the ale with 'is mates' (Sinclair 1999 [1930s–e.40s]: 137). 'We went out on thee ale' (Griffiths 2003: 187). *NR; derivation is clear.

On the pig's back (phr.): well-off, very lucky. 'There are other Gaelicisms … including "cod" for "fool", "on the pig's back" (meaning very fortunate …)' (Shaw 1955a: 6). '*On the pig's back*: lucky; doing well; in the money' (Lane 1966: 78). 'On the pig's back – eh?' (Sinclair 1999 [1930s–e.40s]: 123). Recorded from e.19c.; Irish English; a direct translation of the Gaelic phrase 'ar mhuin na muice'.

On the piss (phr.): out drinking. 'Think she's been on the piss!' (Sinclair 1999 [1930s–e.40s]: 33). 'He went out on the piss' (Griffiths 2003: 205). Recorded from e.20c.; Forces' usage, from e.20c. 'piss', 'alcoholic drink'.

On, you're/it's (phr.): said when a bet or offer is accepted. 'Tell him it's on' (Hignett 1966: 274). 'OK, Moby, you're on' (Sampson 2002: 35). Recorded from m.20c.; from e.19c. racing discourse; an abbreviation of 'the bet is taken on'.

Once round her twice round the gasworks (phr.): fat. 'Once round her, once round the gasworks ... (unkindly of a fat girl)' (Shaw 1963d: 4). 'Once round Maggie, twice round the gasworks' (Lane 1966: 77). *NR; derivation is clear.

Oncer (n.): one pound. '£1 A Oncer, a Plymouth Sound, a Nicker' (Minard 1972: 86). Recorded from m.20c.; derivation is clear.

One-eyed city (n.): Birkenhead. 'This was the land of the "One-eyed" people – a sarcastic nickname given them by less shrewd Liverpudlians. The Mersey separated us. It was an effective separation' (O'Mara 1934: 4). 'De One-eyed City. *Birkenhead*' (Shaw et al. 1966: 30). *NR; there are two possible explanations: either this is a condescending characterisation of their near-neighbours by Liverpudlians, or it is the fact that there is indeed one 'i' in 'Birkenhead'.

One o'clock gun (n.): gun fired at one o' clock every day. 'Waitin, with what seemed to the boy to be a rather excessive air of drama, for the one o' clock gun' (Owen 1921: 61). 'Merseyside's famous "One 'o Clock Gun"' (anon 1944: 3). 'The famous one o' clock gun which used to boom out day by day' (Unwin 1984 [1920s–30s]: 67). 'The boom of the one o' clock gun echoed across the river' (Bainbridge 1989 153). 'The faithful One o' clock gun could hardly be heard' (Sinclair 1999 [1930s–e.40s]: 34). *NR; to keep accurate Greenwich Mean Time, a cannon at Morpeth Dock, Birkenhead, was fired remotely from Bidston Observatory at one o'clock each working day between 1867 and 1969 (except during the Second World War).

One over the eight (phr.): one drink too many; drunk. 'Suffering evidently from having had one over the eight?' (Bower 2015 [1936]: 106). 'What's up with him, one over the eight?' (Russell 1996 [1976]: 221). 'Especially when he'd had "one over the eight"' (Sinclair 1999 [1930s–e.40s]: 79). Recorded from e.20c.; Forces' usage; presumably from the belief that it is the ninth drink that makes you drunk.

Onion (n.): Welsh person. '*Onion*: Name sometimes given to a Welshman' (Lane 1966: 78). *NR; probably from the 'welsh (spring) onion'.

Orange (n.): Protestant. 'These Orange associations are illegal combinations' (Anon. 1819: 9). 'Orange Procession' (Anon. 1855: 8). 'Of south-west Lancashire ... the Toryism is more orange than bucolic in the lower grades, and very much coloured by Liverpool in the upper strata' (Anon. 1884: 2). 'The stumbling block was colour. Mrs Fury's was green – Mrs Postlethwaite's orange' (Hanley 1935: 289). 'Endless battle between Orange and Green' (Ash 1954: 48). 'The Green and the Orange have battled for years' (McGovern 1995 [1961]: 4). 'Some people are Orange, others are Green' (Jacques 1972: n.p.). 'And your creed didn't matter, be it orange or pope' (McGovern 1995: 10). 'The area was solidly Orange – people, churches, pubs' (Maddox 2008 [1930s–40s]: 34). Recorded from l.18c.; sometimes derogatory; from King William of Orange, Protestant Conqueror of Ireland in 1690.

Orange Lodger (n.): Protestant. 'A town full of Orange Lodgers, King Billy's bastards' (Hignett 1966: 143). 'The biggest Orange Lodger in our road' (Bleasdale 1975: 79). *NR; sometimes derogatory; a reference to the Orange Order, the politico-religious body, founded in 1795 and organised into local Lodges, devoted to the ascendancy of Protestant and Loyalist principles in Ireland (and, later, Northern Ireland); there were many Orange Lodges in Liverpool; see *Orange*.

Orange River (n.): the different areas of Liverpool in which Protestants were in the ascendancy. 'In the South, the Protestants have Clive Street and Jerry Hill, and in the North, Netherfield Road and Lodge Lane – scattered bits grouped under the name of the Orange River' (O'Mara 1934: 10). *NR; see *Orange*.

Orangeman/Orangewoman (n.): Protestant. 'Calling the congregation a set of bloody Orangemen, and threatening to pull the preacher from his box' (Anon. 1835: 6). 'The Liverpool Orangemen' (Anon. 1878: 6). 'Liverpool Orangemen abandon 12th July demonstration' (Anon. 1915b: 3). 'Orangemen (perfervid Protestants) and Catholics' (Bower 2015 [1936]: 77). 'She is a Protestant, and ardent Orangewoman' (Kerr 1958: 106). 'It was Liverpool on the twelfth of July, the Orangemen's day' (Robinson 1986 [1920s–30s]: 7). 'At the hands of the Orangemen' (Bryan 2003 [1940s–50s]: 35). 'Silk cords to be clutched by following Orangemen' (Lees 2013: 97). Recorded from l.18c.; sometimes derogatory; see *Orange*.

Ossie (n.): house. 'An emmy oggie. A bap ossie. *An empty house*' (Shaw et al. 1966: 47). *NR; derivation unknown.

Ould/ahl/owd/owl/owld (adj.): old; sometimes signifying fondness. 'He wur wuss nor any owd woman' (Hocking 1966 [1879]: 38). 'I was born thirty two years ago in "Auld" Harris's tenement house in Bridgwater Street' (O'Mara 1934: 11). 'The large number of Irish words which occur in Liverpool's dialect – Gom (a fool), Ould (Old, which is pure Dublin), Feller (fellow), and Youse (You)' (Whittington-Egan 1955a: 6). 'Ould (or owl) not necessarily signifying age is common … Just as our kid may be older than the speaker, ould Joe may be quite a young man and me ould hat a recent purchase' (Shaw 1962a: 10). '*Owd geezer*: An elderly man' (Lane 1966: 79). 'A tanncr and/my owld one for that' (Simpson 1990: 82). 'Shows how right aul' Paulie is' (Sampson 2002: 123). 'And we'll throw owld Johnson in the dock' (Callaghan 2011 [1910s–30s]: 11). The spellings are simple variants of 'old'.

Our (adj.): used to signal kinship or allegiance. '"Our" is generally used for "my" in speaking of other members of the family, for example, "our Alice" for "my sister Alice" (Farrell 1950a: 4). 'Family and possessions will be either "our" (pronounced *awr* or *are*), or "my" (pronounced *me*) thus, *our Flo, our Richie, our Jamesey, me auntie, me 'at*, and a brother, whatever his age, is invariably – *Our Kid* … Children say *Our Mam* as "Can I ave a jam butty, our mam"' (Shaw 1958d: 14). 'Me Gran, me Mam, our Tony, and our Arthur' (Bleasdale 1975: 26). 'Mike McCartney refers to his elder and richer brother Paul as "are kid"' (Spiegl

1989: 12). 'My Mam collected me and our Alec' (Elliott 2006 [1940s–70s]: 6). Recorded from e.19c. to refer to a relative, friend or acquaintance.

Our kid (n.): brother or sister, sometimes friend. '"Our kid's gone to keep me a speck" means "My brother has gone ahead to reserve me a place"' (Farrell 1950a: 4); 'Here you are, our kid' (Hignett 1966: 184). 'Our kid [brother] said' (Parker 1974: 172). 'Our kid's in the police cadets, y'know' (McClure 1980: 333). 'I saw you with our kid' (Grant 1996: 47). 'Our kid was in the war' (Simpson 2011: 341). Recorded from e.20c.; possibly from the l.19c. Americanism, 'kid-brother/ sister'; 'our kid' is north-west England dialectal. Though the phrase usually means 'my brother/sister', it can be used to refer to a close acquaintance, or demeaningly as a term of scolding – 'listen our kid'. See *Kidder*[2]

Our road (n.): the speaker's neighbourhood and its inhabitants. 'What about me mates? What about our road when they come, when they see me at the evenin' performance?' (Bleasdale 1975: 150). *NR; 'road' is metonymic and links place and people. See *round our way*.

Ours (n.): house, home. 'It was only from your 'ouse to ours' (Marenbon 1973 [1920s]: 10). 'I carried on towards ours' (Bleasdale 1975: 66). 'Should see ours' (McClure 1980: 335). 'Come to ours termorrer' (Bryan 2003 [1940s–50s]: 146). Recorded from l.19c.; dialectal; a specific use of the possessive pronoun.

Out (phr.): on strike; unemployed. 'Many weary weeks flew by, but Paul was still out' (Powys 1857: 43). 'He told me how there had been a strike in their trade, how he was out, and what a trifle he had to live on' (Shimmin 1863: 76). 'Joe was only a fool if he came out' (Hanley 1935: 84). Recorded from e.19c.; from 'turn-out', 'strike'.

Over the water (phr.): the Wirral peninsula. '"Over the water", as every Liverpudlian referred to the Cheshire shore' (Ash 1954: 76). 'I don't think he'll know the district. He's from over the water' (Hignett 1966: 194). 'Let's go over the water to New Brighton baths' (Parker 1974: 200). 'Many a Liverpudlian's holiday was a day out "over the water"' (Unwin 1984 [1920s–30s]: 109). 'They move to New Brighton, over the water' (Brown 1989: 47). 'Some lad from over the water that used to go the aways' (Sampson 2001: 42). 'He lives over the water in the Wirral' (Stamper 2010: 154). *NR; the 'water' in question is the River Mersey.

Overhead/overhead railway (n.): Liverpool Overhead Railway system. 'The Overhead Railway has ceased for the day' (Haigh 1907: 313). 'He would walk the seven miles to the Langdon dock to save overhead railway fare' (O'Mara 1934: 22). 'The brown cars of the Overhead Railway' (Mays 1954: 35). 'We'll go on the Overhead!' (Owen 1961: 24). 'There was a railway under the Overhead, the Dock Railway' (Clerk 1971 [c.1900]: 49). 'He could take the overhead railway from the Dingle' (Melly 1984 [1930s–40s]: 181). 'You could travel on the "overhead railway" to the ships' (Elliott 2006 [1940s–70s]: 75). *NR; see *Docker's Umbrella*.

Ovies (n.): overtime. 'Wotsmee oaveez? *How much overtimewill I be given?*' (Minard 1972: 94). *NR, derivation is clear.

Ozzy (n.): hospital. 'I have met with such as "ozzy" (hospital), "rally" (railway), "Pivvy" (the Pavilion Theatre) and "de Pool" (for Liverpool itself)' (Isenberg 1962: 6). 'Will yer send me to de ozzy? *Do I have to go to hospital?*' (Shaw et al. 1966: 56). 'I wuz on me way to de ozzie' (Spiegl 1989: 28). 'This you just out of the ozzy then?' (Griffiths 2003: 13). Recorded from m.20c.; derivation is clear.

P

Pace-egging (n.): Paschal-egging. 'Childwall … pace-egging, oak-apple day and the maypole' (Anon. 1915c: 4). 'I saw a party of children in the Kirkdale district this Easter observing the custom of "pasch", or "pace", egging' ('Postman' 1945a: 2). 'I lived on Gateacre Brow and the "pace eggers" used to visit us every Easter' ('Postman' 1945b: 2). Recorded from l.16c., mainly northern and Scottish; from l.14c. 'Pace', Easter', ultimately Latin 'Pascha', Hebrew 'Pesah'. In older forms of this traditional ritual, eggs were decorated as part of the Easter celebration and distributed by 'pace-eggers' – groups of garishly dressed players who performed a traditional mummers play, recited songs and collected money. Picton noted that 'Pasche eggs, Morris dances, and hot cross buns have lingered here with greater perseverance than in most other parts of the country' (Picton 1875: 2.302).

Padded (adj.): concealing stolen goods. 'Anyway, he could see I wasn't padded' (Clerk 1971 [c.1900]: 30). Recorded from e.20c.; an Americanism; derivation is clear.

Paddy (n.): temper; fit of anger. 'Such a Paddy! Ye could do without it' (Hallowell 1972: n.p.). 'Uncle Vernon flew into a paddy' (Bainbridge 1989: 66). Recorded from l.19c.; based on the stereotypical belief in the fierce temper of Paddy (the Irish).

Paddy Kelly (n.): dock policeman. 'He was copped by a Paddy Kelly nicking a bit a slummy' (Shaw 1957a: 7). 'A "Paddy Kelly" is a dock-policeman' (Channon 1970: 102). 'Paddy Kelly meant policeman in the slang we used those days' (McGovern 1995: 5). '*Paddy Kelly* A docks police officer' (Spiegl 2000b: 100). 'Grunting their Good Morning to/the Paddy Kelly on the gate' (Simpson 2011: 415). Recorded from m.20c.; 'Liverpool dockers' slang for "policeman"' (Partridge *s.v. Paddy Kelly*); derivation unknown.

Paddy Rileys (n.): the dock police. 'The bobbies (known as scuffers in Liverpool, Paddy Rileys on the waterfront) would have to be watched' (Anon. 1955: 6). *NR; see *Paddy Kelly*.

Paddy wack (n.): pea soup; poor meat. 'An' well like dey 'ad dis Paddy Wack an' a pan of scouse … [trans.:] with a menu of pea soup, scouse' (Anon. 1961b: 3). '*Paddywack*: An indigestible ligament of meat' (Lane 1966: 80). 'Blind scouse, paddy wack, hot pot, wet nellas' (Lees 2013: 82). *NR in these senses; derivation unknown.

Paddy Wester (n.): seaman with false papers; incompetent sailor. '*Paddy Wester*. A fake seaman with a dead man's discharge, after a notorious boarding-house keeper in Liverpool who shipped thousands of green men as A.B.'s for a consideration' (Bowen 1929: 100). 'Paddy Wester came to mean any greenhorn' (Channon 1970: 93).

Recorded from l.19c.; immortalised in various sea-shanties, 'Paddy West', was a notorious Liverpool crimp (someone who procures seamen by entrapping or coercing them), operating in the m.19c.

Paddy's Hammer (n.): the bells of St. Patrick's church, Park Road. '"Paddy's Hammer", which is an affectionate term for the bells of St. Patrick's Church, in the south-end of Liverpool' (Unwin 1984 [1920s–30s]: 9). *NR; derivation is clear.

Paddy's Market (n.): Great Homer Street Market (also known as *Greaty*). 'She bought it for her son in Paddy's market' (Anon. 1855: 5). 'I remember one night going to Paddy's Market, and getting a regular rig out for about two shillings' (Shimmin 1863: 152). '"Paddy's Market" has grown old and poor and desolate' (Anon. 1887: 5). 'Midway in this throughfare stands Paddy's Market, also internationally known, where the refuse of the Empire is bought and sold' (O'Mara 1934: 4). 'The goods had been bought in the now blitzed "Paddy's Market", opposite to us in Scotland Road' (Fleming Prout 1950: 4). 'One could get a saucer of Irish stew for a halfpenny, at the side street by Paddy's Market, served out of big "panmugs"' (Ford 1957: 6). 'Lascar seamen on their visits to "Paddy's Market", were invited to have a "Dekko" and assured the goods for sale were the "Gear"' (Holbrow 1964: 6). 'Gorridin Paddy's Maahrkit' (Minard 1972: 58). 'A good part-time job in "Paddy's Market"' (Robinson 1986 [1920s–30s]: 115). 'Paddy's Market in Great Homer Street' (Elliott 2006 [1940s–70s]: 16). *NR; *Paddy's Market* actually refers to

a number of markets on or around the same site in the Great Homer Street/ Scotland Road area from the m.19c. to the present. The name derived from the preponderance of Irish/Liverpool-Irish people who lived locally.

Paddy's Wigwam (n.): the Catholic Cathedral. 'Mersey Funnel ... A general nickname for the new Roman Catholic cathedral, Liverpool, which is funnel, or tent-shaped. Also Paddy's Wigwam' (Lane 1966: 66–7). 'Not forgetting "Paddy's Wigwam" of course, the Catholic cathedral at one end of Hope Street' (McClure 1980: 21). '*Paddy's Wigwam* The Metropolitan Cathedral of Christ the King' (Spiegl 2000b: 52). '"Paddy's Wigwam" (the metropolitan Cathedral)' (Lees 2013: 235). *NR; the unusual shape of the *New Cathedral* explains the 'wigwam' reference.

Pay off (v.): to pay. 'First time I've been paid off in Liverpool' (Owen 1961: 20). 'Going round to London to pay off' (Lane 1987: 10). 'The same old paid-off swaggering ashore' (Simpson 1990: 88). 'I've seen lads paid off many a time' (Fagan 2007 [1950s]: 97). Recorded from m.17c.; an extension of the nautical sense, 'to pay and discharge a ship's crew'.

Pal (n.): term of address which suggests annoyance or aggression. 'Sod off pal' (Jacques 1977: n.p.). 'Who're yer talkin' to, pal?' (McClure 1980: 240). 'Hey now, just hold on pal' (Bleasdale 1985: 215). Recorded from m.20c.; an ironic inversion of l.18c. 'pal', 'partner, associate, friend'; from Romani 'pal', 'brother'.

Palliasse (n.): prostitute; 'promiscuous woman'. '*Promiscuous woman*. Brass,

Pallyass, Good thing, Cert, Charva'
(Minard 1972: 89). Recorded from
l.19c.; part of the repressive discourse
around women's sexuality; from
'palliasse', 'straw bed, mattress'.

Panda (n.): police car. 'Church Street
is swarming with pandas and fuzz'
(Cornelius 2001 [1982]: 162) 'Panda.
Panda car' (Spiegl 1989: 59). Recorded
from m.20c.; from the black and white
colouring of police cars introduced in
the 1960s.

Panel, the (n.): pre-cursor to NHS; later
the NHS. 'I raise my hat to the panel
doctors' (Whittaker 1934: 235). 'I'll
go on UAB [social security] or the
panel [sick leave]' (Parker 1974: 123).
'Pat and Mick fer six weeks, wid no
panel' (Jacques 1979: n.p.). Recorded
from e.20c.; 'the panel' was originally
a list of doctors registered as accepting
patients under the National Insurance
Act (1911) and later the National
Health Service.

Panmug (n.): a large earthenware vessel;
bits of broken pottery. 'A pan-mug of
soapy water stood upon a chair' (Haigh
1907: 192). 'Annie did all her baking
(when there was flour of course) in a big
pan mug' (O'Mara 1934: 62). 'I once
caused consternation in these parts
by asking for a panmug' (Price: 1950:
4). 'One could get a saucer of Irish
stew for a halfpenny, at the side street
by Paddy's Market, served out of big
"panmugs"' (Ford 1957: 6). Recorded
from l.19c.; a north-western dialectal
combination of 'pan' and 'mug'.

Pannymug/bannymug (n.): children's
game, played with broken pottery.
'"Bannymug" was the term, I think,
used by many children for bits of

broken pottery in the once popular
game of "jacks"' (J.A.S. 1950: 2). 'You
never see dat Banny-mug we used to
use when we played shop wid the likkle
girls' (Shaw 1957a: 1). 'Banny-mug:
Pieces of broken pottery used by
children as currency in games and for
making chalk marks on pavements'
(Lane 1966: 6). '"Banny mugs" and
"Jumping Figures"/On the pavement
by the door' (Hallowell 1972: n.p.).
'Bannymug. Broken glazed pottery.
Liverpool' (Howarth 1985: n.p.). See
panmug.

Pantown (n.): Moreton. '*Pantown*: the
township of Moreton' (Lane 1966: 80).
*NR; Moreton, on the north Wirral
peninsula, was once a thriving holiday
town, full of caravan and campsites;
pans were used for transporting water.

Paradise Found (n.): Liverpool One.
'"Paradise Found", the new consumerist
zone of modern Liverpool' (Dudgeon
2010: 52). *NR; a sardonic reference to
the Liverpool One shopping complex;
a play on nearby Paradise Street, and
Milton's *Paradise Lost*.

Paralyse (v.): to beat, hurt, punish. 'Of
like force are the verbs "to paralyse",
"to marmalise", and (a macabre touch)
"to stiffen"' (Farrell 1950b: 4). *NR;
probably from the sense of causing
a person to be unable to think or act
through fear.

Parapet (n.): pavement or footpath.
'The foot paths, called here parapets,
are disagreeable and offensive, they
are all laid with small sharp pebbles,
that render walking in the town very
disagreeable, particularly to ladies'
(Wallace 1795: 273). 'Several persons
were fined in mitigated penalties, for

suffering baskets &c. to remain on the parapets of the streets' (Anon. 1818: 7). 'Meantime the parapet, the carriage road, every court and alley, every nook and cranny, is crowded' (Anon. 1841: 2). 'He started off along the edge of the parapet' (Tirebuck 1891: 6). 'There is one word of the Liverpool vocabulary which seems to have been missed by your correspondents – Parapet for pavement or sidewalk' (R.H.W. 1951: 2). 'Liverpool's exclusive "parapet" for the side-walk is frequently used even by the educated classes' (Whittington-Egan 1955a: 6). 'Along the parapet (sidewalk)' (Shaw 1962f: 12). 'Parapet. Kerbed roadside or footpath. Liverpool' (Howarth 1985: n.p.). 'By which time we were safe on the parapet' (Callaghan 2011 [1910s–30s]: 26). Recorded from 18c.; a Lancastrian term retained in Liverpool; from 'parapet', 'low wall, barrier'.

Parkey/parkie (n.): park-keeper, watchman. 'Parkey (park-keeper)' (Shaw 1954: 4). 'Away from the parkie's hut' (Hignett 1966: 310). 'Five-bob licences obtained from Parkies' (Spiegl 1989: 41). 'Parkie – Park-keeper' (Callaghan 2011 [1910s–30s]: viii). *NR; derivation is clear.

Parkin (n.): gingerbread, usually made from oatmeal and syrup. 'Beef paste sandwiches and a piece of parkin each' (Sinclair 1999 [1930s–e.40s]: 150).

Parlatic (adj.): completely drunk. '"I was absolutely palatic last night." It meant pissed' (Hignett 1966: 76). 'Parlatic. Malapropism for "paralytic"' (Spiegl 1989: 59). 'He'd 've just thought I was pallatic' (Sampson 2001: 119). Recorded from l.19c.; Irish English and Lancashire dialectal; from 'paralytic', in the sense of 'too drunk to do anything'.

Parly/Upper Parly (n.): Parliament/Upper Parliament Street. 'Upper Parly. *Upper Parliament Street*' (Shaw et al. 1966: 33). 'The wagon whizzed past and turned on to Parly' (Murari 1975: 22). '"Where?" "Parly"' (Cornelius 2001 [1982]: 89) 'We cross Parly, past the cathedral' (Sampson 2001: 30). 'An address down Parly, by Somali town' (Griffiths 2003: 179). 'Stanley House on Upper Parly' (Lees 2013: 144). *NR; Upper Parliament Street is one of the main thoroughfares in the south of the city and its fortunes (prosperity, decline, partial regeneration) mirror those of Liverpool itself. 'I'll chase a pup up Upper Parly' was a children's tongue-twister.

Parrot (n.): red and white *ollie*. 'Av loss me parrot, it wuz a tooer. A complaint voiced by children when someone has won a red and white marble from them' (Minard 1972: 42). *NR; supposedly from the plumage of the bird.

Pay out, giving the (phr.): orating, preaching, giving an account. 'Down at the Lanny these days, you get fellas, a bit loopy perhaps, their gates is down, but givin' the pay out' (Shaw 1957a: 15). 'That will be all except for the later account to friends ("Giving the pay out")' (Shaw 1959a: 40). 'He was giving the pay out about ministers and Sunday-school teachers' (Dudgeon 2010: 123). Recorded from l.19c.; from nautical discourse, 'pay out', 'let out a rope or cable'.

Pea whack (n.): pea soup. 'If his mam had made from the cheapest bits of meat some *Pea Whack* (soup) he was contented' (Shaw 1958d: 19). 'Pea wack. *Pea soup*' (Shaw et al. 1966: 40). 'Peawack, scouse or chips' (Jacques 1975: n.p.). 'Peawack. A filling dish made from dried peas and meat. Liverpool' (Howarth 1985: n.p.). '*Peawack* Pea soup' (Spiegl 2000b: 122). *NR; derivation unclear, though possibly *whack*, 'portion, share or allowance'.

Pedlers/peddlers (n.): light clogs. 'To speed things up some kids helped him off with his clothes, of which he had a reasonable amount, socks and pedlers' (Clerk 1971 [*c.*1900]: 62). Recorded as 'Liverpool street arabs': later C.19–early 20' (Beale (1984) *s.v. peddler*); possibly from the footwear of 'pedlars/peddlers', 'itinerant sellers'.

Peggy[1] *(n.)*: menial dogsbody. 'A "Peggy", to the uninitiated, is the "Mary Ann", or "slavey", for the rest of the firemen' (Bower 2015 [1936]: 161). 'Tanjon's now employed a number of elderly labourers to act as Peggies' (Fagan 2007 [1950s]: 181). Recorded from e.20c.; a nautical usage referring to a menial worker on a ship.

Peggy[2] *(n.)*: children's game. 'Peggy. A game … Liverpool' (Howarth 1985: n.p.). 'Peggy, which was played with a stick and a short square peg' (Stamper 2010: 16). *NR; another name for *knurr and spell* and *tip cat*.

Pen (n.): area where men queued for work under the casual labour scheme on the docks. 'Always in the pen (the taking-on stand)' (Shaw 1960b: 5). 'Go down to the Pen (Work on the docks)' (Jacques 1972: n.p.). 'They'd put men into pens and they'd choose them at seven o' clock in the morning, and at

half-twelve they'd have to go back into the pens' (McClure 1980: 399). 'No I won't go down to the docks every morning and stand in a stinking pen' (Bleasdale 1985: 245). 'A dock worker's day in them days consisted of his having to report to "his pen" at 7.45' (Elliott 2006 [1940s–70s]: 77). 'We were hired for work at a control point known as "The Pen"' (Burnett 2011: 8). Recorded from e.20c. in this sense; from 'pen', 'a small enclosure in which animals were kept'.

Pepper thrower (n.): derogatory term for a Catholic. 'Bricks and pepper would be thrown at the lodge. Hence the expression "pepper thrower", to identify a Catholic' (Elliott 2006 [1940s–70s]: 22). *NR; from the practice of throwing pepper at the Orange Lodges as they paraded on July 12th.

Perch Rock Battery (n.): New Brighton. 'The Rock; Perch Rock Battery: New Brighton' (Lane 1966: 90). 'The guiding beacon on Perch Rock' (Channon 1970: 132). *NR; the battery was built to defend Liverpool Bay during the 1820s.

Peter Hudson (n.): a glass of beer containing about a third of a pint. 'My correspondent points out that the "dodger" is known locally as a "Peter Hudson", a name for which he cannot account' ('Postman' 1931c: 5). 'A small glass which contains more than a quarter but rather less than a half-pint of beer. This has been christened locally a "Dodger" or "Peter Hudson"' (Whittington-Egan 1955a: 6). 'A Peter Hudson. *A bastard glass (not Imperial measure)*' (Shaw et al. 1966: 69). 'Peter Hudson. A measure less than half a pint. Liverpool' (Howarth 1985: n.p.). *NR; supposedly named after a l.19c. Liverpool brewer who limited his morning intake to this amount.

Petty (n.): outside toilet. 'Sniffing his way round the petty' (Hanley 1932: 126). '*Petty*: A lavatory' (Lane 1966: 81). 'Outside petties whitewashed for a tanner!' (Unwin 1984 [1920s–30s]: 98). '*Wur's dee petty?* Where is the toilet?' (Spiegl 2000b: 33). Recorded from l.19c.; northern dialectal; from 'petit', 'little', an abbreviation of m.18c. 'little house', 'toilet'.

Phil Garlic (n.): foolish or down-at-heel person. Recorded as a 'Liverpool variant (C. 19–20) of *Pilgarlic*' (Partridge *s.v. Phil Garlic*). A 16c. term of abuse, 'pilgarlic', 'baldy head', extended to mean a pitiable or foolish person; from 'pilled', 'bereft of hair, plucked' and 'garlic'.

Phil, the (n.): The Philharmonic pub, or Philharmonic Hall, Hope Street. 'They'd all be in the Crack or the Phil at nine o'clock' (Hignett 1966: 17). 'They performed in the Philharmonic Hall. The Phil!' (Murari 1975: 52). 'The three corners comprised the Phil, Ye Crack and O'Connor's Tavern' (Cornelius 2001 [1982]: 34). 'The Walker and the Phil are flourishing' (Lees 2013: 274). *NR; derivation is clear.

Phoney (adj.): false, insincere. 'This phony arrest coming so quickly afterwards' (Parker 1974: 166). 'Everything about it was phoney' (Cornelius 2001 [1982]: 51). 'That phoney gas board feller' (Brown 1989: 84). Recorded from l.19c.; an Americanism; an example of a term exported to the USA and then re-imported; possibly originally

from l.18c. 'fawney-rig', a con-trick involving a 'ring' (Gaelic 'fáinne').

Photie (n.): photograph. 'Eer yare tart, wanna fotie?' (Simpson 1995: 22). 'Some shady photie on the website' (Sampson 2002: 123). Recorded from m.20c.; originally Scottish; derivation is clear.

Pick up (v.): earn money. '"She makes more than you've ever picked up"' (Hignett 1966: 61). *NR in this sense; a simple extension of 'to pick up', 'take hold of, gather'.

Pickie (n.): threepenny bit. 'Several other Liverpool expressions of those days – the "Stick": The Landing-stage: a win, one penny: fudge, a farthing: a pickie, threepenny bit' (Bidston 1955: 4). *NR; derivation unknown.

Picture house (n.): cinema. 'The entrance of the picture-house' (Hanley 1932: 83). 'A long time ago there'd been a picture house on the corner' (Murari 1975: 9) 'He pointed over towards a picture house on the other side of the road' (Bleasdale 1975: 131). 'The Forum, which is a Roman picture house' (Brown 1989: 26). Recorded from e.20c.; like *the pictures*, also still in use in Liverpool, *picture house* sounds dated and is probably now older-generational.

Pictures, the (n.): cinema. 'He had denied himself cigarettes and a visit to the pictures' (Hanley 1932: 29). 'I felt as if I was going in the three bobs at the pictures' (Naughton 1945: 21). 'He went to the pictures at five o'clock' (Mays 1954: 104). 'We went to the pictures … The Futurist' (Hignett 1966: 42). 'To take her to the pictures' (Parker 1974: 96). 'One of my mates asked me to go to the pictures' (Robinson 1986 [1920s–30s]: 40). 'Lend us a penny for the pictures please?' (Elliott 2006 [1940s–70s]: 33). 'Our great treat was going to the pictures' (Stamper 2010: 27). Recorded from e.20c.; an Americanism; now dated, though still used.

Pieces (n.): inferior, left-over meat. 'Another [task] we had was to go to Bank's meat shop and stand in the long line to get "two pennorth of pieces"' (O'Mara 1934: 95). *NR in this specific sense; the derivation of this specific sense is clear.

Pier Head jump/jump (n.): taking the place of an absentee sailor to work a passage; unregistered work on a ship. 'Some supported a "Pier Head jump" as the noblest and most heroic course' (Haigh 1907: 26). 'The only thing I could do – was to try to get what is known in Liverpool maritime parlance as a "jump." A "jump" meant filling the berth of an absentee sailor at the last moment' (O'Mara 1934: 261). 'Would you take a jump, Furey, if she turned out to be short-handed?' (Hanley 1935: 540). 'We may have to make a pierhead jump anytime' (Jerome 1948: 129). *NR in this sense; probably an extension of l.19c. American 'jump', 'journey', or, more simply, the act of jumping on board at the very last moment. In Liverpool usage, the term could mean a last-minute decision to engage with a ship, but usually referred to the fact that when sailors who had previously deserted ship (or otherwise lost their registration book), wanted to obtain another passage, they had to find another means of gaining a place on board. The 'jump' was a regular practice, accepted by all concerned; once at sea, the (curtailed) pay of the bookless seaman would be decided, and at the end of the voyage a new 'sea book' would be issued (often under a false name).

Pig and Whistle (n.): crew canteen or bar on ship; a Liverpool pub. 'The "Pig and Whistle" was just one of the 208 public-houses which stood within a stone's throw of the Dock Road' (Hall 2004 [1939]: 22). 'The Crew Bar (called, on every ship, *The Pig and Whistle*)' (Minard 1972: 93). *NR; recorded from 20c.; derivation unknown.

Piggeries, the (n.): high rise flats in Everton. 'Piggeries. Merseyside tower-blocks' (Spiegl 1989: 60). *NR; *The Piggeries*, on William Henry Street in Everton (officially Crosbie, Canterbury and Haigh Heights) were opened in the mid-1960s and uninhabitable by the late-1970s.

Pigs (n.): the police. 'The name for a policeman is pig. Pig!' (Murari 1975: 106). 'The pigs beating P.V. up in the cell' (Cornelius 2001 [1982]: 163) 'Pigs Police' (Spiegl 1989: 60). Recorded from e.19c.; dating to the origin of modern British policing (the Bow Street Runners were called 'pigs'); from 'pig', 'offensive person'.

Pig's foot (n.): pig's trotters, a delicacy, sometimes used in soup. 'Soon mother went in to prepare his spare-ribs or his pig's foot' (Shaw 1957c: 6). 'Ten thousand Spam butties, an' three pigs feet' (Jacques 1972: n.p.). 'Typical Merseyside delicacies in bygone days included tripe and onions, pigs feet or "trotters", cowheels, spice balls, and even sheep's brains' (Unwin 1984

[1920s–30s]: 31). 'Pig's feet, cockles and watercress were favourite snacks sold on every corner' (Lees 2013: 127). Recorded from 15c.; as well as a form of food, the pig's trotter also featured in a phrase commonly used when someone received a blow likely to result in bruising: *it'll be like a pig's foot in the morning.*

Pill (n.): cigarette. '*Pill:* A cigarette' (Lane 1966: 82). Recorded from e.20c.; from 'pill', 'oral medication'.

Pinch (v.): to steal, rob. 'Somebody's pinched those posh pictures' (Hanley 1932: 61). 'He wondered whether his father ever felt scared when he was pinching stuff' (Cross 1951: 17–18). 'There was nothing for anybody to pinch anyway' (Hignett 1966: 133). 'The big boys knew who'd do a screw, smoke drag, pinch a car' (Murari 1975: 122). ''E didn't need ter pinch' (Sinclair 1999 [1930s–e.40s]: 77). 'We seen a boat and we pinched it' (Dudgeon 2010: 87). Recorded from 17c.; originally cant, the term remains common in Liverpool.

Pinky (n.): type of *ollie*. '*Pinky:* A small clay marble' (Lane 1966: 82). *NR; derivation unknown.

Pipe (v.): to watch, notice, inspect. 'A couple of boys were pipe-ing a car' (Parker 1974: 77) 'Looks to me like a livin'-on merchant. We might pipe him' (McLure 1981: 134). 'Pipe. Watch stealthily. Everton' (Howarth 1985: n.p.). 'It was then that I piped my toolbox' (Fagan 2007 [1950s]: 305). Recorded from m.19c.; derivation unclear, possibly from 'peep'.

Piss (n.): any unpleasant drink; weak alcoholic drink. 'He took a gingerly sip of Macon Blanc and declared it piss' (Sampson 1999: 115). '*Whisky,* not povo headfuck cheap piss like that' (Griffiths 2001: 184). Recorded from e.20c.; derivation is clear.

Piss about (v.): waste time; mess around. 'No pissin' about meetin' me half way' (Bleasdale 1975: 56). 'Stop pissin' about' (Robinson 1986 [1920s–30s]: 82). Recorded from e.20c.; from 'to piss', 'urinate', but derivation unclear.

Piss prophet (n.): doctor. '*Piss prophet:* A Physician' (Lane 1966: 82). Recorded from 17c.; from the practice of diagnosis by analysis of urine (once the preserve of market-day quacks, now standard medical procedure).

Pissed (adj.): drunk. 'Pay for us all to get pissed' (Hignett 1966: 94). 'He was pissed. He'd been to this do, y'see' (McClure 1980: 244). 'My dad's a rigger, comes home pissed' (Simpson 1990: 40). 'They were not compos mentis (pissed as newts)' (Stamper 2010: 112). Recorded from e.19c.; derivation unclear.

Pissed off (adj.): angry, annoyed. 'No, I'm pissed off, same as all them down there' (Bleasdale 1975: 13). Recorded from m.20c.; an Americanism (though the contemporary American usage is 'pissed'); possibly derived by analogy with Forces' usage 'browned off'.

Pisseries, the (n.): the Potteries. '*Pisseries, Ther:* The Stoke-on-Trent area' (Lane 1966: 82). *NR; a play on 'the Potteries' (Stoke and surrounding areas), where toilet ware was made.

Pissing down (v.): raining hard or very hard. ''S pissin down It is raining hard' (Spiegl 2000b: 67). Recorded from e.20c.; derivation is clear.

Pisspot (n.): chamber pot. 'A tanner piss-pot' (Robinson 1986 [1920s–30s]: 16). Recorded from 15c.; derivation is clear.

Pisspot jerker (n.): ship steward. 'Pisspot jerker. *A ship's steward*' (Shaw et al. 1966: 57). *NR; presumably from the steward's role of emptying the *pisspot*.

Pitch and Toss (n.): street gambling game. 'Next we played pitch and toss for halfpence under the lamplight' (O'Mara 1934: 133). 'They play pitch and toss or dice in small clusters' (Mays 1954: 72). 'They could still play pitch-and-toss outside Renshaw Hall' (Hignett 1966: 123). 'Shambling off to pitch-and-toss/somewhere against a jigger wall' (Simpson 1995: 27). 'Playing Pitch and Toss, an illegal gambling game' (Callaghan 2011 [1910s–30s]: 24). Recorded as 'pitch-and-hustle' from 17c.; *pitch and toss* was by far the most popular street gambling game (most forms of gambling were not legalised in Britain until 1960), not least because it required only a mark (to pitch) and coins (to toss) – the winner being the coin nearest the mark.

Pivvy (n.): The Pavilion theatre. '"Pivvy" (Pavilion)' (Shaw 1955a: 18). 'I have met with such as "ozzy" (hospital), "rally" (railway), "Pivvy" (the Pavilion Theatre) and "de Pool" (for Liverpool itself)' (Isenberg 1962: 6). 'The old Pavilion theatre in Lodge Lane became known to Liverpool people as the "Pivvy"' (Unwin 1984 [1920s–30s]: 184). 'I remember going to see George Formby at the Pivvy' (Dudgeon 2010: 246). *NR; the Pavilion Theatre, Lodge Lane, was a major South Liverpool entertainment centre in its day.

Placcy (adj.): see *plazzy*.

Plainees (n.): detectives; plain clothes detectives. '*Detectives*. Jacks, Old Bill, Plainees' (Minard 1972: 89). *NR, derivation is clear.

Plant (v.): to punch; hit very hard. 'Aplantudum … *I delivered a punch to his cheek*' (Minard 1972: 83). Recorded from e.19c.; from boxing discourse, probably an extension of 'plant', 'set in the ground'.

Plastered (adj.): very drunk. 'Get plasterd yew basterd, 'appy birthday tew yew' (Minard 1972: 99). 'Pretending to be plastered' (Fagan 2007 [1950s]: 161). Recorded from e.20c.; derivation unclear.

Plazzy/plassy/placcy (adj.): plastic; false, imitation, second-rate. '[We] went down to the Gym with a plassy ball' (Bleasdale 1975: 84). 'Take a good load of plasi bags' (Graham 1988: 152). 'Fuckin plazzy gangsters, the lot of them' (Sampson 1998: 33). 'It's not like thee need placcy fuckin surgery' (Griffiths 2003: 33). Recorded from l.20c.; derivation is clear.

Plonk (n.): wine; alcoholic drink. 'D'you t'ink I'd be any happier in one of dem open-air places wid the plonk and them kewins they call escargots?' (Shaw 1962d: 7). 'A surfeit of plonk and Tankard beer' (Jacques 1972: n.p.). Recorded from e20c.; an Australian coinage; probably rhyming slang for 'vin blanc'.

Plonkie/plonky (n.): a drunk. 'Ee's a plonky. *He is a wine drinker*' (Shaw et al. 1966: 67). 'Plonkie: A wine drinker, usually to excess' (Parker 1974: 213). 'The fella that's in there is violent and a plonkie' (McClure 1980: 72). 'You don't get no auld plonkies hamming it up for their Aussie Whites in G. H. Lees' (Sampson 2001: 239). See *plonk*.

Plug hat (n.): see *blocker*.

Plushbums (n.): the rich. 'Rich folk, plushbums as we called them, were more bent on feeding and clothing natives abroad' (Clerk 1971 [*c*.1900]: 1). Recorded as 'Liverpool low: ca. 1890–1940' (Beale (1984) *s.v. plushbums*); from 'plush', 'comfortable, luxurious' and 'bum', 'idler'.

Pobs (n.): hot milk and bread. 'Milk puddings and pobs were Mr. Mangan's only food' (Hanley 1935: 434). '*Pobs*: Bread and hot milk or any insipid meal similar thereto' (Lane 1966: 83). 'Pobs. Milk and bread as a meal' (Howarth 1985: n.p.). '*Pobs* Porridge' (Spiegl 2000b: 121). Recorded from e.19c.; northern dialectal, possibly from 'pap', 'liquidised food'.

Poke (n.): money. 'Av dun me poke in on dthe gee gees' (Minard 1972: 26). 'You spend yer poke, come home flat broke' (Jacques 1979: n.p.). 'I'd need poke for the move, but I need to think it all out' (Sampson 1998: 128). Recorded from e.20c.; an extension of 19c. Americanism 'poke', 'purse, wallet' ('I've got plenty of scratch in my poke' (Steen 1932: 106).), later 'booty, plunder'; from 14c. 'poke', 'bag'.

Police clothes (n.): clothes given to poor children by the police. 'Many children were wearing the despised police clothes' (Unwin 1984 [1920s–30s]: 47). 'Your parents would be invited to apply for Police clothes' (Elliott 2006 [1940s–70s]: 30). 'They would sooner be in rags than wear police clothes' (Dudgeon 2010: 143). *NR;

police clothes, distributed in e.20c. to the poorest children, carried a social stigma and were despised.

Pong (n.): strong unpleasant smell. 'A dairty great pong. A very bad smell' (Lane 1966: 83). 'The awful pong drifted in' (Sinclair 1999 [1930s–e.40s]: 130). 'Bloody 'ell, what's the pong?' (Fagan 2007 [1950s]: 157). Recorded from e.20c.; derivation unknown.

Ponko (n.): old shawl; worn out blanket. ''E wooden give me a tanner on me ponko' (Lane 1966: 83). *NR; from Spanish 'poncho', 'woollen cape'.

Pony[1] *(n.)*: a quarter of a pint of beer. 'A "dodger" is a glass of beer containing less than a half-pint and more than a "pony" or quarter pint' ('Postman' 1931c: 5). 'That was before the coming of the still smaller "pony"' ('Postman' 1931d: 5). 'A half-pint (quaintly called a *gill*) is bourgeois, a glass less than a half pint ("a pony") being positively effeminate' (Shaw 1959a: 36). 'Pony. A small glass of beer. "A Liverpool half-pint"' (Howarth 1985: n.p.). Recorded from e.18c.; originally 'a small glass or measure of alcohol'; derivation unknown.

Pony[2] *(n.)*: twenty-five pounds. '£25 A Pony' (Minard 1972: 86). Recorded from l.18c.; from gambling discourse; derivation unknown.

Pool, the (n.): Liverpool. 'Next day she went to the 'Pool. Gone on Lime Street as far as I can hear' (O'Flaherty 1925: 110). 'The "Pool" was the capital city of the seven seas' (McColl 1952: 2). 'A barmpot from the Pool' (Martin 1962: 18). 'The toughest part of the Pool to grow up in' (Driscoll 1973: 29). 'All the way back to the 'Pool' (Brown 1989:

18). 'Obviously a couldn't go back ter the Pool after tha' (Griffiths 2000: 312). 'We can go over to the Pool and meet the lads' ((Fagan 2007 [1950s]: 76). Recorded from e.20c.; possibly from Irish English.

Pop (n.): lemonade; alcoholic drink. 'Three bottles of pop' (Hanley 1932: 44). 'Free oranges and bottles of pop' (Hignett 1966: 135). 'I did not want the pop; I needed the empty bottles' (Robinson 1986 [1920s–30s]: 28). 'The two lads ran home as fast as they could with the aspros and pop' (Sinclair 1999 [1930s–e.40s]: 32). 'He's out on the pop every weekend' (Fagan 2007 [1950s]: 76). Recorded from e.19c.; originally any form of fizzy drink (from ginger beer to champagne); from the 'pop' of the cork.

Posh (adj.): smart; (imprecisely) belonging to the middle/upper class; a way of talking. 'Somebody's pinched those posh pictures' (Hanley 1932: 61). 'He was poshing himself up' (Cross 1951: 17). 'I don't like posh people or things' (Kerr 1958: 115). 'I spoke differently and "posher" than they did' (Parker 1974: 217). 'That's what posh people always say when they're going to give you the chop' (Bleasdale 1975: 150). 'One woman in a very posh voice asked for "two nice larm chops"' (Unwin 1984 [1920s–30s]: 39). 'I hope they don't all talk posh' (Robinson 1986 [1920s–30s]: 138). 'Paul McCartney, in respectable middle-age, has almost abandoned Scouse and now talks modified "posh"' (Spiegl 1989: 6). 'Wouldn't have thought she was from the barrio to hear the girl talk … the girl was fucking posh' (Sampson 2002: 42). 'The Wirral did seem posh to working-class Liverpudlians' (Dudgeon 2010: 3). Recorded from e.20c.; this imprecise, usually negative, term connotes social or cultural distinction. Suggestions for its derivation include (in order of plausibility): Romani 'posh-ora', 'money' or 'posh', 'a dandy'; Urdu 'safed-pōś', 'dressed in white, well-dressed'; an acronym for 'port outward, starboard home', i.e. the more expensive (cooler) side for accommodation on ships travelling between Britain and India.

Potty (adj.): crazy, mentally unbalanced. 'She's getting more queer every day. I wonder if she's going potty?' (Hanley 2009 [1936]: 293). 'They were all a bit potty' (Robinson 1986 [1920s–30s]: 19). Recorded from m.19c.; originally 'feeble, indifferent, bad-looking' with the sense of 'craziness' developing in e.20c.; derivation unknown.

Pox Palace (n.): Liverpool Museum of Anatomy. 'Pox Palace, Ther: The famous Liverpool Museum of Anatomy' (Lane 1966: 84). *NR; The Liverpool Museum of Anatomy (closed 1938) was on Paradise Street, in the heart of 'Sailortown'; the dangers of venereal disease figured prominently in the displays.

Pozzy (n.): jam, marmalade. 'Pozzy: Jam or any preserve' (Lane 1966: 84). 'Pozzy Jam or tinned preserve' (Spiegl 2000b: 119). Recorded from e.20c.; Forces' usage; possibly from 'Posy Brand' condensed milk, issued to First World War soldiers.

Pressy/prezzie (n.): present. 'I wanna give y' y' pressy' (Russell 1996 [1975]:

11). 'That was the money we saved up for our Chrissy pressie' (Brown 1989: 86). 'What a nice pressie!' (Sinclair 1999 [1930s–e.40s]: 108). 'It's a fuckin top prezzie' (Griffiths 2003: 207). Recorded as m.20c. 'Aus[tralian] and Merseyside' (Beale *s.v. pressie* n); derivation is clear.

Preston Guild, every (phr.): once in a long time. 'Now you wooden 'eer a good speech evry Preston Guild' (Shaw 1957a: 15). '"Once every Preston Guild" is an expression equivalent to "once in a blue moon"' (Lane 1966: 84). 'Once in a Preston Guild at neap tide' (Lees 2013: 268). *NR; Preston Guilds are held every twenty years.

Prick (n.): annoying person; idiot; general insult. 'Prick, dthat!' (Minard 1972: 81). 'A prick, in my eyes' (McClure 1980: 197). 'Fucking prick' (Griffiths 2003: 9). 'Keep away from that prick' (Burnett 2011: 20). Recorded from 16c.; originally one of a number of distinct though related senses: (male) sweetheart; penis; contemptible or annoying person.

Prig/Prigger (n.): thief, petty thief. 'A "prigger of pomade", as her scientific explorations of the lodger's toilet mysteries, invariably meant a dimunition of Rowland's Kalydor' (Powys 1857: 37). '"You're a poor lot … a poor priggish lot"' (Haigh 1907: 21). 'They are, one might truthfully say, the alma mater of the internationally known Liverpool Prig' (O'Mara 1934: 8). 'This underworld is described as *Rowdies, Bucks, Buckos*, and (rarely now) *Prigs*' (Shaw 1958d: 16). 'He thought these aggressive "prigs" might attack him' (Sanders and Sanders 2009

[1960s]: 121). Recorded from l.16c.; see *prig (v.)*.

Prig (v.): to steal. 'I'll swear I never prigged nothing' nor tried to prig nothin' since' (Roberts 1893: 208). Recorded from l.16c.; cant, derivation unknown.

Pro/prozzie (n.): prostitute. 'She's a pro, that's what she is' (Hanley 1932: 162). 'Druggies, prozzies, dealers' (Grant 2002: 24). 'The pocket dance floor with seasoned "pros"' (Lees 2013: 143). Recorded from m.20c.; derivation is clear.

Prod/Proddie (n.): derogatory term for Protestant. 'You're a prod' (Owen 1961: 17). 'Two Proddies had murdered an innocent Cogger' (Lees 2013: 210). Recorded from e.19c.; derivation is clear.

Proddie/Prot (adj.): Protestant. '*Prot parade*: the annual parade of the Loyal Order of Orange Lodges' (Lane 1966: 84). 'Up to round the Proddie Cathedral just to look at the brasses' (Sampson 2001: 102). Recorded from e.18c.; an Irish English coinage; derivation is clear.

Proddy-dog (n.): derogatory term for Protestant. 'Proddy-dog, Proddy-dog, sittn' on a well;/Up came ther devil an' pulled 'im down ter ell' (Lane 1966: 85). 'Proddydogs Catterlicks' (Jacques 1973: n.p.). 'Catslicks and Prodidogs' (Robinson 1986 [1920s–30s]: 7). 'In search of Proddy dogs, to give them a thrashing' (Grant 1996: 49). '*E's a proddy-dog* He is a Protestant' (Spiegl 2000b: 53). 'Proddy dogs – Catholic taunt for Protestants' (Callaghan 2011 [1910s–30s]: viii). Recorded from e.20c.; 'dog' may be an insulting ironic coinage based on the pronunciation of 'Catholic' as 'Catlick' ('dog' versus 'cat').

Proey (n.): match day magazine at football. 'Anyone gorra proey? *Has anyone purchased a programme?*' (Shaw et al. 1966: 48). '"Proey" is programme' (Channon 1970: 103). *NR; derivation is clear.

Professor Messer (n.): pedant, didact. 'Professor Messer. A didactic person' (Shaw et al. 1966: 29). *NR; derivation is clear.

Prom, the (n.): Otterspool Promenade. 'The prom's in a terrible mess' (Graham 1988: 47). 'Down thee Albert Dock or Otterspool prom' (Griffiths 2003: 86). *NR; Otterspool Promenade (between Dingle Point and Garston) was made between 1925 and 1950 by tipping materials from the excavation of the Mersey tunnel as landfill.

Puck/pug (n.): a hit or blow. 'Poc (pronounced [in Gaelic] puck). – To strike a blow i.e., puck in the gub (a blow on the mouth or nose)' (O'Hanri 1950a: 2). 'Not to mention a "go-along" or a "pug in the gob"' (Shaw 1957c: 6). 'A puck in the gob' (Jacques 1972: n.p.). 'Poc. To strike a blow. Liverpool' (Howarth 1985: n.p.). 'Each received "a puck in the gob"' (Maddox 2008 [1930s–40s]: 15). Recorded from m.19c.; Irish English, from Gaelic 'poc', 'butt' (by a goat), 'stroke of a stick' (as in hurling).

Puckle (v.): pull a face. 'Now don't puckle at me, my girl' (Tirebuck 1891: 244). *NR; probably from 'to pucker', 'to wrinkle, purse lips'.

Pudding eater (n.): pimp. 'Oh aye, a puddin' eater – must be' (McClure 1981: 135). 'PUDDING EATER

A keeper of COWS, a pimp' (Spiegl 1989: 62). Recorded from l.20c.; possibly from 16c. 'pudding', 'vagina'.

Pudding picking (n.): living off immoral earnings. 'Pudden pickin': Living on immoral earnings' (Lane 1966: 85). *NR in this sense; see *pudding eater*.

Puff (n.): derogatory term for homosexual man. 'Like one of them puffy ice skaters on the telly' (Bleasdale 1975: 44). 'A fairy ... a puff! A guy who sleeps with other guys' (Robinson 1986 [1920s–30s]: 152). 'Yeh great big fuckin puff' (Griffiths 2003: 58). Recorded from c.19c.; probably from 16c. 'puff', 'insubstantial, inconsequential person'.

Pug (n.): boxer, fighter. 'Toma was every inch a "pug"' (Jerome 1948: 36). 'Punch-drunk ancient pugs shamelessly labelled Instructors' (Cross 1951: 116). Recorded from m.19c.; an abbreviation of 'pugilist'.

Pulverise (v.): beat up severely. 'The woman fell in her hall and Mrs B. would have "pulverized her"' (Kerr 1958: 140). 'I seen Moby pulverising him' (Sampson 2002: 161). *NR in this sense; an extension of 'pulverise', 'grind, reduce to powder'.

Pump (n.): piss. '"I think I'll nip over yonder for a pump" ... "Me too!" ... The two men hurried across the urinal' (Hanley 1935: 488). Recorded from e.20c.; from m.18c. 'pump ship', 'to pump the ship dry of water'.

Pumps (n.): cheap gym shoes. 'I'm only in me pumps' (Bleasdale 1975: 109). 'He found his pumps' (Sinclair 1999 [1930s–e.40s]: 5). Recorded from 16c.; a type of slipper, probably from 'pomp', 'splendid display'.

Punk (n.): derogatory term for male homosexual. '*Homosexual*. Shirtlifter, Punk, Queer, Turd burglar' (Minard 1972: 89). Recorded from 16c.; a complex word with a variety of negative senses, almost all related to sexuality; the homophobic meaning is a m.20c. American development; derivation unknown.

Punk grafter (n.): beggar. Recorded as 'Liverpool street arabs': late C.19–early 20' (Beale (1984) *s.v. punk grafter*); from 'punk', 'contemptible' and 'grafter', 'beggar'.

Purring (n.): fighting by means of kicking opponent with clogs. 'The grand old English sport of Purring' (Hall 2004 [1939]: 61). Recorded from e.19c.; from 16c. 'purr', 'thrust, prod', extended to dialectal 'kick'.

Push-buggy (n.): pram. 'Push-buggy (American heard in Liverpool). Perambulator' (Ware 1909: 203). *NR; 'baby buggy' is a m.19c. Americanism.

Pusher[1] (n.): girlfriend, wife, woman. 'For a while after the First World War *Pusher* was frequently heard, and later, *Skin*' (Shaw 1958d: 15). Recorded from e.20c.; Forces' usage; 'square pushing' meant 'to "walk out" with a girl'.

Pusher[2] (n.): auctioneer's accomplice. '*Pusher*: A mock-auctioneer's accomplice' (Lane 1966: 85). Recorded from l.19c.; an Americanism; someone who 'pushes' a purchase (as later, 'drug-pusher').

Puss in four corners (n.): children's game. 'You could play "tick", "blind man's buff", "puss in four corners", and so on, without going out of the court' (Roberts 1893: 9). *NR; usually played in a court or square, the game featured four players in corners with one in the middle; the aim was to swap corners without the person in the middle getting there first.

Put the blocks on (v.): to stop, prevent. 'I'm putting' the blocks on heavy pettin'' (Jacques 1975: n.p.). Recorded from e.20c.; derivation unclear.

Putter-on (n.): official who hired workers at docks. 'The putter-on from the firm came out' (Hanley 1932: 92). 'Familiar faces the "putter-on" already trusted were invariably picked' (Lees 2013: 121). *NR in this sense; under the casual work system at the docks, the *putter-on* picked men from the *pen* for the morning or afternoon shift; the role allowd for much discrimination.

Q

Queen (n.): woman, old woman; term of address to woman. 'Yis, I know queen' (Jacques 1977: n.p.). 'Then he says, "Tarra queen"' (Brown 1989: 66). 'Kate was glad to see her and called her "queen"' (Sinclair 1999 [1930s–e.40s]: 80). 'Ahl queen dropped me change' (Griffiths 2003: 61). 'You'll be needin' that ye self, Queen' (Sanders and Sanders 2009 [1960s]: 144). Recorded in this weakened sense from 16c.; often used with affection or respect in Liverpool.

Queen Anne front and Mary Ann back (phr.): pretentiously deceptive. 'Queen Anne front an' Mary Ann back: Said of a woman considered uppish ... [and] of a house thought to be all show with nothing behind it' (Lane 1966: 87). 'She's Queen Anne front – Mary Ann back She is all show and pretence' (Spiegl 2000b: 57). *NR; the force of the phrase lies in the incongruity between 'Queen Anne' and a Mary Ann.

Queen of the wash-house (n.): a gossip. 'Queen o' ther wash-house: An authoritative gossip; a persistent scandal-monger' (Lane 1966: 87). *NR; apparently pejorative, though the term could refer to someone of significant social status since the wash-house was a crucial centre of working-class women's lives, and a good source of news was highly valued.

Queenie (n.): an 'effeminate' man. 'Queenie: an effeminate male' (Lane 1966: 87). Recorded from e.20c.; an Americanism.

Queer (n.): derogatory term for male homosexual. 'It was becoming a reflex, spitting at queers' (Hignett 1966: 272). 'Homosexual. Shirtlifter, Punk, Queer, Turd burglar' (Minard 1972: 89). Recorded from e.20c.; from 'queer', 'strange, odd'; the term was used until its recent reappropriation.

Queer feller/quare feller (n.): strange, odd fellow; whatshisname. 'He's a queer feller' (Hanley 1932: 81). 'A feckless acquaintance is "the queer feller" (or "the quare feller")' (Farrell 1950b: 4). 'De quare feller in de green gansey' (Whittington-Egan 1955c: 216). 'Queer (or quare) feller: Whozit, whatsizname' (Lane 1966: 87). 'The queer feller himself clocks in' (Brown 1989: 6). 'Look who's der – it's dat queer feller' (Sinclair 1999 [1930s–e.40s]: 133). 'The bleedin' queer fella knows what's on the agenda' (Fagan 2007 [1950s]: 102). Recorded from e.19c.; from Irish English; there is no allusion to homosexuality in this long-established usage.

Queg(g) (n.): derogatory term for male homosexual. 'Queggs always seem to have a good sense of humour' (Sampson 2001: 55). 'Coupla fuckin homs ... Two fuckin quegs them, lar' (Griffiths 2003: 210). *NR; a l.20c. variant of queer.

Quick-sticks, in (adv.): very quickly. 'I an' my mates 'll help you out quick sticks'

187

(Hocking 1966 [1879]: 120). 'Two men wuz called in an they landed him out in quick-sticks' (Tirebuck 1891: 437). Recorded from m.19c.; derivation unknown.

Quod (n.): prison. 'Bob Blazes should be sent to quod' (Maginn 1844: I, 239). 'I can't be wuss off in quod than knockin' about, as I 'ave been lately' (Roberts 1893: 209). 'Everybody expected that Michael would soon be captured and taken off to "quod"' (Haigh 1907: 23). Recorded from l.17c.; cant; derivation unclear, though possibly simply from 'quadrangle'.

R

Rack (n.): frame for drying clothes. 'Underclothes that were airing on the rack above the fireplace' (Cross 1951: 137). 'The rack/above the bath hangs heavy' (Simpson 1990: 15). 'The daily, rusty hoist of the rack over the kitchen table' (Bryan 2003 [1940s–50s]: 163). Recorded from 14c. in this sense; glossed as 'rare' though in common use in Liverpool until l.20c.; originally a frame for the drying of skins and cloth; the *rack* was often attached to the kitchen ceiling and could be raised to save space.

Rack, the (n.): see *Monkey Rack*.

Raddled (adj.): drunk; confused. '*Raddled*: Bewildered, confused' (Lane 1966: 88). Recorded from l.17c.; possibly by association with 'addled'.

Rag and bone man/Ragman (n.): a dealer in rags or old clothes. 'A man like a ragman or hawker overtook her on the road' (Anon. 1833b: 3). 'Daniel Healy, a ragman living in the same yard' (Anon. 1867: 5). 'He told her that a ragman gave it to him' (Anon. 1891: 7). 'He saw the defendant arguing with a ragman' (Anon. 1915a: 4). 'Look at Paddy McGee, the ragman' (Hall 2004 [1939]: 29). 'De ragman. *The old-clothes man*' (Shaw et al. 1966: 24). 'I've borried a ragman's bugle' (Jacques 1975: n.p.). 'The rag and bone men with goldfish and balloons in exchange for woollens and jamjars' (Unwin 1984 [1920s–30s]: 79). '*Dee ragman* The old-rags man'

(Spiegl 2000b: 51). 'Rag and bone men, midden men and knife grinders were galoshermen' (Lees 2013: 131). Recorded from 17c.; rags were used for the manufacture of paper, while bones were used in making toys, ornaments, household implements and soap.

Ragged school (n.): free school for poor children. 'The Story of a Ragged School Boy' (Shimmin 1863: 148). 'After a peep in at a ragged school' (Haigh 1907: 118). 'At first elementary education – except in the "ragged school" – charming name – cost a penny a week' (Shaw 1959a: 41). 'The Reverend Lester's ragged school, probably Liverpool's first poor kids shelter' (Clerk 1971 [*c*.1900]: 75). Recorded from m.19c.; *Ragged Schools* were established from the 1840s for the education of the poor (there were around thirty in Liverpool); the 1870 Education Act replaced them with state-provided Board schools.

Ran-tan (n.): loud noise or knocking. 'After giving a good *ran-tan* the other night' (Anon. 1813: 7). 'A ran-tan at every man's door which has startled the inmates' (Anon. 1868: 3). 'Said the policeman briskly ran-tan-tanning Nathan on the shoulder, as if knocking at a door' (Tirebuck 1891: 49). 'Lissen to is rantan. *He is knocking loudly*' (Shaw et al. 1966: 24). 'Ran-tan. Banging loudly and with fervour at a door. Liverpool' (Howarth 1985: n.p.).

Recorded from e.17c.; possibly echoic of the sound of drumming.

Rat catchers (n.): derogatory term for Catholics. '*Rat catchers*: R.Cs. Roman Catholics'. *NR; a play on the acronym 'R.C.'

Ratbag (n.): general insult. 'The landlady, an "old ratbag", came in' (Parker 1974: 130). 'An old rat bag who hated kids' (Robinson 1986 [1920s–30s]: 18). 'The rat bag's bin listenin'' (Fagan 2007 [1950s]: 102). Recorded from l.19c.; derivation is clear.

Rattlers (n.): stairs; trams. 'Let's run up de rattlers (dancers). *Let us go upstairs*' (Shaw et al. 1966: 66). '*Rattler*: A tram or street-car, or (plural) the stairs thereof, or any stairs' (Lane 1966: 88). Recorded from e.17c.; originally 'a vehicle that rattles'; the 20c. extension to 'stairs' is unexplained.

Readies (n.): money; cash. '*Money*: Readies, Poke, Bran Mash, Ackers' (Minard 1972: 89). 'Enormous extra payments in "readies"' (Sayle 1984: 48). 'It was all readies to him' (Grant 1996: 348). 'Lie down and take the readies' (Sampson 2002: 38). Recorded from m.20c.; the plural form of 17c. 'ready', 'cash in hand', from 'ready money', 'funds available for immediate use'.

Ream (adj.): beautiful, good. '*Beautiful*. Custy, Ream' (Minard 1972: 88). Recorded from m.20c.; an extension of m.19c. 'ream', 'genuine'; possibly from Romani 'rumni', 'gypsy'.

Red Biddy (n.): fortified red wine. 'Red Biddy. *Cheap red wine*' (Shaw et al. 1966: 69). '*Red biddy* Cheap red wine, plonk' (Spiegl 2000b: 85). Recorded from e.20c.; Irish English; derivation unknown.

Red meg (n.): fictional therefore worthless coin. '*It ain't worth a red meg*: It is completely worthless' (Lane 1966: 89). *NR; see *meg*.

Red-raddle (n.): red-coloured stainer for steps and window sills. 'Red raddle or yellow ochre, on windows and door steps' (Anon. 1868b: 7). 'The steps and waterway red-raddled' (Anon. 1899: 9). 'Two housewives giving the front doorsteps their usual scrubbing and raddling' (Anon. 1941b: 3). 'The steps all red-raddled right out on to the parapet and arf-way up the broo' (Shaw 1957a: 7). '*Red raddle*: A hard block of red powder, used for cleaning and colouring window-sills, doorsteps and brickwork' (Lane 1966: 89). '*She's red-raddlin* She is colouring the doorstep Cardinal red' (Spiegl 2000b: 48). 'There was red-raddle for window sills, sandstone for the front step' (Callaghan 2011 [1910s–30s]: 17). *NR in this sense; recorded from 14c. in sense of 'raddle', 'red ochre' (oxide of iron), used in rural areas for marking sheep; the m.19c. urban sense refers to the use of *red-raddle* for colouring front steps, tiles, window-sills and so on. It was a matter of pride in working-class areas of Liverpool to have shiny, raddled steps.

Redneck (n.): derogatory term for a Catholic. '*Redneck*: A Catholic. *Also "Cogger" or "Left-footer" or "Ail Mury, "Rat Catcher" or "Crate Egg"*' (Lane 1966: 89). 'Rednecks Papes' (Jacques 1973: n.p.). Recorded from m.19c.; Lancashire dialectal; derivation unknown.

Redner (n.): blush. 'Ee looks around with a redner, obviously feeling daft now'

(Griffiths 2000: 294). *NR; derivation is clear.

Reds, the (n.): Liverpool F.C. 'I could see the rally of the Reds coming' (Anon. 1945f: 3). 'Up the blues, up the reds' (Hignett 1966: 224). 'Dthe redz lost' (Minard 1972: 23). 'He don't play for Everton, nor even the Reds neither' (Brown 1989: 23). 'Devotees of the reds or the blues' (Fagan 2007 [1950s]: 76). *NR; one of the nicknames of Liverpool F.C., based on the red home strip.

Redskin (n.): trouble-maker. 'A redskin. *A trouble maker*' (Shaw et al. 1966: 58). 'Red-skin. A troublemaker. Liverpool' (Howarth 1985: n.p.). 'I'm no redskin with arl the answers' (Simpson 1995: 22). *NR in this sense; an extension of a l.18c. Americanism, now considered offensive, that translates a phrase used in a variety of Native American languages; the extension owes more to the skewed conception of American history which informed Hollywood Westerns than to an accurate representation of historical fact.

Relalio/relievo/re-allyo/Lally Ho (n.): children's game. 'Remember the time we used to play Lally Ho' (Hanley 2009 [1940]: 443). 'The Liverpool version of Prisoner's Base (called Relievo or – from the call Rally O – Relalio) is still popular' (Shaw 1960: 36). 'How about the game "Reliev-oh"?' (Hallowell 1972: n.p.). 'The kids playing alley-oh' (Bleasdale 1985: 251). 'Relieve-o … Done Ya, one, two, three' (Moloney 2001: 11). 'There was re-allyo (a game not unlike hide and seek)' (Stamper 2010: 17). Recorded from l.19c.; northern dialectal; from 'relieve';

a game of chase and catch: the chasing team captured opposing players, while the running team's aim was to release the captives from the base in which they were held (and to shout 'relalio!', 'relievo!' or 'alley-oh' while so doing).

Rhody/rody (adj.): streaky, as in bacon. 'A quarter a rhody bacin' (Shaw 1957a: 18). 'Rodey bacon. *Streaky bacon*' (Shaw et al. 1966: 38). '*Rodey* Streaky bacon' (Spiegl 2000b: 111). Recorded from e.19c.; Lancashire dialectal; from 'roded' (with the same meaning); derivation unknown.

Rig-out (n.): set of clothes; suit. 'I recollect going one night to Paddy's Market and getting a regular rig out for about two shillings' (Shimmin 1863: 152). 'Don't you think we could get the boy a rig-out?' (Haigh 1907: 323). 'I reckoned that was an Australian rig out you got on' (Hanley 1935: 63). 'All the rest of his fancy rig-out' (Hall 2004 [1939]: 72). Recorded from e17c.; an extension of the naval term 'to rig', 'to prepare a ship for sea'.

Riley, living the life of (phr.): having an easy time. 'Having a good time, "leading the life of Riley"' (Shaw 1955: 6). Recorded from e.20c.; an Americanism; derivation unknown.

Ring taw (n.): game of marbles. 'How convenient the court was to play marbles in from "ring taw" to "three holes"' (Roberts 1893: 9). *NR; 'taw', 'large, choice or fancy marble', hence 'game of marbles', is recorded from e.18c.; derivation unknown.

Ring the bell (v.): to make someone pregnant. 'Said of the father of a large family: *'e rings the bell every time*' (Lane 1966: 90). '*Ev'ry time e looks at me e rings da bell* I conceive easily' (Spiegl 2000b: 42). Recorded from m.20c.; possibly an extension of 15c. 'ring the bell', 'to have sex' or 20c. 'ring the bell', 'to achieve success' (as at a fairground challenge).

Rip (n.): old, worn out horse, person; old woman. '"It's no harder for a horse, I suppose; though a rip of a thing it is"' (Tirebuck 1891: 82). 'I'm half in love with the aul' rip' (Sampson 2002: 95). Recorded from l.18c.; dialectal; possibly from 'rep', 'reprobate'.

Road (n.): way, manner. 'For goodness' sake, don't cry a that road. Whatever is to do with the lad?' (Shimmin 1863: 94). 'That's what he would have done had he had his road' (Hanley 2009 [1940]: 572). Recorded from m.19c.; northern dialectal; an extension of 'road', 'way'.

Rob (v.): to steal. 'Robbing your poor mother' (Hanley 1932: 117). 'The man who robbed the shop was found' (Kerr 1958: 120). 'He's a robbing bastard' (Hignett 1966: 273). 'They came here to rob the place' (Murari 1975: 105). 'Going to rob a shop or somebody does take a degree of courage' (McClure 1980: 97). 'ROB. All-purpose scaly word for stealing' (Spiegl 1989: 63). 'When we rob it' (Griffiths 2003: 59). 'Ye friggin' robbin' bastard' (Sanders and Sanders 2009 [1960s]: 100). Recorded from 13c.; now glossed as colloquial, regional and 'incorrect'; more commonly used than 'steal' in Liverpool.

Rob, on the (phr.): intent on, or engaged in, stealing. 'He's still "on the rob" to try and pay off fines which threaten his freedom' (Parker 1974: 209). 'The McQueens decide to go out on the rob and wear decoy pregnancy bumps to stash the stolen items' (Anon. 2009: 5). Recorded from m.19c.; see *rob*.

Robber (n.): a thief. 'The first "Jew man" they went to "was a robber"' (Kerr 1958: 40). 'They're the biggest robbers of the lot' (Parker 1974: 41). 'Burglars and robbers and muggers' (McClure 1980: 119). 'The worst robbers on these docks are the so-called security guards' (Bleasdale 1985: 119). 'I was a robber and he was Plod' (Sampson 2002: 21). 'Not everyone was a robber' (Burnett 2011: 18). Recorded from Old English; more common than 'thief' in Liverpool; see *rob*.

Rockery (n.): the complex set of quays, locks and basins in Liverpool's seven miles of dock. 'The 7-mile line behind which lie nearly forty miles of quays, locks and basins known to the port's pilots as "The Rockery"' (Channon 1970: 139).

Rofe (n.): four pounds. '£4 A Rofe' (Minard 1972: 86). Recorded from 19c.; back-slang for 'four', usually with reference to money.

Roller/roll-boy (n.): religious person. '*Roller* or *roll-boy*: A very pious person' (Lane 1966: 90). Recorded from m.20c.; from the 19c. Americanism, *Holy Roller*, a pejorative reference to Pentecostalists who 'rolled' in the aisles when inspired.

Rollie/rolly (n.): self-rolled cigarette. 'ROLLIES Roll-ups' (Spiegl 1989: 64). Recorded from m.20c.; American prison usage; derivation is clear.

Rolling (v.): stealing from; robbing. 'But we weren't rollin kids really' (Clerk 1971 [c.1900]: 69). 'ROLLIN' Robbing a person' (Spiegl 1989: 64). Recorded from m.19c.; an Americanism; originally 'to rob someone, especially someone drunk'; from 'roll over'.

Rope (n.): cheap lodging house. 'A Rope – a tuppeny kip, we kids knew them as Lascar Ropes' (Clerk 1971 [*c*.1900]: v). Recorded from e.19c.; a reference to a lodging house in which the beds consisted of ropes, suspended from the ceilings and walls, over which sacking was thrown.

Rope (v.): to stitch (a wound). 'Gorra borrivva gash 'n' dthee roped me up' (Minard 1972: 82). *NR; derivation is clear.

Ropey (adj.): bad; poor quality; dangerous; unwell. 'A *ropey do*: A disappointing affair' (Lane 1966: 90). 'Things look like getting pretty ropy' (Brown 1989: 80). 'I like the ropy bints' (Sampson 2002: 85). 'I was still feeling ropey' (Fagan 2007 [1950s]: 315). Recorded from m.20c.; Forces' usage; derivation unclear.

Rotten (adj.): completely drunk. '*Rotten*: Very drunk' (Lane 1966: 60). 'You missed a good night last night, we all got rotten' (Parker 1974: 92). 'You see someone staggerin' and you think they're rotten' (McClure 1980: 363). Recorded from l.19c.; an Australian coinage; an extension of 16c. 'rotten', 'in a poor state'.

Round our way (phr.): in our neighbourhood. 'They wouldn't last long around our way' (Bleasdale 1975: 129). 'Y' can't tell them that round our way' (Russell 1996 [1980]: 285). *NR; this interesting usage can mean 'nearby' ('there are no decent pubs round our way'), but by extension

also something like 'the way we do things' ('round our way, you behave yourself').

Round the bend (phr.): crazy, insane. 'The unfortunate type thought by his workmates to be "round the bend"' (Shaw 1958c: 6). 'Gone round the bloody bend?' (Cornelius 2001 [1982]: 50). Recorded from e.20c.; a nautical phrase; derivation unclear.

Round the twist (phr.): crazy, insane. 'He knew we knew he was around the twist' (Bleasdale 1975: 97). Recorded from l.20c.; probably a derivative of *round the bend*.

Rowdies (n.): gangsters, roughs; the underworld. 'Scrawny children who had grown up exactly as they could have been expected to have grown up – rowdies one and all' (O'Mara 1934: 221). 'This underworld is described as *Rowdies, Bucks, Buckos*, and (rarely now) *Prigs*' (Shaw 1958d: 16). 'It was Christmas night and no one about but a few rowdies who cuffed us' (Clerk 1971 [*c*.1900]: 84). 'A focal point for revellers, vagrants and young rowdies' (McClure 1980: 119). Recorded from e.19c.; an Americanism; originally 'unruly or noisy person, a troublemaker'; the Liverpool usage narrowed to refer to criminals (though the older sense evidently remained); from 'row', 'noisy or violent argument'.

Royal Liver (n.): a five pound note. 'A five pound note [is generally known] as a "royal liver"' ('Postman' 1937a: 6). 'You never hear a five-pound note referred to as a "Royal Liver" these days' (Whittington-Egan 1955a: 6). 'Royal Liver. A five-pound note. Liverpool' (Howarth 1985: n.p.). *NR; this e.20c.

term is probably rhyming slang, 'royal liver', 'fiver'.

Rozzer (n.): policeman. 'I could guess the meaning of rozzer and Judy' (Anon. 1958: 3). 'The word "rozzers" seems to be dying out' (Anon. 1963b: 8). '*Rozzer*: A police constable' (Lane 1966: 91). 'ROZZER Slang for policeman' (Spiegl 1989: 64). Recorded from l.19c.; possibly from 'Robert' ('Sir Robert Peel', founder of the modern British police force), or Romani 'ruzlus', 'strong'.

Rube (n.): fairground or circus worker. '*Rube*: A fairground or circus attendant' (Lane 1966: 91). Recorded from l.19c.; an Americanism; a derogatory term meaning 'unspohisticated rustic, yokel, hick'; an abbreviation of e.19c. 'Reuben', with the same sense.

Ruck (n.): dogshit. 'Mind dat ruck on der parapet. *Beware of the (dog) mess on the pavement*' (Shaw et al. 1966: 45). '*Mind dat ruck* … Beware of the dog-mess' (Spiegl 2000b: 40). Recorded from m.20c. in this sense; originally 13c. 'ruck', 'heap, pile' (of combustible material); later northern dialectal 'untidy heap, tangle'.

Runner, do a (v.): to run away, escape. 'DOIN A RUNNER Running away' (Spiegl 1989: 26). 'She ain't going to be doing no runners' (Sampson 2001: 63). Recorded from l.20c.; derivation is clear.

Runner, ship's (n.): someone who rounded sailors up. 'He was a ship's runner, a man who earned his living partly from the kip houses and partly from the shipping companies' (Jerome 1948: 11). '*The runner*, a rather despicable type' (Hughill 1967: 83). 'The swarms of runners and crimps who waited on the quayside' (Hall 2004 [1939]: 19). *NR in this l.19c. sense; derivation is clear.

Runs, the (n.): diarrhoea. '*Go like a bookie wit' ther runs*: To move very fast' (Lane 1966: 91). '*I got Rangoon runs* I have diarrhoea' (Spiegl 2000b: 108). Recorded from e.20c.; probably from 'to run' to the toilet (hence also 'the trots'), and 'run', 'a flow of liquid'; from 'diarrhoea', Greek διάρροια, 'flowing through'.

S

Sack/Sack something off (v.): to stop, bring to an end; leave, reject. 'It wouldn't be the end of the world if they had to sack it' (Sampson 1999: 442). 'Tempted to sack the whole friggin thing off' (Griffiths 2003: 95). Recorded from l.20c.; an extension of m.20c. 'sack', 'reject a suitor, partner'; from e.19c. 'sack', 'dismiss from a job'.

Saddy (adj.): cruel. '*Saddy*: Cruel' (Lane 1966: 92). *NR; from 'sadistic'.

Sag (v.): to play truant. 'In defiance of the Education Act and Liverpool Education Committee, I "sagged" (played truant)' (Whittaker 1934: 149–50). 'If a lad should *sag* school (i.e., play truant …)' (Shaw 1950b: 4). '*Sagging*. This is definitely the prevailing term [for playing truant] amongst delinquents in all parts of Liverpool' (Opie and Opie 1959: 372). 'Sagging is playing truant' (Armstrong 1966: 6). 'We often go up there when we're sagging school' (Bleasdale 1975: 43). 'Bunk off (i.e. school) Playing truant, i.e. Sagg off' (Spiegl 1989: 19). 'Lerrim go cos we sagged a few classes together?' (Griffiths 2003: 50). 'Sagging – Playing truant' (Callaghan 2011 [1910s–30s]: viii). Recorded from e.20c.; all sources specify '*sag*' as local to Liverpool; possibly an extension of 16c. nautical sense of 'movement or tendency to leeward', hence drifting or being carried out of the intended course.

Sage a mint a parsley (phr.): herb-sellers' cry. 'Sage-ermint-er-parsley!: A very old street cry shouted by female vendors, mostly outside St. John's Market' (Lane 1966: 92). 'Mary Ellens cried their wares of "sage-a-mint-a-parsley"' (Unwin 1984 [1920s–30s]: 76). *NR; this was a familiar call in Liverpool city centre until the 1960s.

Sailortown (n.): area of Liverpool dominated by seamen. 'Sailortown was the main district, lying close to the river' (Hall 2004 [1939]: 10). 'Liverpool's Sailortown sprawled over a large area' (Huggill 1967: 95). *NR; Liverpool's *Sailortown* developed from the e.19c. and eventually took up large parts of the *south end* and *north end*; it was effectively that part of the city that catered for sailors.

Salchester (n.): Liverpool. 'They lived in Falkland Square, one of the best residential parts of Salchester' (Duke 1939: 5). *NR; *Salchester* was Winifred Duke's fictional name for Liverpool.

Sally Gash (n.): Salvation Army. '*Sally Gash*: The Salvation Army' (Lane 1966: 92). *NR; possibly from Scots 'gash', 'foolish, inconsequential talk'.

Salt dolly (n.): salt fish. 'We had codfish, we called "salt dolly", and we would spread margarine over the salt fish' (Stamper 2010: 5). *NR; see *salt fish*.

Salt fish (n.): dried and salted fish (traditionally cod). 'Pork and beans is a Yankee dish,/But give me Sunday morning and the ould salt fish …' (Shaw 1957c: 6). 'You can pop down the road for a piece of salt-fish any day you like' (Rush 1966: 6). 'Sunday without salt fish was akin to Christmas Day without turkey' (Unwin 1984 [1920s–30s]: 31). 'Tell yer mam to give yer salt fish' (Sinclair 1999 [1930s–e.40s]: 78). '"Salt Fish" was and still is to a lesser extent, a Liverpool delicacy' (Elliott 2006 [1940s–70s]: 29). 'Salt fish and bacon for breakfast' (Callaghan 2011 [1910s–30s]: 21). *NR; also known as *bacalhoa*, *salt fish* was a traditional seafarer's dish; particularly popular (on fish-only Fridays) in areas in which large numbers of Catholics lived; from Portuguese 'bacalhau', 'cod'.

Sandgrounder/soundgrubber (n.): person from Southport; Southport F.C. 'The Sandgrounders expect to be able to place a very strong eleven in the field' (Anon. 1916: 6). 'Crewe held the Sandgrounders in the first half' (Anon. 1942a: 3). '*Sandgrounders or sandgrubbers*: Citizens of Southport' (Lane 1966: 92). *NR; Southport has sandy beaches.

Sandstone (v.): to clean front steps with sandstone. 'Another daily routine was the sandstoning of the front steps' (Unwin 1984 [1920s–30s]: 41). 'She was sandstoning the steps of the house' (Sinclair 1999 [1930s–e.40s]: 14). *NR as a verb; front steps were scrubbed with a piece of sandstone or a *donkeystone*.

Sanny (n.): sanitary hygiene inspector. 'We've 'ad ther sanny round ter find ther pong' (Lane 1966: 92). *NR; derivation is clear.

Sap (v.): to make someone bleed. '"Did they sap yer?" a kid asked me' (Clerk 1971 [c.1900]: 21). *NR; Clerk glosses *sap* as 'bleed' (in the context of birching

at a police station); possibly from 'sap', 'vital juice or fluid'.

Sarnie (n.): sandwich. 'The ould fella's sarnies was burnt so he give her down the banks' (Shaw 1963d: 4) 'If they caught yer 'aving a sarny' (Jacques 1975: n.p.). 'Stuck his nose in my sarneys' (Graham 1988: 89). '*Sarneys* sandwiches' (Spiegl 2000b: 121). 'You know that sarnie you scrounged off me' (Fagan 2007 [1950s]: 94). Recorded from e.20c.; Forces' usage; glossed as 'since ca. 1925, Liverpool slang' (Partridge *s.v. sarnies*); derivation is clear.

Sass (n.): Sarsparilla (soft drink). '*Sass*: Sarsaparilla, a soft drink' (Lane 1966: 92). 'Bollasass. *One container of your Sarsaparilla, please*' (Minard 1972: 54). *NR; sarsaparilla was sold in *herbys* and was a legacy of the Temperance movement; derivation is clear.

Savager cane (n.): police signalling stick. 'The police, from police sergeant up, still carry what some might think is a walking stick, or something corresponding to a savager cane' (Clerk 1971 [c.1900]: 42). *NR; some of the higher ranks of Liverpool police carry thick wooden sticks tipped with metal; before modern telecommunications, these were used to send reports by striking the metal against the pavement to send pre-arranged signals. See *signalling sticks*.

Savoury ducks (n.): faggots, meatballs. 'Nothing worth eating – veal pies, sausages, and savoury ducks excepted' (Anon. 1849: 2). '"Savoury ducks" – a compound of onions, flour, and small pieces of pork' (Anon. 1880: 8). 'Blood sausages, black puddings, faggots and savoury ducks' (Anon. 1918: 3). 'Faggots, rissoles, savoury ducks, black puddings, white puddings' (Anon. 1942, 'Are weddin' breakfast was spice-balls. (If that delightful dish, called elsewhere "savoury ducks", is still obtainable it will not be at the rate of 2d a bowlful including gravy)' (Shaw 1959b: 6). '*Savoury ducks*: Faggots' (Lane 1966: 93). '*Faggots, savoury ducks* Meatballs wrapped in cauls' (Spiegl 2000b: 114). *NR; a cheap dish made from minced scrag ends of meat; derivation unknown.

Scadge (v.): to beg, borrow. '*Scadge*: To beg or borrow' (Lane 1966: 93). Recorded from 19c.; an extension of 'scadger', 'mean fellow, always looking for a loan', possibly from Cornish 'scadgan', 'tramp'.

Scalded (adj.): worried, vexed, annoyed. ''E 'as her 'eart scaldid' (Shaw 1957a: 13). Recorded from 19c.; Irish English and Scottish; from 'to scald', 'to trouble, pain, vex; to disgust; esp. in phr. to scald the heart'; an extension of 'scald', 'burn with hot liquid'.

Scaldie, the (n.): the Liverpool–Leeds Canal. 'We went swimmin' in the Scaldie or up at the Cassie' (Shaw 1957a: 4). '*Scaldy. A swimming-hole; part of canal warm with industrial effluents*' (Shaw et al. 1966: 44). 'Scaldie. A canal waterway. Liverpool' (Howarth 1985: n.p.). 'Clarke would dive into the Scaldy and swim' (Lees 2013: 81). *NR; from the fact that the water was 'scalding' from the pollution.

Scaler (n.): descaler on ships. 'Some of them may become scalers and some go to sea' (Haigh 1907: 59). 'Condron was a scaler and a riveter' (Hanley 1932: 5).

'Five went to sea, three were scalers' (Mays 1954: 100). 'Two ship's scalers went into the tank' (Stamper 2010: 84). Recorded from m.19c.; descaling was one of the dirtiest, hardest and most essential jobs in ship maintenance.

Scallicon Valley (n.): Wavertree Technology Park. '[Yours Truly] was among the first to get on the Scallicon Valley trail' (Sampson 2001: 31). *NR; coined somewhat ambitiously after 'Silicon Valley'.

Scallops (n.): potatoes in batter in the shape of a scallop, 'When the parade had passed I was loaded down with the remnants of fish and chips and scallops' (O'Mara 1934: 98). '"Scallops" – sliced potatoes fried in fat' (Unwin 1984 [1920s–30s]: 32). *NR; derivation is clear.

Scally/scal[1] (n.): misbehaving, irresponsible, anti-social person; general insult. 'SCAL(LY) Scouse abbreviation of the nationally used "scally-wag", i.e. a miscreant' (Spiegl 1989: 65). 'They look smart, miniature scals in cords, trainies and Adidas windcheaters' (Sampson 1998: 5). 'Say a bunch of scallies steal a BMW' (Grant 2002: 156). 'Scallies offered to look after the cars' (Lees 2013: 190). Recorded from l.20c.; a Liverpool coinage first associated with young working-class men interested in football and fashion; it soon pejorated to take on anti-social connotations; an abbreviation of *scallywag*.

Scally, scal[2] (adj.): like a *scally*. 'Scally Nige heading for small screen stardom' (Chapple 2007: 3). See *scally*[1].

Scally (v.): to behave like a *scally*. 'I can see us, little rats, scallying around that

Garden Festival' (Sampson 2001: 7). See *scally*[1].

Scallywag (n.): rough, irresponsible, anti-social person; general insult. 'He is a real scallywag, always playing truant' (Shaw 1957a: 13). 'To deal with these scallywags living round here' (McClure 1980: 91–2). 'There are a lot of evil scallywags out there' (Kelly 2006 [1930s–40s]: 77). 'A Liverpool 8 scallywag' (Lees 2013: 143). Recorded from 19c.; an Americanism; originally either a native white of the southern states who was willing to accept post-Civil War Reconstruction, or, in Trade Union discourse, someone unwilling to work.

School board (n.): school attendance officer. 'The attendance officer – then called the "School Board" for some reason' (Unwin 1984 [1920s–30s]: 10). 'I'll tell the school board (truant officer) about you' (Elliott 2006 [1940s–70s]: 39). 'Failure to attend school meant a visit from the school board, Mr. Percival' (Callaghan 2011 [1910s–30s]: 29). *NR in this specific sense; School Boards were set up to administer public elementary schools after the 1870 Education Act.

Schoolie (n.): school pupil; young girl. 'Schoolie. Juvenile still at school' (Spiegl 1989: 66). 'Little posses of hooched-up schoolies and shopgirls' (Sampson 2001: 112). Recorded from l.20c.; an extension of l.19c. 'schoolie', 'schoolteacher'.

Scoff (n.): food. 'I went to work in the kitchen, ladling out the "skoff"' (Whittaker 1934: 252). 'The generic word for food ("scoff")' (Farrell 1950b: 4). 'So feed him if he wants scoff; give him a bevy if 'e's thirsty' (Anon. 1967b: 4). 'His Chinese scoff' (Jacques 1972: n.p.). 'In common parlance, he's having his scoff' (McClure 1980: 36). 'A mensive or "posh-scoff"' (Moloney 2001: 48). 'Chicken scoff' (Sanders and Sanders 2009 [1960s]: 80). Recorded from l.18c.; from the South African Cape Dutch borrowing of Dutch 'schoft', 'quarter of a day' (hence each of the four meals of the day).

Scoff (v.): to consume voraciously. 'Before … Lynch and Bob Steele get back and scoff the lot' (Martin 1963: 160). 'I was scoffin' one of the sarnies me Mam had made for me' (Bleasdale 1975: 93). 'We scoffed it right from the pan' (Robinson 1986 [1920s–30s]: 84). 'We'd scoffed the lot' (Jones 1999: 26). 'Scoffing his breakfast' (Fagan 2007 [1950s]: 215). See *scoff (n.)*.

Sconehead (n.): generic insult, stupid or ugly. 'The reason for Sconehead is obvious, and not very clever' (Shaw 1954: 4). 'Beat it, scone 'ead' (Jacques 1972: n.p.). 'No, scone'ead, this is it' (Bryan 2003 [1940s–50s]: 138). *NR; derivation is clear.

Scooby (n.): clue. 'Have not got a fucking scooby where he's going with this' (Sampson 2001: 292). '"Guess what he sees?" "Norrer scooby"' (Griffiths 2003: 180). An e.21c. coinage; rhyming slang (Scooby Doo).

Scoot (off) (v.): to leave in a hurry, run off. 'I have heard "scoot", "skelp" and "slavey"' (D.W.F.H. 1951: 3). 'Lordy, but he did scoot' (Cross 1951: 206). I scoot along, legs kicking wildly' (Robinson 1986 [1920s–30s]: 67). Recorded from m.18c.; originally 'scout' and probably nautical, the term became obsolete and was revived as an American import; from Old Norse *skióta, 'to shoot', hence perhaps 'to shoot off'.

Scoots (n.): roller skates. '*Scoots*: roller skates' (Lane 1966: 93). *NR; a variant of 'skates' playing on 'to scoot'.

Score (n.): twenty pounds. '£20. A Score of Quids' (Minard 1972: 86). 'Give the lad a score' (Sampson 2002: 199). Recorded from e.20c.; an extension of 'score', 'set of twenty'.

Score, know the (v.): to understand. '"Knowing the score" about theft' (Parker 1974: 6). 'You know the score Chrisse – there's nothin' down for y'' (Bleasdale 1985: 52). 'Everyone in the family knew the score' (Simpson 1995: 31). 'She knows the fuckin' score' (Burnett 2011: 81). See *score*.

Score, the (n.): how things stand; the state of affairs. 'If he hadn't come back to see what the score was' (Hignett 1966: 245). 'What's the score, Tommy?' (Smith 1998 [1971]: 76). 'What's the score then?' (Graham 1988: 41). Recorded from e.20c.; an extension of sports' 'score', 'record of points, goals'.

Scotchman (n.): Pedlar (usually draper) who sells on credit. 'My husband had swore if I ever ordered anything from a "Scotchman" again what he would do' (Shimmin 1863: 14). Recorded from 17c.; glossed as dialectal, and with a general sense of 'nuisance', from 'Scotch', with the same meaning.

Scotty/Scotty Road (n.): Scotland Road. 'Scotland Road is known (by the people who do not live on it) as "Scottie Road"' (Farrell 1950a:

4). 'Scotty Road wassen too clever neether' (Shaw 1957a: 5). 'After seeing her back to Scotty Road' ('Postman' 1961a: 4). 'The old Scottie Road was always a flurry of activity' (Unwin 1984 [1920s–30s]: 60). 'Going down Scotty Road like the clappers' (Brown 1989: 10). 'We don't really talk different to the Scotty Road crew' (Sampson 2002: 24). 'Scottie was divided into parishes' (Dudgeon 2010: 66). *NR; impoverished, and much mythologised, working-class area just to the north of the city centre, once composed of a variety of immigrant communities (mostly Irish but also Scottish, Welsh and to a much lesser extent Italian and German) and often the site of bitter sectarianism.

Scouse[1] *(n.)*: a type of stew; the Liverpool dish. '14 Measures potatoes for scouse Onions for ditto' (Eden 1797: 2.336). 'The prison diet … consists principally, of oatmeal porridge, scouse, herrings, and bread' (Anon. 1824: 6). 'They liked this scouse better than they did potatoes' (Anon. 1847: 7). 'It is a kind of stew or scouse, or something of that sort' (Anon. 1870: 3). 'Liverpool Workhouse "Scouse"' (Anon. 1895: 6). 'The custom is to provide scouse, or, as the writer calls it, "stew", three times a week' (Barrett 1915: 7). 'Memories of many a feed of scouse in my old home in the city's dockside area' (Anon. 1939b: 4). 'Years ago … "scouse" was the main midday meal for seamen and dockers in Liverpool, and all the dockside public houses made it one of their specialities' ('Postman' 1942c: 2). 'A good pot of scouse' (Ash 1954: 135). 'A pan of scouse' (Hignett 1966: 134).

'Brung up on Guinness and scouse' (Jacques 1975: n.p.). 'Dinner a plate of cheap but nourishing scouse' (Unwin 1984 [1920s–30s]: 9). 'We'd be sittin there eatin ar scouse like' (Griffiths 2003: 112). 'The term Scouse referred to a recipe born out of poverty and the cheapest cuts of meat' (Callaghan 2011 [1910s–30s]: 28). Recorded from l.18c.; a Liverpool abbreviation of e.18c. 'lobscouse', a type of poor gruel served on ships; derivation unclear but suggestions range from 'lob's course' ('lob' meaning 'clown, lout'), to the more plausible (given the trade links to the Baltic) Latvian 'labs', 'good', 'kauss', 'bowl'.

*Scouse*² *(n.)*: native of Liverpool. 'The term "scouser", which is now applied in the Navy to ratings from Liverpool, seems to be derived from an expression in common use in dockland when I was a youth … "Hello Scouse", was how one man would hail another in jocular greeting' ('Postman' 1942b: 2). 'A member of the Royal Navy said to me the other day, "When any chap from Liverpool joins our ship, we immediately christen him Scouse"' (Hill 1945: 2). 'The Army knows its "Scouses" and their sense of humour. From personal experience I can confirm that where there's a "Whacker" (a pal), there's a quip and a quake of laughter' (Anon. 1945b: 8). 'You're not a Taffy – you're a Scouse' (Owen 1961: 89). 'A dirty, lazy, lousy, shiftless, no-good scouse' (McColl 1952: 9). 'Have you ever heard anybody calling anybody else scouse?' (Hignett 1966: 90). 'At present it is not in vogue to use the word "scouse" on Merseyside' (Jacques

1973: n.p.). 'Go on Scouse!' (Robinson 1986 [1920s–30s]: 151). 'Come on, Scouse. You're the boss, eh?' (Sampson 1998: 85). 'Don't worry, Scouse' (Kelly 2006 [1930s–40s]: 122). '[Scouse]: Applied to an individual it meant that person was the lowest of the low, a remark often leading to bloodshed' (Callaghan 2011 [1910s–30s]: 29). See *Scouser*.

*Scouse*³ *(n.)*: the language of Liverpool. 'Scouse Lingo – How It All Began' (Shaw 1950b: 4). 'What the last few weeks prowling around the whilom Scouse-speaking territory has shown me – the dialect is disappearing' (Whittington-Egan 1955a: 6). 'Some bits, as most old Merseyside readers will detect, are not old enough to be real "Scouse"' (Dwyer 1957: 6). 'Save our Scouse – the dying language of Liverpool' (Hodgkinson 1960: 11). 'Liverpoolese, Yes, But I Don't Like "Scouse"' (Shaw 1962c: 8). *Lern Yerself Scouse* (Shaw et al. 1966: title). 'Scouse isn't what it used to be' (Whittington-Egan 1972: 10). 'In the sixties, all over Britain, it was the trendy thing to adopt a scouse accent' (Cornelius 2001 [1982]: 29). 'Well finally I made it and I bought that house/First thing I did was stop talking scouse (McGovern 1995: 6). 'Scouse is the name given to the accent and dialect of Liverpool' (Briscoe 2003: 5). 'Scouse is sharp, fast, colourful and chatty' (Lees 2013: 133). Recorded from m.20c.; the evidence clearly indicates that the use of *Scouse* to refer to the language of Liverpool dates no further back than 1950 (and indeed it might be observed that central to its coinage was the belief that it was dying out – a persistent if mistaken belief about dialects); an extension of *Scouse*[2].

Scouse alley (n.): foodsellers in Paddy's Market. '"Scouse Alley", the line of refreshment booths on the waste ground in Fontenoy Street, known as Paddy's Market' (Anon. 1939b: 4). 'St. Martin's Hall, off Scotland Road, which was one of the cheapest eating places in the city. "Scouse Alley" they called it' (Unwin 1984 [1920s–30s]: 61). *NR; see *scouse*[1].

Scouse boat (n.): market cart selling scouse. 'A cart selling cheap stew in a poor area at the turn of the century was popularly known as the "Scouse boat"' (Shaw 1958d: 18). 'A penny a plate at the Scouseboat' (Lees 2013: 1331). *NR; see *scouse*[1].

Scouse shops (n.): early twentieth-century dockland cafés. '"Scouse shops" were the dock-road eating houses' (Anon. 1939b: 4). *NR; see *scouse*[1].

Scoused (adj.): drunk. 'A person who was well "lit up" or a customer well-beaten was said to be "scoused"' (Anon. 1939b: 4). 'She says evryt'ing but her prurs if I get scoused' (Shaw 1957a: 7). *NR; derivation unclear.

Scouseland (n.): Liverpool. 'A book he hopes to publish shortly on the lingo of Scouseland' (Anon. 1951: 4). 'And you're from Scouse Land?' (Owen 1961: 128). 'Come on, Scouseland's not too bad' (Brown 1989: 47). Recorded as 'Liverpool: nautical and (Liverpool) dockers': late C. 19–20' (Partridge *s.v. Scouseland*); see *scouse*[1].

Scouseology (n.): the study of all things Scouse. 'If ever anyone wants an Anthology of Scouseology' (Shaw 1963b: 6). 'During the hooley an honorary degree in Scouseology will be conferred on guest Frank Shaw' ('Postman' 1968: 4). *Whitbread Book of Scouseology* (Young and Bellew: 1986: title). 'It is part of Scouseology that the Wirral is alien and distinct' (Dudgeon 2010: 3). *NR; in 1968, at the inaugural meeting of the Warwick Wackers Club at the University of Warwick, Frank Shaw, the first 'professional Scouser', was awarded an honorary degree in Scouseology – B.Sc[ouse].

Scouseport (n.): Liverpool. '"Blocker", which often puzzles strangers in Scouseport' (Shaw 1964a: 12). 'Scouseport. In my young day the river was full of boats, great windjammers and liners queuing up for the Stage' (Clerk 1971 [c.1900]: 61). *NR; derivation is clear.

Scouser (n.): person from Liverpool. 'They have a special nickname in the "Silent Service" for ratings from Liverpool. Men from these parts are known as "scousers", a name I have not heard before' ('Postman' 1942a: 2). 'An old Liverpool seafarer who has been familiar with the term "scouser" for many years suggests that it actually does owe its origin to the stew or hot-pot colloquially known as "scouse". Years ago of course, this "scouse" was the main midday meal for seamen and dockers in Liverpool, and all the dockside public houses made it one of their specialities … Many a time he has heard one seaman remark to a Merseyside man: "Oh, you come from the place of scouse". And from this it is only a short step to calling a Liverpool man a "scouser"' ('Postman' 1942c: 2). 'The Army nickname for a Liverpool man is "Scouser" and the members of the "Scouser" club are his brothers' (Anon. 1943c: 2). '"Scouse", the local stew, gave to native members of the armed Forces (N.C.O.s and men) the name "Scousers". This term is hardly ever used as a mark of affection' (Farrell 1950b: 4). 'How the "Scousers" found their dialect' (Smith 1955: 5). 'The name Scouser for the Liverpool man is modern and I should say was created by the Royal Navy' (Wynn 1957: 6). 'I was born in Liverpool in 1879 ... I came South in 1913 and it was not until years after that I heard the unlovely term "Scouser" used, and I feel fairly certain it was a wartime affectionate mark of disrespect that crept into circulation via the Army' (Bindloss 1957: 6). 'Whenever the term "scouser" originated, it seems to have crept into general use in the Scotland Road area of Liverpool after the First World War' (Anon. 1957a: 6). 'D'y'mean that scouser?' (Owen 1961: 127). '*Scouser*, an inhabitant of Merseyside, not necessarily a Liverpudlian' (Lane 1966: 93). '"Scouser" was a name not used in my youth ... when Dicky Sam was the nickname' (Shaw 1971: 20). 'Quite a colony of Scousers (a term I dislike using)' (Jacques 1972: n.p.). 'Brenda and Mary, two girls from Liverpool. Real Scousers' (Flame 1984: 108). 'The Scousers still see us as Wools' (Sampson 1998: 3). 'Another Scouser who left the city' (Griffiths 2003: 40) 'The Sergeant Major then said "You're

a scouser aren't you?" I had never heard the expression before' (Elliott 2006 [1940s–70s]: 141). 'The Scouser defends England against the evils of vanity and intellectual self-deception' (Lees 2013: 137). Recorded from m.20c.; Partridge claims that *scouse*² and *Scouseland* were l.19c. and e.20c. 'nautical and (Liverpool) dockers' usage (Partridge (1961) *s.v scouse*; *Scouseland*), and there seems to be some evidence in the quotations cited above in relation to both terms to support the claim. What is clear, however, is that both *scouse*² and *scouser* were not generally used to refer to people from Liverpool until the Second World War and after, and that the appellation was created in Forces' usage. Before that time the more widely used terms were *Dicky Sam* and, much later, *whacker*. It is also evident that *scouse*² and *scouser* were often considered negatively until relatively recently, and that their full acceptance can be dated only to the last fifty years or so at most.

Scouserism (n.): Scouse linguistic ways; the philosophy of Scousers. 'The language side of "Scouserism" is based upon economy' (Anon. [L. Iver] 1957: 4). *NR; the coiner of the term discriminates between *Liverpoolese* and *Scouserism* thus: 'If one calls a cat a "moggie" or an entry a "jigger", that is "Liverpoolese" but if one says "Act soft and I'll buy yer a coalyard", when someone pretends they cannot understand what you are getting at, then that's a "Scouserism"'.

Scousette (n.): woman scouser. '"Scousette"? ... A friend of mine in the W.A.A.F., home on leave, tells me that she has several times been called a "scouser" when people have found out where she comes from. As she is rather a smart young woman, the rather rough title of "scouser" seems inappropriate' (Anon. 1945a: 2). *NR; the term didn't catch on.

Scow (v.): to play truant, idle. 'He'd ha been laffin bags if this blockerman hadden a found him scowing in the shed uv a monkey boat' (Shaw 1957a: 7). '*Sagging* ... is definitely the prevailing term [for playing truant] amongst delinquents in all parts of Liverpool. A student, however, adds "scowing" as a Liverpudlian expression' (Opie and Opie 1959: 372). 'I wuz on der welt; I wuz scowing, I was having an unofficial spell of leisure time' (Shaw et al. 1966: 58). '"Scowing" is idling' (Channon 1970: 102). 'Scowe. To be idle on the job. Liverpool' (Howarth 1985: n.p.). Recorded from l.19c.; a l.19c. northern dialectal abbreviation of 18c. 'scowbanker', 'dishonest businessman', which became 19c. 'idler, loafer'.

Scran (n.): food, meal. 'A surfeit of nicknames with which to describe the stuff of life. It may have the general name of "scran" or "mungy"' (Anon. 1917: 3). 'Scran. Food. Liverpool' (Howarth 1985: n.p.). 'Bit of scran downstairs, bottle of wine' (Sampson 2002: 44) 'We went out on thee ale an we're down Hardman Street an she wants some scran. Gets a chicken burger' (Griffiths 2003: 187). Recorded from l.19c.; a 19c. nautical extension of 18c. cant 'scran', 'a reckoning at a boozing-ken' (pub).

Scrap (n.): fight. 'Let's see a damned good scrap' (Whittaker 1934: 256). 'It won't do either of us any good to start scrappin' (Jerome 1948: 138). 'The Liverpudlian says "Come on I'll 'ave you a go" ... or "I'll have you a scrap"' (Opie and Opie 1959: 197). 'A Fight. A Scrap, a Lumber, a Go' (Minard 1972: 89). 'If yer wants ter scrap' (Sinclair 1999 [1930s–e.40s]: 14). Recorded from m.19c.; from boxing discourse; possibly from 'scrape'.

Scratch (n.): money. 'I've got plenty of scratch in my poke' (Steen 1932: 106). 'Scratch is – money, not dope' (Smith 1998 [1971]: 14). Recorded from e.20c.; an Americanism; derivation unclear.

Screeve (n.): car. 'Car. Screeve' (Minard 1972: 88). Recorded from m.20c.; from Romani 'skreev', 'car'.

Screw[1] (n.): prison warder. 'Screw: A prison officer' (Lane 1966: 93). Recorded from e.19c.; probably an extension of l.18c. 'screw', 'skeleton or false key' hence 'warder', 'turnkey'.

Screw[2] (n.): sexual partner, usually female. '"A bloody good screw" might refer to an attractive girl' (Lane 1966: 93). Recorded from e.19c.; an extension of e.18c. cant 'screw', 'prostitute' (see *to screw*[2]).

Screw[3] (n.): a job. 'I preferred a straight screw with none of the responsibility for breakdowns and broken contracts' (Melly 1965: 142). Recorded from m.20c.; an extension of m.19c. 'screw', 'wages or salary'.

Screw[4] (n.): a robbery. 'Breaking and entering. It was a stupid screw' (Murari 1975: 28). See *screw*[1] *(v.)*.

Screw[1] (v.): to break into, rob, steal from. 'They had robbed him, and screwed him, and bullied him' (Powys 1857: 30). '*Screw* can also mean to commit a burglary or to have sexual intercourse, or wages' (Lane 1966: 93). 'We was trying to screw the perfume in Boots side window' (Bleasdale 1975: 48). 'I was draggin' a fella out of the bullring one day – for screwin' a car' (McLure 1980: 51). 'There's the place … we're gunner screw' (Griffiths 2003: 58). Recorded from e.19c.; an extension of l.18c. 'screw', 'skeleton or false key'.

Screw[2] *(v.)*: to have sex with. 'You come here to screw all our birds?' (Hignett 1966: 221). 'The tarts round here don't all screw' (Parker 1974: 135). 'More drag, a beef to screw, a car ride' (Murari 1975: 85). Recorded from e.18c.; cant; 'screw', 'to copulate with a woman'.

Screwy (adj.): silly, insane. 'Screwy, that was what she was' (Cross 1951: 77). '*Screwy*: Daft' (Lane 1966: 94). 'He was a bit queer, screwy like' (Parker 1974: 28). 'The screwy ta-ta gives him the right one' (Brown 1989: 9). Recorded from m.19c.; an Americanism; probably from 'a screw loose', 'something wrong'.

Script (n.): prescription, usually for narcotic drugs. 'Script. Abbreviation for a prescription' (Spiegl 1989: 66). 'All aloof to them crusties around her, must be script day for em' (Griffiths 2003: 64). Recorded from m.20c.; an Americanism; an abbreviation of 'prescription'.

Scrubber (n.): prostitute; general insulting term for woman. 'A scrubber was a girl who slept with a jazzman but for her own satisfaction as much as his' (Melly 1965: 172). '*Scrubber*, used instead of "tart" which has a non-derogatory meaning. "A right scrubber" is a girl who's rough-looking, whore-like' (Parker 1974: 213). 'Don't call me a soft owl get, ye fuckin' scrubber' (Sanders and Sanders 2009 [1960s]: 103). Recorded as 'Liverpool (C.20), a prostitute' (Partridge *s.v. scrubber* n. 7); a derogatory evaluation of women in general and working-class women in particular; an extension of 'scrubber', 'a woman who scrubs' (a *charwoman*).

Scruff (n.): insult, generally referring to working-class people. 'Ordinary low people are Scruffs' (Shaw 1958d: 16). 'You're behaving like a gang of common scruffs' (Russell 1996 [1976]: 126). 'It, well, like, sets you apart from the scruffs' (McClure 1980: 39). 'Me a Bootle scruff' (Simpson 1990: 39). Recorded from m.19c.; a dialectal extension of 16c. 'scruff', 'worthless waste'.

Scruffy King's (n.): The King's Regiment (Liverpool). 'It is, however, not unlikely that one of "The Scruffy Kings" had given it to the Army before that' (Shaw 1950b: 4). 'It is strange to find the Army generally calling the Liverpool Regiments The Scruffy Kings' (Shaw 1958d: 16). Recorded from e.20c.; the 8th King's Regiment became known as The King's (Liverpool Regiment) in 1881; it disappeared through amalgamation in 1958.

Scuffer (n.): policeman. '"Scuffer", policeman' (Jones 1935: 5). 'Dowse lads, here's the scuffer' (O'Hanri 1950a: 2). 'Dodging the *Jacks* (detectives), the *Scuffers* (Police, *Slops*, also being used) or their friends' (Shaw 1958d: 16). 'The place was swarming with scuffers' (Hignett 1966: 116).

'Dthe scuffers nicked him' (Minard 1972: 56). 'The whole shop is alive with scuffers' (Brown 1989: 14). 'Make sure that the scuffers don't spot you' (Kelly 2006 [1930s–40s]: 84). Recorded from m.19c.; probably either from dialectal 'scuff', 'nape or "scruff" of the neck', hence 'to seize or shake by the nape of the neck', or 'to strike with an open hand' ('she "scufts him" for being in the way' Shimmin 1863: 49).

Scuird/scard (n.): splash (drink). 'A scuird of tea' (O'Hanri 1950b: 6). '"Scuird", despite its foreign-seeming, is generally regarded as the Gaelic loan-form of English "squirt"' (D.W.F.H. 1951: 3). Recorded from m.20c.; from Irish English 'scaird', 'jet, squirt or splash', from the Gaelic 'scáird', 'squirt, splash, gulp'.

Scuppered (v.): beaten; finished with, done for. '"E orter be 'ung, drawn an' scuppered*: He should be punished' (Lane 1966: 94). Recorded from l.19c.; supposedly derived from the fact that a man who died on deck might fall into a ship's scuppers.

Sea-pie (n.): Scouse. 'Sea-pie*: Scouse' (Lane 1966: 94). *NR; presumably from the nautical origins of *scouse*[1].

See (v.): to make a bet. 'See (American). To "bet" … a word which now may often be heard in Liverpool commercial cotton circles' (Ware 1909: 218). Recorded from 16c.; originally from the card game 'brag'; the Liverpool usage marks an interesting extension from gambling to the stock market (another form of gambling).

See that wet? (phr.): what follows is true. 'See that wet?*: I am about to tell the truth' (Lane 1966: 94). *NR; this e.20c. saying derives from a children's oath which involved licking a finger, holding it up, and reciting: 'See that wet, see that dry? Cut my throat if I tell a lie' (Opie and Opie 1959: 127).

See yer at the Assizes (phr.): see you later. Recorded from m.20c.; 'the Liverpool version of the more general catch phrase "see you in court"' (Beal (1985) *s.v. see you in court*).

Seen (v.): past tense of see. "E done it – I seen him' (Lane 1966: 94). 'Pete seen it parked there since last night' (Murari 1975: 90). 'That's so's you know why I never seen you' (Sampson 2002: 210). 'I seen our Marge' (Simpson 2011: 415). See *come, done, give* etc.

Segs on his arse (phr.): lazy. 'Segs: Areas of thickened skin … got segs on 'is arse is said of a lazy, shiftless person' (Lane 1966: 94). *NR; 'seg' from m.19c.; northern dialectal, ultimately Old Norse 'sigg', 'hard skin'.

Serang (n.): Indian seaman; *Lascar* officer. 'He looked like a Lascar … Jim had used the word "serang" or something similar' (Baird 1957: 66). 'Followed by the SERANG, an Indian bo'sun' (Owen 1961: 19). 'A common sight at the Landing Stage were the Lascars … often accompanied by a sword-wearing serang of higher caste' (Lees 2013: 79). Recorded from l.18c.; *serang* is the Indian English rendering of Persian 'sarhang', 'commander' and referred to the native captain of a Lascar crew.

Sett (n.): large paving stones. 'Setts: Granite road-blocks' (Lane 1966: 95). 'It was cobbled or made of stone sets' (Kelly 2006 [1930s–40s]: 100). 'Most of the dock road was made up with granite sets' (Stamper 2010: 200). Recorded from l.19c.; derivation unknown.

Seven Hedges (n.): 'top of Dingle Lane' (Jones 1935: 5). *NR; derivation unknown.

Sevvy/Seffy Park (n.): Sefton Park. 'We might go to Shawrie or Seffy an' try ketchin' jackies' (Shaw 1957a:2). 'In Seffy Park, wid Micky keepin' douse' (Anon. 1965: 4). 'I'm goin' fishin' in Sevvy Park' (Spiegl 1989: 41). 'Kickin back in Sevvy Park with a spliff' (Griffiths 2003: 52). *NR; one of Liverpool's most important municipal parks, Sefton Park was opened in 1872.

Shaddle (n.): seesaw. '"Shaddle", a word used by all Liverpool children to denote the see-saws used in children's playgrounds' (Griffith 1950: 2). 'The was climp shaddles in the Mizzie' (Shaw 1957a: 4). 'Why should to see-saw be to shaddle?' (Armstrong 1966: 6). 'Shaddle. A children's see-saw. Liverpool' (Howarth 1985: n.p.). *NR; derivation unknown.

Shag¹ (n.): sexual intercourse. '"Tap one" for "a quick shag"' (Parker 1974: 137). 'The Busy tries to keep things light, saying he's on for a shag if he gets home early today' (Sampson 1999: 10). 'I wish I had thee energy for a fuckin shag' (Griffiths 2002: 183). Recorded from e.20c.; see *shag (v.)*.

Shag² (n.): sexual partner. 'A good shag for her age. Ripe. Juicy' (Bleasdale 1975: 171). 'Victor, me prospective shag' (Griffths 2002: 174). Recorded from l.20c.; see *shag (v.)*.

Shag (v.): to have sex with. 'I'd go out shagging' (Flame 1984: 38). 'And I could step in and shag her behind his

back' (Griffiths 1999: 128). 'All hands reckoned they'd shagged her' (Sampson 2002: 86). Recorded in this sense from l.17c.; possibly from 14c. 'to shag', 'to toss about, to shake'.

Shagged/shagged out (adj.): tired out. 'Lazy, fat-gutted, half-shagged bunch of palookas' (Cross 1951: 151). 'Praps shagged out' (Simpson 1995: 23). Recorded from m.20c.; an extension of *shag (v.)*.

Shammy round the block (n.): chase. 'Shammy Round the Block (a chasing game)' (Shaw 1957a: 4). *NR; derivation unknown.

Shandry (n.): light cart. 'A man in a milk shandry offered her a ride' (Tirebuck 1891: 125). Recorded from m.19c.; north-western dialectal, derivation unknown.

Shanghai (v.): to kidnap a sailor and place him on a vessel. 'Sam had got rotten drunk in some rum shop off the Dock Road and had been shanghaied aboard a ship' (Hall 2004 [1939]: 131). '"To shanghai", meaning the kidnapping of a crew for a ship' (Hughill 1967: 83). 'Well Daniel have yer ever been Shanghaied?' (Jacques 1977: n.p.). 'Dishonest landladies and shanghaiers' (Lees 2013: 79). Recorded from l.19c.; originally from the idea of a voyage that a sailor didn't want to undertake (to Shanghai, for example).

Shank's pony (n.): walking. 'It was "Shank's pony" all the way there and back' (Unwin 1984 [1920s–30s]: 14). 'It was a question of Shank's pony … you had to do a lot of walking' (Dudgeon 2010: 313). Recorded from l.18c.; from 'shank', 'shin', by extension 'leg'.

Sharrer/chara/charry (n.): coach. 'Going out to climb on the charas again' (Bower 2015 [1936]: 169). 'They go for mystery charry drives' (Kerr 1958: 106). '"Sharrer" derived from charabanc, or excursion motor coach' (Lane 1966: 102). 'Chara. A charabanc. Liverpool' (Howarth 1985: n.p.). 'Every now an' again a charra load of cops come up' (Fagan 2007 [1950s]: 67). Recorded from e.20c.; an abbreviation of 19c. 'charabanc', from the French 'char-à-banc' (carriage with benches).

Shawlie (n.): old woman. 'A rhyming fable about the origins of scouse, which had three shawlies on the Cast Iron Shore round a cauldron' (Anon. 1961b: 3). 'Mary Ellen; a working-class Liverpool woman, usually elderly and of scruffy appearance. Once known as a *shawlie* from the Irish habit of wearing a shawl' (Lane 1966: 72). 'The old Scottie Road [with] its shawlies' (Unwin 1984 [1920s–30s]: 60). '*A shawlie, a Mury Ellen* A Liverpool (Irish) woman' (Spiegl 2000b: 57). Recorded from l.19c.; from Irish English, hence also used in other cities where there were large populations of Irish descent (such as Glasgow); derivation is clear.

Shebeen (n.): illegal drinking club. 'Lodging houses, clubs, brothels and shebeens' (Mays 1954: 44). '*Shebeen*: Any place in which liquor is sold illegally, usually at an extortionate price' (Lane 1966: 95). 'Parties, shebeens, boat cruises on the Mersey' (Murari 1975: 64). '*Less go to a shebeen* Let us visit an illegal drinking den' (Spiegl 2000b: 88). 'Shebeens (drinking clubs) in the south end of town' (Elliott 2006 [1940s–70s]: 129).

Recorded from l.18c.; an Irish English coinage, from Gaelic 'síbín', ultimately from 'séibín', 'little mug', hence 'ale, esp. bad ale'.

Shed (n.): old, poorly maintained car. 'In some fucked-up ahl shed of a car drivin inter fuckin Wales' (Griffiths 2003: 52). Recorded from l.20c.; an ironic reversal of e.20c. Americanism 'shed', 'solid-top car'.

Sheepshagger (n.): general insult. 'Don't like this fuckin place … Fuller fuckin woollybacks, sheepshaggers' (Griffiths 2003: 56). Recorded from l.20c.; supposedly derived from the sexual proclivities of the inhabitants of rural areas (North Wales and Lancashire).

Sheet (n.): one pound. 'Half a sheet for prescriptions' (Smith 1998 [1971]: 81). 'Cheap stuff he'd bought for six sheets' (Murari 1975: 1). Recorded from e.20c.; from 'sheet' of paper, hence 'note'.

Sherper (n.): socially ambitious person. '*Sherper*: An ambitious person' (Lane 1966: 96). *NR in this sense; an extension of 'sherpa', the Himalayan mountain guides (hence 'social climber').

Shift (v.): move (house). 'The neighbourhood was no better than that from which she had shifted' (Hanley 2009 [1940]: 64). '*Shiftin*': Moving to another address' (Lane 1966: 97). 'How they shifted, my kin, flitted/about the sandstone city' (Simpson 2011 [2001]: 3). Recorded from l.16c.; the specific sense of 'changing lodgings' has been retained in Liverpool.

Shifter (n.): removals man. '*Shifter*: A removal man' (Lane 1966: 97). Recorded from l.16c.; originally a general term, then specifically a scene-mover in a theatre; the narrowing to 'removals' is local to Liverpool.

Shin off (v.): run away; get lost. '*Shin off*: Go away; get to hell out of it' (Lane 1966: 97). 'Less juss shin off me an yooze' (Simpson 1995: 21). Recorded from m.20c.; an extension of the m.19c. Americanism 'to shin', 'to move quickly'; 'shin' is a metonym for 'leg'.

Shindig (n.): party, dance. '*They 'ad a whizzo shindig after ther wedd'n*' (Lane 1966: 97). Recorded from m.19c.; an Americanism; derivation unknown.

Shindy (n.): argument, fight. 'Harry had kicked up the deuce of a shindy' (Hall 2004 [1939] 135). '*To kick up a shindy*: to start a row' (Lane 1966: 97). Recorded from e.19c.; possibly from the name of a sailors' dance, or the game of 'shinty'.

Ship's Mary (n.): male prostitute. '*Ship's Mary*: An effeminate man or a male prostitute' (Lane 1966: 97). *NR; this derogatory m.20c. coinage reflects a common confusion between 'effeminacy' and homosexuality; an extension of m.20c. 'Mary', 'male prostitute'.

Shippen/shippon (n.): cowshed. 'Our milkman kept his cows in a shippen at the back' (Forrester 1974: 136). 'One stable for horses and two shippons for cows' (Lane 1987: 93). 'The shippen which housed his six cows was directly under our back bedroom (Callaghan 2011 [1910s–30s]: viii). Recorded from Old English (same root as 'shop'); glossed as 'now dialectal'; up to the m.20c., livestock (horses, cattle) were a familiar sight on Liverpool's streets.

Shirt out, get your (v.): to become angry. '"All right", he said, "don't get your shirt out about it. I'll go out"' (Hanley 1935: 423). Recorded from m.19c.; a number of similar terms appear from m.19c: 'shirty', 'get up someone's shirt', 'take your shirt off', 'keep you shirt on'; probably from stripping to the waist in order to fight.

Shirtlifter (n.): derogatory term for male homosexual. '*Homosexual.* Shirtlifter, Punk, Queer, Turd burglar' (Minard 1972: 89). 'BUM CHUM. Homosexual friend. See also SHAIRTLIFTER' (Spiegl 1989: 19). Recorded from m.20c.; an Australian coinage; derivation is clear.

Shit creek (n.): River Mersey. '*Shit creek*: The River Mersey' (Lane 1966: 97). *NR; a reference to the practice of sewage disposal in the river, with an echo of the l.19c. Americanism, 'up shit creek without a paddle'.

Shit hot (int.): excellent, outstanding. '*Shit 'ot*: Very good, excellent, wonderful' (Lane 1966: 97). 'He wasn't going to be shit hot. He wasn't going to compete' (Sampson 1999: 17). Recorded from m.20c.; a reversal of the American interjection expressing enthusiasm, 'hot shit!'.

Shit oneself (v.): to be very frightened. 'He was shitting himself because he knew there was plenty more to fuck him' (Parker 1974: 143). 'Near fuckin shit meself then I did' (Griffiths 2003: 109). 'They just shit themselves' (Stamper 2010: 111). Recorded from m.18c.; derivation is clear.

Shit-scared (adj.): terrified. '*Shit-scairt*: Badly frightened' (Lane 1966: 97). 'He's shit scared of me Mam; always was' (Bleasdale 1975: 27). 'He'd be shit-scared of what people would say' (Sampson 2002: 122). Recorded from m.20c.; an extension of the e.20c. Americanism 'scare the shit out of'.

Shitcart (n.): bed. '*Bed*. Flock, Wagon, Shitcart' (Minard 1972: 87). *NR in this sense; derivation unclear.

Shite[1] *(n.)*: offensive, despicable person; general insult. 'Y' know why – 'cos the likes of you, y' shite. You're nothing' (Bleasdale 1985: 119). 'They're pure Wrexham shite, those two' (Sampson 1998: 10). Recorded since 18c.; a variant of 'shit', probably imported from Irish English in 20c.

Shite[2] *(n.)*: rubbish, nonsense; worthless stuff. 'Stinking shitty load of SHITE!' (Russell 1996 [1975]: 92). 'Ploughing through the shite of all them fucking dons' (Simpson 1990: 40). 'Good gear like? Not cut with too much shite, no?' (Griffiths 2000: 4). 'That's shite … Pure unadulterated shite' (Fagan 2007 [1950s]: 263). Recorded from l.19c.; a variant of 'shit'.

Shite[3] *(n.)*: aggravation. 'I can't support my family, my wife's giving me shite' (Bleasdale 1985: 133). 'There's a lot of shite that comes with having a gaff in town' (Sampson 2002: 8). Recorded from m.20c.; an extension of the m.20c. Americanism, 'to give someone shit'.

Shite (int.): exclamation of concern, annoyance, frustration. 'Shite. Wish I could have that money la' (Murari 1975: 22). 'Oh shite!' (Bleasdale 1985: 226). 'Then say "shite" cos you've forgotten to leave the milk out' (Griffiths 2003: 3). Recorded from e.20c.; Irish English variant of *shite*[1] *(n.)*.

Shitehawk (n.): seagull; term of abuse. 'How come you write him up like a messiah when you know he's a phoney little shitehawk?' (Sampson 1999: 131). 'Look at those fucking shitehawks, they'd eat anything' (Burnett 2011: 106). Recorded from m.20c.; originally referred to the scavenging herring gull, but later extended.

Shithole (n.): dreadful place. 'Three years of playing in shitholes' (Sampson 1999: 7). 'Next time he needs summin sorted in this bleedin shithole' (Griffiths 2003: 95). 'They came back to the shitholes they left behind' (Stamper 2010: 4). Recorded from m.20c.; an extension of e.16c. 'hole', the worst cell in a debtor's prison.

Shithouse[1] *(n.)*: toilet. '*Shittus*: A lavatory' (Lane 1966: 97). 'If they fell down the shit-house – they'd come up smellin' o' roses' (Sinclair 1999 [1930s–e.40s]: 9). Recorded from 17c.; derivation is clear.

Shithouse[2] *(n.)*: nasty, mean person. 'You pair of dirty shithouses' (Hignett 1966: 300). 'Fella's properly a shithouse' (Sampson 2001: 88). Recorded from m.19c.; an extension of *shithouse*[1].

Shithouse[3] *(n.)*: coward. 'They call you a shithouse 'coz you won't do a car with them' (Parker 1974: 93). 'Bit of a shithouse. I tried to get everyone calling him Danny Jekyll – he's always hiding' (Sampson 1998: 9). 'Ye soft shithouse' (Sanders and Sanders 2009 [1960s]: 29). Recorded from l.20c.; an extension of *shithouse*[2].

Shoe nuts (n.): cashew nuts. '*Shoe nuts*: Oleo nuts … from their fancied resemblance to clogs *Cf. Also Cashew Nuts*' (Lane 1966: 97–8). *NR; a simple abbreviation.

Shooting gallery (n.): men's urinal. 'The "shooting gallery" (Liverpudlian for the "gents")' (Channon 1970: 116). '*Wur's dee shoot'n gallery?* Where is the urinal' (Spiegl 2000b: 88). *NR in this sense; derivation is clear.

Short arse (n.): small person. 'C'mon short-arse' (Graham 1988: 68). 'HEY, short arse' (Fagan 2007 [1950s]: 8). Recorded from e.18c.; originally 'short arse', 'small, despicable person'; derivation is clear.

Short-arsed (adj.): small. '*Shortarsed*: Of small stature' (Lane 1966: 98). 'A looked over at the bar like an saw iss fuckin short-arsed twat in a blew jumper' (Griffiths 2000: 97). Recorded from e.20c.; an extension of *short arse*.

Short-handed (adj.): under-staffed. 'Would you take a jump, Fury, if she turned out to be short-handed?' (Hanley 1935: 540). 'I was a bit short-handed' (Jacques 1979: n.p.). 'I thought y' might have been short-handed' (Bleasdale 1985: 45). Recorded from l.18c.; a nautical usage that meant sailing without a full complement of sailors; the extension to any type of shortage of labour was a m.19c. development; from 'short', 'lacking', 'hands', 'sailors' ('all hands on deck').

Shout the odds (v.): to make a loud fuss. 'Some mouthy fuckin no-mark shoutin the friggin odds' (Griffiths 2003: 52). Recorded from e.20c.; Forces' usage; from bookmakers shouting the odds loudly at a racecourse.

Shuftie (n.): look, glance. 'Leaning out of her bedroom window to get a shuftie at the goings on' (Bainbridge 1973: 34). 'Asks if he can have a shuftie in the boot' (Sampson 2001: 50). 'Let's have a fuckin' shufti' (Burnett 2011: 114). Recorded from m.20c.; Forces' usage; from Arabic 'šufti', 'have you seen?'.

Side (n.): pavement. 'She stepped off the side' (Tirebuck 1903: 90). '"Side" for sidewalk or pavement' (Farrell 1950b: 4). 'He wouldn't give you a push off the side' (Elliott 2006 [1940s–70s]: 77). *NR; an abbreviation of the 18c. British coinage 'sidewalk' later taken up in American English.

Side (v.): to tidy up, clear away, put in order. 'Liddy was, as she terms it, busy in siding up and preparing for the next day' (Shimmin 1863: 74). 'Siding his table and darning his combs' (Bainbridge 1973: 6). Recorded from e.19c.; northern dialectal; derivation unknown.

Signalling stick (n.): policeman's walking stick. 'Signalling sticks they called them – and still do, as it happens, although the brass ferrule is no longer needed for rapping out nocturnal messages on the pavement' (McClure 1980: 163). *NR; see *savager cane*.

Silver (n.): silver coins for the meter. 'I went their house the other day to get some silver for the meter' (Bleasdale 1975: 90). *NR; 'silver' is recorded as 'silver coin' from Old English, but the reference here is to the silver coins accepted by gas and electricity meters.

Sin-shifter (n.): clergyman. '*Sin-shifter*, a parson, priest, or rabbi' (Lane 1966: 98). Recorded from e.20c.; Australian Forces' usage; derivation is clear.

Sis (n.): familiar term of address. 'When the girl brought the tea and cakes, he said, "Right Cis"' (Hanley 1932: 72). 'We can stop seeing him, sis' (Ash 1954: 59). 'If, on one day, you are cordially hailed as "mate", "sis" (sister), "la" (lad), "Mac" (favoured by bus conductors), "chuck", "wack" or even simply "yew" (plural "youse") do not be annoyed' (Shaw 1963e: 4). 'Ah, stay a bit longer, sis' (Bryan 2003 [1940s–50s]: 180). Recorded from l.17c.; a simple abbreviation of 'sister'.

Skallan (n.): scallion, spring onion. 'The vocabulary of the Irish area contains several genuine Anglo-Irish and Irish (= Gaelic) words, such as "skallan" (young onion), "caubeen" (hat), "bothered" – ear, deaf (ear)' (Oakes Hirst 1951: 4). 'Skallon. A young onion. Liverpool' (Howarth 1985: n.p.). *NR; a variant of 'scallion', probably from Irish English; from Ascalon, the name of a seaport in Palestine.

Skank (v.): steal, rob. 'He's been skanking him bad style' (Sampson 2002: 2). 'I thought yeh were gunner skank the place there an fuckin then!' (Griffiths 2003: 61). Recorded from e.21c.; an extension of l.20c. British black English 'skank', 'to con, cheat'; originally from Caribbean English; derivation unknown.

Skedaddle (v.): to move quickly away; escape. 'So I skedaddled off' (Roberts 1893: 209) 'I advise you to skidaddle and bring her back' (Hanley 2009 [1940]: 311). 'Skeddadling off to London' (Bainbridge 1989: 22). 'Soon's I was legally allowed to, that was me – fwit. Gone. Skedaddle' (Griffiths 2003: 46). Recorded from m.19c.; glossed as an Americanism, but found previously in north-east dialectal usage; derivation unknown.

Skelp (v.): to slap, smack. 'I have heard "scoot", "skelp" and "slavey"'

(D.W.F.H. 1951: 3). Recorded from 15c.; chiefly northern and Scottish dialectal; from the Gaelic 'sceilp', 'slap'.

Skem (n.): Skelmersdale. '*Skem*. The township of Skelmersdale, Lancashire' (Lane 1966: 99). 'Runcorn, Skem, Winsford, others?' (Jacques 1973: n.p.). 'Lads from Kirkby and Crocky and Skem' (Sampson 2001: 34). *NR; Skelmersdale was one of two 'new towns' (the other was Runcorn), built to alleviate the post-Second World War housing problem in Liverpool.

Skew-whiff (adj.): crooked, askew. 'Above his head, skew-whiff on a nail, hung the head of an animal' (Bainbridge 1989: 17). 'Cap skew-whiff across his brow' (Simpson 1995: 30). Recorded from m.18c.; glossed as dialectal; derivation unclear.

Skimmer (n.): small flat stone used for skimming water. '*Skimmer* or *skipper*: A small flat stone or piece of slate' (Lane 1966: 98). Recorded from 19c.; Lancashire dialectal; derivation is clear.

Skin[1] (n.): woman, girl. '*Tart* is also used for girl, and usually has no offensive intent. For a while after the First World War *Pusher* was frequently heard, and later, *Skin*' (Shaw 1958d: 15). Recorded from m.19c.; nautical and American usage; from 'skin', metonym for 'body'.

Skin[2] (n.): person, usually a man. 'Well me old skin' (Owen 1961: 16). 'He was a good skin and you couldn't help hating him on a day like this' (Hignett 1966: 256). 'He was a good skin, me dad' (Bleasdale 1975: 27). 'Oh, sorry, skin! Sorry. Didn't realise' (McClure 1981: 75). 'Jim is a good skin' (Brown 1989: 39). 'Bosun, foreman-rigger, real good skin' (Simpson 2011 [2001]: 290). Recorded from e.20c.; Irish English, though glossed as used 'mostly in Liverpool' (Beale (1984) *s.v. good skin*); see *skin*[1].

Skin the dog (v.): to get someone to buy drink. '*Skin ther dog*: To encourage a person to spend all his money on drink' (Lane 1966: 98). *NR; derivation unknown.

Skinful (n.): quantity of alcohol. 'But the next night they're down the Boundary or the Black Horse having a skinful' (Bleasdale 1975: 34). 'Yer old man comes 'ome from sea an' gets a skinful' (Sinclair 1999 [1930s–e.40s]: 11). 'Hit the town and have a proper skin full' (Fagan 2007 [1950s]: 275). Recorded from l.16c.; probably from 'skin', 'container made of animal skin'.

Skinny (adj.): mean, stingy. '*Skinny*: Mean, parsimonious' (Lane 1966: 98). '"Skinny old bag!" Jimmy complained to Art' (Sinclair 1999 [1930s–e.40s]: 33). Recorded from m.19c.; derivation unclear.

Skint (adj.): penniless, completely broke. ''E wooden cod on wen I waned mugged, aldo I was skint' (Egan 1955: 216). '*Skint*: Penniless' (Lane 1966: 98). 'Skint: Without money' (Parker 1974: 213). 'Make it three pence, wack, I'm skint' (Robinson 1986 [1920s–30s]: 135). 'George replied that he was skint' (Elliott 2006 [1940s–70s]: 124). Recorded from e.20c.; Forces' usage; a variant of 'skinned', from e.19c. 'to skin', 'to win everything from someone at cards' (clothes, money).

Skip (v.): to board or take a form of transport. 'He did a lot of lorry-skipping but never took anything off the back'

(Mays 1954: 190). 'Skip dis buzz. – Let us get on this omnibus' (Shaw 1962f: 12). 'People always boarded and skipped off the trams while they were on the move … The local term was "skipping on" or "skipping off"' (Robinson 1986 [1920s–30s]: 110). 'Skip a lorry (jump on the back of it)' (Elliott 2006 [1940s–70s]: 56). 'Skippin' leckies was exciting but risky' (Callaghan 2011 [1910s–30s]: 26). *NR; from 'skip', 'leap, jump', presumably onto an open-doored tram or bus.

Skirt (n.): a woman; sex. 'Be running after the skirts soon, fumbling with them in the alleyways after dark' (Cross 1951: 14). 'It's gold we're here for, not skirt' (McGovern 1995: 12). 'You should see all the loose skirt that gets in there' (Fagan 2007 [1950s]: 276). Recorded from l.19c.; a derogatory extension of 'skirt', 'lower part of woman's dress'.

Skit (v.): to joke, make fun of. 'The whole street was laughing and skitting behind her back' (Hanley 1932: 133). 'My own pronunciation, although occasionally "skitted" at' (Parker 1974: 217). Recorded from 19c.; dialectal extension of e.18c. 'skit', 'satirical comment' (hence 'parody or caricature').

Skive (v.): to avoid work. 'Skived off at lunchtime and left me' (Parker 1974: 94). 'He'd know you'd been skiving' (Graham 1988: 54). 'What d'yer think you're doing skiving over there?' (Fagan 2007 [1950s]: 337). Recorded from l.19c.; an Americanism popularised in First World War Forces' usage; possibly from French 'esquiver', 'to escape'.

Skrike (n.): scream, shriek. 'Didn' I hear the man skrike more like a pig' (Tirebuck 1891: 438). Recorded from 14c.; glossed as now dialectal, with additional sense of 'weep, cry'; derivation unknown.

Sky, have a (v.): watch, look for. 'A drop a fender ale and a sky a the telly' (Shaw 1957a: 1). 'We'd go up to the golf links skyin' balls and nick 'em' (Shaw 1957a: 2). 'Sky. To watch. Liverpool' (Howarth 1985: n.p.). Glossed as 'mostly Liverpool: since ca. 1920' (Partridge *s.v. sky*).; probably rhyming slang, 'sky-hook', 'look'.

Sky-blue pink wit' a finny-addy border (phr.): the acme. '*Sky-blue pink wit' a finny-addy border*: said of something regarded as having everything, such as an imposing mansion or a Rolls-Royce car' (Lane 1966: 54). *NR; derivation unclear.

Sky pilot (n.): clergyman. 'Them there sky-pilots as runs the 'ome' (Hall 2004 [1939]: 40). 'Sky pilot. A padre' (Howarth 1985: n.p.). Recorded from l.19c.; presumably from the idea of 'steering to heaven'.

Slab (n.): sink, washing place. 'Most of the houses had many families and there was only one slab and tap for the lot' (Clerk 1971 [c.1900]: 80). *NR; sinks in working-class houses were often thick stone slabs.

Slack (n.): cheap, small inferior coal. 'It seemed so strange not to see the pile of slack and cinders heaped upon [the fire]' (Hanley 2009 [1936]: 367). 'Bags of nutty slack' (Russell 1996 [1975]: 70). 'There wasn't so much as a spoonful of slack left' (Bryan 2003 [1940s–50s]: 163). 'A quantity of slack shovelled, weighed and poured' (Callaghan 2011 [1910s–30s]: 41). Recorded from 15c.; used to *back*

up a fire at night; derivation unknown.

Slang (n.): watch chain. 'He could lift … slangs a' yeller clocks, yooks, twerns an' jarks with such ease and frequency' (Clerk 1971 [c.1900]: 69). Recorded from m.19c.; from Dutch 'slange', 'snake'.

Slapper (n.): insulting term for a woman. 'But you couldn't say she's a slapper. She's a sexy girl' (Sampson 2001: 236). Recorded from m.19c.; possibly from Gaelic 'slapóg', 'slut, untidy woman' (from 'slapaire' 'a sloven, awkward, untidy' person).

Slash (n.): urine, urination. 'You'd probly start drinkin yer own slash before the fuckin water ran out' (Griffiths 2003: 185). 'We wer having a slash into the hedge' (Stamper 2010: 101). Recorded from m.20c., derivation unclear, possibly Scots 'slash', 'splash'.

Slavey (n.): a servant. 'I have heard "scoot", "skelp" and "slavey"' (D.W.F.H. 1951: 3). 'Slavies. A skivvy, a young woman in domestic service. Everton' (Howarth 1985: n.p.). Recorded from e.19c.; originally a 'servant of either sex', but in later Irish English use, women servants.

Sledder (n.): thief. '"You're no sledder", he said, "you're a bloody gip and I'll learn yer something"' (Clerk 1971 [c.1900]: 37). Recorded as 'Liverpool street arabs': late C.19–mid-20' (Beale (1984) *s.v. sledder*); derivation unknown.

Slice, get a/knock off a (v.): to have sex (especially with married woman). 'Once they're gettin' a regular slice, they soon go off statues an' altar rails' (Bleasdale 1975: 179–8). 'Knockin' a slice off somebody's wife' (Mc Clure 1981: 96). Recorded from l.18c.; 'to take a slice' is glossed as 'to intrigue; particularly with a married woman, because a slice of a cut loaf is not missed' (Grose (1788) *s.v. slice*).

Sling your hook (v.): to go away; leave; resign; die. '*Sling yer 'ook*: Clear off; go away' (Lane 1966: 99). 'Ah go sling yer 'ook' (Jacques 1975: n.p.). 'Her father's slung his hook' (Simpson 1995: 30). '*E slung is hook* He has resigned' (Spiegl 2000b: 102). 'Sling yer 'ook, ye soft old get' (Sanders and Sanders 2009 [1960s]: 103). Recorded from m.19c.; possibly from the docker's *Liverpool hook* (if there was no work he was told to *sling your hook*).

Slobbergob (n.): general insult. '*Slobbergob*: Name given to a person with a thick-lipped, drooling kind of mouth' (Lane 1966: 99). *NR; derivation is clear.

Slog (v.): to labour, work hard. '*Slog*: To work hard' (Lane 1966: 99). Recorded from m.19c.; probably from 'to slug', 'to strike hard'.

Slog (n.): hard work. '*A rill slog*: A difficult or tiring job' (Lane 1966: 99). See *slog (v.)*.

Slop (n.): policeman. 'She was in the family way by a slop' (Hanley 1932: 89). 'Slop. Policeman' (Price: 1950: 4). 'Dodging the *Jacks* (detectives), the *Scuffers* (Police, *Slops*, also being used) or their friends' (Shaw 1958d: 16). '*Slop*: A police constable' (Lane 1966: 99). 'My name's Dinky Doo/And my number's twenty two/I'm not the only slop but I'm a few' [children's rhyme] (Clerk 1971 [*c*.1900]: 46). 'Slops. Policemen. Liverpool' (Howarth 1985: n.p.). Recorded from m.19c.; probably back-slang.

Slummy[1] *(n.)*: slum dweller. '*The Autobiography of a Liverpool Irish Slummy*' (O'Mara 1934: title). 'It was a typical slummie's house' (Prior 1964: 158). '*'Ey look at 'er wit' ther raggety kecks* implies that the person referred to is a slummy' (Lane 1966: 88). 'Many "slummies" were uprooted against their will' (Lees 2013: 159). Recorded from e.20c.; O'Mara's use is the first recorded in this sense; from e.19c. cant 'slum', 'room', though 'very poor housing' is more or less contemporaneous.

Slummy[2] *(n.)*: waste material; 'He was copped by a Paddy Kelly nicking a bit a slummy' (Shaw 1957a: 7). 'Ee musta seen yer nick de slummy. *He must have see you steal the dunnage*' (Shaw et al. 1966: 64). 'This ain't slummy, it's for me mantlepiece' (Graham 1988: 39). '"Slummy" was the local name for scrap cable ends, strips of lead, brass bars' (Fagan 2007 [1950s]: 200). Recorded from m.20c.; an extension of the e.20c. Americanism 'slum', 'virtually worthless prizes offered at fairs'.

Slummy[3] *(n.)*: coppers or loose change. 'Think you can take the piss? Think you can get me to count out your slummy?' (Sampson 2001: 86). *NR; a m.20c. extension of *slummy*[2].

Sly (adj.): unfortunate, pitiable. '"Fucking state of that fella's dick" ... "It's sly, isn't it?"' (Sampson 2002: 32). *NR in this sense; a m.20c. extension of 'sly', 'mean, nasty', that refers to the effect of slyness.

Sly jack (n.): store detective. '*Sly jack*: A shop or store detective' (Lane 1966: 55). *NR; from 'sly', 'stealthy, underhand', and *jack*, detective.

Smack (n.): slap, punch, blow. 'Little more than a smack across the ears' (Whittaker 1934: 156). '*Unmerciful hiding* (a smack: typical hyperbole)' (Shaw 1952: n.p.). 'A young constable who gave him a real smack' (Parker 1974: 167). 'Maybe I should just give him a smack' (Sampson 2001: 23). Recorded from l.18c.; an extension of 'smack', 'loud noise made by lips'.

Smart[1] (adj.): clever; cheeky. 'You lectured me on being too smart' (Hall 2004 [1939]: 219). 'One cannot help being smart and the other being touchy' (Naughton 1945: 47). 'The "divvy" is the antithesis of the smart, quick person' (Parker 1974: 150). 'That's fuckin' smart' (Cornelius 2001 [1982]: 94). 'If any of you boys passes any uncomplimentary remarks, or tries to get smart' (Sinclair 1999 [1930s–e.40s]: 54). 'While you, Smart Lad, were lovey-doveying with that tart' (Simpson 2011: 415). Recorded from 15c. 'cheeky' and 16c. 'clever'; an extension of 'smart', 'quick or well-executed'.

Smart[2] (adj.): in good health. '*Smart*: Well, healthy' (Lane 1966: 99). Recorded from l.18c.; an Americanism and English dialectal usage; primarily used negatively ('not too smart', 'not very well'); an extension of 'smart', 'quick or well-executed'.

Smashing (adj.): great, wonderful. 'Smashin' suit you got there Red' (Cross 1951: 10). '"Smashing", the ubiquitous adjective of appraisal, has already replaced "De Gear" and the much older "It's climp"' (Whittington-Egan 1955a: 6). 'It tastes smashing' (Hignett 1966: 139). '"A'right Chalky?"

"Smashin"'' (McClure 1980: 511). 'Everything goes smashing at first' (Brown 1989: 13). 'It's smashin' Bob, ta' (Sinclair 1999 [1930s–e.40s]: 158). 'That's it. Smashin'' (Burnett 2011: 80). Recorded from m.19c.; popularised in First World War (and, more particularly, Second World War) Forces' usage; probably an extension of l.18c. 'smasher', 'anything unusually large or excellent'.

Smoked Irishman (n.): racist term for black person. 'Smoked Irishman. A *coloured person*' (Shaw et al. 1966: 28). '*Smoked Irishman*: A Negro, a coloured person' (Lane 1966: 100). '"Smoked Irish" teenagers dressed for the kill' (Lees 2013: 146). *NR; the author of the introduction to *Lern Yerself Scouse* claimed that there is 'nothing abusive' about this term and that it demonstrates 'how the Liverpudlian accepts the negro as only another immigrant "Irishman" but with a different skin colour'. He added that 'there is, incidentally, no colour problem in Liverpool' and that he had 'never heard a Scouse-speaking Liverpudlian use the word *nigger*' (Shaw et al. 1966: 12). Such delusional complacency was unfortunately all too commonplace in the disastrous history of racism in Liverpool.

Snadger (n.): house sparrow. '*Couldn't kick a snadger up its arse* is said of a person considered weak and ineffectual' (Lane 1966: 100). *NR; see *spadger*.

Snapper rigs (n.): old clothes. 'Nothing under our outer cover such as it was, snapper rigs' (Clerk 1971 [c.1900]: 81). Recorded as 'Liverpool street arabs' late C.19–mid-20' (Beale (1984) *s.v. snapper*

215

rigs); from the nautical Americanism 'snapper rigged', 'a ship which is poorly rigged', or 'a man with few clothes'; from 'rig', 'the arrangement of sails and masts on a sailing ship'.

Snappin (n.): packed lunch. Glossed as 'a packed lunch; hence, any packed food: Merseyside workers': since ca. 1910' (Beale 1984 *s.v. snappin*). Recorded from e.20c.; from 19c. dialectal 'packed food' for workers', from 17c. 'snap', 'slight or hasty meal or mouthful; a snack'.

Sneaker (n.): underarm bowl in cricket. '"No sneakers" was the appeal which stopped underam' (Shaw 1960a: 39). '"No sneakers" and other rigid rules' (Shaw 1966c: 6). Recorded from m.19c.; presumably from the belief that underarm bowling was legitimate but sneaky.

Sniffer (n.): investigator from the Department of Social Security. 'Two sniffers from the dole' (Bleasdale 1985: 42). Recorded from l.20c.; derivation is clear.

Snippet (n.): female pudenda; sexual intercourse. Recorded as 'the female pudend. Liverpool: late C. 19–20. 2. Hence intercourse with a girl: Liverpool: C. 20' (Partridge *s.v. snippet*); possibly from 19c. English dialectal 'snicket', 'dirty, careless, impudent woman' or 'narrow passage'.

Snitch¹ (n.): an informer. 'The biggest snitch in the whole school' (Brown 1989: 16). 'The girl he's got in there is a snitch' (Sampson 2002: 97). Recorded from l.18c.; an extension of *snitch¹ (v.)*.

Snitch² (n.): nose. 'She hugs him so hard his snitch gets jammed down the top of her blouse' (Brown 1989: 60). Recorded

from l.17c.; derivation unknown.

Snitch¹ (v.): inform on someone. '"Don't snitch", Don't tell, or Don't give me away' (Jones 1935: 5). 'I'll snitch on yer. *I will report you*' (Shaw et al. 1966: 45). 'He will go and snitch to Basher' (Brown 1989: 66). 'He won't snitch when I'm done with him' (Sampson 2002: 206). 'To my eternal shame I snitched on him' (Callaghan 2011 [1910s–30s]: 8). Recorded from e.18c.; see *snitch² (n.)*.

Snitch² (v.): to steal. 'Is it something you snitched from the docks' (Cross 1951: 17). '*Snitch*: To steal' (Lane 1966: 100). Recorded from l.19c.; South Lancastrian dialectal; probably from 'snatch'.

Snookered (adj.): in difficulty. 'All hands were snookered' (Jacques 1975: n.p.). 'I was well and truly snookered' (Fagan 2007 [1950s]: 235). *NR; from being forced to play a difficult shot in snooker.

Snot gobbler (n.): term of abuse. 'I bet he's only an old snot gobbler like you' (Bleasdale 1975: 18). *NR; derivation is clear.

Snot pie (n.): cowheel pie. '*Snot pie*: Cowheel pie, a glutinous concoction typifying Northern fondness for offal' (Lane 1966: 100). *NR; derivation is clear.

Snot pudding (n.): sago or tapioca. '*Snot pudden*: Sago or tapioca pudding' (Lane 1966: 100). *NR; derivation is clear.

Snotty-nosed (adj.): poor, pitiable. 'She was smiling at snotty-nosed kids on the see-saw' (Hanley 1932: 127). 'The snotty-nosed kids in care' (Robinson 1986 [1920s–30s]: 110). 'Sum snotty-nosed little Tilly Mint' (Simpson 1995:

23). 'Yer snot-nosed little bitch' (Bryan 2003 [1940s–50s]: 154). Recorded from l.17c.; almost always used to refer to children.

Snout[1] *(n.)*: tobacco; cigarette. '*Snout*: Tobacco, especially when smuggled into prison' (Lane 1966: 101). 'Goin down the city fer a booze an a snout' (Moloney 1966: 54). Recorded from l.19c.; from prison discourse; derivation unknown.

Snout[2] *(n.)*: nose. '*Ow'd yer like a bang on ther snout?*' (Lane 1966: 101). Recorded from e.14c.; an extension of the slightly earlier 'snout', 'trunk of an elephant'.

Snuck/snucked (v.): past tense of sneak. '*I snucked it in from 'Ong Kong*' (Lane 1966: 101). 'I cud juss snuck out off one' (Simpson 1995: 22). *NR; from the Americanism 'snuck' (past tense of 'sneak') and 'ed' as regular marker of past tense.

Snurge (n.): informer; obnoxious person. 'Now then snurge, we're gonna try you' (Cross 1951: 91). Recorded from e.20c.; possibly from 'sneak' or 'snitch'.

Soak (v.): beg, borrow. '*Can I soak yer fer a coupler bob*' (Lane 1966: 101). Recorded from l.19c.; an Americanism; originally with the sense of 'extortion or excessive borrowing'; derivation unclear.

Soapville (n.): Port Sunlight. '*Soapville*: The district of Port Sunlight' (Lane 1966: 101). *NR; Port Sunlight is the 'model village' on the Wirral Peninsula that was built (1899–1914) to house the workers at the Lever Brothers soap-making business.

Sod (n.): term of abuse, sometimes mild. 'What gets me is that sods like us get by and chaps like him go!' (Jerome 1948: 172). 'Are you de self-same unrelenting Sod?' (Shaw et al. 1966: 77). 'The miserable sod went straight past' (Bleasdale 1975: 23). 'Daft little sod' (Sinclair 1999: 12). Recorded from e.19c.; an abbreviation of 'sodomite' which lost its sexual connotation and weakened to refer to an unpleasant person. The first text written entirely in 'Scouse', Frank Shaw's play *The Scab* (1952), was censored by the Lord Chamberlain's Office for its use of *sod*.

Sod/sod off (v.): go away, emphatic. 'Well, sod 'em' (Cross 1951: 14). 'Patsy too, sod her' (Hignett 1966: 36). 'Oh! Sod off Chrissie' (Bleasdale 1985: 171). 'An I don't give two fucks what it means so sod off and shurrup' (Griffiths 2003: 79). Recorded from m.20c.; derivation unclear, though clearly related to *sod*.

Soda batch (n.): Welsh soda-bread. '*Soady batch*. Welsh soda bread' (Lane 1966: 101). Recorded from m.20c.; 'batch' is recorded from 15c. to refer to the product of baking.

Sodding (adj. and adv.): derogatory intensifier. 'Every sodding day, and as flat as hell' (Cross 1951: 13). 'Do your sodding job' (Smith 1998 [1971]: 33). 'I've had enough of that – if you don't laugh, you'll cry – I've heard it for years – this stupid soddin' city's full of it' (Bleasdale 1985: 177). 'Its as soddin borin as/someone avin der appendicks out' (Simpson 1995: 21). Recorded from e.20c.; see *sod*.

Soft (adj.): foolish, idiotic, simple; too easy-going. 'I's just soft, I is' (Hocking 1966 [1879]: 12). 'Dorrie didn't want to look soft' (Tirebuck 1891: 243). 'As for that soft little shit' (Hanley 1932: 156). 'A person who expects favour to be readily granted [is] "a soft feller"'

(Farrell 1950b: 4). 'Don't be soft' (Kerr 1958: 100). 'D'you think I'm soft or something?' (Hignett 1966: 208). 'The lads called me soft, even though I could beat them physically' (McClure 1980: 311). 'You soft get' (Bleasdale 1985: 134). 'Yeh reckon that Tommy's too *soft*?' (Griffiths 2003: 48). 'You don't think I'm that fuckin' soft, do ya?' (Burnett 2011: 127). Recorded from 12c.; the term is long-established and had a number of early senses: 'gentle or mild in nature or character'; 'easily influenced or swayed; having little power of resistance to the influence of other persons or things; facile, compliant'. These meanings were retained but a 17c. extension – 'more or less foolish, silly, or simple; lacking ordinary intelligence or common-sense; easily imposed upon or deceived' – is the dominant Liverpool sense.

Soft arse (n.): general insult. 'You stay out of it, softarse' (Bleasdale 1979: 63). 'Pullin soft arsed faces' (Simpson 1995: 23). 'It ain't going to be softarse here' (Sampson 2002: 200). *NR; see *soft*.

Soft lad (n.): idiot, fool. 'That's you that soft lad!' (Russell 1996 [1976]: 189). 'It was George first. Then soft lad yesterday'. (Sampson 2002: 6). 'No not friggin *now* softlad' (Griffiths 2003: 58). *NR; see *soft*.

Soft Joe/Sam/Mick (n.): imaginary figure of negative comparison. 'She'd eat as much as Soft Joe' (Shaw 1957a: 12). 'You must take me for Soft Sam' (Hignett 1966: 48). 'More excuses for not wearing his teeth than soft Mick' (Smith 1998 [1971]: 34). Recorded from m.20c.; a poor Everyman, from e.19c. 'Joe', 'an imaginary person', particularly in the USA; 'Sam', Lancashire dialectal for 'fool', 'Mick', 'Irishman'.

Soggy (adj.): dilapidated, worn out; second rate. '*A soggy dump*: a dirty, tumbledown place. *A soggy do*: A disappointing and inferior affair' (Lane 1966: 101). *NR; an extension of the general negative connotation of 'soggy'.

Soojy-moojy (v.): to scrub paintwork (on a ship). 'Much painting and soojy-moojying [scrubbing paint work]' (O'Mara 1934: 240). 'There are no sailors to-day … only Sugi-Mugi men' … Mere washers of paint' (Hanley 1934: 131). Recorded from e.20c.; an extension of l.19c. 'soogee-moogee', 'a caustic soda-based mix' used to clean paintwork and woodwork on ships and boats; derivation unknown.

Sooner (n.): lazy person. 'Yewr an ould sooner (would sooner idle than work)' (Shaw 1959a: 41). Recorded from l.19c.; an Australian coinage; Shaw's suggested derivation is probably correct.

Sort (v.): to provide for; arrange; pay. 'Sort us some powder' (Sampson 1999: 59). 'Can yer lay us on another rock like? Al sort yer next week' (Griffiths 2000: 262). 'If Nina Perkins-West is getting sorted then it's not her fella that's doing the honours' (Sampson 2001: 110). 'I'll just sort the lads out' (Elliott 2006 [1940s–70s]: 114). Recorded from l.20c. in this sense; used with pleasurable connotations (money, sex, drugs, match tickets); an extension of 'sort', 'arrange, put in order'.

Sort out (v.): fight; defeat. '*Sort out*: To pick a fight' (Lane 1966: 102). 'He needs sortin' out doesn't he? (Russell 1996 [1976]: 152). 'I'll soon sort you out' (Elliott 2006 [1940s–70s]: 149). Recorded from m.20c.; an extension of 'to sort', 'arrange, put in place'.

Sorted (adj.): arranged; finished. 'Soon as this is sorted – off. Gone' (Sampson 2001: 242). 'Buzzwords like "sorted" and "chilled out"' (Lees 2013: 252). See *sort (v.)*.

Sough (n.): gutter. 'I'd sooner she was passing under me now, down in the sough there, dead and done with' (Tirebuck 1891: 244). Recorded from 16c.; a variant of northern dialectal 'sheugh', 'ditch, drain'; derivation unknown.

Soul case, give one's (v.): to give a great deal. 'I'd give me soul case for a good hooley' (Shaw 1957a: 1). *NR; presumably from the value attached to the heart, the 'soul's case'.

Sound (adj.): general term of approbation; safe, okay. 'You're sound, miss' (Russell 1996 [1976]: 107). 'You're all right boys, you're sound, y' can kid them soft' (Bleasdale 1985: 144). 'Sound. No problem … Yis can rent the newer one' (Griffiths 2000: 120). 'Go on your tod. You'll be sound' (Sampson 2001: 127). '"Sound" (good guy)' (Lees 2013: 137). Recorded from l.20c.; glossed as 'Liverpool colloquial' (*OED s.v. sound* adj. Draft additions 2003), though it has become general; an extension of 12c. 'sound', 'in good health'.

Sound as a pound (adj.): very good. 'Alright Aldo Sound as a pound/I'm cushty la but there's nothing down' (Johnson 1988). 'Everything's sound as a pound' (Sampson 2002: 125). 'Sound as a pound and gud nuff ter

win de league' (Lees 2013: 294). *NR; see *sound*.

South End (n.): the southern part of Liverpool (variably defined). 'So far the South end of the town has been spoken of. We will now go to the North' (Shimmin 1863: 121). 'I'm going to see your sisters in the south end' (Haigh 1907: 465). 'Though she lived in the south end, most of her material was garnered around Scotland Road' (O'Mara 1934: 118). '"Jigger", an old word used in the south end of the town to denote a back-passage or entry between two rows of houses' ('Postman' 1945c: 5). 'A memory going back to the end of the last century pictures such individuals as "Captain", who haunted the south end of the city' (Dawson 1951: 4). 'A Liverpool councillor took me recently to see the specially made olly holes, half a century old, in his South End constituency' (Shaw 1966c: 6). 'On my way from the south end to the Landing Stage' (Unwin 1984 [1920s–30s]: 92). 'The Black lads that we grew up with round the South End, once they got to a certain age they did all start talkin Yardie' (Sampson 2001: 25). 'He's one of the hardest cases in the south-end' (Fagan 2007 [1950s]: 33). *NR in this sense; originally used to refer to the southern end of the city centre, the term came to mean the southern end of the city itself – effectively from Toxteth to Speke (although the limits are imprecise and historically variable). The *South End* and the *North End* of Liverpool think of themselves as being culturally distinct from each other: 'south and north in Liverpool are almost as far apart as the poles' (Haigh 1907: 480).

South-ender (n.): someone from the south end of the city. 'The Vale: Walton Vale to Liverpool north-enders, Aigburth Vale to south-enders, St. Domingo Vale to in-betweeners' (Lane 1966: 113). 'See *south end*.

SP (n.): information, facts. 'Now I'll give youse the full SP' (Jacques 1977: n.p.). 'Cormack's given us a bit of the SP about some of the thinking behind the development' (Sampson 2002: 20). Recorded from l.20c.; an acronym for 'starting price' in the discourse of horse racing.

Spadger (n.): sparrow; child, usually a boy. 'My own likkle spadger' (Shaw 1957a: 5). 'Spadger. Sparrow' (Williams 1971: 179). 'Spadger. A sparrow' (Howarth 1985: n.p.). 'A couple of spadgers an hoodies in the garden' (Griffiths 2003: 28). Recorded as m.19c. dialectal; extended to 'child' from l.19c.; derivation is clear.

Spalpeen (n.): rogue. 'Ye spalpeens' (Melville 1849: 335). 'Where are you rushing to, you spalpeen' (Haigh 1907: 159). Recorded from m.18c.; from the Irish 'spailpín', 'agricultural labourer', 'scamp'.

Spammie (n.): love-bite. 'SPAMMIE A "love-bite"' (Spiegl 1989: 70). *NR; from the 'spam' colours left from the 'bite'.

Spar (n.): friend. 'The regular meeting-place for him and his spars' (Murari 1975: 8). 'Why do these black blokes call everyone "spar"?' (Cornelius 2001 [1982]: 145). Recorded from l.20c.; black British usage, an abbreviation of 'sparring partner'.

Spare-rib (n.): rib of pork (often cooked in *pea whack*). 'Drinking may stop for a good feed of scouse or spare rib or a dish or two of winkles ("kewins")' (Shaw 1959a: 36). 'The only things that are missing from a Liverpool menu are spare-ribs and salt fish' (Anon. 1961b: 3). 'Give me a plate of spare ribs and cabbage' (Unwin 1984 [1920s–30s]: 31). 'Spare ribs and cabbage – delicious' (Callaghan 2011 [1910s–30s]: 106). Recorded from 16c.; a Liverpool culinary speciality; 'spare' refers to the undressed or simple quality of the meat.

Spec/speck (n.): place or space. 'Our kid's gone to keep me a speck' (Farrell 1950a: 4). 'I ope to tap the brother for a coupla sprowser for a cheap spec at the pics' (Shaw 1957a: 7). 'Spec [is] a view or position' (Armstrong 1966: 6). 'Finds himself a good speck to leeward' (McClure 1980: 377). 'The best spec, right next to the directors' box' (Brown 1989: 8). 'Ere's a good spec Here is a good vantage point' (Spiegl 2000b: 135). 'You had little chance of a speck in the mess room' (Burnett 2011: 39). *NR; an abbreviation of 'place from which to spectate'.

Spelk/spell (n.): splinter. 'Spell. Splinter' (Howarth 1985: n.p.). 'This spelk/ (yes, that's the word) or rotten wood splinter' (Robinson 2008: 115). Recorded from 15c.; northern dialectal, from Old English 'spelc', 'surgical splint'.

Spew (v.): to leave something; to reject. 'I was there eighteen months ... then I spewed it [left]' (Parker 1974: 69). 'Bang a few more beauty queens an' then finally spew it t' the South of

France' (Bleasdale 1975: 192). *NR in this sense; an extension of 'to spew', 'vomit, eject'.

Spew your ring (v.): to vomit copiously. "*E spewed his ring up*: he vomited' (Lane 1966: 49). 'Head stuck half-way down the lavvy pan, spewing his ring up' (Brown 1989: 10). 'Yatsiz Wine Loge /where thee spew der rings up' (Simpson 1995: 21). Recorded from m.20c.; 'ring' means 'anus' from l.19c.

Spiceballs (n.): meatballs. 'Spiceballs. *Meatballs, faggots, savoury ducks*' (Shaw et al. 1966: 39). 'Spice balls … were the equivalent of today's savoury ducks' (Unwin 1984 [1920s–30s]: 32). '*Spiceballs* Meatballs' (Spiegl 2000b: 112). *NR; see *savoury ducks*.

Spiky, the (n.): 'a short cut from Dingle-lane to the shore' (Jones 1935: 5). *NR; derivation unknown.

Spit (v.): preach, sermonise. 'Kids would say "the gaffer twanged" or "the beak spat at me"' (Clerk 1971 [c.1900]: 24). Recorded from l.19c.; probably from 17c. 'to spit out', 'to speak plainly'.

Spit blood (v.): become angry. 'When I think of it I could spit blood' (Lane 1966: 102). Recorded from l.20c.; derivation is clear.

Spit feathers (v.): to be thirsty. 'I'm spittin feathers. *I am thirsty; dry*' (Shaw et al. 1966: 67). 'Spittin' feathers and rootin' all over the shed for a bevvie' (Jacques 1973: n.p.). '*I'm spitt'n feathers* I am thirsty' (Spiegl 2000b: 87). Recorded from e.20c.; an Americanism; derivation is clear.

Spit of, the (n.): the image of, likeness of. 'You are the living spit of your eldest son' (Hanley 1935: 52). 'That ther

kid's ther dead spit of 'is gramp' (Lane 1966: 25). Recorded from the l.18c.; derivation unclear.

Split (v.): to inform, tell on. 'If you'll be a trump an' not split on a poor little chap' (Hocking 1966 [1879]: 70). 'I saw too much of what happened to those who "squealed" or "split"' (Whittaker 1934: 116). 'Well either *they've* split, or you' (Hanley 2009 [1940]: 76). 'I wouldn't split to the cops if I was you' (Cross 1951: 94). 'We wanted no mumtip. No matter what a yen did with us … we didn't split' (Clerk 1971 [c.1900]: 43). 'Grass: To "stooley", to "split", to tell Authority of a misdemeanour' (Parker 1974: 213). Recorded as a l.18c. cant coinage; glossed as 'Liverpool street arabs': late C. 19 early 20' (Bale (1984) *s.v. split* v. 9).

Splosh (n.): money. 'We never 'ad much splosh' (Shaw 1957a: 2). 'Splosh. *Money*' (Shaw et al. 1966: 34). Recorded from l.19c.; possibly echoic, from 'splash', 'splash out'.

Sponds (n.): money. 'SPONDS Money' (Spiegl 1989: 70). *NR; an abbreviation of m.19c. Americanism 'spondulics', 'money'; derivation unknown.

Sporran (n.): female pubic hair. '*Er sporran* Her pubic hair' (Spiegl 2000b: 68). Recorded from l.19c.; the gendered sense is recent; from Gaelic 'sparán', 'purse made of animal skin with hair left on'.

Spraza/sprazy (n.): a sixpence. '"Spraza" … in the Liverpool gambling world this term denotes a sixpenny piece' ('Postman' 1937a: 6). '6d. A sprarzy, a Tanner' (Minard 1972: 85). Recorded from e.20c.; from Romani 'spars', 'sixpence'.

Spreck up (v.): ejaculate. 'I feel like I'm going to spreck up there and then' (Sampson 2002: 88). *NR; derivation unknown.

Spree (n.): drinking bout, bender. 'You never was the kindest of neighbours, and you never was worth anythink in a spree' (Shimmin 1863: 19). 'Many times during the spree I became afraid for my mother' (O'Mara 1934: 277). 'Sea-faring men intent on a spree' (Hall 2004 [1939]: 9). Recorded from e.19c.; possibly from French 'esprit'.

Sprowser (n.): sixpenny piece. 'I ope to tap the brother for a coupla sprowser' (Shaw 1957a: 7). 'Sprowser. *Sixpenny piece*' (Shaw et al. 1966: 34). See *spraza*.

Spud (n.): hole in a sock. 'With your patched up kecks and spuds in your socks' (Fagan 2007 [1950s]: 77). *NR; presumably from the resemblance between the shape of the hole and a potato.

Squallies (n.): rubbish, leftovers. 'Another kid said, "it's ya stomik, it's them squallies what y'ate"' (Clerk 1971 [*c*.1900]: 29). *NR; derivation unknown.

Squashies (n.): squashed or broken chocolates sold cheaply. 'At one time a Scouser child's dream of paradise was three penny-worth of *squashies*' (Lane 1966: 102). *NR; derivation is clear.

Squatter (n.): toilet. ''E sits fer ars on ther squatter mumblin' to hisself' (Lane 1966: 102). *NR; derivation is clear.

Squelcher (n.): crushing blow. 'That kid has nearly got a squelcher! … Luk how she staggers; she'll put the stunners on it afore long' (Shimmin 1863: 7). Recorded from m.19c.; an extension of 'squelch', 'heavy blow on a soft body'.

Squidge (v.): to look at, examine. '*Let's 'ave a squidge at it*' (Lane 196: 102). *NR; possibly a variant of 'squint'.

Squirrel dance (n.): foreplay. 'You don't know what a squirrel dance is?' (Fagan 2007 [1950s]: 114). *NR; glossed by Fagan as 'twice round the floor an' straight outside for your nuts' (ibid.).

Stage, the (n.): the Landing Stage. 'Waiting for the railway boat to come up to the end of the stage' (Hocking 1966 [1879]: 95). 'The iron plates of the bridge leading to the stage throw off a paint-laden heat' (Tirebuck 1891: 192). 'It would have been an event, this walking along the Stage, in sight and sound of the river traffic' (Hanley 1935: 86–7). 'The turning tide, coming up the stage alongside them' (Hignett 1966: 178). 'We'd struggled with weights around Liverpool from quite an early age, bags heavier than ourselves from Lime Street to the Exchange or the Stage' (Clerk 1971 [*c*.1900]: 7). 'A walk down to the famous stage became almost a ritual' (Unwin 1984 [1920s–30s]: 66). 'There was always some activity going on at the stage' (Stamper 2010: 197). *NR; derivation is clear.

Stan, the (n.): Stanley Road, Bootle. '*Ther Stan*: Stanley Road, Liverpool' (Lane 1966: 103). *NR; Stanley Road is one of central thoroughfares running north from Liverpool city centre.

Stand (n.): area in which men queued for work under the dock casual labour scheme. 'Don't come near my stand ever again' (Hanley 1932: 70). 'I'd be on the stand at seven-thirty every morning' (Lane 1987: 41). 'You had to "get on the stand", and if your face fitted, you got a job' (Dudgeon 2010:

91). *NR in this sense; a specialised sense of 'stand', 'stall, booth'.

Starved (adj.): very cold. '*I'm bloody starved*: I am very cold' (Lane 1966: 103). '*I am starved* I am very cold' (Spiegl 2000b: 70). Recorded from 16c.; the sense, 'perished with cold', was retained in northern dialects; a weakened extension of the original sense of 'to starve', 'to die'.

Starving (adj.): hungry. 'Dey going 'ome starvin' ungry and drownded' (Shaw 1957a: 15). 'Hey Mam, what's for tea? I'm starvin'' (Bleasdale 1975: 30). 'Let's stop for our tea, we're starving' (Brown 1989: 69). 'Fuck me, am starvin'' (Griffiths 2003: 13). *NR in this sense; an example of Liverpool hyperbole.

State of (phr.): expression of disbelief or disapproval (regarding clothing, behaviour). 'State of yous last night, lad' (Parker 1974: 220). 'Look at the state of yer' (Sinclair 1999 [1930s–e.40s]: 82). 'Fucking state of our Anthony' (Sampson 2002: 194). 'The state of these two bean poles' (Fagan 2007 [1950s]: 280). Recorded from l.20c.; derivation is clear.

Steadier (n.): handrail outside a pub. 'Thick brass rails for protection and steadiers when the stewed turned out at midnight bellies inflated' (Clerk 1971 [c.1900]: 32). *NR in this sense; derivation is clear.

Stem-winder (n.): watch. 'Stem-winder (American Liverpool). Keyless watch' (Ware 1909: 233). Recorded from l.19c.; an Americanism; derivation is clear.

Step-dash (v.): to clean front steps. 'Me ould girl, a real Murry Ellen, goes out step-dashin'' (Shaw 1957a:

7). 'Step-dashing is washing the door-step' (Armstrong 1966: 6). 'And thoughts of dashin',/never entered her head' (Hallowell 1972: n.p.). 'She's step-dashin. She is scrubbing the doorstep' (Spiegl 2000: 48). *NR; from 17c. 'dash', 'throw water on'. A clean front step, scrubbed with a piece of sandstone or a *donkeystone*, was a matter of pride.

Sterry/sterry milk (n.): sterilised milk. 'Sterry. *Sterilised milk*' (Shaw et al. 1966: 38). '*Sterry* Sterilised milk' (Spiegl 2000b: 111). *NR; popular before the advent of mass home refrigeration because it could be stored for long periods, sterilised milk (the alternative was 'fresh milk') was subject to prolonged heat treatment to destroy bacteria; it had a very distinctive taste.

Stevedore (n.): overseer on the docks. 'The language of the stevedores and truckmen' (Melville 1849: 250). '"It's always like this", said the foreman stevedore' (Hall 2004 [1939]: 225). 'The master stevedore to see the mate' (Lane 1987: 41). 'Stevedore – Docker elected in the gang to tell the others what to do' (Burnett 2011: 13). Recorded from l.18c.; an Americanism, from Spanish, 'estivador', from 'estivar', 'to stow cargo'.

Stewbum (n.): drunkard. 'The goms had gigs with fast trotting ponies. But they weren't convenient for collecting up stewbums' (Clerk 1971 [c.1900]: 32). Recorded as 'Liverpool street arabs': late c.19–earlier 20' (Beale (1984) *s.v. stew bum*); see *stewed*.

Stewbum palace (n.): local lock-ups. 'In different parts of the city there were stewbum palaces, miniature gaols where the goms dumped the stewbums to sober up' (Clerk 1971 [*c*.1900]: 32). *NR; see *stewbum*.

Stewed (adj.): drunk. 'On occasion leading chaps too stewed to get aboard their ships' (Clerk 1971 [*c*.1900]: 27). Recorded from e.20c.; from an 18c. Americanism.

Stick, the (n.): the Landing Stage at the Pier Head. '"Stick" (Landing Stage)' (Jones 1935: 5). 'The "Stick", Liverpool Landing Stage' (O'Hanri 1950a: 2). 'Down at the Stick (Landing Stage)' (Shaw 1964b: 4). 'Most people knew the Landing Stage as "The Stick"' (Unwin 1984 [1920s–30s]: 79). *NR; probably from the floating wooden pontoons of which the Landing Stage was made.

Stick-man (n.): dapper or finicky man. '*Stick-man*: A carefully dressed and very dapper individual' (Lane 1966: 103). *NR in this sense; from e.20c. Forces' usage, 'got the stick'; the most smartly turned out soldier was given a 'stick', which enabled him to evade onerous duties.

Stickjaw (n.): toffee. '*Stickjaw*: A glutinous form of toffee' (Lane 1966: 103). 'A quarter pound of coconut stick-jaw' (Robinson 1986 [1920s–30s]: 66). *NR; derivation is clear.

Sticky lice (n.): liquorice. '"Sticky-lice" is liquorice' (Channon 1970: 102). '"Sticky-lice" which looked like a twig of wood, and was in fact that root of the liquorice tree' (Stamper 2010: 26). *NR; the derivation is unclear; *sticky lice* was used as a mouth freshner.

Stiff moo/stiff tit (n.): condensed milk. See *conny-onny*.

Stiffen (v.): punish severely. 'If ah stayed out that late me dad id stiffen me'

(Farrell 1950b: 4). 'I stiffened 'im. I 'alf et 'im' (Shaw 1950a: 40). Recorded from l.19c.; a weakening of 'stiffen', 'kill'.

Stipe, the (n.): Stipendiary Magistrate. 'The ould Stipe makes it a caution' (Shaw 1957a: 7). '*De Stipe*, the Liverpool Stipendiary Magistrate' (Shaw et al. 1966: 65). '(DE) STIPE The Stipendiary Magistrate' (Spiegl 1989: 71). Recorded from m.19c.; a simple abbreviation.

Stop (v.): stay, remain. 'I'm stopping at home tonight' (Hanley 1932: 118). 'A real fuckin' stop-in' (Parker 1974: 137). 'Don't be tight, let's stop for our tea' (Brown 1989: 68). 'I'll try and stop a bit longer next time' (Sinclair 1999 [1930s–e.40s]: 85). Recorded from 19c.; derivation is clear.

Stopout (n.): someone who stays out late/all night. 'Yer a dirty stopout. *You are a nocturnal reveller*' (Shaw et al. 1966: 27). 'Though Julia has renamed it the "stopouts dish"' (Russell 1981: xi). 'Here's another dirty stop-out coming home' (Fagan 2007 [1950s]: 166). Recorded from m.20c.; the connotation is often mocking; see *stop*.

Strag (n.): stray pigeon. 'The name given to a lost, stray, homing pigeon' (Howarth 1985: s.v. strag). 'Mr. Know sold the "strags" he caught' (Elliott 2006 [1940s–70s]: 55). *NR; probably an abbreviation of 'straggler'.

Straightener (n.): a fight to decide an argument; punishment. 'He's starting to get a bit aerated, but I've half got a feeling that's down to tomorrow, the straightener and that' (Sampson 2001: 194). 'Yeh don't send two of yer best boys off on a straightener in a fuckin shed like this' (Griffiths 2003: 10). 'Local disputes were settled by "straighteners"' (Lees 2013: 127). Recorded from l.20c.; an extension of 'straighten', 'make straight, clear up, put in order'.

Street school (n.): street gambling. 'A *street-skule* is a group of gamblers playing pitch-and-toss' (Lane 1966: 99). *NR; from e.19c. 'school', 'a party of persons meeting for the purpose of gambling'.

Strides (n.): trousers. 'STRIDES for trousers is our very own. The word comes, via the theatre, from tailors' cant' (Shaw 1959a: 34). '*Trousers*. Strides' (Minard 1972: 46). 'Strides. Slang for trousers. Liverpool' (Howarth 1985: n.p.). Recorded from e.19c.; from the discourse of tailors and the theatre.

Strong as a bad egg (phr.): a weakling. '*You're strong as a bad egg*' (Shaw 1950b: 4). 'G'wan yewr strong as a bad egg (i.e. you are a weakling)' (Shaw 1959a: 41). *NR; derivation is clear.

Stroppy (adj.): bad-tempered, awkward. '"Have you got a licence for it?" "Oh, don't be so stroppy"' (Burke 1964: 80). 'They're not so stroppy and aggressive' (McClure 1980: 240). Recorded from m.20c.; probably an abbreviation of 'obstreperous'.

Stuck up (adj.): snobby, pretentious. 'A stuck-up, proud, penniless pauper!' (Powys 1857: 190). 'If one woman in a court or street is bent on keeping herself to herself … she is called "proud" or "stuck-up" or a "touch-me-not"' (Shimmin 1863: 33). 'If he isn't like all the other stuck-up pigs, I'll have somebody to talk to' (Hanley 2009 [1936]: 408). 'Bein' too stuck up to belong to the gang' (Cross 1951: 92). 'The middle classes who are "stuck up" and "toffee nosed"' (Parker 1974: 159). 'The boys of the family, in particular, saw her as "stuck up"' (Bryan 2003 [1940s–50s]: 85). Recorded from e.19c.; derivation unclear but possibly 'nose stuck up in the air'.

Sub (n.): loan. 'I'll get a sub for you' (Hanley 1932: 159). 'He's a man without money and on the lookout for a sub!' (Shaw 1958a: 3). 'Sub. *A loan*' (Shaw et al. 1966: 35). 'A sub as most people know is a small loan' (Jacques 1973: n.p.). 'You could get a sub off the captain out of your wages' (Dudgeon 2010: 84). Recorded from m.19c.; originally 'payment of wages on account', then more generally 'a loan' ('to sub' means 'to lend'); probably from either 'subsistence money' or 'subvention'.

Suck (n.): sweet. 'Ool swap a bloody jark for a suck!' (Clerk 1971 [c.1900]: 69). Recorded from 19c.; dialectal; derivation is clear.

Suckhole (n.): toady, arse-licker. 'Des, he's a real fucking suckhole' (Parker 1974: 94). 'Get the suckholes like Jez Sully an his creepin fuckin mates' (Griffiths 2003: 182). '"Suck 'ole" a familiar voice muttered' (Fagan 2007 [1950s]: 256). Recorded from e.20c.; Australian usage, from 'hole', 'anus'.

Sudner (n.): someone from the South of England. '*Sudner*: Anyone whose speech suggests that he comes from a town in the South of England, such as Chester' (Lane 1966: 104). Recorded from l.19c.; Lane's gloss illustrates the significance attached to language in relation to the distinctiveness of Liverpudlian identity.

Sunbeam (n.): pious person. '*Sunbeams*: children who regularly attend Sunday School or adults who are persistent church-goers' (Lane 1966: 104). 'Proper little sunbeams we're gonna be' (Sinclair 1999 [1930s–e.40s]: 129). *NR; probably from the hymn, 'Jesus wants me for a sunbeam'.

Suss/suss out (v.): to suspect; work out. 'I sussed it out ten minutes ago' (Murari 1975: 49). 'They're not going to suss him' (McClure 1980: 95). 'I'd sussed that he was gay' (Flame 1984: 38). 'Trying to sus where I'm going' (Sampson 2002: 38). 'Nipper had already sussed it out' (Fagan 20017 [1950s]: 194). Recorded from m.20c.; a simple abbreviation of 'to suspect'.

Sussed (adj.): found out; worked out. 'Well sussed. Found out' (Spiegl 1989: 83). 'Paul seems to have it sussed' (Sampson 2002: 238). Recorded from l.20c.; see *to suss*.

Swallow the anchor (phr.): retire from the sea. 'He could do that. Swallow the anchor for good and all. Bury himself between bricks and mortar again' (Hanley 2009 [1936]: 90). '"I'm swallowin' the anchor" indicates that the man has given up the sea' (Jacques 1972: n.p.). 'We "swallowed the anchor", the navy term for resigning' (Stamper 2010: 68). Recorded from l.19c.; derivation is clear.

Sweat cobs¹ (v.): to worry greatly. '"To sweat cobs" is to show excessive anxiety' (Farrell 1950b: 4). Recorded from m.20c.; possibly from 'cob', 'roundish mass, lump'.

Sweat cobs² (v.): to sweat profusely. 'You're sweating cobs' (Bainbridge 1978: 66). 'I'm going to sweat cobs today' (Graham 1988: 63). '*She wuz sweat'n cobs* The lady was perspiring profusely!' (Spiegl 2000b: 91). See *sweat cobs¹*.

Sweat on (v.): await anxiously. '"To sweat on something" is to experience considerable anxiety about the outcome of a certain event' (Farrell 1950b: 4). '*Sweat on*: To wait anxiously for a given result' (Lane 1966: 104). 'Sweatin' on number one' (Jacques 1973: n.p.). Recorded from e.20c.; an Americanism; probably originated in gambling discourse, but now refers to any fretful expectation.

Swede (n.): head. 'It's doing everyone's swedes in that the Scousers still see us as Wools' (Sampson 1998: 3). 'Mashed her friggin swede big time' (Griffiths 2003: 111). Recorded from e.20c.; Forces' usage; presumably a comparison between the shape of a swede (Swedish turnip) and a head.

Swill (n.): wash. 'Both lads had a quick swill' (Sinclair 1999 [1930s–e.40s]: 172). *NR in this sense; an extension from Old English 'swillan', 'wash or rinse out a vessel'.

Swing a free leg (phr.): unmarried. Recorded as 'overheard in Liverpool 1966' (Beale (1984) *s.v. swing a free leg*); derivation unclear.

Swipe (v.): steal. '*'Oo's the bastard what swiped me moo?* Who is the person who has stolen the milk?' (Lane 1966: 104). Recorded from l.19c.; an Americanism; probably from 'sweep', 'clear away'.

Swipes (n.): beer, dregs. '*Swipes*, as I learned, was a sort of cheap substitute for beer; or a bastard kind of beer;

or the washings and rinsings of old beer-barrels' (Melville 1849: 173). 'Brawn, bread and pickle washed down with "swipes"' (Lees 2013: 78). Recorded from l.18c.; originally the weak beer served by the purser to a ship's crew, but by extension any beer (Melville notes that *swipes* 'is drunk in large quantities by the poor people about Liverpool'); from English dialectal 'to swipe', 'to drink hastily and greedily'.

Swiper (n.): hard drinker; boozer (insult). 'Go away you dirty rotten auld swiper or oi'll batter your bloody face in for you' (O'Mara 1934: 49). See *swipes*.

T

Tabbie (n.): elderly person; old woman. 'TABBIE elderly person' (Spiegl 1989: 73). '*Tabbies* Pensioners' (Spiegl 2000b: 63). Recorded from 18c.; the dimunitive form of 'Tabitha'.

Take a powder (v.): to leave, escape. '"They're goin ter hang me" "Then you'd best take a powder"' (Jacques 1973: n.p.). '*Take a Powder*: Meaning, "get lost", or "go away"' (Sanders and Sanders 2009 [1960s]: 185). Recorded from e.20c.; an Americanism; an abbreviation of 'run out powder'.

Take one's coat off, I'll (phr.): threat to fight. 'The threat may be made "I'll take me coat off t'year" but there's nothing in it' (Shaw 1959a: 36). 'Says one Huyton councillor: "I'll after take me coat off to um"' (Shaw 1966d: 6). *NR; presumably from the perceived need to take your coat off before fighting.

Take someone's kecks down (v.): to humiliate someone. '*Take 'is kecks down*: To put a person in his place, to expose somebody' (Lane 1966: 105). *NR; derivation is clear.

Takers-on (n.): men employed to select workers under the casual labour scheme on the docks. '"Takers-on" displayed favouritism often based on religious and political issues' (Shaw 1959c: 6). *NR; the casual labour system entailed workers queuing for the morning and afternoon shifts; the system was open to abuse on sectarian or political grounds.

Talent (n.): the local nubility (women – usually – and men – occasionally). 'All de talint was dere an' ev'body wus bevvied' (Shaw 1959a: 34). 'Dur's no talint ere. *There are no pretty women here*' (Shaw et al. 1966: 62). 'There's no talent in the pub' (Russell 1996 [1976]: 203). 'Weighing up the talent, just as we would at other venues' (Fagan 2007 [1950s]: 109). Recorded from m.20c.; usually collocated with 'local'; from 'talent' 'measure of weight', hence value.

Talk Blundellsands (v.): to talk posh. '*She talks Blendellsahnds*: Said of a woman considered to have an affected accent' (Lane 1966: 96). *NR; Blundellsands is an affluent area to the north of Liverpool.

Tally (n.): docket confirming work under casual labour system at the docks, or union membership. 'All three boys had handed in their workers' tallies to the woman' (Hanley 1932: 30). 'In the bad old days of casual labour the docker's tally became worth its weight in gold' (Unwin 1984 [1920s–30s]: 107). 'A tally was a ticket confirming employment often for half a day's work only' (Dudgeon 2010: 91). *NR in this sense; the *tally* played a central role in the casual labour system.

Tallyman (n.): collector of payment for goods on credit. 'De tallyman. *The hire purchase collector*' (Shaw et al. 1966: 24). 'Tally-man. Hire purchase agent. Everton' (Howarth 1985: n.p.).

'Them pawnbrokers and that tally man' (Bryan 2003 [1940s–50s]: 108). 'Tallyman – The man who collected payments at the door for things bought on "tick"' (Callaghan 2011 [1910s–30s]: ix). Recorded from 17c.; from 'tally', 'stick used to record debt or payment'; by extension, *As ard as a breathless tally-man*. To be pressing and insistent' (Lane 1966: 105).

Tank (n.): money. 'Could use the tank and all too' (Sampson 2001: 4). '"Goulash" or "tank" was money' (Lees 2013: 242). Recorded from e.21c.; derivation unknown.

Tanner (n.): sixpence. 'I haven't got three bob. Give you one and a tanner for it' (Hanley 2009 [1936]: 537). '*Tanner*: sixpence' (Shaw 1952: 4). 'Rattling down to add the tanners' (Hignett 1966: 148). 'Lenza tanner' (Minard 1972: 10). 'Sixpence or a "tanner", would buy ten top quality cigarettes, or five Woodbines, with twopence change' (Unwin 1984 [1920s–30s]: 36). 'A tanner postal order' (Sinclair 1999 [1930s–e.40s]: 154). 'Tanners – Sixpences' (Callaghan 2011 [1910s–30s]: ix). Recorded from l.18c.; cant; derivation unknown.

Tanner doctor (n.): inferior doctor, charging less than the going rate. 'Dr. Walker (the "tanner doctor", just dismissed as the head doctor from the South Dispensary' (O'Mara 1934: 68). *NR; see *tanner*.

Tanner-megger (n.): cheap football, medium rather than full-sized. 'We played footee with any old ball, from a golfie to a tanner-megger' (Shaw 1957a: 1). 'Tanner-megger. *Small football*' (Shaw et al. 1966: 44). 'Tanner-meggar.

A small ball. Liverpool' (Howarth 1985: n.p.). *NR; see *tanner*; *megger* is unknown.

Tanroagan (n.): scallop. '*Tanrogans*: Escallops' (Lane 1966: 105). 'Tanrogans. Escallops. Liverpool' (Howarth 1985: n.p.). *NR; an Isle of Man food specialty; from Manx, 'tanroagan', 'scallop-shell'.

Tap¹ (v.): to borrow. 'Didden you tap me for fourpence for a pint the other night to get into Cains?' (Shaw 1952: n.p.). 'I ope to tap the brother for a coupla sprowser' (Shaw 1957a: 7). Recorded from m.20c.; an extension of 18c. 'tap', 'to open the purse or pocket; to spend freely'.

Tap² (v.): to importune. 'The Boys wil go hoping to "tap one" for "a quick shag"' (Parker 1974: 137). 'Don't be tappin' 'er up, either' (Fagan 2007 [1950s]: 32). Recorded from m.20c.; either from 'tap' (on shoulder), or a weakening of l.17c. 'tap', 'deflower a woman'.

Tap stopped (phr.): barred from a pub. 'Should one protest, he'll have his "tap stopped" i.e. he won't be served next time he comes in' (Shaw 1959a: 37). 'Pack it in or Ile stop yer tap. *If the customer continues to offend he will not be served*' (Shaw et al. 1966: 70). '*I'll stop yer tap* I'll refuse to serve you more drink' (Spiegl 2000b: 80). *NR; the 'tap' in question is the 'beer tap'.

Tara/Ta-ra well (int.): goodbye. 'That phrase, spoken at parting to mitigate sweet sorrow: "Tar-ra well!"' (Farrell 1950b: 4). '"Ta-ra." Lynch said' (Martin 1962: 29). 'T'sarrahwell. *Farewell!*' (Shaw et al. 1966: 18). '"Tarrah, Valerie!" called Rita up the stairs' (Bainbridge 1973: 39). '"Tirrah!"

Boom goes the door' (McClure 1980: 146). 'He says "Tar-rar", and goes in his house' (Brown 1989: 39). 'OK, ta-ra girl' (Sinclair 1999: 9). 'We said ar taras and I leave' (Griffiths 2003: 28). Recorded from m.20c.; a northern dialectal adaptation of e.19c. 'ta ta'.

Tarpaulin muster (n.): pooling or collection of money. 'I often took part in these "tarpaulin musters" (a navy term)' (Elliott 2006 [1940s–70s]: 33). Recorded from l.19c.; an Australian nautical coinage; from 'tarpaulin', 'sailors' ('tars') pooling resources.

Tart (n.): girl, woman, girlfriend, wife. 'Like good sailormen, they were talking about women, one of them saying something about a "tart's" expecting him to marry her' (O'Mara 1934: 290). 'Suppose we pick up two tarts and take them in the boats' (Hanley 2009 [1940]: 425). 'Not like the tarts around Peacock's Buildings' (Cross 1951: 24). 'When he's tart and mine get janglin'' (Shaw 1957a: 1). 'That little tart' (Hignett 1966: 31). 'Me judy, me tart, me gerl. *My lady-friend; my fiancée; my* wife' (Shaw et al. 1966: 25). 'Tart: the girlfriend, not a derogatory term' (Parker 1974: 213). 'Like a big soft tart' (Brown 1989: 23). 'I don't know that I can have a tart telling myself what's what' (Sampson 2002: 38). 'Fuckin' big tart' (Burnett 2011: 80). Recorded from m.19c. in this sense; Shaw et al. claim that 'though the name has come to be a rather opprobrious one', in Liverpool the term has 'remained pleasant' (Shaw et al. 1966: 25); the *OED* reinforces this interpretation: 'applied, *gen[erally]* (orig[inally] often endearingly) to a girl or woman; freq. in Australia and N.Z. Also in Liverpool dial[ect]' (*OED s.v. tart* n. 2 a). As with *judy*, however, claims as to the neutrality of *tart* have to be met with scepticism; the *OED* documents another common use of *tart*: a woman 'of immoral character; a prostitute. Also *loosely* as a term of abuse' (*OED s.v. tart* n. 2 b).

Tatter/rag-tatter (n.): the rag and bone man. '*Tatter*, the name for the old-clothes collector who shouts "Mugs for rags"' (Shaw 1950b: 4). 'De tatter. *The rag collector*' (Shaw et al. 1966: 24). 'A tatter was rootin' in the bin' (Jacques 1973: n.p.). '"Tatters", who, of course, were the rag and bone men' (Unwin 1984 [1920s–30s]: 69). 'The rag-tatter called again' (Sinclair 1999 [1930s–e.40s]: 87). Recorded from l.19c.; from m.19c. 'tat', 'to gather rags'; probably from Hindi ṭāṭ, 'coarse canvas made from various fibres'.

Tatting (n.): rag and bone collecting. 'The Liverpool slang term "tatting" as applied to collecting rags and bones' ('Postman' 1932a: 5). 'The aunt, the old girl's sister, she goes out tattin'' (Shaw 1957a: 7). 'Tatting is collecting rags' (Armstrong 1966: 6). 'He had resorted to rag-tatting to earn a few shillings' (Sinclair 1999 [1930s–e.40s]: 20). See *tatter*.

Tatty-bye (int.): goodbye. *Tatty Bye* (Dodd 1965b: title). Recorded from m.20c.; this was the Liverpool comedian Ken Dodd's catch-phrase; a conflation of 'ta-ta' and 'bye-bye'.

Tatty-head (n.): mostly affectionate term of address. ''Ere, tatty-ead! *I say, young woman*' (Shaw et al. 1966: 17). 'Nit Nurse came/to scratch the muck of war/from tattyheads' (Simpson

1990: 19). '*'Ere, tatty'ead!* I say, young woman!' (Spiegl 2000b: 37). '"Tatty head", because of his curly hair' (Elliott 2006 [1940s–70s]: 38). *NR in this sense; 'tatty' has been used in Scots to describe hair since 16c.

Tea (n.): evening meal. 'He came home one night from his work … she gave him his tea, and made him as comfortable as she could' (Roberts 1893: 88). 'That evening, after the inevitable bacon and eggs for "tea"' (O'Mara 1934: 175). 'He would never dream of missing five o'clock teatime' (Cross 1951: 190). 'It wasn't just his evening meal the all-important "tea", being spoilt which made him eggy' (Shaw 1959a: 38). '*Dinner = lunch. Tea = supper. Supper = a late night snack*' (Lane 1966: 26). 'The light was fading … it was time for tea' (Murari 1975: 117). 'He'd come home from work every day, expecting his tea to be ready' (Flame 1984: 13). 'Friday night was special. We had bacon and eggs for tea' (Callaghan 2011 [1910s–30s]: 21). Recorded from e.20c. in this sense; the term varies regionally and with class; it can refer to tea and light refreshments in the late afternoon, but in the north, Scotland and Ireland, it can refer to a cooked evening meal (any time from around five o'clock).

Tear-arse (n.): busy, impatient person. '*Tear-arse*: A busy person; one who refuses to dawdle or waste time' (Lane 1966: 106). 'Terry Collins, better known to everyone as Tear-Arse' (Fagan 2007 [1950s]: 220). Recorded from e.20c.; an Americanism that combines 'tear', 'move violently, with impetuosity' and 'arse', general pejorative for 'person'.

Tear-away (n.): irresponsible, usually badly behaved person. 'A proper tearaway he is, alwis saggin' schule' (Shaw 1957a: 12). 'He was a tear-away' (Grant 1996: 47). Recorded from e.20c.; see *tear-arse*.

Them (pron.): those. 'Them two were a pair' (Hanley 2009 [1940]: 429). 'Dem. They; these' (Shaw et al. 1966: 25). 'Remember them sex lessons I signed up for' (Brown 1989: 22). 'Them 'oles 'll be full o' water' (Sinclair 1999 [1930s–e.40s]: 87). 'Them days there were cinemas everywhere' (Dudgeon 2010: 249). Recorded from e.19c.; the use of *them* as a demonstrative pronoun is glossed as 'regional and nonstandard'.

There's hair on baldy (phr.): general insult. '*There's hair on baldy!*: shouted derisively by Liverpool street girls' (Beale 1985: *Liverpool Catch Phrases*). Recorded from e.20c.; derivation unclear.

Thick (adj.): stupid, idiotic. 'You are as thick as you look, Kilkey, but you've got a good heart all the same' (Hanley 2009 [1936]: 316). '*So thick 'e can't leak*: Very stupid' (Lane 1966: 107). 'Hell! You're thick' (Sinclair 1999 [1930s–e.40s]: 11). 'They're all stupid thick cunts' (Griffiths 2003: 169). Recorded from e.17c.; original meaning, 'slow-witted'; an extension of 'thick' in relation to perception (sight, hearing).

Thick as pigshit/shite (adj.): really stupid. 'Fucking thick as shite, she is' (Sampson 2002: 48). 'Thick as shite, aren't yeh? Thick as fuckin pigshit' (Griffiths 2003: 59). Recorded from l.20c.; an addition to the list of comparisons made to emphasise stupidity (Shakespeare has 'thick as Tewksbury mustard'). See *thick*.

Thick as two short planks (adj.): stupid, idiotic. 'I wus thick as two short planks, I cooden learn from a big clock' (Shaw 1957a: 15). '*Thick as two short planks*: Extremely stupid' (Lane 1966: 107). Recorded from m.20c.; the emphasis is produced by the specificity of the comparison: 'two', 'short', 'planks'; see *thick*.

Thingy/Thingio (n.): unnamed object; said when word can't be recalled or is not known. 'It's a thingy, isn't it?' (Russell 1996 [1975]: 14). 'The one that's always on at this time of year, thingio – the Dickens one' (Sampson 2001: 105). Recorded from l.20c.; an abbreviation of 18c. 'thingummy'.

Thisavvy/isavvy (phr.): this afternoon. See *savvy*.

Thrap (n.): masturbation. 'Only easy thing to do with one hand is to have a thrap' (Griffiths 2003: 4). Recorded from l.20c.; possibly an extension of e.19c. dialectal variant 'thrap', 'to bind tightly' (from 'frap').

Three holes (n.): game of marbles. 'How convenient the court was to play marbles in from "ring taw" to "three holes"' (Roberts 1893: 9). 'The noble game of marbles called "Three Holes"' (Unwin 1984 [1920s–30s]: 62). Recorded from e.19c.; the aim was to get the marbles into the holes.

Three on the hook and three on the book (phr.): part-time employment at the docks. 'They had just done three on the hook and three on the book, meaning three days at work and three on the dole' (Anon. 1955: 6). 'T'ree on der ook – t'ree on de book' hree on the hook",

the dockers' tool of trade, and "three on the book", that is signing on at the Labour Exchange' (Shaw 1959c: 6). '"Three on the hook and three on the book" – which meant three days work and three days on the dole' (Unwin 1984 [1920s–30s]: 107). *NR; O'Mara explained the system in the 1930s: 'one could work three days at the dock for thirty-six shillings and draw the dole at three shillings per day to boot … if one worked four days at the dock, there would be no dole, so the trick was to see to it that only three days were worked' (O'Mara 1934: 302). O'Mara's explanation is misleading in one respect; dockers were lucky to find three days work in a week in the 1930s. From 'hook', the docker's tool, and 'book', the unemployment register.

Thundermug (n.): chamber-pot. '*Thundermug*: a chamber-pot' (Lane 1966: 108). ''Aven't yer forgotten somethin' – yer thunder-mug' (Sinclair 1999 [1930s–e.40s]: 131). Recorded from l.19c.; an Americanism; presumably from the sound of its use.

Tiddler[1] (n.): small fish. 'It was lake water, full of cack an' tiddlers' (Bleasdale 1975: 116). Recorded from l.19c.; originally a stickleback and by extension other small fish; probably from 'tiddly', 'little'.

Tiddler[2] (n.): silver threepenny bit. 'Tiddler. *Silver Threepenny piece*' (Shaw et al. 1966: 33). *NR; the last silver threepenny bits were minted in 1945; an extension of *tiddler[1]*.

Tiger-nuts (n.): sedge nut; chufa sedge. 'The popularity of monkey-nuts and tiger-nuts has somewhat waned' (Collinson 1927: 18). '*Tiger nuts*:

European sedge-nuts, popular among children' (Lane 1966: 108). Recorded from l.19c.; the popular name for Cyperus esculentus, an edible tuber rather than a nut; common in West Africa and imported through Liverpool.

Tight/Tight-arsed (adj.): repressed; mean. 'Fuck off yourself, you tight bastard' (Parker 1974: 48). 'All titty lipped and tight arsed' (Bleasdale 1975: 159). 'Ah eh Missis, don't be tight' (Brown 1989: 68). 'Yer tight-arsed twat. Why not give the poor bastard a coin?' (Griffiths 2000: 133). 'So tight he'd once been put on probation for breaking into a ten bob note' (Fagan 2007 [1950s]: 99). Recorded from e.20c.; originally 'chaste, close-legged', extended to 'stingy'.

Tilly Mint (n.): a general name, often used to scold young women, sometimes in jest. 'You'd often hear her shout across to her mint-selling pal, "Hey, Tilly Mint!"' ('Postman' 1964a: 4). 'Tilly Mint stood in Mill Street, in the South End of Liverpool, for many years' ('Postman' 1964b: 6). '*Tilly Mint*: Whozit, whatsername' (Lane 1966: 109). 'Wot wud be the use if sum/snotty-nosed Tilly Mint went an told yer/y werent on afterorl?' (Simpson 1995: 23). 'Yer can leave Tillie-mint 'ere to me' (Bryan 2003 [1940s–50s]: 124). *NR; supposedly the name of one of the women who sold bunches of herbs outside St. John's Market on the steps of the Fish Market ('sage-er-mint-er-parsley!', their cry), though she was also identified as a herb-seller on Mill Street in the Dingle.

Tin Can Alley (n.): Otterspool Promenade. 'Al see yerrin Tin Can Alley. *Let's meet*

at Otterspool Promenade' (Minard 1972: 40). *NR; see *Prom.*

Tip-cat (n.): children's game. '*Tip-cat*: a game in which a piece of wood is rapped to make it jump and is then struck while in mid-air' (Lane 1966: 109). 'There was a game we used to play called "Tip Cat"' (Unwin 1984 [1920s–30s]: 19). Recorded from 17c.; a children's game of which varieties are played throughout the world; the aim is to hit the small piece of wood (the 'cat') as far as possible.

Tip-scrabbler (n.): rubbish dump scavenger. '*Tip-scrabbler*: A person who searches ash-heaps for small quantities of burnable fuel' (Lane 1966: 109). *NR; one of the legacies of Thatcherism was the re-appearance of *tip-scrabblers* in the 1980s.

Tit/Tit-end/Tithead (n.): idiot, fool. 'I kept on looking for that tit-end, Robin Day' (Bleasdale 1975: 147). 'His dad calls him Tithead' (Bleasdale 1975: 212). 'Mancs and tits getting respect on the street' (Sampson 2001: 26). Recorded from l.20c.; a combination of l.19c. 'tit', 'fool' and e.20c. 'tit' (variant of 'teat'), 'breast'.

Tocky (n.): Toxteth. 'Debbi's from Tocky. Windsor Street. Tocky proper' (Sampson 2001: 25). 'No rich cunts in Tocky, lar' (Griffiths 2003: 57). 'Toccy had a myriad of shebeens' (Lees 2013: 146). *NR; Toxteth is one of the oldest areas of Liverpool and appeared in the Domesday Book ('Tochstede'). The 1981 Toxteth riots brought a new pronunciation along with notoriety; local people stress the first syllable, media visitors the second; derivation is unclear.

Tod (n.): clever, crafty person. 'You can play around with the grammar tods from the 'igh school' (Cross 1951: 92). Recorded from 16c.; glossed as Scottish, a figurative extension of 12c. 'tod, 'fox' (hence 'sly, crafty').

Tod, on one's (phr.): alone. '*On me tod*: by myself' (Lane 1966: 109). 'So Adam went to live on his tod' (Jacques 1975: n.p.). 'On my tod!' (Graham 1988: 138). 'Go on your tod. You'll be sound' (Sampson 2001: 127). Recorded from m.20c.; an abbreviation of the slightly earlier rhyming slang 'on one's Tod Sloan'; Tod Sloan was an American jockey.

Toe-rag (n.): term of abuse; worthless person. 'Take the toe rag with y'' (Bleasdale 1985: 120). 'You've got no fucking respect you ... you little toe rag!' (Sampson 1999: 106). 'Peddling guns in Toxteth and Speke and Garston. A toe-rag' (Grant 2002: 158). Recorded from l.19c.; originally the rags worn by tramps inside their shoes, extended to the tramps themselves.

Toffees/Toffeemen, the (n.): nickname for Everton Football Club. *NR; see *Everton toffee*.

Togee/togo (n.): brown sugar. 'Togo. *Brown sugar*' (Shaw et al. 1966: 38). '"Togo" is brown sugar' (Channon 1970: 102). 'Togee – Lumps of brown sugar, usually picked up from the back of Tate and Lyle's sugar refinery' (Callaghan 2011 [1910s–30s]: ix). *NR; sugar cane was grown in Togo (the Togolese Republic), on what was once known as the Guinea Coast.

Togs (n.): clothes; swimming costume. 'In *Madagasky* there, they don't wear any togs at all' (Melville 1849: 130).

'Get on yer best togs and let's be off' (Hocking 1966 [1879]: 73). 'He'd lend you togs' (McColl 1952: 3). 'Sailors from Asian and African ports still make a beeline for Paddy's to buy secondhand togs' (Channon 1970: 120). 'I don't have any swimming togs' (Robinson 1986 [1920s–30s]: 29). Recorded from e.18c.; from cant 'togeman', 'coat', extended in l.18c. to mean 'clothes', with later specialised senses of 'landsmen's clothes' ('shore clothes, or "*long* togs", as the sailors call them' Melville 1849: 97), and 'swimming costume'.

Tom off (v.): to stack cargo neatly on a ship. 'Learning to batten hatches, tom-off cars down holds' (Simpson 1990: 48). 'Stabilizing cargo in the ships, which was known as "chocking" or "tomming off"' (Stamper 2010: 80). *NR; derivation unknown.

Tom Pepper (n.): liar. 'Eez a Tom Pepper, 'im: *That man lies very frequently*' (Minard 1972: 26). Recorded from m.19c.; in nautical folklore, Tom Pepper was kicked out of hell for lying.

Ton (n.): one hundred pounds. '£100 A Ton' (Minard 1972: 86). 'Still n all tho, it's a ton for a day's work' (Griffiths 2003: 52). Recorded from m.20c.; an extension of 'ton' in sports (cricket, darts), 'score of one hundred'.

Tonka-beans (n.): tonka beans. '*Tonka-beans*: Tonquin beans, used in snuff-making' (Lane 1966: 110). Recorded from l.18c.; the beans, from the South American tree dipterix odorata, were used in snuff, tobacco and perfume; from Guyanese Creole 'tonka'.

Tontine (n.): savings club. 'Are you in a tontine?' (Haigh 1907: 267). '*Tontine*: A club whose members save money for holidays, Christmas or other special occasions' (Lane 1966: 110). 'So the communal ton-tine wuz raided' (Jacques 1975: n.p.). 'Our mothers' simple tontine dreams' (Simpson 1990: 35). 'Molly started a Tontine – the poor man's savings club' (Bryan 2003 [1940s–50s]: 31). Recorded from l.19c. extension in this sense; from the name of a 17c. Neapolitan banker who invented an annuity scheme.

Tony/toney (adj.): stylish. 'The young Liverpudlian was always TONEY' (Shaw 1959a: 33). 'Worrabowt me/all toney, kecks up t the knees' (Simpson 1995: 24). Recorded from l.19c.; an Americanism; also used in Irish English; from 'tone', 'style'.

Top hat/put the top hat on it (phr.): the last straw; to finish. '*Put the top hat on it* (the last straw). (Shaw 1952: n.p.). '"Dat's put the top 'at on ut." – Finis coronat opus' (Shaw 1955b: 18). '*Dat's put dee top 'at on it!* The End' (Spiegl 2000b: 149). Recorded as '20c. Liverpudlian' (Partridge *s.v. top-hat on it*); possibly an extension of 'to top', 'to complete by putting the top on' or e.20c. Forces' usage 'to put a tin hat on it'.

Topshiner (n.): top-hat. '"Topshiner" for the then still fashionable top-hat or silk hat' (J.A.S. 1950: 2). 'The reader who wrote on "topshiner" may be pleased to know that in my verbal wardrobe it is well established with a straw gussie and a pair of kecks' (Shaw 1950c: 2). 'Topshiner. *Top hat*' (Shaw et al. 1966: 37). *NR; top hats were commonly worn in e.20c. ('toppers' was a game

that involved attempting to knock them off)' probably from 'shiner', 'silk hat'.

Tosh (n.): neutral form of address. '*Think yer posh, tosh, don'tcher?*' (Lane 1966: 110). Recorded from m.20c.; from l.19c. Scottish adjectival 'tosh', 'friendly, intimate'.

Tosheroon (n.): see *tusheroon*.

Toss (v. and n.): pitch and toss. 'Betting at Jem Ward's, making their books at Radley's, or "tossing" at Jack Lanagan's' (Maginn 1844: I, 14). 'Bill is tossing for quarts of ale at ––' (Shimmin 1863: 87). 'Don't ever let me catch you or your mates on that corner playing toss!' (O'Mara 1934: 98). See *pitch and toss*.

Touch-me-not (n.): snob. 'If one woman in a court or street is bent on keeping herself to herself … she is called "proud" or "stuck-up" or a "touch-me-not"' (Shimmin 1863: 33). Recorded from l.19c.; an extension of the slightly earlier meaning, 'prudish'; 'touch me not' are Christ's words to Mary Magdalene (the first person to see him after the Resurrection).

Tout (v.): to solicit (for prostitution); importune, try to sell. 'We'd been touting for ladies and after Newington for ourselves too. We'd see a chap or chaps coming along and we'd stop them, "me or my sister, mister"' (Clerk 1971 [*c.*1900]: 21). Recorded from e.20c.; an extension of l.17c. 'tout', 'to look out, peep'; Clerk's account relates to the prostitution of 'street arabs' in Liverpool.

Towels on/up (phr.): Time! 'If you seek another [drink] you'll be brusquely told "Towels is on!"' (Shaw 1959a: 27). 'The towels were up and the bar was drifting out' (Hignett 1966: 224). 'The manager sneered/as he put on the towels' (Jacques 1972: n.p.). 'There was a shout from the barman "Time Please" hence "the towel on"' (Stamper 2010: 188). *NR; from the practice of placing bar towels over the beer pumps in a pub to signal that opening hours were over.

Town (n.): Liverpool city centre; Liverpool. 'I'll be in town in the afternoon with my ma' (Hignett 1966: 63). 'Walking round town as if they owned it' (Parker 1974: 13). 'Shoes I've bought in town' (Simpson 1990: 49). 'It's not like it's *town* town' (Sampson 2002: 8). 'This many mountains an lakes and woods, it's not fuckin right … Wanner be back in town' (Griffiths 2003: 56). 'He preferred to drink with his friends in town' (Elliott 2006 [1940s–70s]: 130). The use of 'town', often without an article but following a preposition, to refer to a specific place, is recorded from 16c. in English; in Liverpool it means very specifically the city centre or, when out of the city, Liverpool itself.

Towns (n.): testicles. 'It was hairy from the age of nine, Moby's dick. Not just his towns and that, by the way. The whole package' (Sampson 2001: 12). Recorded from l.20c.; an abbreviation of 'town halls', rhyming slang for 'balls'.

Trackie(s) (n.): tracksuit. 'He watches Ally stand and brush his trackie down' (Griffiths 2003: 60). 'I just look down at my trackies' (Sampson 2002: 158). Recorded from l.20c.; derivation is clear.

Trainies (n.): training shoes. 'Now to me, trainies equals adidas' (Sampson 2001: 13). 'Baseball hat and tracksuit, trainies' (Griffiths 2003: 80). Recorded from l.20c.; derivation is clear.

Tramstopper (n.): large *butty*. 'A large one [sandwich], (a *Tramstopper)*' (Shaw 1958d: 19). 'A tramstopper; doorstopper. *A large piece of bread*' (Shaw et al. 1966: 41). *'A tramstopper, or doorstopper* A thick piece of bread' (Spiegl 2000b: 120). *NR; derivation is clear.

Tranny (n.): transistor radio. 'It was dead easy over there to take trannies' (Parker 1974: 45). 'He played "Sound of Music" on his trannee' (Jacques 1977: n.p.). Recorded from m.20c.; derivation is clear.

Trimmer (n.): labourer working in ship's boiler-room as an aide to the fireman. 'The lot of the coal trimmer' (O'Mara 1934: 253). 'The trimmers and donkeymen' (McColl 1952: 10). 'He was registered initially as a trimmer' (Sinclair 1999 [1930s–e.40s]: 79). 'As a trimmer, my father would be regarded at sea and shore as the lowest form of life' (Callaghan 2011 [1910s–30s]: 73). Recorded from l.19c.; an extension of l.18c. 'trim', 'to stow or arrange coal or cargo in the hold of a ship' ('the boys prevailed on me to go below and trim coal' Bower 2015 [1936]: 162).

Turd burglar (n.): derogatory term for male homosexual. '*Turd burglar*: homosexual man' (Lane 1966: 111). '*Homosexual*. Shirtlifter, Punk, Queer, Turd burglar' (Minard 1972: 89). 'TURD-BURGLAR Same as a SHAIRTLIFTER' (Spiegl 1989: 78). 'The cheeky fucking turd-burgling faggot' (Sampson 2002: 221). Recorded from l.20c.; another term in the abusive litany directed towards homosexuality; derivation is clear.

Tush/tosh (n.): half a crown. See *tusheroon*.

Tusheroon (n.): half a crown. 'I'd give you 'arf a tosh, but the old girl would soon 'ave it out of you!' (Steen 1932: 106). 'A half-crown [is generally known] as a "tusheroon"' ('Postman' 1937a: 6). 'Most of our slang currency, like *tosheroon* [came from the race track]' (Shaw 1962a: 9). '2/6d: A Tosheroon, Half a Dollar' (Minard 1972: 86). Recorded from m.19c.; derivation unknown.

Twang (v.): to preach, sermonise. 'Kids would say "the gaffer twanged" or "the beak spat at me"' (Clerk 1971 [c.1900]: 24). *NR; *twang* refers to the words of wisdom uttered by a magistrate to 'street arabs' in l.19c. Liverpool; possibly from 'twang', 'to play on an instrument'.

Twat[1] *(n.)*: term of abuse. 'Halloran, you soft twat, kick it' (Hignett 1966: 270). 'These fuckin' big twats with big cars' (Parker 1974: 85). 'They are such twats that nobody will go with them' (Sayle 1984: 20). 'Birrova twat' (Simpson 1995: 23). 'Safer than you still, yeh twat' (Griffiths 2003: 109). 'Ya thick twat' (Burnett 2011: 135). Recorded from e.20c.; an extension of m.17c. 'twat', 'female genitalia'.

Twat[2] *(n.)*: idler: '"Gom come", I answered, "the twat near broke my arm"' (Clerk 1971 [c.1900]: 43). *NR; glossed by Clerk as 'idler, loafer'; used by Liverpool street children in l.19c.; derivation unclear but presumably related to *twat*[1].

Twat (v.): to hit hard. 'She reckoned I threw her down the steps and twatted her' (Parker 1974: 136). 'Then she twatted me on the head with the cash register' (Sayle 1984: 126). Recorded from l.20c.; derivation unclear.

Twelfth, the (n.): the 12th of July. 'The Twelfth of July, or, as we were raised to call it, "King Billy's Day"' (O'Mara 1934: 86). 'The Twelfth (nothing to do with grouse; it is the 12th July' (Shaw 1952: n.p.). 'The Glorious Twelfth' (Sinclair 1999: 5). *NR; as in Northern Ireland and Glasgow, Liverpool Protestants commemorate the 12th July, the date of the victory of King William of Orange at the Battle of the Boyne, with Orange Lodge marches.

Twern (n.): swivel of watch chain; watch. 'He could lift … slangs an' yeller clocks, yooks, twerns an' jarks with such ease and frequency' (Clerk 1971 [c.1900]: 69). *NR; Clerk glosses 'yooks and twerns' as 'swivels' (on which a watch chain hung); derivation unknown.

Twig (v.): to drink. 'Some kids longing for a twig of their parents' pints' (Clerk 1971 [c.1900]: 83). Recorded from l.19c.; dialectal; 'twig', 'to drink deeply or continuously'; derivation unknown.

U

Uncle (n.): pawnbroker. 'Uncle was an outlet though often getting things for nought [by] threatening to gom us' (Clerk 1971 [*c*.1900]: 69). Recorded from m.18c.; derivation unclear; probably a euphemism.

Under the arm (phr.): second rate, very inferior; unpleasant; unwell. '*Under the arm* – worst, terrible' (Anon. 1964a: 20). 'I'm under de arm, doctor. *I am feeling rather poorly, doctor*' (Shaw et al. 1966: 54). 'British ale which is under the arm' (Brown 1989: 28). '*I'm feelin under dee arm, doctor* I am feeling rather poorly, doctor' (Spiegl 2000b: 104). Recorded from e.20c.; derivation unclear.

Under the crotch (phr.): very unwell. '*I'm feelin under der crotch, doctor* I am feeling worse than poorly' (Spiegl 2000b: 106). *NR; emphatic version of *under the arm*.

Under the doctor (phr.): being treated by a doctor; by extension, on sick leave. 'I wus undher the doctor for tree weeks' (Shaw 1957a: 12). Recorded from m.19c.; an extension of 'under', 'subordinate to, controlled by'; used with special reference to medical supervision.

Up the chute (phr.): in trouble; pregnant. '*Up ther shute*: To be in serious trouble' (Lane 1966: 98). '*E's got 'er up ther shute*: He has made her pregnant' (Lane 1966: 98). 'Are y'sure it's you … What's put her up the shoot?' (Bleasdale 1975: 163). Recorded from m.20c.; an Australian coinage; derivation is clear.

Up the entry eyes (phr.): sexually promising. 'She's got up-de-entry eyes … She has a come hither look' ('Postman' 1966a: 6). '*She got up-dee-entery eyes* She gave me a come-hither look' (Spiegl 2000b: 92). *NR; derivation is clear ('entry' is 'back alley').

Up the pole (phr.): crazy, at wit's end. '*Up the pole*: Crazy, irresponsible' (Lane 1966: 112). Recorded from e.20c.; derivation unclear; distinct from the Irish English 'up the pole', 'pregnant'.

Up the spout (phr.): game played with *cherrywobs* (a form of *ollies*). 'Up the Spout (of a house's gutter-pipe)' (Shaw 1957a: 4). '"Cherry-wabs" there up the spout' (Hallowell 1972: n.p.). 'The only one of our games where "rain stopped play". What did we call it? "Up the spout", of course' (Callaghan 2011 [1910s–30s]: 14). *NR; the aim was to flick a *cherrywob* up the spout.

Up the wall (phr.): annoyed, frustrated, very angry; crazy. 'Sends me up ther bloody wall' (Lane 1966: 40). 'And all our friends are around the bend. Nearly all of them are up the wall' (Bleasdale 1975: 153). Recorded from m.20c.; derivation unclear.

Us (pron.): me, I. 'I'll just have my nightcap with old Bob; ler us have hould of the basket' (Shimmin 1863: 6). 'Where shall us go?' (Hocking 1966 [1879]: 23). 'Here, give us one and I'll take it to him' (Owen 1961: 81). 'Do us a favour. Don't tell him I called' (Smith 1998 [1971]: 109). 'Give us a tanner!' (Robinson 1986 [1920s–30s]: 135). 'Puts her arms around us and slides her hand down me trackies and starts giving us a gam' (Sampson 2001: 217). 'Not realising Warren had said "the café by us"' (Lees 2013: 242). Recorded from m.19c.; dialectal (also Scottish and Irish English) and often in unemphatic use with 'give'; if there is a Royal 'we', 'us' belongs to the people.

V

Vale, The (n.): the (specific) Vale. 'The Vale: Walton Vale to Liverpool north-enders, Aigburth Vale to south-enders, St. Domingo Vale to in-betweeners' (Lane 1966: 113). There are a number of vales in Liverpool place names, including: Walton Vale, Everton Vale, Dingle Vale, Woolton Vale, Gateacre Vale.

Vamoose (v.): leave, escape. 'If he really intended to vamoose' (Cross 1951: 101). 'Vamoosed. Not that you could imagine the lad vamoosing anywhere' (Sampson 2002: 164). Recorded from e.19c.; an Americanism that passed into English use almost immediately though the 20c. usage probably came from Westerns; from Spanish 'vamos', 'let's go'.

Vaults (n.): pub. 'A narrow lane [in Liverpool], filled with boarding-houses, spirit vaults and sailors' (Melville 1849: 168). 'With a sly look Jack steps into the large vaults which have a back entrance in [Mill Street]' (Shimmin 1863: 5). 'Repulsive, granite-faced "Vaults" recurrent every five hundred yards' (Cross 1951: 112). 'The little pub opposite is called Curiosity Vaults''' (Channon 1970: 119). Recorded from 16c.; originally a 'cellar or store for liquor', extended to South Lancashire dialectal 'vault': 'a place where intoxicating liquors are sold at the counter only'.

Vauxy (n.): Vauxhall Road. 'Voxey: Vauxhall Road, Liverpool' (Lane 1966: 113). *NR; Vauxhall Road is one of the main thoroughfares in the north of the city, lying between Great Homer Street and Scotland Road.

Veil (n.): caul. 'Shortly after the baby's birth a man came to the house and offered £25 for the "veil"' (Kerr 1958: 130). Recorded from m.19c.; dialectal; the membrane that surrounds the foetus at birth was considered by sailors to be protection against drowning and was highly valued.

Vinegar trip (n.): wasted journey. 'She's gone on a vinegar trip' (Bainbridge 1973: 115). 'Vinegar-trip. A wasted journey' (Howarth 1985: n.p.). *NR; derivation unknown.

W

Wack/Whack/Wacker/Whacker (n.): Liver-pudlian. 'If it be true, he must be a wacker e'cod' (Boulton 1768: 31). '"Hey, Whacker!" they said as he passed' (Kavanagh 1949: 179). 'The Liverpool whacker who brought us some much-needed laughter' during the war' (Egan 1955: 216). 'Ta-ra, me old whack' (Hignett 1966: 152). 'What am I paying you for, wack?' (Smith 1998 [1971]: 74). 'The Wackers' (Title: BBC TV series 1975) 'Ow much for the trousers, wack?' (Robinson 1986 [1920s–30s]: 135). '[In the 1920s–30s] Whacker was used as a form of greeting between fellow-scousers' (Garnett 1995: 124). 'Ha, wacker! Leave the kid alone' (Kelly 2006 [1930s–40s]: 93). Recorded from 18c.; from the e.20c. this was the term used commonly by Liverpudlians to refer to each other (it displaced *Dicky Sam* and was in turn replaced by *Scouse/Scouser*). Derivation unclear; possibly a combination of 'whack', 'to divide or share' and 'whack', short for *paddy whack*.

Wagon (n.): bed. '*Bed*. Flock, Wagon, Shitcart' (Minard 1972: 87). *NR in this sense; presumably from the flat shape.

Walk out (n.): a failure. 'Walk out (American–English Theatrical, 1890 on). Failure, from the American habit of condemning a bad play before it is over by going home. Reached England by way of Liverpool' (Ware 1909).

Recorded from l.19c.; an extension of the slightly earlier Americanism, 'to walk out' (specifically of a performance).

Wallasey lad (n.): derogatory term for male homosexual. '*Wallasey Lad*: homosexual man' (Lane 1966: 114). '*E's a Wallasey lad* He is a homosexual' (Spiegl 2000b: 54). *NR; from an e.20c. scandal surrounding a homosexual brothel in Wallasey.

Wank (v.): to masturbate. 'Was it, he asked politely, permitted for the audience to wank during the recital?' (Melly 1965: 178). 'I used to wank myself daft' (Sampson 2001: 101). Recorded from m.20c.; derivation unclear; possibly from l.18c. Scottish 'whang', 'to beat, whip, flog, thrash'; 19c. English dialectal 'whang', 'throw, drive, pull'; or l.19c. Americanism 'whang', 'penis'.

Wank (n.): masturbation. '"OK for a finger" or "a wank"' (Parker 1974: 138). 'One of last year's Leavers wrote "wank" on every line for ten pages' (Bleasdale 1975: 46). 'I'm dying for a wank off' (Robinson 1986 [1920s–30s]: 146). 'A posh wank would set the world to rights' (Sampson 1999: 317). 'Fuckin wankmags' (Griffiths 2003: 168). Recorded from m.20c.; see *wank (v.)*.

Wank (adj.): second-rate, inferior. 'Pay's wank, but yer can make it up in ovies' (Griffiths 2002: 141). Recorded from l.20c.; an extension of *wank (n.)*.

Wanker (n.): general insult. 'He's a bit of a wanker really' (Russell 1996 [1980]: 358). 'Wanker. Abuse term' (Spiegl 1989: 83). 'It was Billie, the wanker, who was holding his hand' (Sampson 1999: 367). '*Wanker!* You despicable person!' (Spiegl 2000b: 41). Recorded from l.20c.; from *wank (n.)*.

Wanky (adj.): nasty, unpleasant. 'Just one of those wanky things that this fuckin life's full of' (Griffiths 2002: 7). Recorded from l.20c.; from *wank (n.)*.

Was (v.): were. 'I wish you was dead' (Baird 1957: 109). 'You was always down here' (Parker 1974: 34). 'There was a time when we was mates' (Brown 1989: 6). 'We was a law unto ourselves' (Sampson 2001: 11). *NR; this irregular past tense is one of a number of much-stigmatised dialectal forms (see *done, drug, give, see*).

Wash-house (n.): public laundry. 'Queues at the lavatory and the wash-house' (Hanley 2009 [1940]: 46). '"She's the talk of the wash-house." – Her moral character is in doubt' (Shaw 1955b: 18). 'The Wash-house in Beamish Street' (Hallowell 1972: n.p.). 'The public wash houses were a boon to the busy housewife' (Unwin 1984 [1920s–30s]: 43). 'My grandma's Liverpudlian/ wash-house talk' (Simpson 1990: 14). 'The pawnshop was near the old wash-house' (Sinclair 1999 [1930s– e.40s]: 33). 'To the washhouse for a well-earned gossip' (Callaghan 2011 [1910s–30s]: 25). Recorded from e.19c. in this specific sense; the public wash-house and private baths were invented in Liverpool by Kitty Wilkinson, a Derry woman who settled in the city, as a response to a cholera outbreak in 1832; wash-houses were important sites of labour and socialisation for working-class women.

Waterloo Cup (n.): hare-coursing event run at Altcar, just north of Liverpool. '*E'd take a day off fer ther Waterloo Cup*: Said of a worker who frequently absents himself on petty pretexts' (Lane 1966: 115). *NR; the Waterloo Cup was run from 1836 to 2005; not the most popular sporting event on Merseyside.

Wayo (int.): hold on, just wait. ''Ere, wayo' (Shaw 1957a: 16). '*Wayo*: Wait a moment' (Lane 1966: 115). *NR; an abbreviation of 'wait on', or 'wait' and 'hold on'.

Webs (n.): feet. 'Certainly from Ireland we received *gob, gom, mam, the queer feller, webs, lug, moider*' (Shaw 1950b: 4). 'You never see lads selling papers in dur bare webs' (Shaw 1957a: 15). 'Me webs. *My* feet' (Shaw et al. 1966: 36). Recorded from e.20c.; Forces' (naval) usage; by analogy with the webbed feet of sea birds.

Weighed in/off (phr.): paid. 'Avyer bin weighed off yea? *Have they paid you what they owe you?*' (Minard 1972: 31). 'As though it's a bonus to get weighed in' (Sampson 2002: 76). Recorded from l.19c.; in horse racing, successful punters are not paid until the jockeys 'weigh in/off' after the race.

Well away/well on (phr.): drunk or nearly so. 'His father is "at the Globe, getting well on"' (Shimmin 1863: 99). 'He's alright, missus, he's well away' (Hanley 2009 [1950]: 245). 'Mr Mander is well away and no mistake' (Bainbridge 1973: 6). 'When ee's well away, a put im on thuh couch in thuh spare room' (Griffiths 2000: 32). Recorded from m.19c.; from 'well on the way to getting drunk'.

Well in (phr.): in an advantageous position. 'If he could get through a day like yesterday without that kind of help, he was well in' (Hignett 1966: 185). 'He wanted to get well in with John' (Murari 1975: 11). 'Clear indication that he was well-in' (Callaghan 2011 [1910s–30s]: 88). Recorded from m.19c.; an Australian abbreviation of 18c. 'well in with', 'having established a good relationship with someone'.

Well-stacked (adj.): with large breasts. 'She looked a well-stacked piece too' (Bleasdale 1975: 113). Recorded from e.20c.; an Americanism; derivation is clear.

Wellied (adj.): drunk. 'I'm fairly wellied by the time Quox stands up' (Griffiths 2002: 45). Recorded from l.20c.; an extension of *welly (v.)*.

Wellies (n.): Wellington boots. '*Wellies*: Gumboots' (Lane 1966: 115). 'Soldiers in leather wellies heading for a parade ground' (Bleasdale 1975: 127). 'That's Swiftie/in the wellies' (Simpson 1990: 30). Recorded from m.20c.; an abbreviation of the name given to the knee-length boots worn by the famous Irishman Arthur Wellesley (also known as the Duke of Wellington).

Wells Farthole type (n.): see *Cabbage Hall Yank*.

Welly (v.): to kick, hit; beat up. 'Eee wuz wellied. *He was kicked*' (Shaw et al. 1966: 48). 'There's this buck wellying shite out of the wings of the car' (McClure 1980: 37). 'Let's go and welly this one-armed cunt' (Griffiths 2003: 37). Recorded from m.20c.; from *wellies*.

Welsh-butty (n.): see *butty*.

Welsh letter (n.): defective condom. '*Welsh letter*: A defective contraceptive' (Lane 1966: 115). 'A defective condom is a "Welsh letter"' (Redfern 1984: 3). *NR; a play on 'leek'.

Welt (n.): unauthorised time-off. 'Meanwhile readers might like to trace the origins of … *welt*' (Shaw 1950b: 4). 'A cup a tea an' a long sit down like in the cokes during the welt' (Shaw 1957a: 7). 'I wuz on der welt; I wuz scowing. *I was having an unofficial spell of leisure time*' (Shaw et al. 1966: 58). 'Goan ommec welt' (Minard 1972: 17). 'WELTING Also "bobbing" and "ghosting". Time-honoured practices perfected by Liverpool dockers' (Spiegl 1989: 83). 'He was going full belt, not working the "welt"' (McGovern 1995: 12). 'Up Brownlow Hill, to take me welt' (Moloney 2001: 23). 'Working the welt – Eight men in a gang … Four men go to work and the other four absent themselves' (Burnett 2011: 13). Recorded from m.20c.; a practice whereby some members of a team of dockers would take an unauthorised break while the rest worked; derivation unknown.

Westport (n.): Liverpool. 'Westport admires commercial success' (Owen 1921: 20–1). *NR; *Westport* was John Owen's name for Liverpool in *The Cotton Broker*.

Wet (n.): an (alcoholic) drink. 'I'll skip off for a wet' (Hanley 2009 [1936]: 47). 'If they just get a bob or two, they'll go and 'ave a "wet"' (Hallowell 1972: n.p.). Recorded from 17c.; interchangeable with 'whet' in early uses; derivation is clear.

Wet Nellie/Wet Neller (n.): Nelson Cake. 'Various correspondents agree in identifying the "wet Nellie" (or "Neller") as the once popular Nelson Cake' ('Postman' 1932b: 5). 'Tommy Handley spoke affectionately of "Wet Nellies" (strictly "Wet Nellers") or Nelson cakes' (Farrell 1950b: 4). 'Wet neller, wet nelly. *Nelson cake.* A cake made from compressed, broken biscuits, pastry remnants etc. with dried fruit added: the whole soaked in syrup or burnt sugar and stacked in great piles' (Shaw et al. 1966: 42). 'A "Wet Nelly" (much used in ITMA scripts' (Channon 1970: 102). '"Wet Nellies" Or, to give them their more dignified title – Nelson Cakes' (Unwin 1984 [1920s–30s]: 32). 'You could have knocked me down with a wet Nellie!' (Sinclair 1999 [1930s–e.40s]: 170). 'You could get a big wet Nellie – you know, a square pudding cake' (Dudgeon 2010: 139). Recorded from m.19c.; derivation is clear.

We've got a right one here (phr.): reference to an odd person or idiot. Recorded as a catch-phrase: 'Usually A to B (official) about C … : mainly Liverpool: c. 1940' (Beale (1985) *s.v. We've got a right one (or 'un) 'ere!*).

Whack (n.): share. '*Whack* can also mean portion or share, as in *yer've 'ad yer wack, wack*' (Lane 1966: 114). Recorded from l.18c.; originally 'a share of a booty obtained by fraud', but quickly extended to the more general 'share or division'.

Whack (v.): to share. 'Did the Army or Navy give us, say, *jack*, for detective, *chatty, have a cob on, whack* (to share)?' (Shaw 1950b: 4). See *whack (n.)*.

Wheel him in (phr.): insult. '*Wheel 'im in*: A catch-phrase meaning "here he is, the feeble fellow"' (Lane 1966: 116). Recorded as 'a 20c. Liverpool catch-phrase': '*There he is – wheel him in. There he is – bail him out* … Or just *Bail him out* – shouted after any unpopular person' (Beale (1985) *s.v. Liverpool Catch Phrases. Wheel him in*). Recorded from e.20c.; an insult based on the idea that the addressee was always in trouble.

When Donnelly docked (phr.): a long time ago. 'Donnelly, from whose arrival in the port events are dated – "it wus whin Donnelly docked"' (Shaw 1955a: 6). '"When Donnelly docked" ("A long time ago")' ('Postman' 1966a: 6). '"When Donnelly docked" meaning "long ago"' (Lees 2013: 136). *NR; derivation unknown.

When Nelson gets his eye back (phr.): a long time in the future (never). '"When Nelson gets his eye back" (long-term doubtful repayment of loan)' (Anon. [L. Iver] 1957: 4). 'When …? When Nelson gets his fuckin' eye back' (Robinson 1986 [1920s–30s]: 98). *NR; the counter-part of *when Donnelly docked*; derivation is clear.

Where did you get the Rossa? (phr.): challenge to pomposity or pretentiousness. 'When Rossa said his name was Jeremiah O'Donovan Rossa, Mrs Dudley asked, 'Where did you get the Rossa?' … It was supposed that the Rossa was a flight of fancy. This phrase commenced in New York, thence went to Liverpool and over all England' (Ware 1909: 262). From the name of the Irish Fenian, O'Donovan Rossa, who was wounded in New York in 1885 by Mrs Dudley (who may have been a British agent). As she approached him in the street she asked his name and said, *Where did you get the Rossa?* (in his name), before shooting him. 'Rossa' was an agnomen, derived from Rossmore, in Kilmeen, County Cork.

Where the bugs wear clogs (phr.): rough, unsalubrious. 'Some of the ould houses, bugs wid clogs on in um' (Shaw 1957a: 15). '*Brutal Bootle where the bugs wear clogs*' (Lane 1966: 13). 'Liverpool! Where only the bugs wear clogs' (Robinson 1986 [1920s–30s]: 76). 'Bootle – where the bugs wear clogs' (Simpson 1990: 46). *NR; derivation is clear.

Whicker (n.): suit. 'Meanwhile readers might like to trace the origins of … *whicker*' (Shaw 1950b: 4). 'Their best whicker, from the first word of the rhyming slang "whistle and flute"' (Anon. 1955: 6). 'Whicker for suit' (Armstrong 1966: 6). 'Whicker. A suit. Liverpool' (Howarth 1985: n.p.). *NR; probably from rhyming slang 'whistle and flute'.

Whip (v.): to steal. 'His line was whipping stuff' (Cross 1951: 78). '*Whip*: To confiscate or steal' (Lane 1966: 116). 'There was Half A Dog whipping four packets of chocolate marshmallows' (Bleasdale 1975: 23). 'One of them … whips my sketch-pad from under my arm' (Cornelius 2001 [1982]: 90). Recorded from m.19c.; an extension of 15c. 'whip', 'to make a sudden brisk movement'.

Whip behind (phr.): warning to carters about children bunking rides. 'A kid "snitching" on another, taking a free ride behind a cart, would shout to the carter, "Whip be'ind, master"' (Shaw 1963e: 4). '*Whip behind*: Warning cry shouted by children at carters' (Lane 1966: 116). 'Carters … shouted "whip behind" as they drove away' (Robinson 1986 [1920s–30s]: 28). 'We rode on the axles of hansom cabs … until someone shouted "whip behind"' (Callaghan 2011 [1910s–30s]: 26). *NR; derivation is clear.

Whizz (v.): pickpocket; steal. 'Plenty of whizzing going on up an' down Duke Street. Catherine knew that whizzing meant pickpocketing' (Steen 1932: 107). 'Whizzed: Stolen, robbed, taken surreptitiously' (Parker 1974: 213). Recorded from e.20c.; an Americanism; from 'on the wizz', probably an extension of 16c. 'to whizz', 'to move swiftly'.

Who d'you do? (phr.): greeting among criminals. Recorded as 'a C20 Liverpool petty crooks' fraternal greeting', meaning 'whom have you cheated or defrauded recently' (Beale (1985) *s.v. who d'you do?*).

Who told you to say that? (phr.): mocking comment. Recorded as a retort 'to a chap trying to be witty. Liverpool: since 1920s' (Beale (1985) *s.v. Who told you to say that?*).

Whoof (n.): fart. '*Whoof like a booze-moke*' (Lane 1966: 117). *NR; an extension of e.20c. 'whoof', 'to make a sound as of air being expelled'.

Wick, get on someone's (phr.): to annoy or irritate. '*Gets on me wick*. Annoys me very much' (Lane 1966: 117). 'There was one feller who really got on me wick from the start' (Bleasdale 1975: 200). 'The same line over and over. It's getting on Alastair's wick' (Griffiths

2003: 178). Recorded from e.20c.; an abbreviation of 'Hampton Wick', rhyming slang for 'prick'.

Win (n.): a penny. '"Win", penny' (Jones 1935: 5). 'The use of "meg" for halfpenny and "win" for penny, seems to be dying out' (Farrell 1950b: 4). '"Fudge" for a farthing, "meg" for a half-penny and "win" for a penny are no longer current coin' (Whittington-Egan 1955a: 6). '"Fudge" for a farthing, "meg" for a half-penny and "win" for a penny … flourished in the [18]80s and [18]90s' (Jones 1955: 4). 'Win. One old penny (1d). Liverpool' (Howarth 1985: n.p.). Recorded from l.16c.; derivation unclear.

Win (v.): to beat. 'We wundem eezy' (Robinson 1986 [1920s–30s]: 31). Recorded from l.20c.; this transitive form is glossed as obsolete.

Windy Hill (n.): James Street. '*Windy Hill*: James Street, Liverpool' (Lane 1966: 117). *NR; James Street runs down to the waterfront and thus catches the wind.

Winger (n.): ship steward. '[What are] wingers? … These are ship stewards' (Shaw 1962g: 6). 'A winger. *A ship's steward*' (Shaw et al. 1966: 57). Recorded from l.19c.; a nautical extension of e.19c. 'winger', 'small cask or tank stowed in the wing of a ship's hold'.

Wingy (adj.): one-armed. 'Wingy. *A person with one arm*' (Shaw et al. 1966: 29). Recorded from l.19c.; from e.19c. nautical 'wings', 'arms'.

Winnick (adj.): insane, crazy; thick. 'Have you all gone winick?' (Hanley 1932: 154). 'She's doolally, not elevepence for a shillin', winnick, if yez ask me' (Shaw 1957a: 12). '*Winnuck* or *Winnick*: Daft, dotty' (Lane 1966: 118). 'Winnick. Not intelligent, not very bright. Liverpool' (Howarth 1985: n.p.). '*She's winnucky* She is mad, insane' (Spiegl 2000b: 59). Recorded from e.20c.; an abbreviation of e.20c. 'to be or to go winick'; from Winwick mental hospital (1902–97), just outside Liverpool.

Wobbler, throw a (v.): to lose one's temper; to lose control or panic. 'The Parish Priest threw a wobbler' (Bleasdale 1975: 13). Recorded from l.20c.; an extension of the m.19c. Americanism 'wobbly', 'fit of nerves, of panic, of bad temper'.

Woodbine/Woody/Woodies (n.): Woodbines (brand of cheap cigarette). 'The great guy was busy shielding a Woodbine from the wind' (Cross 1951: 9). 'CIGGY, of course, is cigarette, the cheap kind being a WOODY' (Shaw 1959a: 39). 'He asked me for a light for a Woody' (Hignett 1966: 239). 'He slipped me a Woodbine and asked me to do it for him every Sunday' (Bleasdale 1975: 50). 'Sixpence or a "tanner", would buy ten top quality cigarettes, or five Woodbines with twopence change' (Unwin 1984 [1920s–30s]: 36). 'She lit a "Woody"' (Sinclair 1999 [1930s–e.40s]: 14). 'Woodbines and Player's Weights were five for twopence' (Callaghan 2011 [1910s–30s]: 100). Recorded from m.20c.; 'Woodbines' were a strong, unfiltered cigarette sold from l.19c. and discontinued in l.20c.

Wooden hill (n.): stairs. 'He'll wink/ to nudge you up/the wooden hill' (Simpson 1990: 93). Recorded from l.19c.; derivation is clear.

Wool/woolly (n.): abbreviated form of *woollyback*. 'Woolly. Short for "woolly-back" – someone who lives outside Liverpool, i.e. St. Helens, Skelmersdale, Prescot, the Wirral, etc. And therefore not strictly a true Scouser' (Spiegl 1989: 85). 'She talks like a wool, in fairness – Carlisle' (Sampson 2002: 35). Recorded from l.20c.; see *woollyback*.

Wool/woolly (adj.): adjective from *wool (n.)*. 'These teds though – pure wool, they are' (Sampson 2002: 146) 'So yer've got woolly fuckin' blood then? Explains a lot' (Griffiths 2003: 57). 'Penny-pinching wool adverts' (Lees 2013: 278). Recorded from l.20c.; see *woolly*[1].

Woollyback (n.): originally someone from just outside Liverpool (particularly Lancashire or North Wales); now simply anyone not from Liverpool. 'The whole woollyback school, all the woollyback teachers, even the woollyback headmaster' (Jacques 1979: n.p.). 'A "woolly back" … means a county bobby, but the implication is he's had a hard life' (McClure 1980: 20). 'And you thought with me being new here, a woolly-back from Wigan' (Bleasdale 1985: 44). 'I've never known a game so eagerly anticipated as this local spat with the despised woollyback foes' (Sampson 1998: 2). '*A wooly (back)* Someone who sounds like a Scouser but comes from the countryside' (Spiegl 2000b: 56). 'Don't like this fuckin place … Fuller fuckin woollybacks, sheepshaggers' (Griffiths 2003: 56). 'Woollybacks foolish enough to try to breach Fortress Anfield' (Lees 2013: 191). Recorded from l.20c.; the derivation of this Liverpool term of contempt is unclear; 'woolly' is an e.20c. term for a peasant or country person, but it was also used in the Liverpool police force from the 1960s to refer pejoratively to uniformed officers (the uniforms were made of wool).

Word and a blow (phr.): quick to fight. 'Many men … prided themselves on being "a werd and a blow" persons' (Shaw 1957c: 6). Recorded from 16c.; derivation is clear.

Work an hour about (phr.): work the *welt*. 'Working an hour about was accepted practice' (Sanders and Sanders 2009 [1960s]: 42). *NR; the practice of working an hour followed by an hour off. See *welt*.

Wrecked (adj.): very drunk; intoxicated; generally confused. 'Wrecked. Totally ruined by excesses, usually drugs and/ or alcohol' (Spiegl 1989: 85). 'That's wrecked my head that has' (Sampson 2002: 64). 'Djer wanner get wrecked or not?' (Griffiths 2003: 125). Recorded from l.20c.; an Americanism; a simple extension of 'wrecked', 'damaged, destroyed'.

Wynd (n.): lane. 'From Liverpool and Manchester and Stockport and from all the wynds and vennels' (McColl 1952: 7). 'Wynd – narrow path snaking through the houses' (Callaghan 2011 [1910s–30s]: ix). Recorded from 15c.; glossed as Scottish and northern dialectal.

Y

Yankee (n.): a complex horse-racing bet on four selections, consisting of 11 separate gambles: 6 doubles, 4 trebles and a fourfold accumulator. 'I had a successful Yankee bet' (Shaw 1957a: 19). Recorded from m.20c.; derivation unknown.

Yak (v.): nag, talk incessantly. 'Yak: To nag' (Lane 1966: 119). 'Yakking at him harder than ever' (Brown 1989: 11). 'She does yak on a bit' (Smith 1998 [1971]: 21). Recorded from m.20c.; an extension of e.20c. 'yack', 'chatter'; supposedly onomatopoeic.

Yard dog (n.): an insult; lowly esteemed person. 'A yard dog. A customs officer' (Shaw et al. 1966: 57). *NR in this sense; a m.20c. extension of l.18c. 'yard dog', 'watchdog'.

Yeller clock (n.): gold watch. 'He could lift … slangs an' yeller clocks, yooks, twerns an' jarks with such ease and frequency' (Clerk 1971 [c.1900]: 69). *NR; glossed by Clerk; derivation is clear.

Yen (n.): derogatory term for male homosexual. 'He was a bit of a yen and would take us to a cabbie shelter at the bottom of Leece Street and do what he liked with us and yonk us' (Clerk 1971 [c.1900]: 16). Recorded as 'Liverpool street arabs': late C.19–20 (Beale (1984) s.v. yen 3); glossed by Clerk; derivation unknown.

Yez/yiz/yis (pron.): you. 'A muckin' conchie with yez' (Hanley 2009 [1940]: 461). 'Yis'll all go to Hell!' (Callaghan 2011 [1910s–30s]: 1). See youse.

Yimkin (int.): expression of disbelief; rubbish! 'Yimkin, nonsense; I don't believe it' (Lane 1966: 120). 'Yimkin Oh yeah? Nonsense!' (Spiegl 2000b: 143). Recorded from e.20c.; Forces' usage; from Iraqi Arabic 'yimkin', 'perhaps'.

Yip (v.): to inform. 'Rhuie asked if I'd yipped. But he knew I hadn't' (Clerk 1971 [c.1900]: 43). Recorded as 'Liverpool street arabs': late C.19–mid-20' (Beale (1984) s.v. yip); glossed by Clerk as 'to split, give away'; derivation unknown.

Yocker (v.): to spit. 'Ee yockered on me. He spat on me' (Shaw et al. 1966: 45). 'The chucker out looks/like eez gonna yocker on uz on the way out' (Simpson 1995: 23). 'Clearing their noses and throats and yockering' (Kelly 2006 [1930s–40s]: 99). Recorded from m.20c.; given the Liverpudlian fricative pronunciation of 'ck', possibly imitative of the sound of spitting.

Yocker (n.): spit. 'She kept hitting me with the board duster because someone put yocker on her back. But it was Ryan … what spat at her' (Bleasdale 1975: 14). 'Shurrup, will yeh. Yer coverin me in fuckin yocker' (Griffiths 2003: 13). See yocker (v.).

Yodel (v.): to abuse. '"Did he yodel yer?" Jim said' (Clerk 1971 [c.1900]: 43). Recorded as 'Liverpool street arabs': late C.19–early 20' (Beale (1984) s.v. yodel); glossed by Clerk as 'abuse'; derivation unknown.

Yonk (v.): to draw. 'He was a bit of a yen and would take us to a cabbie shelter at the bottom of Leece Street and do what he liked with us and yonk us' (Clerk 1971 [*c*.1900]: 16). *NR; glossed by Clerk as 'draw'; derivation unknown.

Yonks (n.): ages, long time. 'Long "yonks" and ages later' (Jacques 1975: n.p.). 'I haven't played for yonks' (Cornelius 2001 [1982]: 98). 'We've known him for yonks' (Grant 2002: 56). 'Best news I've 'eard for yonks' (Fagan 2007 [1950s]: 234). Recorded from m.20c.; derivation unknown.

Yook (n.): swivel of watch chain; watch. 'He could lift … slangs an' yeller clocks, yooks, twerns an' jarks with such ease and frequency' (Clerk 1971 [*c*.1900]: 69). Recorded from l.19c.; glossed by Clerk as a 'swivel' (on which a watch chain hung); possibly from l.18c. 'yack', 'watch', ultimately Romani 'yacorah', 'hour'.

You (pron.): You (specific use). 'You Mam' (Farrell 1950a: 4). *NR in this sense; Farrell noted that 'to draw the attention of a boy or girl, especially out-of-doors, the expression used is "Hey you la" or "Hey you girl"'. He commented that 'the use of "you" in this connection is interesting, for young children calling to their mother, particularly when they feel the need for her intervention, say "You Mam"'.

You couldn't punch a hole in a wet Echo (phr.): you're a weakling. 'Yew cudden punch an ole in a wet Echo' ('Postman' 1966b: 6). *NR; there were variants of this phrase – 'You couldn't knock the skin off a rice puddin'!' (Bryan 2003 [1940s–50s]: 76); The *Liverpool Echo* is the local newspaper.

You say everything but your prayers (phr.): you talk too much. '"Yew say everythink but yer prayers" means "You talk too much"' ('Postman' 1966a: 6). 'You say everyt'ink but your prurrs' (you are loquacious)' (Channon 1970: 104). *NR; the implication being that the person addressed says everything except the one thing they need to say (their prayers).

You'll know me next time (you see me) (phr.): fighting talk; a challenge effectively. 'G'wan now don't be gawpin', you'll know me nex' time' (Shaw 1957a: 12). 'Had a good look! You'll know me next time, won't you!' (Owen 1961: 25). 'You'll know me next time you see me' (Marenbon 1973 [1920s]: 46). Recorded from e.20c.; usually addressed to someone staring; probably from Irish English.

You're only in the meg specks (phr.): uninformed, ignorant. '"You're only in the meg specks" (you lack *savoir-faire*)' (Shaw 1964a: 12). *NR; presumably those seated in the cheap seats (*meg*, 'halfpenny') did not have a good view.

Your penny a week was wasted (phr.): you are ignorant. 'YEWR PENNY A WEEK WUS WASTED. "You are ill educated"' (Shaw 1959a: 41). *NR; a reference to the penny a week fee for schooling before the introduction of universal elementary education in 1870.

Yous/youse[1] *(pron.)*: you (second person pronoun plural). 'Now, ladies, if youse will get out of the cab, we'll have the old gentleman aboard in two ticks' (Hanley 2009 [1936]: 392). 'From [older more Irish people] we get *youse* (plural of you), *ye* (you)' (Shaw 1952:

n.p.). 'The large numbers of Irish words which occur in Liverpool's dialect – Gom (a fool), Ould (Old, which is pure Dublin), Feller (fellow), and Youse (You)' (Whittington Egan 1955a: 6). 'Roll on, till youse get to that sign' (Hignett 1966: 304). 'If I see yous round here again' (Parker 1974: 87). 'I've done three years for the likes of youse twats!' (Bleasdale 1985: 244). 'Only *youse* can help yourselves' (Sampson 2002: 205). Recorded from e.19c.; this plural form of the pronoun is common in forms of English used in Ireland, the USA, Canada, Australia, New Zealand, South Africa and indeed elsewhere in Britain.

Yous/youse[2] *(pron.)*: you (second person pronoun singular). 'Dan ... would wake me with "Come on, youser! You're last out again"' (O'Mara 1934: 71). 'Are youse the foreign fella?' (Bainbridge 1978: 126). 'While youse is in the ale-house with the lady, Mister' (Brown 1989: 6). 'Eh yooze mate d wanna nuther bevvy?' (Simpson 1995: 24).

'Cheeky little sod – I'm gonna have ter look after youse, so yer better behave yersel – d'yer 'ere?' (Sinclair 1999 [1930s–e.40s]: 105). Recorded from l.20c.; the use as the singular form is both recent and apparently distinctive to Liverpool; see *yous*[1].

Yowge (adj.): emphatically huge. 'Not just a fatty, this lad, by the way, this one is fucking yowge' (Sampson 2002: 163). 'I see the yowge Chinatown gates through the window' (Griffiths 2002: 263). Recorded as 'l.20c. Liverpool dialect' (Dalzell and Victor (2007) *s.v. yowge*); derivation is clear.

Yowler (n.): child; cat. 'Yes, yowler. You know what I mean. The copper's kid' (Hanley 1932: 47). '*Yowler*: A cat' (Lane 1966: 120). Recorded from m.20c.; from 'yowl', 'the wauling of cats'.

Yunnuck (adj.): uninterested in sex. '*Yunnuck*: Frigid, not interested in sex' (Lane 1966: 120). '*Wudden take no notice uv me, the yunnucky bastard*' (Spiegl 2000b: 93). *NR; a variant of 'eunuch', 'castrated male'.

Z

Z-Cars (n.): police series. *Z Cars* (Martin 1963: title). 'Remember the old TV series *Z-Cars*? That was all based in Kirkby' (Dudgeon 2010: 312). Recorded from l.20c.; *Z-Cars* (1962–78) was based in 'Newtown' (Kirkby); it was notable both for its northern setting and its social realist depiction of modern policing.

Select Bibliography

Anonymous (1699) *A New Dictionary of the Terms Ancient and Modern of the Canting Crew*, London.

—— (1725) *A New Canting Dictionary*, London.

—— (1813) 'A False Alarm', *Liverpool Mercury*, 26th November, 7.

—— (1818) 'Police', *Liverpool Mercury*, 30th January, 7.

—— (1819) 'Orange Clubs', *Liverpool Mercury*, 16th July, 8.

—— (A Dicky Sam) (1820) Letter to the Editor, *Liverpool Mercury*, 25th February, 278.

—— 'D[icky].[Sam]' (1821), *The Kaleidoscope; or, Literary and Scientific Mirror*, 96.

—— (1824) 'New Prison at Kirkdale', *Liverpool Mercury*, 7th May, 6.

—— (1833a) 'A Trip to Paris with Mr Jorrocks', *New Sporting Magazine*, vol. 5, no. 25, 30–41.

—— (1833b) 'Robbery at Windsor [St]', *Liverpool Mercury*, 27th December, 3.

—— (1835) 'Disturbing a Congregation', *Liverpool Mercury*, 17th July, 6.

—— (1837) 'Terrible Tidings for the Dicky Sams, alias Liverpudlians', *Liverpool Mercury*, 24th February, 8.

—— (1839) 'Jerry Building', *Liverpool Mercury*, 12th April, 6.

—— (1845) 'To Correspondents', *Liverpool Mail*, 22nd November, 8.

—— (1841) 'The Show Nuisance', *Liverpool Mail*, 6th March, 2.

—— (1847) 'American Hominy', *Liverpool Mercury*, 5th February, 7.

—— (1848) 'Liverpool Weather', *Liverpool Mercury*, 18th August, 2.

—— (1849) 'Chief Events of the Week', *Liverpool Mail*, 3rd February, 2.

—— (1850) 'Soup for the Poor', *Liverpool Mercury*, 18th January, 6.

—— (A Dicky Sam) (1854) 'The Amusements at Liverpool', *The Era*, 11.

—— (W.T.M.) (1855a) 'Dickey Sam', *Notes and Queries*, 1st series, XII, 226.

—— (1855b) 'Liverpool Police Court', *Liverpool Daily Post*, 24th October, 5.

—— (1857) 'Orange Procession', *Liverpool Daily Post*, 14th July, 8.

—— [Margaret Oliphant] (1862) *John Arnold by The Author of 'Mathew Paxton' &c*, London: Hurst and Blackett.

—— (1865) 'Reverend, Great and Good', *Newcastle Chronicle*, 17th June, 3.

—— (1866) 'The Grand Billiard Tournament', *The Sportsman*, 11th December, 3.

—— (1867) 'Death from Violence in Liverpool', *Liverpool Mercury*, 8th January, 5.

—— (1868a) 'The Improvement Committee', *Liverpool Mercury*, 8th October, 3.

—— (1868b) 'Education in France and England', *Liverpool Mercury*, 28th November, 7.

—— (1870) 'The Liverpool Workhouse', *Liverpool Mercury*, 4th March, 3.

—— (1872) 'Municipal Elections', *Liverpool Mail*, 5th October, 11.

—— (1878b) 'The Liverpool Orangemen', *Liverpool Mercury*, 16th July, 6.

—— (1880) 'Savoury Ducks', *Liverpool Mercury*, 21st August, 8.

—— (1884) 'Of South-West Lancashire', *Pall Mall Gazette*, 16th September, 2.

—— (1885) 'Football', *Liverpool Mercury*, 28th January, 7.

—— (1886) 'Comments on Current Things', *East & South Devon Advertiser*, 15th May, 7.

—— (1887) 'Paddy's Market', *Liverpool Mercury*, 31st October, 5.

—— (1891) 'Liverpool Assizes', *Liverpool Mercury*, 10th December, 7.

—— (1895) 'Liverpool Workhouse "Scouse"', *Liverpool Mercury*, 23rd August, 6.

—— (1897) 'Mayor's Sunday', *Liverpool Mercury*, 15th November, 8.

—— (1898) 'Notes', *Dundee Evening Telegraph*, 8th July, 3.

—— (1899) 'Concerts in Alley and Court', *Liverpool Mercury*, 31st May, 9.

—— (1906) 'Spion Kop', *Liverpool Echo*, 14th June, 3.

—— (1914a) 'Tramways under the Mersey', *Liverpool Evening Express*, 3rd January, 4.

—— (1914b) 'Everton Always Win', *Liverpool Echo*, 19th January, 7.

—— (1914c) 'To and from Readers', *Liverpool Echo*, 19th February, 7.

—— (1914d) 'Liverpolitans Shiver', *Liverpool Evening Express*, 21st February, 10.

—— (1914e) 'Bee's Notebook', *Liverpool Echo*, 12th March, 7.

—— (1914f) 'The Spion Kop Army at Anfield', *Liverpool Echo*, 3rd September, 3.

—— (1915a) 'Seized by the Nose', *Liverpool Echo*, 6th February, 4.

—— (1915b) 'Liverpool Orangemen', *Liverpool Daily Post*, 28th May, 3.

—— (1915c) 'The Week-end Ramble', *Liverpool Echo*, 22nd October, 4.

—— (1916) 'Football News', *Liverpool Echo*, 9th March, 6.

—— (1917) 'A Way They Have in the Navy', *Liverpool Echo*, 9th May, 3.

—— (1918) 'Changes in Meat Rations', *Liverpool Daily Post*, 23rd March, 3.

—— (1921) 'Merseyside', *The Times,* 22nd April, 7.

—— (1926) 'Spion Kop', *Liverpool Daily Post*, 29th May, 9.

—— (1929a) 'The Talkies', *Liverpool Daily Courier*, 4th September, 9.

—— (1929b) 'Stop that Man', *Lancashire Evening Post*, 28th December, 5.

—— (1933) 'L.M.S. Merseyside Trip for "Exiled" Liverpolitans', *Western Daily Press*, 3rd February, 9.

—— (1939a) 'A Man Who Calls a Pool a Puddle', *Liverpool Daily Post*, 26th January, 1.

—— (1939b) 'Scouse', *Liverpool Daily Post*, 3rd March, 4.

—— (1939c) 'Pilot Sports Log', *Liverpool Evening Express*, 4th April, 8.

—— (1939d) 'Liverpool Leave it Late', *Liverpool Evening Express*, 4th March, 1.

—— (1941a) 'Everton Win at Anfield', *Liverpool Daily Post*, 10th February, 5.

—— (1941b) 'Day to Day in Liverpool', *Liverpool Daily Post*, 22nd March, 3.

—— (1941c) 'Tommy Still Playing', *Liverpool Evening Express*, 26th July, 3.

—— (1942a) 'New Meat Prices', *Liverpool Daily Post*, 15th July, 3.

—— (1942b) 'Pilot's Sports Log', *Liverpool Evening Express*, 5th October, 3.

—— (1943a) 'Bombers over Merseyside', *Liverpool Daily Post*, title of special edition.

—— (1943b) 'Taught Fellow-Prisoners to Cook', *Liverpool Daily Post*, 19th November, 3.

—— (1943c) '"Scousers" are all Brothers', *Liverpool Evening Express*, 4th December, 2.

—— (1944a) 'You Asked Me', *Liverpool Evening Express*, 2nd March, 3.

—— (1944b) 'Mersey's Famous Time Signal', *Liverpool Daily Post*, 15th August, 3.

—— (1945a) 'Scousette?', *Liverpool Daily Post*, 10th April, 2.

—— (1945b) 'Fine Record of Joking "Scousers"', *Liverpool Evening Express*, 6th July.

—— (1945c) 'Pilot's Sports Log', *Liverpool Evening Express*, 17th September, 3.

—— (1945d) 'Pilot's Sports Log', *Liverpool Evening Express*, 29th October, 3.

—— (1945e) 'Liverpool Lord Mayor in Native Parish', *Liverpool Daily Post*, 19th November, 3.

—— (1945f) 'Pilot's Sports Log', *Liverpool Evening Express*, 31st December, 3.

—— (D.W.F.H.) (1951) 'Gaelic Words', *Liverpool Echo*, 3rd January, 3.

—— (R.H.W.) (1951) 'Parapet', *Liverpool Echo*, 9th January, 2.

—— (1951) 'Propurorful: Liverpool is Dialect Shy', *Liverpool Daily Post*, 31st March, 4.

—— (1954) 'We All Talk Sailors' Slang', *Liverpool Echo*, 9th October, 4.

—— (1955) 'A Proper Jangle in Scouser Lingo', *Liverpool Daily Post*, 1st July, 6.

—— (1957a) [Editorial Comment], *Liverpool Daily Post*, 27th June, 6.

—— (L. Iver) (1957b) 'The Scouser's Philosophy', *Liverpool Echo*, 7th November, 4.

—— (1958) 'The First Lesson', *Liverpool Weekly News*, 6th November, 3.

—— (1959) 'Malapudlianisms' *Liverpool Echo*, 31st January, 4.

—— (1961a) 'Still Going …', *Liverpool Daily Post*, 13th April, 4.

—— (1961b) 'Dese Scousers, Like, Said De Scouse was Gear', *Liverpool Daily Post*, 6th June, 3.

—— (1962) 'The Vicar Makes His Point', *Liverpool Daily Post*, 2nd August.

—— (1963a) 'The Liverpool Sound', *Daily Mail*, 20th September, 4.

—— (Rancid Ronald) (1963b) 'Scouse Not So Exclusive', *Liverpool Echo*, 4th September, 8.

—— (1963c) 'In Defence of Dicky Sam', *Liverpool Echo*, 9th September, 8.

—— (1964a) 'Child Care Officers "Get with it"', *The Guardian*, 4th January, 20.

—— (1964b) 'It's De Gear!', *Liverpool Echo*, 29th January, 6.

—— (Mistrolis) (1964c) 'About Dem Scuffers', *Liverpool Echo*, 19th October, 8.

—— (1965) 'The Rubaiyat's Gone Scouse', *Liverpool Daily Post*, 16th June, 4.

—— (1967a) 'The Mersey Tunnel', *The Universe*, 21st April 1967.

—— (1967b) 'Spreading the Gospel in Scouse', *Liverpool Daily Post*, 22nd April, 4.

—— (1973) *The Guardian*, 4th June, 16, cited in *OED s.v. Merseysider*.

—— (1974) *The Liverpool Echo*, 6th April, 16, cited in *OED s.v. Kop*.

—— (2007) 'Liverpool', *Daily Telegraph*, 4th December, 9, cited in *OED s.v. Liverpool sound*.

—— (2009) *Liverpool Echo*, 14th January, 5, cited in *OED s.v. rob n*^{2}.

Armstrong, Harold (1966) 'Scouse as She is Spoken', *Liverpool Echo*, 25th July, 4.

Armstrong, Isobel (1982) *Language as Living Form in Nineteenth Century Poetry*, Brighton: Harvester.

Ash, Bernard (1954) *Omega Street*, London: Staples.

Atkinson-James, Rachel (2014), *Liverpool Dialect*, Sheffield: Bradwell Books.

Bailey, Nathaniel (1724) *An Universal Etymological English Dictionary*, London: Bell.

Bainbridge, Beryl (1973) *The Dressmaker*, London: Fontana.

—— (1978) *Young Adolf*, London: Duckworth.

—— (1989) *An Awfully Big Adventure*, London: Abacus.

Baird, Alexander (1957) *The Mickey-Hunters*, London: Heinemann.

Barrère, Albert and Charles Leland (1889–90) *A Dictionary of Slang, Jargon and Cant*, Edinburgh: Ballantyne.

Barrett, W. S. (1915) 'David Lewis Northern Hospital', *Liverpool Daily Post*, 30th January, 7.

Bartlett, John Russell (1860) *Dictionary of Americanisms*, 3rd edn, Boston: Little, Brown and Company.

Beale, Paul (ed.) (1984) *A Dictionary of Slang and Unconventional English* (8th edn of Partridge), London: Routledge.

—— (ed.) (1985) *A Dictionary of Catch Phrases British and American from the Sixteenth Century to the Present Day*, 2nd edn, London: Routledge.

Beekman, Gerald and P. L. White (1956) *The Beekman Mercantile Papers 1746–1799*, 2 vols, New York: New-York Historical Society.

Belchem, John (2000), *Merseypride: Essays in Liverpool Exceptionalism*, Liverpool: Liverpool University Press.

Bidston, T. J. (1955) untitled letter, *Daily Post*, 19th April, 4.

Bindloss, R. H. (1957) 'Why Scouser?', *Liverpool Daily Post*, 28th June, 6.

Bleasdale, Alan (1975) *Scully*, London: Hutchinson.

—— (1977) *Who's Been Sleeping in My Bed?* London: Hutchinson.

—— (1979) *No More Sitting on the Old School Bench*, London: Woodhouse.

—— (1985) *Boys from the Blackstuff: Studio Script*, Cheltenham: Thornes.

Bobbin, Tim (1746) *A View of the Lancashire Dialect*, London.

Bowen, F. C. (1929) *Sea Slang: A Dictionary of the Old-Timers' Expressions and Epithets*, London: Sampson Low and Marston.

Bower, Fred (2015 [1936]) *Rolling Stonemason: An Autobiography*, London: Merlin.

Bradshaigh, Robert (1670) 'Letter to Gilbert Ireland', in *Transactions of the Historic Society of Lancashire and Cheshire* (1854), vol. 6, appendix, 15.

Brandon, Henry (1839) 'Dictionary of the Flash or Cant Language', in W. A. Miles, *Poverty, Mendacity and Crime*, London: Shaw.

Briscoe, Diana (2003) *Wicked Scouse English*, London: Michael O'Mara.

British National Corpus (BYU– BNC) http://corpus.byu.edu/bnc

Brooke, Richard (1853) *Liverpool as it was during the Last Quarter of the Eighteenth Century, 1775 to 1800*, Liverpool: Mawdsley and Son.

Brophy, John (1934) *Waterfront*, New York: Macmillan.

Brophy, John and Eric Partridge (1930) *Songs and Slang of the British Soldier: 1914–18*, London: Scholartis.

—— (1931) *Songs and Slang of the British Soldier: 1914–18*, 3rd edn, London: Scholartis.

Brown, Robert (1989) *The Courtship of Nocker Yates*, Birkenhead, Countryvise.

Bryan, Tony (2003) *99 Heyworth Street*, Liverpool: Bluecoat Press.

Burchfield, Robert (ed.) (1996) *Fowler's Modern English Usage*, 3rd edn, Oxford: Clarendon Press.

Burke, John (1964) *The Beatles in A Hard Day's Night*, New York: Dell.

Burnett, Len (2011) *Rogue Docker: A Life of Crime in Birkenhead Docks*, Stroud: Amberley.

Callaghan, James (2011) *Candles, Carts and Carbolic. A Liverpool Childhood between the Wars*, Lancaster: Palatine.

Carter, W. H. (1955) 'Liverpool Dialect', *Liverpool Echo*, 15th April, 4.

Chandler, George (1957) *Liverpool*, London: Batsford.

Channon, Howard (1970) *Portrait of Liverpool*, London: Robert Hale and Company.

Chapple, Mike (2007) 'Scally Nige', *Liverpool Daily Post*, 3rd October, 3.

Clerk, Andie (1971) [*c.*1900] *Arab. A Liverpool Street Kid Remembers (The Autobiography of an Early Century Street Arab)*, Liverpool: n.p.

Clough, Arthur Hugh (1888) *Prose Remains of Arthur Hugh Clough*, London: Macmillan.

Coles, Gladys Mary (1993) *Both Sides of the River. Merseyside in Poetry and Prose*, West Kirkby: Headland.

Collinson, W. E. (1927) *Contemporary English. A Personal Speech Record*, Berlin: Teubner.

Cornelius, John (2001 [1982]), *Liverpool 8*, Liverpool: Liverpool University Press.

Corpus of Contemporary American English (COCA) http://corpus.byu.edu/coca/

Corpus of Historical American English (COHA) http://corpus.byu.edu/coha/

Costello, Ray (2001) *Black Liverpool: The Early History of Britain's Oldest Black Community 1730–1918*, Liverpool: Picton.

Coupland, Nikolas and Hywel Bishop (2007) 'Ideologised Values for British Accents', *Journal of Sociolinguistics*, 11: 74–103.

Critchfield, Richard (1990) *Among the British*, London: Hamish Hamilton.

Cross, H. J. (1951) *No Language but a Cry*, London: John Murray.

Crowley, Tony (2012) *Scouse: A Social and Cultural History*, Liverpool: Liverpool University Press.

Curry, Matt (1964) 'About Dem Scuffers', *Liverpool Echo*, 19th October, 4.

Dalzell, Tom and Terry Victor (eds) (2006) *The New Partridge Dictionary of Slang and Unconventional English*, 2 vols, London: Routledge.

—— (eds) (2007) *The Concise New Partridge Dictionary of Slang and Unconventional English*, London: Routledge.

Davie, Donald (1991) *Collected Poems*, Chicago: Chicago University Press.

Dawson, G. K. (1951) 'Oldsters Will Remember Them. Street Characters of a Bygone Day', *Liverpool Echo*, 5th January, 4.

De Kerchove, René (1948) *International Maritime Dictionary*, New York: Nostrand.

De Quincey, Thomas (2000) 'Confessions of an Opium Eater' (1821, 1856), vol. 2, *The Works of Thomas De Quincey*, ed. Barry Symonds et al., 21 vols, London: Pickering & Chatto.

Dictionary of the Scots Language (2004) http://www.dsl.ac.uk/index.html

Dodd, Kath (2007) *Sugar Butties on the Doorstep*, Liverpool: Lulu.

Dodd, Ken (1965a) *The Song of the Diddymen/Doddy's Diddy Party*, London: Polydor.

—— (1965b) *Doddy and the Diddymen*, London: Polydor.

Dolan, Terence (2004) *A Dictionary of Hiberno-English*, 2nd edn rev., Dublin: Gill and Macmillan.

Drabble, Margaret (1964) *The Garrick Year*, New York: Morow.

Driscoll, Peter (1973) *The Wilby Conspiracy*, London: Macdonald.

Dudgeon, J. P. (2010) *Our Liverpool. Memories of Life in Disappearing Britain*, London: Headline.

Duke, Winifred (1939) *Household Gods*, London: Jarrolds.

D.W.F.H. (1951) 'Gaelic Words', *Liverpool Echo*, 3rd January, 3.

Dwyer, Harry (1957) 'Scotland Road's King of Entertainers', *Liverpool Echo*, 27th August, 4.

Eden, Sir Frederic Morton (1797) *The State of the Poor or, An History of the Labouring Classes in England, from the Conquest to the Present Period ... Together with Parochial Reports*, 3 vols, London: Davis.

Egan, Pierce (1823) *Grose's Classical Dictionary of the Vulgar Tongue, Revised and Corrected*, London: Egan.

Elliott, Jim (2006) [1940s–70s] *Once Upon a Time in Liverpool*, Bebington: Middleview.

Fagan, John (2007) [1950s] *Spots, Pimples and Bum Fluff. An Apprentice's Tale*, Birkenhead: Appin.

Farmer, John (1905) *Dictionary of Slang and Coloquial English. Past & Present; a Dictionary Historical and Comparative of the Heterodox Speech of All Classes of Society for more than Three Hundred Years with Synonyms in English, French, German, Italian, etc. Compiled and edited by J.S. Farmer & W.E. Henley*, London: n.p.

Farmer, John and W. E. Henley (eds) (1890–1904) *Slang and its Analogues Past and Present: A Dictionary, Historical and Comparative of the Heterodox Speech of all Classes of Society for more than Three Hundred Years*, London: printed for subscribers only.

Farrell, John (1950a) 'About That Liverpool Accent (Or Dialect)', *Liverpool Daily Post*, August 8th, 4.

—— (1950b) 'A Guide to the Slang of Merseyside. This Half-Secret Tongue of Liverpool', *Liverpool Daily Post*, 25th August, 4.

Ferguson, Otis (1944) 'Vocabulary for Lakes, Deep Seas, and Inland Waters', *American Speech*, 19.2, 103–11.

Flame (1984) *Flame. A Life on the Game*, London: Gay Men's Press.

Fleming Prout, Leonard (1950) 'Fleming's Phrase', *Liverpool Echo*, 18th December, 4.

Fockleyreen: Manx–English Dictionary, http://dictionaryq.com/gaelg/

Ford, William C. (1957) 'Who Was Dicky Sam?', *Liverpool Echo*, 21st August, 6.

Forrester, Helen (1974) *Twopence to Cross the Mersey*, London: Jonathan Cape.

—— (1979) *Minerva's Stepchild*, London: The Bodley Head.

Francis, M. E. (1898) *Maime O' The Corner*, London: Harper and Brothers.

Frank, Robert (1966) 'That Scouser Accent … It's AN ASSET now', *Liverpool Echo*, 2nd March, 8.

Fraser, Edward and John Gibbons (eds) (1925) *Soldier and Sailor Words and Phrases*, London: Routledge.

Garrett, George (1999) *The Collected George Garret*, Nottingham: Trent.

Giles, Howard and Peter F. Powesland (1975) *Speech Style and Social Evaluation*, London: Academic Press.

Google Books: American English http://googlebooks.byu.edu/

Google Books: British English http://googlebooks.byu.edu/

Graham, Louis (1988) *The Binmen are Coming*, Birkenhead: Countryvise.

Grant, Anthony and Clive Grey (eds) (2007) *The Mersey Sound. Liverpool's Language, People and Places*, Ormskirk: Open House Press.

Grant, Linda (1996) *The Cast Iron Shore*, London: Granta.

—— (2002) *Still Here*, London: Little, Brown.

Grant, Peter (2008) *Talk Like the Scousers*, Liverpool: Trinity Mirror.

Green, Jonathon (ed.) (2010) *Green's Dictionary of Slang*, 3 vols, London: Chambers.

Gribble, Joseph (1957) 'Liverpudlian Views', *Liverpool Echo*, 23rd February, 4.

Griffith, R. (1950) 'Liverpool Slang', *Liverpool Echo*, 14th December, 2.

Griffiths, Niall (2000) *Grits*, London: Jonathan Cape.

—— (2001) *Sheepshagger*, London: Jonathan Cape.

—— (2002) *Kelly + Victor*, London: Jonathan Cape.

—— (2003) *Stump*, London: Jonathan Cape.

—— (2008) *Real Liverpool*, Bridgend: Seren.

Grose, Francis (1785) *A Classical Dictionary of the Vulgar Tongue*, London: Hooper.

—— (1787) *A Provincial Glossary, with a Collection of Local Proverbs, and Popular Superstitions*, London: Hooper.

—— (1788) *A Classical Dictionary of the Vulgar Tongue*, 2nd edn, London: Hooper.

—— (1790) *A Provincial Glossary, with a Collection of Local Proverbs, and Popular Superstitions*, 2nd edn, London: Hooper.

—— (1796) *A Classical Dictionary of the Vulgar Tongue*, 3rd edn, London: Hooper.

—— (1811) *Lexicon Balatronicum*, London: Chappel.

Haigh, J. L. [1907] *Sir Galahad of the Slums*, Liverpool: The Liverpool Booksellers.

Hall, J. Francis (2004 [1939]) *The Dock Road. A Seafaring Tale of Old Liverpool*, Liverpool: Book Clearance Centre.

Hallowell, Nora (1972) *Dingle Born – and Proud of it!*, Liverpool: Raven Books.

Hanley, James (1932) *Ebb and Flood*, London: The Bodley Head.

—— (1935) *The Furys*, London: Chatto & Windus.

—— (2009 [1936]) *The Secret Journey*, London: Chatto & Windus.

—— (2009 [1940]) *Our Time is Gone*, London: Faber and Faber.

—— (2009 [1950]) *Winter Song*, London: Faber and Faber.

—— (2009 [1958]) *An End and a Beginning*, London: Faber.

Harman, Thomas (1567) *A caueat for commen cursetors vvlgarely called uagabones*, London.

Harrison, George (1964) 'Scouse – 'The Great Whodunit', *Liverpool Echo*, 29th January, 2.

Harvey, Ted (1950) 'Liverpool Lingo', Liverpool Echo, 20th December, 2.

Henri, Adrian, Roger McGough and Brian Patten (1967) *The Mersey Sound*, Harmondsworth: Penguin.

Hignett, Sean (1966) *A Picture to Hang on the Wall*, New York: Coward-McCann.

Hill, Judy (1945) 'Let's Talk It Over', *Liverpool Evening Express*, 18th November.

Hilton, Nick (2012) 'Barrie Wells has the Kids Boxed Off', *Liverpool Echo*, 28th March.

Hocking, Silas (1966 [1879]) *Her Benny*, Liverpool: Gallery Press.

Hodgkinson, Kenneth (1960) 'Save Our Scouse – The Dying Language of Liverpool', *Liverpool Daily Post*, 2nd December, 11.

Holbrow, F. G. (1964) 'It's De Gear!', *Liverpool Echo*, 29th January, 6.

Honeybone, P. (2001) 'Lenition Inhibition in Liverpool English', *English Language and Linguistics*, 5.2, 213–49.

—— (2007) 'New Dialect Formation in Nineteenth-Century Liverpool: A Brief History of Scouse', in *The Mersey Sound. Liverpool's Language, People and Places*, ed. Anthony Grant and Clive Grey, Ormskirk: Open House Press.

Honeybone, P. and Kevin Watson (2013) 'Salience and the Sociolinguistics of Scouse Spelling: Exploring the Phonology of the Contemporary Humorous Localised Dialect Literature of Liverpool', *English World-Wide*, 34, 305–40.

Hotten, John Camden (1860) *A Dictionary of Modern Slang, Cant, and Vulgar Words*, 2nd edn, London: printed by the author.

—— (1869) *The Slang Dictionary: or, the Vulgar Words, Street Phrases, and 'Fast' Expressions of High and Low Society*, 2nd edn, London: printed by the author.

—— (1874) *The Slang Dictionary, Etymological, Historical and Anecdotal. A New*

Edition, Revised and Corrected, with Many Additions, 5th edn, London: Chatto & Windus.

Howarth, K. (1985) *Sounds Gradely. A Collection of Dialect and Other Words Used in Lancashire Folk Speech*, Manchester: North West Sound Archive.

Hughes, Glyn (1963) 'Taking Proper', *Liverpool Daily Post*, 30th January, 4.

Hughill, Stan (1967) *Sailortown*, London: Routledge & Kegan Paul.

Ireland, Sir Gilbert (1670) 'Letter to Lord Derby', in *Transactions of the Historic Society of Lancashire and Cheshire* (1854), vol. 6, appendix, 8.

Isenberg, David (1962) 'A Second Language – Standard English', *Liverpool Echo*, 9th July, 6.

Jacques, J. B. (1972) *Yennoworrameanlike*, Liverpool: Raven Books.

—— (1973) *Get yer Wack*, Liverpool: Raven Books.

—— (1975) *According to Jacques: A Mersey Bible*, Liverpool: Raven Books.

—— (1977) *Scouse with the Lid Off*, Liverpool: Raven Books.

—— (1979 *Jakestown My Liverpool*, Liverpool: Raven Books.

J.A.S. (1950) 'Other Words', *Liverpool Echo*, 13th December, 2.

Jerome, J. A. (1948) *Chinese White. A Story of Chinatown*, Molesey: Hampton Court Books.

Johnson, Samuel (1775) *A Dictionary of the English Language to which are Prefixed, a History of the Language, and an English Grammar*, 4th edn, Dublin.

Johnston, C. (1988) *Anfield Rap*, cited in *OED s.v. sound*.

Jolliffe, Grace (2005) *Piggy Monk Square*, Birmingham: Tindal Street Press.

Jones, Florence (1999) *From the Stripper with Love*, Prescot: Liverpool.

Jones, J. W. (1955) 'Liverpool Dialect', *Liverpool Daily Post*, 19th April, 4.

Jones, T (1935) 'Liverpool Slang', *Liverpool Post and Mercury*, 15th June, 5.

Joyce, P. W. (1910) *English as We Speak it in Ireland*, Dublin: Gill.

Kelly, Bryan (2006) [1930s–40s] *For what it's Worth: My Liverpool Childhood*, Stroud: Sutton.

Kelly, Stan (1964) *Liverpool Lullabies: The Stan Kelly Songbook*, London: Sing.

Kerr, Madeleine (1958) *The People of Ship Street*, London: Routledge & Kegan Paul.

Kersh, Gerald (1942) *The Nine Lives of Bill Nelson*, London: Heinemann.

Kidson, Frank (1891) *Traditional Tunes: A Collection of Ballad Airs*, Oxford: Taphouse.

Kipling, Rudyard (1898) *The Day's Work*, London: Macmillan.

Lane, Linacre (1966) *Lern Yerself Scouse*, vol. 2, *The ABZ of Scouse*, Liverpool: Scouse Press.

Lane, Tony (1987) *Liverpool. Gateway of Empire*, London: Lawrence & Wishart.

Lees, Andrew (2013) *Liverpool, The Hurricane Port*, London: Mainstream.

Liddell, Billy (1960) *My Soccer Story*, London: The Soccer Book Club.

Lovegreen, T. J. (1955) 'Daddy Bunchy', *Liverpool Echo*, 16th March, 6.

Lowry, Malcolm (1933) *Ultramarine*, London: Cape.

—— (2000) [1947] *Under the Volcano*, London: Penguin.

Lynd, Robert (1947) *Things One Hears*, London: Dent.

McClure, James (1980) *Spike Island: Portrait of a British Police Division*, London: Macmillan.

McColl, Ewan (1952) 'Scouse. A Collection of Shanties, Yells and Forebitters about a Great City', BBC Radio, North of England Home Service, 9th December (unpublished transcript).

McDermott, Lalla (1984) *Orrell Klondyke Gateway to the Past*, Liverpool: n.p.

McGovern, Pete (1995) [1961] *In My Liverpool Head*, Liverpool: L: Scene.

MacIlwee, Michael (2011) *The Liverpool Underworld: Crime in the City, 1750–1900*, Liverpool: Liverpool University Press.

Mackay, Rod (1985) *Hard Knocks (Nutters and No-Marks)*, Birkenhead: Countyvise.

Maddox, Jack (2008) [1930s–40s] *In the Shelter of Each Other: Growing up in Liverpool in the 1930s and 40s*, Stroud: The History Press.

Maginn, William (1844) *John Manesty, The Liverpool Merchant*, 2 vols, London: Mortimer.

Marenbon, Zena (1973) [1920s] *Don't Blow Out the Candle: A Liverpool Childhood 1921–1931*, London: Hart-Davis MacGibbon.

Martin, Troy Kennedy (1963) *Z Cars*, London: Herbert Jenkins.

Masefield, John (1933) *The Conway*, London: Heinemann.

Mays, John (1954) *Growing up in the city*, Liverpool: Liverpool University Press.

Melly, George (1965) *Owning Up*, London: Weidenfeld & Nicolson.

—— (1977) *Rum, Bum and Concertina*, London: Weidenfeld & Nicolson.

—— (1984) [1930s–40s] *Scouse Mouse. Or, I never got over it*, London: Futura.

Melville, Herman (1849) *Redburn: His First Voyage*, New York: Harper & Bros.

Mignolo, Walter (2012) *Local Histories/Global Designs Coloniality, Subaltern Knowledges and Border Thinking*, Princeton, NJ: Princeton University Press.

Minard, Brian (1972) *Lern Yerself Scouse*, vol. 3, *Wersia Sensa Yuma?*, Liverpool: Scouse Press.

Moloney, Peter (1966) *A Plea for Mersey. Or, The Gentle Art of Insinuendo*, Liverpool: Gallery Press.

—— (2001) *Tales You Win. Merseydotes in Merseydotage, a Sorto-Biography in Chapter and Verse*, Birkenhead: Countyvise.

Murari, Timeri (1975) *The New Savages*, London: Macmillan.

Naughton, Bill (1945) *A Roof Over Your Head*, London: Pilot.

Neal, Frank (1988) *Sectarian Violence: The Liverpool Experience 1819–1914*, Manchester: Manchester University Press.

Nodal, J. H. and G. Milner (1875) *A Glossary of the Lancashire Dialect*, Manchester: Manchester Literary Society.

O'Flaherty, Liam (1925) *The Informer*, New York: Knopf.

O'Hanri, Hari [an scríob] (1950a) 'It's The Irish In Us', *Liverpool Echo*, 13th December, 2.

—— (1950b) 'Letter', *Liverpool Echo*, 29th December, 4.

—— [Harry O'Henry] (1955) 'Irish Influence in Speaking Scouse', 16th March, 6.

O'Henry, see O'Hanri.

O'Mara, Pat (1934) *The Autobiography of a Liverpool Irish Slummy*, London: Hopkinson.

Oakes Hirst, T. (1951) 'Liverpool Speech: Some Local Pronunciations', *Liverpool Daily Post*, 29th January, 4.

Opie, Iona and Peter Opie (1959) *The Lore and Language of Schoolchildren*, Oxford: Clarendon Press.

—— (1997) *Children's Games with Things*, Oxford: Oxford University Press.

Oswyn, Powys (1857) *Liverpool Ho! A Matter-of-Fact Story*, London: Hope.

Owen, Alun (1961) *Three TV Plays: No Trams to Lime Street After the Funeral Lena, Oh My Lena*, London: Jonathan Cape.

Owen, John (1921) *The Cotton Broker*, London: Hodder & Stoughton.

Oxford English Dictionary (1989) 2nd edn, prepared by J. A. Simpson and E. S. C. Weiner, 20 vols, Oxford: Clarendon Press.

Parker, H. J. (1974) *View from the Boys*, Newton Abbott: David & Charles.

Partridge, Eric (1949) *A Dictionary of the Underworld*, London: Macmillan.

—— (1961) *Dictionary of Slang and Unconventional English*, 5th edn rev., London: Macmillan.

Partridge, Eric and Paul Beale (1985) *A Dictionary of Catch Phrases from the Sixteenth Century to the Present Day*. 2nd edn rev., London: Routledge.

Partridge, Eric, Wilfred Granville and Francis Gerard Roberts (1948) *A Dictionary of Forces' Slang 1939–45*, London: Secker & Warburg.

Phelan, Jim (1948) *The Name's Phelan. The First Part of the Autobiography of Jim Phelan*, London: Sidgwick & Jackson.

Picton, Sir James A. (1875) *Memorials of Liverpool. Historical and Topographical*, 2nd edn rev., 2 vols, Liverpool: Walmsley.

—— (1883) *City of Liverpool: Selections from the Municipal Archives and Records, from the 13th to the 17th Century Inclusive*, 2 vols, Liverpool: Walmsley.

—— (1888) 'Does Mr. Gladstone Speak with a Provincial Accent', *Notes and Queries*, 7th series, vol. 6, 210–11.

'Postman' (1931a) 'Nix', *Liverpool Post and Mercury*, 20th October, 5.

—— (1931b) 'With Sugar', *Liverpool Post and Mercury*, 26th October, 5.

—— (1931c) 'The Artful Dodger', *Liverpool Post and Mercury*, 27th November, 5.

—— (1931d) 'The Artful "Dodger"', *Liverpool Post and Mercury*, 28th November, 5.

—— (1932a) 'Tatting', *Liverpool Post and Mercury*, 21st January, 5.

—— (1932b) 'More About the "Wet Nellie"', *Liverpool Post and Mercury*, 18th February, 5.

—— (1937a) 'Liverpool Language', *Liverpool Post and Mercury*, 15th March, 6.

—— (1942a) 'Scousers', *Liverpool Daily Post*, 28th July, 2.

—— (1942b) 'Hello Scouse', *Liverpool Daily Post*, 30th July, 2.

—— (1942c) 'Scouse and Scouser', *Liverpool Daily Post*, 1st August, 2.

—— (1945a) 'Easter Custom', *Liverpool Daily Post*, 5th April, 2.

—— (1945b) 'Those "Pace-Eggers"', *Liverpool Daily Post*, 9th April, 2.

—— (1945c) 'Jigger', *Liverpool Daily Post*, 11th December, 5.

—— (1947a) 'Another "Jigger"', *Liverpool Daily Post*, 24th June, 4.

—— (1947b), 'Jowlers', *Liverpool Daily Post*, 25th June, 6.

—— (1950) 'Correct Form', *Liverpool Daily Post*, 27th September, 4.

—— (1961a) 'Still Going …', *Liverpool Daily Post*, 13th April, 4

—— (1961b) 'Another Delly' *Liverpool Daily Post*, 19th April, 4.

—— (1964a) 'They Called Her Tilly Mint', *Liverpool Echo*, 31st July, 4.

—— (1964b) 'She Remembers "Tilly Mint"', *Liverpool Echo*, 6th August, 6.

—— (1965b) 'Classic Course', *Liverpool Daily Post*, 15th July, 4.

—— (1966a) 'Lern Yerself Scouse Den', *Liverpool Daily Post*, 12th July, 6.

—— (1966b) 'The Vicar Makes His Point', *Liverpool Daily Post*, 2nd August, 6.

—— (1966c) 'Learning Themselves', *Liverpool Daily Post*, 3rd August, 4.

—— (1968) 'Paradise Lost', *Liverpool Daily Post*, 9th June, 4.

Price, George (1950) 'Liverpool Slang', *Liverpool Daily Post*, 15th August, 4.

Prior, Alan (1964) *Z Cars Again*, London: Jenkins.

Redfern, Walter (1984) *Puns*, Oxford: Blackwell.

Redmond, Phil (1982) *Tucker and Co: Stories of Life in and Out of Grange Hill*, London: HarperCollins.

Reed, Sir Edward James (1869) *Shipbuilding in Iron and Steel: A Practical Treatise*, London: Murray.

Robberds, John (1862) 'History of Toxteth-Park Chapel', *The Christian Reformer*, new series, 18, 343–61.

Roberts, Eleazar (1893) *Owen Rees: A Story of Welsh Life and Thought*, Liverpool: Foulkes.

Roberts, S. (1955) 'Liverpool Dialect', *Liverpool Daily Post*, 25th April, 4.

Robinson, Jack (1986) *Teardrops on my Drum*, Swaffham: Gay Men's Press.

Robinson, Peter (2008) *The Look of Goodbye*, Exeter: Shearsman.

[Romani] Project. Angloromani Dictionary, http://romani.humanities.manchester. ac.uk/angloromani/dictionary.html

Roscoe, William (1853) *The Poetical Works of William Roscoe*, Liverpool: Young.

Rush, Len (1966) 'Let's Give the Cult a Rest', *Liverpool Daily Post*, 5th January, 6.

Russell, Willy (1996 [1975; 1976; 1980]) *Plays: 1*, London: Methuen.

Sampson, John (1911) 'Jacob Bryant: Being an Analysis of His Anglo-Romani Vocabulary', *Journal of the Gypsie Lore Society*, new series, 4, 162–94.

Sampson, Kevin (1998) *Awaydays*, London: Jonathan Cape.

—— (1999) *Powder*, London: Jonathan Cape.

—— (2001) *Outlaws*, London: Jonathan Cape.

—— (2002) *Clubland*, London: Jonathan Cape.

—— (2014) *The House on the Hill*, London: Jonathan Cape.

Sanders, Tony and Lorraine Sanders (2009 [1960s]) *Heave a Bit Driver Seven Miles of Laughter*, Milton Keynes: Authorhouse.

Sayle, Alexei (1984) *Train Ride to Hell*, London: Methuen.

Scott, Dixon (1907) *Liverpool*, London: Black.

Sexton, Carole (1996) *Confessions of a Judas-Burner*, Little Neston: Cherrybite.

Shaw, Frank (1950a) 'Liverpool's Dialect is His Hobby', *Liverpool Daily Post*, 1st November, 5.

—— (1950b) 'Scouse Lingo – How It All Began', *Liverpool Echo*, 8th December, 4.

—— (1950c) 'Liverpool Lingo', *Liverpool Echo*, 21st December, 2.

—— (1951) 'Propurorful: Liverpool is Dialect Shy', *Liverpool Daily Post*, 3rd March, 5.

—— (1952) 'The Scab: A One Act Play Set in Liverpool during the General Strike, 1926. With a Note on the Liverpool Way of Talking', typescript (author's personal copy), Liverpool Record Office.

—— (1954) 'City of Nicknames', *Liverpool Echo*, 1st July, 4.

—— (1955a) 'Do You Want to Speak Scouse?', *Liverpool Echo*, 3rd March, 6.

—— (1955b) 'Death of a Dialect', *Manchester Guardian*, 20th April, 18.

—— (1955c: 4) 'A Proper Jangle in Scouser Lingo', *Liverpool Daily Post* (n.d.) [July], 4.

—— (1957a) 'Scouse Talks (text, with translations, of tape sound recordings made in Liverpool City Library)', Liverpool Record Office.

—— (1957b) 'Scouse Lingo is Preserved for Posterity', *Liverpool Echo*, 16th July, 6.

—— (1957c) 'What Songs will be Sung about Speke and Kirkby?', *Liverpool Echo*, 20th August, 6.

—— (1958a) 'Beware of a "Destroyer" when at the Docks. He may be after a Sub', *Liverpool Weekly News*, 30th January, 3.

—— (1958b) 'The Talking Streets of Liverpool', *Liverpool Echo*, 25th October, 6.

—— (1958c) 'Malapudlianisms', *Liverpool Echo*, 30th December, 6.

—— (1958d) 'Dialect of a Seaport I', *Journal of the Lancashire Dialect Society*, vol. 8, 12–19.

—— (1959a) 'Dialect of a Seaport II', *Journal of the Lancashire Dialect Society*, vol. 9, 32–41.

—— (1959b) 'It's Quicker than Cockney', 30th March, 6.

—— (1959c) 'Strange Charm of the Lingo of Liverpool's Dockland', *Liverpool Echo*, 30th July, 6.

—— (1960a) 'Dialect of a Seaport III', *Journal of the Lancashire Dialect Society*, vol. 10, 30–42.

—— (1960b) 'Ink, Lino and the Lenient Judge', *Liverpool Echo*, 20th June, 5.

—— (1961) 'Malapudlianisms. They're still at it in Liverpool', *Liverpool Echo*, 12th June, 4.

—— (1962a) 'Origins of Liverpoolese: Evolution of a Lingo', *Liverpool & Merseyside Illustrated*, January 1962, 9–10.

—— (1962b) 'What Dreams May Come …', *Punch*, 21st February, 8.

—— (1962c) 'Liverpoolese, Yes, But I don't Like Scouse', *Liverpool Echo*, 14th June, 8.

—— (1962d) 'A Scouser in Paris', *Labour Voice*, Liverpool, n.p., 7.

—— (1962e) 'A Skinful of Words', *Liverpool Echo*, 11th October, 6.

—— (1962f) 'Parlez Vous Scouse, La?, *Liverpool Echo*, 14th November, 12.

—— (1962g) 'Twenty Scouser Questions – "How Well Do You Know Your Liverpoolese?"', *Liverpool Echo*, 21st December, 6.

—— (1963a) 'Merseyside Should Nurse its Scouse, but Reject Bad English', *Liverpool Daily Post*, 28th January, 6.

—— (1963b) 'In Love with the Pier Head Budgies', *Liverpool Echo*, 7th March, 6.

—— (1963c) 'A Wacker's Musical?', *Liverpool Echo*, 27th May, 4.

—— (1963d) 'This is Frank Shaw's Spec' ['Scouser Quiz'], *Liverpool Echo*, 4.

—— (1963e) 'Mac, Wack and Chuck', *Liverpool Echo*, 28th August, 4.

—— (1964a) 'It's the Gear! – But how did the Expression Start?', *Liverpool Echo*, 17th January, 12.

—— (1964b) 'That's Why They're Called Scuffers', *Liverpool Echo*, 6th October, 6.

—— (1966a) 'Are Scousers Always Trying to be Funny?', *Liverpool Echo*, 18th January, 4.

—— (1966b) 'Liverpool Doctors Hear the Strangest Things', *Liverpool Echo*, 2nd February, 8.

—— (1966c) 'Ollies in the Liverpool Olympics', *Liverpool Daily Post*, 8th August, 4.

—— (1966d) 'Diddy Men Man the Boundary', *Liverpool Daily Post*, 12th August, 6.

—— (1969) *You Know Me Anty Nelly? Liverpool Children's Rhymes. Compiled with Notes on Kids' Games and Liverpool Life*, Liverpool: Gear Press.

—— (1971) *My Liverpool*, London: Wolfe.

Shaw, Frank, Fritz Spiegl and Stan Kelly (1966), *Lern Yerself Scouse. How to Talk Proper in Liverpool*, Liverpool: Scouse Press.

—— (2000), *Lern Yerself Scouse. How to Talk Proper in Liverpool* (Millenium Reprint), Liverpool: Scouse Press.

Shimmin, Hugh (1863) *Liverpool Sketches*, Liverpool: Gilling.

Silberman, Leo and Betty Spice (1950) *Colour and Class in Six Liverpool Schools*, Liverpool: Liverpool University Press.

Simpson, David (2013) *All About Scouse*, Durham: My World.

Simpson, Matt (1990) *An Elegy for the Galosherman*, Newcastle: Bloodaxe.

—— (1995) *Catching up with History*, Newcastle: Bloodaxe.

—— (2011 [1998; 2001]) *Collected Poems*, Nottingham: Shoestring.

Sinclair, James (1999 [1930s–e.40s]) *A Way Out Including its Sequel Welsh Scouse*, Liverpool: Bluecoat.

Skeat, W. W. (ed.) (1882) *An Etymological Dictionary of the English Language*, Oxford: Clarendon Press.

Smith, Don (1955) 'How the "Scousers" Found their Dialect', *Daily Herald*, 25th February, 5.

Smith, Neville (1998) [1971] *Gumshoe*, London: Fontana.

Smith, Wilfred (ed.) (1953) *A Scientific Survey of Merseyside*, Liverpool: Liverpool University Press.

Smyth, W. H. (1867) *The Sailor's Wordbook: An Alphabetical Digest of Nautical Terms*, London: Blackie and Son.

Spiegl, Fritz (1962) 'Scouser Songs: An Entertaining Evening of Old Liverpool Street Ballads, Sea Shanties and Folk Songs', programme for concert at Philharmonic Hall, 3rd March, Liverpool: n.p.

—— (1989) *Lern Yerself Scouse*, vol. 4, *Scally Scouse. The Language of Law and Disorder*, Liverpool: Scouse Press.

—— (2000a) 'Foreword to the Millenium Reprint', in Shaw et al. (2000).

—— (2000b) *Scouse International. The Liverpool Dialect in Five Languages*, Liverpool: Scouse Press.

Stamper, Jack (2010) *#4 Hatch. An Autobiography*, Birkenhead: Countyvise.

Steen, Marguerite (1932) *The Wise and the Foolish Virgins*, London: Victor Gollancz.

Strang, Barbara (1970) *A History of English*, London: Methuen.

Syers, Robert (1830) *The History of Everton*, Liverpool: Robinson.

Tafari, Levi (1993) *Rhyme Don't Pay*, West Kirkby: Headland.

—— (2006) *From the Page to the Stage*, West Kirkby: Headland.

Thomas, T. L. (1963) 'Scouse Words', *Liverpool Daily Post*, 30th January, 4.

Tirebuck, William (1891) *Dorrie: A Novel*, London: Longmans, Green and Co.

—— (1903) *'Twixt God and Mammon*, New York: Appleton.

Tomlinson, Ricky (2008) *Celebrities My Arse!* London: Sphere.

Unwin, Frank (1984) *Reflections on the Mersey Memoirs of the Twenties and Thirties*, Leighton Banastre: Gallery Press.

Utting, J. E. (1992) 'Editorial: The Era of Relaxant Anaesthesia', *British Journal of Anaesthesia*, 69.6, 551–3.

Vaux, James Hardy (1819) 'Vocabulary of the Flash Slang', *Memoirs of James Hardy Vaux*, vol. 2, London: Clowes.

Vickery, Roy (1983) 'Lemna Minor and Jenny Greenteeth', *Folklore*, 94: 2, 247–50.

Wallace, James (1795) *A General and Descriptive History of the Ancient and Present State of the Town of Liverpool*, Liverpool: Phillips.

Walsh, Helen (2004) *Brass*, Edinburgh: Canongate.

Ward & Lock (1881) *Ward and Lock's (late Shaw's) Tourists' Picturesque Guide to Liverpool and its Environs*, 5th edn, London: Ward, Lock and Co.

Ware, James Redding (1909) *Passing English of the Victorian Era: A Dictionary of Heterodox English, Slang and Phrase*, London: Routledge.

Watson, Kevin (2002) 'The Realisation of Final /t/ in Liverpool English', *Durham Working Papers in Linguistics*, 8, 195–205.

—— (2006) 'Phonological Resistance and Innovation in the Northwest of England', *English Today*, 22/02, 55–61.

—— (2007b) 'Liverpool English', *Journal of the International Phonetics Association*, 37/3, 351–60.

—— (2007c) 'Is Scouse Getting Scouser? Exploring Phonological Change in Contemporary Liverpool English', in A. Grant and C. Grey (eds), *The Mersey*

Sound: Liverpool's Language, People and Places. Liverpool: Open House Press, 106–40.

Weekley, Ernest (1921) *Etymological Dictionary of Modern English*, London: Murray.

Welsh, Jack (1964) 'We Owe These Wackers More Than We Know', *Liverpool Echo*, 23rd March, 8.

Whittaker, James (1934) *I, James Whittaker*, London: Rich and Cowan.

Whittington-Egan, Richard (1955a) 'Liverpool Dialect is Dying Out', *Liverpool Echo*, 14th April, 6.

—— (1955b) 'Liverpool Dialect', *Liverpool Echo*, 18th April, 6.

—— (1955c) 'Is Liverpool Dialect Dying Out?', in *Liverpool Colonnade*, Liverpool, Philip, Son and Nephew, 216–20.

—— (1972) 'Scouse isn't what it used to be', *Liverpool Echo*, 20th July, 10.

Williams, Bill (1962) 'Boys were "Snitched on" for "Saggin"', *Liverpool Echo*, 8th June, 12.

Williams, Dick and Frank Shaw (1967) *The Gospels in Scouse*, Liverpool: Gear Press.

Williams, Peter Howell (1971) *Liverpolitana*, Liverpool: Merseyside Civic Society.

Williams, Raymond (1965) *The Long Revolution*, Harmondsworth, Penguin.

—— (1973) *The Country and the City*, London: Chatto & Windus.

Woollaston, Victoria (2013) 'Scousers Have the "Least Intelligent and Least Trustworthy" Accent', http://www.dailymail.co.uk/sciencetech/article-2433201/ Scousers-intelligent-trustworthy-accent--Devonians-friendliest.html

Wozyer (1950) 'Strange Word', *Liverpool Echo*, 27th December, 2.

Wright, Joseph (ed.) (1896–1905) *The English Dialect Dictionary. Being the Complete Vocabulary of All Dialect Words Still in Use, or Known to Have Been in Use During the Last Two Hundred Years*, 6 vols, London: Frowde.

Wright, M. (1951) 'Word Explained', *Liverpool Echo*, 1st January, 4.

Wynn, R. H. (1957) 'Lob-Scouse', *Liverpool Daily Post*, 8th July, 6.

Young, Phil and Jim Bellew (1986) *The Whitbread Book of Scouseology*, Liverpool: Brunswick.

—— (1988) *The Whitbread Book of Scouseology*, vol. 2, *Merseyside Life 1900–1987* Liverpool: Scouse Promotions.